GOD'S GUIDE TO THE END OF THE WORLD

WHEN EVEN YOU CAN BE SAVED

THE CONCLUSION OF ELLEN G. WHITE'S *THE GREAT CONTROVERSY*
& THE SOLUTION TO *DANIEL'S RIDDLE*

THE END OF THE

ISRAEL BREAKS THE COVENANT	THE 2,625 YEAR LONG ISRAELITE

605 BC

NEBUCHADNEZZAR

CONQUERS ISRAEL AT THE BATTLE OF CARCHEMISH, 605 BC, ENDING ISRAEL'S CONTINUAL, RIGHTFUL, BLOOD SACRIFICES MEANT TO PROTECT ISRAEL FROM OUTSIDE INVADERS (DANIEL 12:11)

3 PRO-CHINA, CONSECUTIVE HORNS/KINGS

CLINTON   W. BUSH   OBAMA

CLINTON TOOK A BRIBE AND HAD AMERICANS BUY COMMUNIST-MADE-GOODS, FUNDING CHINA'S KING, TURNING AMERICA INTO MAGOG, MEANING THOSE WHO ENRICH THE WORLD-ENDING BEAST OF TEN KINGDOMS (DANIEL 7:8,20-25, DANIEL 8:24, ZECHARIAH 11:8,17, ISAIAH 14)

BEGINS THE END

JEREMIAH'S INCURABLE
EZEKIEL'S "ASCENDING
GOG'S LAND OF TEN KINGDOMS

COVID
JEREMIAH'S INCURABLE PLAGUE
(JEREMIAH 30:12-15)

ASCENDING PASSENGERS
(EZEKIEL 38:9)

MAGOG
THOSE WHO ENRICH GOG

ISRAELITE PUNISHMENT

PUNISHMENT (DANIEL 12:11)

"IN DAYS TO COME, GOG, I WILL BRING YOU AGAINST MY LAND, SO THAT THE NATIONS MAY KNOW ME WHEN I (GOD) AM PROVED HOLY THROUGH YOU BEFORE THEIR (THE GENTILES') EYES". (EZEKIEL 38:16)

2020 AD

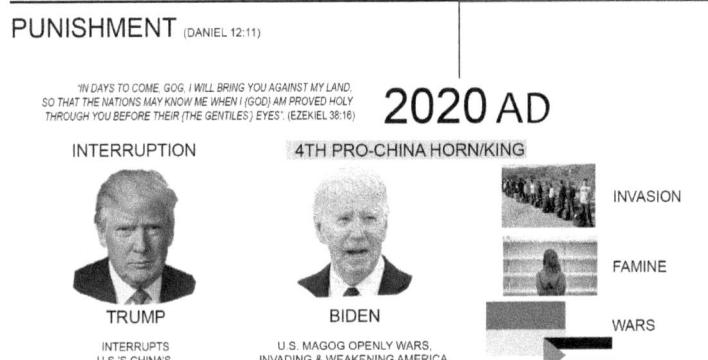

INTERRUPTION

TRUMP
INTERRUPTS U.S.'S CHINA'S ENRICHMENT
(DANIEL 7:8)

4TH PRO-CHINA HORN/KING

BIDEN
U.S. MAGOG OPENLY WARS, INVADING & WEAKENING AMERICA, TO ENRICH CHINA
(DANIEL 7:8,20-22,25, ZECHARIAH 11:7)

INVASION

FAMINE

WARS

OF THE WORLD

PLAGUE SPREAD BY PASSENGERS" FROM SHOWN TO DANIEL

THE WORLD ENDING BEAST OF TEN KINGDOMS WIPES OUT HUMANITY
(DANIEL 7:7,23)

GOG'S INVASION PACIFIC THEATER

CHINA
THE LAND OF TEN KINGDOMS
TEN KINGDOM PERIOD IS THE FIRST NAME OF A UNITED MAINLAND CHINA CIRCA 909-960 AD

GOG
KING OF THE LAND OF TEN KINGDOMS
(DANIEL 7:7)

☐ SOVEREIGN
NATIONS ENRICHING THEMSELVES

GOG IS MADE POWERFUL BY OTHERS
(DANIEL 7:23-25, DANIEL 8:23-25, EZEKIEL 38,39)

YOUR GOD COMES

IN A SINGLE DAY
(ZECHARIAH 3:9)

THE EARTHQUAKE WILL STRIKE AMERICA'S WEST COAST
(EZEKIEL 38:19, EZEKIEL 39:4-8, 17-29, ISAIAH 59:19)

THEY WILL GRAB THEIR STOMACH WITH PAIN OF A PREGNANT WOMAN
(JEREMIAH 30:5-8)

EARTHQUAKE AFTERMATH

"THERE SHALL BE A GREAT EARTHQUAKE IN THE LAND...I WILL SEND FIRE ON MAGOG AND ON THOSE WHO LIVE IN SAFETY IN THE COASTLANDS, AND THEY WILL KNOW THAT I AM THE LORD."
(EZEKIEL 38:19, 39:6-7)

"I WILL BRING ONE-THIRD THROUGH THE FIRE."
(ZECHARIAH 13: 8-9)

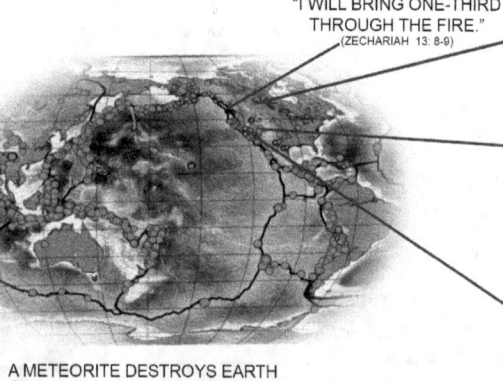

A METEORITE DESTROYS EARTH
(DANIEL 2:34-35, ISAIAH 24:19, ISAIAH 34:1-23, ISAIAH 51:6, ISAIAH 62:1, MALACHI 3:2, MALACHI 4:1, AMOS 5:18, ZEPHANIAH 3:8, ZEPHANIAH 1:18, JOEL 2:1-32)

ANNIHILATES GOG
TO SAVE

WITH VENGEANCE

IN A SINGLE MONTH
(ZECHARIAH 11:8)

THREE OF THE FOUR
MAGOG KINGS
ARE REMOVED
(DANIEL 7:24) (ZECHARIAH 11:8)

THE WORST OF THE SHEPERD'S
RIGHT EYE IS BLINDED &
RIGHT ARM IS PARALYZED
(ZECHARIAH 11:17)

"THE KING OF BABYLON", WHO
ENDED CIVILIZATION BORN FROM
BABYLON, EARNING HIM THE NAME
HELEL BEN SHACHAR, MEANING
SHINING SON OF THE MORNING
LIGHT, OFTEN MISTRANSLATED AS
LUCIFER

FOR SEVEN MONTHS
HE WILL CALL ALL THE ANIMALS
TO FEAST ON THE BODIES
(EZEKIEL 38:19, EZEKIEL 39:17-29)

YOU WILL BECOME EXPERTS
AT REMOVING HUMAN REMAINS
(EZEKIEL 39:11-13)

AND WILL BURY THE REMAINS IN A NOSE-SHAPED
CEMENTARY IN THE VALLEY OF HAMON-GOG TO
FINALLY PLUG THE NOSES OF THE PASSANGERS
SPREADING THE INCURABLE DISEASE
(EZEKIEL38:11-16)

AND MAGOG
YOU

GOD RETURNS TO EARTH
(DANIEL 7:9-14, 21-27, AMOS 4:12)

NATIONS ARE ALLOWED TO LIVE FOR A TIME
(DANIEL 7:11-12)

A SMALL REMINANT ARE SAVED FROM EARTH'S DESTRUCTION
(ISAIAH 1, ISAIAH 24:1-3, EZEKIEL 34:11, MALACHI 3:17)

GOD'S GUIDE TO THE END OF THE WORLD

WHEN EVEN YOU CAN BE SAVED

THE CONCLUSION OF ELLEN G. WHITE'S *THE GREAT CONTROVERSY*
& THE SOLUTION TO *DANIEL'S RIDDLE*

OTHER WORKS BY BENNETT JOSHUA DAVLIN

BOOKS FICTION

MEMORY
Penguin Books U.S., Random House Australia, Blanvalet Germany, Sony Books Japan

DREAMSPACE: Escape C19
Centered America Books & Various Foreign Publishers

THE MODERN ART OF DATING
Centered America Books & Various Foreign Publishers

UNION 57
Centered America Classic Books & Various Foreign Publishers

MAJOR MOTION PICTURES

THE MEDALLION
Sony Entertainment & Columbia TriStar Pictures

MEMORY
Warner Bros. & EBE

BOOKS NONFICTION

HOW TO WIN THE WAR THE PLAN TO SAVE THE U.S.A.
Centered America Books

SAINT MICHAEL STOOD UP
China Is Gog
Centered America Books

**GOD'S GUIDE TO THE END OF THE WORLD,
WHEN EVEN YOU CAN BE SAVED**
Centered America Books

AUDIOBOOK EXPERIENCE

GOD'S GUIDE TO THE END OF THE WORLD
When Even You Can Be Saved
Centered America Books

**SAINT MICHAEL STOOD UP
CHINA IS GOG**
Centered America Books

CINE-GRAPHIC NOVEL

DREAMSPACE: Escape C19
Centered America Classic Books

POLITICAL ONLINE ESSAYS

THE "ESSENTIAL" ESSAYS
www.centeredamerica.com

GOD'S GUIDE TO THE END OF THE WORLD

WHEN EVEN YOU CAN BE SAVED

THE CONCLUSION OF ELLEN G. WHITE'S *THE GREAT CONTROVERSY*
& THE SOLUTION TO *DANIEL'S RIDDLE*

Anthologized by
B. Joshua Davlin

CENTERED AMERICA PUBLISHING GROUP
Published by the Centered America Books
A Division of Davlin Productions LLC
269 South Beverly Dr., Suite 537 Beverly Hills, CA 90212

GOD'S GUIDE TO THE END OF THE WORLD: WHEN EVEN YOU CAN BE SAVED: THE CONCLUSION OF ELLEN G. WHITE'S *THE GREAT CONTROVERSY* & THE SOLUTION TO *DANIEL'S RIDDLE*

This book is an original publication of Centered America Books

This is a work of nonfiction.

Copyright 2024, Davlin Productions LLC, all rights reserved

No part of this book may be reproduced, scanned, or distributed in any printed or electronic forms without permission. Please do not participate in or encourage piracy of copyrighted materials in violation of the author's rights. Purchase only authorized editions.

CENTERED AMERICA PUBLISHING GROUP and CENTERED AMERICA BOOKS are a trademark of Davlin Productions, LLC

PRINTING HISTORY
Centered America Publishing Group trade paperback edition / November 17, 2023

An application to register this book for cataloguing has been submitted to the Library of Congress.

ISBN: 979-8-9881466-2-9

PRINTED IN THE UNITED STATES OF AMERICA.

10 9 8 7 6 5 4 3 2 1

*For my Great Grandmother, beheaded in Brest Litovsk
on September 22, 1920 for trying to worship the Most High,
for President Trump, America's most High,
for Ellen G. White, Dr. Geert Vanden Bossche, Dennis Prager,
Col. Douglas Macgregor, Dr. Scott Atlas, Friedrich Hayek, &
Thomas Sowell, just some of the Saints of the Most high,
and for Americans and believers worldwide
who can now be freed by God.*

O Lord,…The Gentiles shall come to You
From the ends of the earth and say,
"Surely our fathers have inherited lies,
Worthlessness and unprofitable things."
Will a man make gods for himself,
Which are not gods?
"Therefore behold, I will this once cause them to know,"
Jeremiah 16:19-21

"Thus says the Lord of hosts: 'In those days ten men from every language of the nations shall grasp the sleeve of a Jewish man, saying, "Let us go with you, for we have heard *that* God *is* with you." ' "
Zechariah 8:23

'Behold, I will save My people from the land of the east…And from the land of the west;
Zechariah 8:7

"The Lord calls for a reformation all through our ranks. When the church is awakened, decided changes will be made. Men and women will be converted, and so filled will they be by the Spirit of God…"
Ellen G White, *The Need For Reform (1902)*

AUTHOR'S NOTE

As a child, my father told me we were Jewish, which meant we were born into a cult formed by an ancient man named Abraham. I never held an interest in religion or the bible; instead, I majored in philosophy, taking continual college courses in varied subject for over thirty years, later living the life of a Hollywood film writer, producer, director, and internationally translated author who knew projects about God were not commercially viable in a global marketplace. Then on the evening of October 27th, 2017, my wife and I experienced a metaphysical event that set me on the path of producing this work. Now, I grasp why out of all the Jews, He anointed me. As a philosopher, there's nothing I won't question and through my craft I was able to synthesize the Hebrew Bible and 6,500 years of Israelite history to provide God's message without the conflicts of interests of spiritual intermediaries. True to His promise, God used a Jew named Joshua, although I know I may be a disappointment for those who expected Joshua, misnamed Jesus, would descend in a cloud because they've read the wrong liturgy, as will be shown. Now, in the end, God is interested in one thing: can you distinguish between good and evil? In a time when you can't speak freely, you simply must confess to Him in the inner temples of your mind and He will now talk to you and save you from your wicked U.S. pro-Communist China leaders and the lying pro-life, pro-sodomy spiritual leaders, and save you from the Earth He will soon destroy. This Guide includes what we have done wrong and must confess and the proper policies needed to restore us as a united people. In the end, the message is political; and politics is about treating each other well.

BENNETT JOSHUA DAVLIN
PICTORIAL BIOGRAPHY

A brief genealogy of Bennett Joshua Davlin. This guide explores how after his anointing by Saint Michael on 10/27/17, he would later unmask Gog and Magog and write the *Mishpat*, a political plan to treat all American citizens fairly regardless of race, creed, etc. His anointing revealed him to be the *Nasi*, the *Branch, the slave of the Lord*, possessing 7 spirits termed *lamps* or *eyes of the Lord*, including the spirit of David, Elijah the Tishbite, and one of the two Joshua messengers symbolized by two olive trees revealed in Zechariah 3 & 4.

Bennett's Grandfather, Mr. Louis Davlin came to America as a penniless immigrant following the death of his father, saddled with seven younger siblings to support, later serving in the U.S. infantry in the French trenches of WWI.

Bennett's Grandparents, Mr. & Mrs. Louis Davlin, who by the 1930s was one of the largest manufacturers of plumbing fittings in America.

Their son, Bennett's father, Irwin Davlin.

Bennett's great-grandfather and namesake Mr. Bennett J. Orkin, with grandson Irwin Davlin.

Irwin Davlin with his father Mr. Louis Davlin.

BENNETT JOSHUA DAVLIN

Bennett's Parents, Mr. & Mrs. Irwin Davlin. After Army service in WW2, Irwin became the world's largest manufacturer of oil & gas fittings. His wife, a *Ford* fashion model, would be a leading fashion designer before becoming the largest manufacturer of high-end, home accessories in America. A year before their wedding photo (above) while driving in rural MA, they were struck by a magical light from the night sky, immobilizing Irwin's car, and inexplicably passing through the vehicle's hardtop roof, striking their lower extremities and making them glow in the dark.

A young Bennett Joshua Davlin at his family's Newport, RI summer home, *Seafair*.

The 14-year-old novelist Bennett with family while dining with his early mentor, famed author James A. Michener in the *Queen's Grill* on the cruise ship *Queen Elizabeth II*.

making films with his 8 mm home movie camera.

Before serving as a war correspondent in Osijek, Croatia during the Yugoslavia conflict, Bennett was on safari in Kenya, Africa. Shortly after this photo was taken, he was unexpectedly bestowed the honor of a Maasai Chieftain's royal walking stick. The Chief asserted Bennett would one day do a great thing for the world and asked Bennett to remember his tribe, further explored in Appendix (f) on pg. 414 of this guide.

while working in heavy industry.

with Mexico's 62nd President & businessman Vicente Fox.

Multimillion-dollar-turnaround CEO of the largest U.S. manufacturer of home decorative accessories.

GOD'S GUIDE TO THE END OF THE WORLD   xiii

Bennett became Hong Kong's highest-paid screenwriter for Jackie Chan's Sony Tristar 35 million dollar film *The Medallion*.

with friend & fellow director David Anspaugh introduced by actor Dennis Hopper whom they both directed.

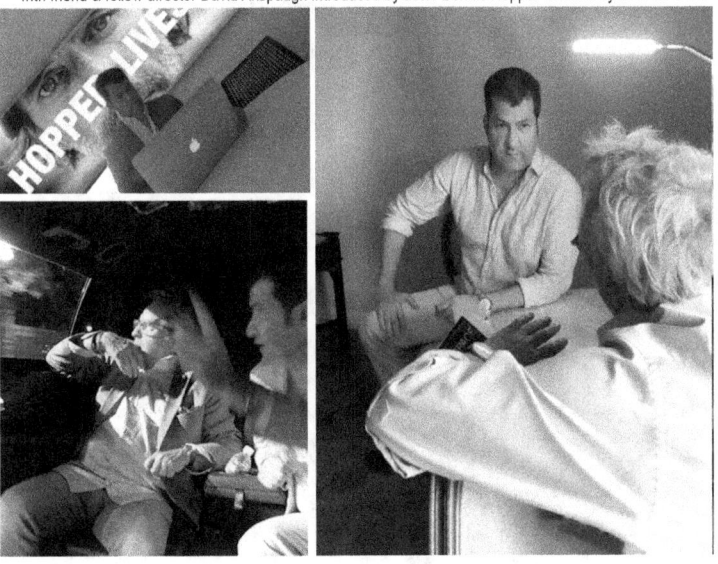

Joking for the camera while on set directing two, two-time Academy Award Nominees, Dennis Hopper & Ann-Margret on the Warner Bros. film *Memory*.

Under *a first-look deal at CBS Paramount* writing, producing, & directing the pilot project *Panic*.

With actress Ann-Margret at the premiere of Warner Bros. and Echo Bridge's *Memory*. Davlin became the first screenwriter to adapt his own novel and serve as the film's director & producer within a single film project.

The successful film garnered international distribution.

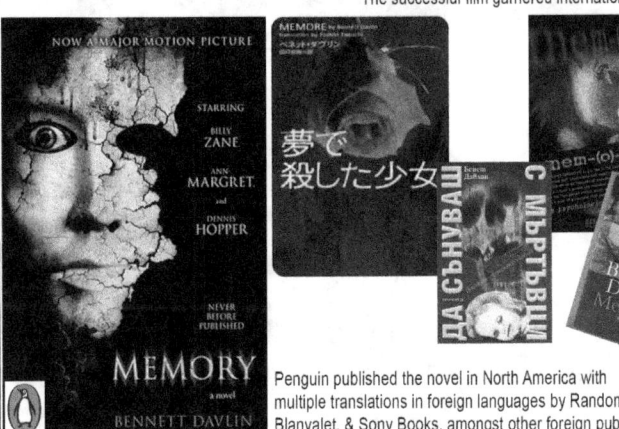

Penguin published the novel in North America with multiple translations in foreign languages by Random House, Blanvalet, & Sony Books, amongst other foreign publishers.

xvi BENNETT JOSHUA DAVLIN

Mr. and Mrs. Bennett Joshua Davlin.
His wife, a third-generation cinematographer, military sharpshooter, and maritime search & rescue veteran.

Family life.

WORK TIMELINE
1998

Government analyst Tom Grant tries to stop a terrorist attack on the Union 57 petrochemical refiner outside New York City that unfolds into a mystery surrounding a cryptic figure, Yves Alexander Dussant, long-jailed by the U.S. government without even a trial. Because Dussant claims to be the Messiah and has a special power to prove it; for anyone listening to the sound of his voice suffers permanent neurological changes, contaminating their mind, and making them

At the intersection of free will and opportunity you'll find out who you really are...1990s Hollywood agent trainee, Cullen Gersh, has his life upended after he steals his boss's invitation to the most exclusive Hollywood party. Cullen will lose nearly everything when he's presented with the ability to explore his unknown desires without judgment or repercussion. Are you who you think you are?

Sony Entertainment & Columbia Tristar Pictures' action comedy stars Jackie Chan as a Hong Kong Police Inspector who teams up with Lee Evans and Claire Forlani as Interpol agents to capture the mysterious crime lord known as Snakehead played by Julian Sands and stop him from kidnapping a chosen boy with special powers and a magical medallion that grants superhuman power and immortality.

Bennett wrote the psychological thriller novel about a medical researcher, Dr. Taylor Briggs, played by Billy Zane, who accidentally ingests a mysterious drug stolen from remote Amazonian Indians. Dr. Taylor Briggs is drawn into a hallucinogenic odyssey where he can temporarily access the memories of his parents proceeding his birth. He realizes one of his parents was a killer whose innocent victims' final moments come to life through these memories.

Variety's Chief film critic Peter Debruge wrote "Over-the-top finale would be right at home in a Brian De Palma movie, but still manages to surprise." Warner Bros. & EBE released the feature film adaptation of the original novel by Davlin in 2007 in the U.S. and all major, worldwide markets. Bennett's Davlin adapted his original book into a screenplay with his producing partner Anthony Badalucco. Bennet also produced and directed the film starring Billy Zane and two-time Academy Award nominees Dennis Hopper & Ann Margret.

2017

Our American Founders knew God birthed science on 11/10/1619. They also warned that a president like Clinton would end U.S. manufacturing and enslave the U.S. to a foreign king then making our goods. Washington said only faith in God could save us. Now in 2020 His words are unsealed with proclamations in undeniable Old Testament Scripture and the plan to save us.

This is the plan for returning manufacturing to win the trade war China declared on America. We'll employ both citizens and tens of millions of noncitizens moved along our borders. Our long-suffering came from Clinton, W. Bush, and Obama allowing in Chinese slave-made goods that also as in ancient Rome made slaves of citizens and divide politicians from the peoples' interest. Now we make nothing and have nothing. Our president is censored by a media lying about the slave-nature of Communism. While our president was illegally wiretapped in a crime eclipsing Watergate before we were virally attacked by China. The needless horror of three corrupt presidents enriching rather than containing Communism. Here's how to cleanse and restore it all.

China entombed the world. Now humanity found an escape. BY 2059 Chinese manufacturing pollution triggered the worldwide flood predicted to last 7,000 years. Plagued with COVID-19 and restricted within flood-walled-zones, humanity prepares to perpetually online on Dreamspace, a digital diversion platform that's as real as life. To play the perpetual game, users must first find a compatible game-mate in the dating module. Once merged, the couple's minds are immersed online permanently gaming with each other, while their offline bodies are maintained in medical body-vaults.Before the worldwide drop, FCC Web Agent Ray Kemper must solve the murder of a beta-tester who may have met his killer on Dreamspace's dating module. The mystery unravels as the detective falls for a suspect who could be the love of his life or the end of it, forcing him to question whether our species is worth saving if doing so means giving up the very thing that makes us human.

2024

FOREWORD
BY GOD TO AMERICA FOR THE BENEFIT OF THE WORLD
SOLELY FROM HIS WORDS IN THE HEBREW BIBLE

*"I pledge allegiance to the flag of the United States of America, and to the republic for which it stands, one nation <u>**UNDER GOD**</u>, indivisible, with liberty and justice for all."*

"You shall not swear by my name falsely, and so profane the name of your God. From the least to the greatest, all are greedy for gain, prophets and priests alike, all practice deceit. They dress the wound of my people as though it were not serious. 'Peace, peace,' they say when there is no peace. My people…women rule over them…your guides mislead you and they have swallowed up the course of your paths. A man's heart plans his way, but the Lord directs his steps. I have struck you as an enemy would and punished you as would the cruel because your guilt is so great and your sins so many…your injury beyond healing."…declares the Lord God, I have no pleasure in the death of the wicked, but that the wicked turn from his way and live…turn back from your evil ways, for why will you die? You shall not take vengeance or bear a grudge against the sons of your own people, but you shall love your neighbor as yourself…{then} He will hide me in His shelter in the day of trouble.

Behold, I send my messenger, and he will prepare the way before me. For it is precept upon precept…line upon line…here a little, there a little…as a light to the Gentiles. Then the eyes of the blind shall be opened, and the ears of the deaf unstopped; For by {this} wise guidance you can wage your war…Keep silent before me, oh wicked coastlands! Let them speak. For the Lord God does nothing without revealing his secret to his servants…"

"The Lord has anointed me to bring good news to the poor; to proclaim the year of the Lord's favor, and the day of vengeance of our God; to comfort all who mourn."
"{It's} a time of doom for the nations...behold, a fourth beast with ten horns {horns signifying ten kingdoms} terrifying and dreadful...It had great iron teeth; it shall devour the whole earth, and trample it down, and break it to pieces {To the first U.S. president William Clinton who enriched the Land of Ten Kingdoms, China's historic name} you are an...abominable branch...Because you...destroyed your land, and slain your people. {For} out of this kingdom ten kings shall arise {the land of 10 Kingdoms, China's historic name}, and another shall arise after them; he shall be different from the former ones, and shall put down three kings {whom history unmasks as Clinton, W. Bush, and Obama}, As I watched, this {fourth pro-Chinese} horn {history proves is Biden} was waging war against the holy people and defeating them...And the Lord said to Satan, "The Lord rebuke you, O Satan! The Lord who has chosen Jerusalem rebuke you! Then I annihilated the three shepherds in one month, for my soul was impatient with them...Woe to the worthless shepherd, who deserts the flock!...May his arm be completely withered, his right eye totally blinded!

You were in Eden...an anointed guardian cherub...till...in the abundance of your trade you were filled with violence in your midst, and you sinned; 'Because you think you are wise, as wise as a god, I am going to bring foreigners against you, the most ruthless of nations...Until {God} the Ancient of Days came and pronounced judgment in favor of the holy people of the Most High, and the time came when they possessed the kingdom. I will discipline you but only in due measure; I will not let you go entirely unpunished. Behold I am against you O Gog. I will turn you around {Gog}, put hooks into your jaws, and lead you out, with all your army...all splendidly clothed, passengers...who will ascend, coming like a storm, covering the land...whose people were gathered from many nations.

'Your wound is incurable, your injury beyond healing. I have struck you as an enemy would and punished you as would the cruel, because your guilt is so great and your sins so many. 'Cries of fear are heard—terror, not peace. Ask and see: Can a man bear children? Then why do I see every strong man with his hands on his stomach like a woman in labor, every face turned deathly pale? How awful that day will be! No other will be like it. It will be a time of trouble for Jacob, but he will be saved out of it. When Gog attacks the land...my hot anger will be aroused, declares the Sovereign Lord. Surely on that day there shall be a great shaking in the land. Call out to every kind of bird and all the wild animals: 'Assemble and come together from all around to the sacrifice I am preparing for you...you will eat flesh and drink blood...of mighty men and...princes. I will break the yoke off their necks and will tear off their bonds. No longer will foreigners enslave them.

And I will send fire on Magog {meaning those who enriched China's king who I codenamed Gog for reasons my messenger shall explain} and on those who live in security in the coastlands. It will come to pass in that day that I will give Gog a burial place in the valley of those who pass by east of the sea, it shall stop the noses of the passengers: and there shall they bury Gog and all his multitude: and they shall call it The valley of Hamon-gog {meaning the multitude serving China's Gog, our west coast and treasonous sanctuary cities}...Behold, the day of the Lord comes, cruel, with wrath and fierce anger, to make the land a desolation and to destroy its sinners from it. And no aliens shall ever pass through her again. I will gather all nations...I will put them on trial for what they did to my inheritance, my people Israel...At that time shall arise Michael, the great prince who has charge of your people {who anointed me on 10/27/17}. And there shall be a time of trouble, such as never has been since there was a nation till that time. But at that time your people shall be delivered...On the day when I act," says the Lord Almighty, I will spare them...And you will again see the distinction between the righteous and the wicked, between those who serve God and those who do not. "

<u>Biblical citations were presented in order of appearance:</u>

Leviticus 19:12, Jeremiah 6:13-14, Isaiah 3:12, Proverbs 16:9, Jeremiah 30:14,12,3, Ezekiel 33:11, Leviticus 19:18, Malachi 3:1, Isaiah 28:10, Isaiah 35:5-6, Proverbs 24:6, Isaiah 41:1, Ezekiel 30:3, Isaiah 61:1-2, Ezekiel 30:3, Daniel 7:7,23, Isaiah 14:19-2, Daniel 7:24-25, Daniel 7:21, Zechariah 3:1-10, Zechariah 11:8,17, Ezekiel 28:13-14, 6-7, Daniel 7:22, Isaiah 9:6, Isaiah 28:12, Proverbs 24:6, Isaiah 41:1, Amos 3:7, Isaiah 61:1-2, Ezekiel 30:3, Daniel 7:7,23, Isaiah 14:19-2, Daniel 7:24-25, Daniel 7:21, Zechariah 3:1-10, Zechariah 11:8,17, Ezekiel 28:13-14, 6-7, Daniel 7:22, Jeremiah 30:11, Ezekiel 38:3,4-7, Ezekiel 39:11, Ezekiel 38:9,12 Jeremiah 30:12,14, 5-7, Ezekiel 38:18-19, Ezekiel 39:17-18, Jeremiah 30:8, Ezekiel 39:6, Jeremiah 6:14-15, Ezekiel 39:7,11, Isaiah 13:9, Joel 3:17, Joel 3:2, Daniel 12:1, Isaiah 65:17, Malachi 3:17-18

ACKNOWLEDGMENT

Aspects of this message were previously web-published in 2017's *Essential Essays* found at centeredamerica.com, later anthologized in 2020's *How To Win The War: The Plan To Save The USA* as well as 2020's *Saint Michael Stood Up: China Is Gog*, calling out the threat from Communist China's tyrant, while this omnibus message, as will be shown, had to tarry until now.

The science fiction novel and film simulation *Dreamspace*, completed in 2015 with the novel published in 2020 are "an extension of the mission born of the writings of Ellen G. White" according to Saint Michael and the experience White prophesied her followers would now need, available at no charge at centeredamerica.com. This film would have validated White's movement and thus, according to God, could have saved the world before it was too late.

Beyond speculation on Michael's visitation, everything herein is grounded in scientific facts or *Hebrew Bible* verse for reasons to be explained. The so-called New Testament is solely quoted in appendix (c) rebuking the pro-life movement with their own liturgy. This work along with its accompanying audiobook or the audio visual experience can be found at major retailers and is provided free of charge at *centeredamerica.com*.

CONTENTS

Citations for the short film for this book are in Section V, pg. 176

DEDICATION	i
OPENING QUOTATIONS	iii
AUTHOR'S NOTE	v
PICTORIAL BIOGRAPHY	vii
FOREWORD BY GOD TO AMERICA & THE WORLD	
SOLELY FROM HIS WORDS IN THE HEBREW BIBLE	xxi
ACKNOWLEDGEMENT	xxv
TABLE OF CONTENTS	xxvi

SECTION I
PART 1, A MESSAGE TO THE NEW JERUSALEM OF
GENTILES, THE ORIGIN OF SCIENCE & ITS DIRE IMPLICATIONS   1
PART 2, THE ECONOMY UNDER GOG, YOU ARE MAGOG,
MADE IN THE USA   8

SECTION II
GOD'S MESSAGE TO YOU
GOD EXPOSES CHINA'S GOG VIA JEREMIAH, EZEKIEL, & DANIEL   16
TROUBLE FOR BOTH JERUSALEMS VIA JEREMIAH   19
HIS PROPHECY TO AMERICA VIA EZEKIEL   28
HIS PROPHECY TO AMERICA VIA DANIEL   39

SECTION III
MISHPAT, ONE NATION UNDER GOD**   54

SECTION IV
PREPARING HIS WAY, THE GREAT GUILT & THE MANY SINS   72
PART I OVERVIEW   75
PART II THE REBUKE OF HASMONEAN JUDAISM
& CONSTANTINIAN CHRISTIANITY   93
PART III ALIENS & MESSENGERS   111
PART IV THE DETAILED PRESENTATION   123

SECTION V
(WITH WORKS CITED)
A MESSAGE TO THE NEW JERUSALEM OF GENTILES
THE ORIGIN OF SCIENCE & ITS DIRE IMPLICATIONS   176

APPENDICES

(a) Analysis On The Solution To *Daniel's Riddle*	**317**
(b) Further Support For Political Policies**	**321**
(c) Scriptural Refutation Of The Pro Life Movement*	**363**
(d) Scriptural Index By Key Topics	**375**
(e) The Image of The Archangel Saint Michael**	**407**
(f) Other Academic Sources, Further Proof Of God's Condemnation of Barack Obama, & Speculation On The Timing Of The Meteorite Impact	**411**
(g) A Complete Summary of This Guide	**417**

EPILOGUE 433

*reprinted from *Saint Michael Stood Up: China Is Gog (2020)*
**reprinted from *How To Win The War: The Plan To Save The USA* (2020)

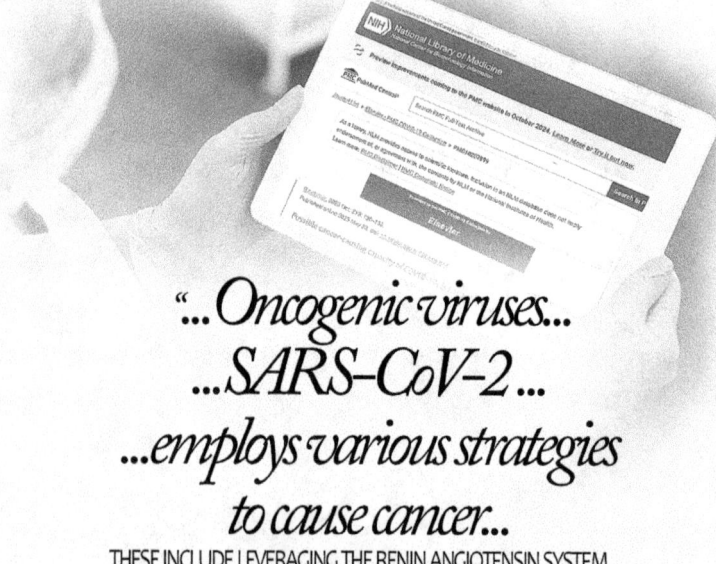

"... *Oncogenic viruses*...
... *SARS-CoV-2* ...
... *employs various strategies
to cause cancer*..."

THESE INCLUDE LEVERAGING THE RENIN ANGIOTENSIN SYSTEM, ALTERING TUMOR SUPPRESSING PATHWAYS BY MEANS OF ITS NONSTRUCTURAL PROTEINS, AND TRIGGERING INFLAMMATORY CASCADES BY ENHANCING CYTOKINE PRODUCTION IN THE FORM OF A "CYTOKINE STORM" PAVING THE WAY FOR THE EMERGENCE OF CANCER STEM CELLS IN TARGET ORGANS.

JAHANKHANI, K., AHANGARI, F., ADCOCK, I. M., & MORTAZA, E. (2023)

JAHANKHANI, K., AHANGARI, F., ADCOCK, I. M., & MORTAZA, E. (2023). POSSIBLE CANCER-CAUSING CAPACITY OF COVID-19: IS SARS-COV-2 AN ONCOGENIC AGENT? BIOCHIMIE. 213, 130–138. HTTPS://DOI.ORG/10.1016/J.BIOCHI.2023.05.014

A MESSAGE TO THE
NEW JERUSALEM OF GENTILES
THE TRUE ORIGIN OF SCIENCE AND ITS DIRE IMPLICATIONS

A message to the New Jerusalem of the Gentiles...

Did you really think they were just coming for your freedom of speech? This is the end but it's also a new beginning. But to understand you must know one thing: that science proves God's existence; for God visited the mercenary soldier Renee Descartes on the night of 11/10/1619, allowing Descartes to invent science. Although God's hand behind science would be hidden by Descartes' later followers, science reunited the lost Israelite tribes through cheap DNA tests and ended the world as the cost of covering up God who caused science's invention.

While God's message dictated in the Hebrew Bible comes alive only now once we have admitted COVID to be incurable. God foretold COVID would come from China, the land of 10 kingdoms, mainland China's historic name; and He will explain why it came in 2020 AD, the exact year following the end of the Israelite's punishment of 2,625 years following the loss of their rightful, blood sacrifices.[1] China is the half-mechanized, world ending *beast with 10 horns*, horns signifying kingdoms, ten kingdoms, shown to Daniel.

All the end-time prophesies are about this same nation's incurable plague. So God foretold to Ezekiel that soldiers from that land would be splendidly clad as "passengers", descending in flying chariots to infect our land in a "storm" that turned out to be Jeremiah's incurable disease. History proves Democrats and Republicans both funded Gog's Wuhan COVID research lab. But God proves China's king intentionally leaked COVID to kill us all to take our unguarded homes and lands. Gog's viral murder masked as an act of God is the reason why God codenamed China's king Gog, a name so close to God's own. All after the U.S. poisoned Gog's land, buying his slave-made Chinese goods so cheap for they were made with no environmental protections, sowing an unheralded pollution poisoning China. God in his ancient, dictated words now damns our 4 presidents shown to Daniel who enriched Gog, Clinton, W. Bush, Obama, and Biden who now reigns as a king from absentee ballots thanks to Gog's virus. Clinton will be unmasked as the world-ending King of all civilization first begun in Babylon, a leader shown to be born from our modern lack of belief in God Himself. For Clinton was a literal *bastard* warned by

---

[1] Some might assert that one year should be deducted for the missing year 0 between the AD and BC dating system created by Dionysius Exiguus, marking the pandemic's start in late 2019 when COVID's spread had begun, infecting the world by early 2020; both are accurate. As for the Jewish chronology, its dating system is purposefully missing 166 years probably obfuscating the year of the Messiah's appearance , which could be calculated by extending 2,625 years from the first unrightful sacrifices as foretold to the prophet Daniel, commencing with the Battle of Carchemish.

God to never make our leader for bastards remove the landmarks and reverse morality. For Clinton first made us enrich Communist China instead of containing Communism, making us part of Magog, meaning those who enrich China's Gog. As our founders noted, we were always slaves to our reigning business elites. Once Clinton outsourced manufacturing to Gog, George Washington rightly prophesied we would be enslaved and ultimately killed by this foreign king God unmasked as China's Gog.

While God calls our spiritual leaders "madmen" for allowing sodomy's spread, forbidden by God as history proves it turns all nations into pedophile ones. Do I not address a nation of adults molested as kids? The offspring of whores, God adds, who quit mothering and ended it all. Some of the only remaining prophesies left in fact are God soon ending our west coast in an unheralded earthquake killing Gog's Chinese passengers planted there to release Gog's new strains. Their remains to be buried in a nose-shaped cemetery marking the stopping of the noses of the passengers and Gog's American supporters who born to liberty stole it. God will eventually vaporize the bodies of our wicked American, Magog elite where they stand. Those breaking God's forbidden, sexual commandments will 'lose their vitality". Finally, God will end all of Gog and Magog, ending earth from a meteorite in an event called the *Day Of The Lord*.

But God promises to save those willing to get real and rescue them. So Americans and believers worldwide who wish to be saved are now told by God to return to their inner temples within them, confessing their political crime of enriching Communism, funding North Korea's nuclear arsenal, China's navy, the Mexican cartels' drug and alien invasion, American sanctuary city ports funded by Gog's products to invade America via illegal aliens. Culminating in our own politicians unthinkably funding Gog's COVID virus to end the free world. Herein is what all need to know to properly confess and find rescue and reform our republic. For after Constantine I ended Christ's rightful return to the Hebrew Bible in antiquity, that Roman king condemned most to the wrong sabbath and end-time scripture. Now the sacrifice of all humanity not returning to God is set, the guests according to Him are all invited and present. While this anointed messenger who was previously sent to leaders of the Seventh Day Adventist faith and to rebuke the Catholic church will show that God promises even the most wicked can now find rescue in ways exceeding even that of the Israelites from Egyptian bondage in Exodus. And if you're willing to stop enriching Gog, then here's how to do it.

Section V, A Message To The New Jerusalem of The Gentiles, The Origin of Science & Its Dire Implications, With Works Cited on page 176 support every word in this section with relevant Hebrew Bible verses and supporting media articles.

THE ECONOMY UNDER GOG

YOU ARE MAGOG

(film transcript)
A caption appears with "Made In The USA" as we hear:

George Washington warned that only a manufacturing economy can ensure your freedom. You must buy what you make. Your work each day is converted from the motions of your body and mind to money. And when you spend that money on American things, our energy stays here in this country and increases. But when you spend that money to buy things made in China, your energy converted to money, leaves the country and flows to one man, Xi Jinping; because no one in China, despite how the media may portray it, has wealth or can own property: they can only rent it. The price of all those cheap goods that you're putting in your recyclable bags are zero environmental protections, which have belched out radioactive particles, mercury, and contaminants that you can't even begin to imagine, which have already wrecked the ozone layer and is soon going to wreck the rest of the atmosphere and bring death to all life on Earth. Those goods are the most expensive ever purchased in all of human history. They come at the cost of your life and all life forms on this planet. And that's what happens when you don't buy Made in the USA.

George Washington warned that only a manufacturing economy can ensure your freedom. You've spent the past 25 years in Clinton's *Servitude Economy* working for Xi Jinping. Do you see the homeless in your street? Do you see the retail stores shuttering? Do you see the lack of opportunity for kids graduating from college, where the average college graduate lives at home? That's the price of all those cheap goods, on top of losing most of your politicians who turned against you; when the made in the USA markings on your grocery store beef may not be made in the USA. It can actually be toxic Chinese cattle that never lived in our nation. And you lost your media, which controls everything you see. And Xi Jinping's got you bottled up; and the only way to break free is to follow my path to restore manufacturing.

I know how to do it. I'm a third-generation manufacturer who Bill Clinton forced to offshore to China. I'm going to take their economic opportunity zone in their southern border they created with Hong Kong and I'm going to duplicate it here in our southern border: a wall of factories where Mexican day workers will come over and work at decreased wages. And those basic cheap goods that they build will have a tax, which will fund our border wall to secure our border like every other country in the world does. And along our secure border, Mexicans will be able to work and live as temporary workers as they slowly take back their nation from chaos.

And those goods will flow to our cities. And I'm going to fund startups out of millennials and everybody else as manufacturers. And we're going to immediately get back to making *Made in the USA* products, environmentally sound that don't need to be trekked across oceans. And together we will enrich ourselves and Mexico and we will have future economic, expansion zones through the Americas.

We will become richer, our neighbors will become richer. With that richness, we will have more freedom, security and liberty. And on top of that, we're going to have an incredible next generation of Americans, because I'm going to institute tax credits and subsidies to make sure that every single American family can have one parent stay at home and raise their children. All that tax basis that my traitorous state is giving to non-citizens that's going to go to citizens. That's where it's supposed to go. It's supposed to help you.

And I'm your only option in the Democrat Party. And you have only one other option in the Republican Party, which is Donald J. Trump. And we're the only two people in this nation to speak out to Xi Jinping that controls it all. I have been given skill-sets of such vast and diverse nature, like John Irving's book, A Prayer for Owen Meany, my life has been an assemblage of all the skills and knowledge and tool sets that I require to come at this moment and fix this country immediately.

I'm going to end crime in your cities immediately. I'm going to bring back the police. I'm going to half your rent. I'm going to keep one parent staying at home. I'm going to make the American experience what it used to be. We're growing our homes. Those homes are fostering philosophical and spiritual wellsprings for our people. And where has all this madness led us? We're the only mammal that doesn't take care of its young; with a level of child abuse because parents aren't around to the point that we have so many molested males now coming out as homosexuals and their parents wanting to throw a parade and say, well, that's just the way it is and not face the hard truths. You have to be there to protect your children. No one is going to protect your child like you, the parent. This is true of the whole primate kingdom. Citizenship as the framers of our Constitution created it begins at birth; and no bureaucrat is going to tell a woman that she has to be a mother when she desires not to be. And bureaucrats aren't going to get in the way of you being able to have a gun to protect your body from intruders. And our politicians are not allowed to change the basics of citizenship. Everything that I'm here to do, is to reassert the Constitution and our laws.

Now is a time for all of us to come together to renew the compact that we have as citizens to each other and to call out those traitors who are against us within our nation; when we quit fighting our Cold War enemy, a complete totalitarian regime, and began funding it; and then imprisoned the marginalized black and Latinos who should have had their fathers manufacturing jobs: the largest mass incarceration in human history.

And this must stop because every day you are going to work to kill yourselves, my fellow Americans, to poison you and your children to death. And Donald Trump is your *John the Baptist* telling you you're in trouble, America needs fixing; and you don't even want to believe it as you poison yourself to your death because you followed these leaders, because politics for Americans has always been tribal. No more. No more debates. No more little soundbites. No more slogans like *Hope*. Make me your elect so I can save the lives of every one of you and your children and free this nation. Or you choose death; because death is the option of every other candidate in the Democrat Party. I am Bennett Joshua Davlin, candidate for president of the United States of the Democrat Party. Thank you for your time, America.

When absentee ballot stole your vote, you can make me your Elect in your heart.

The next section further supports these political policies.

"You people have a wound that cannot be cured. Your injury cannot be healed...

...I hurt you as an enemy would. I punished you very hard. I did this because your guilt was so great. I did this because your sins were so many...

...Though I completely destroy all the nations among which I scatter you, I will not completely destroy you..."

JEREMIAH 30

GOD'S MESSAGE TO YOU

THE TIME OF TROUBLE FOR BOTH JERUSALEMS

In 605 BC, a foreign king finally conquered ancient Israel, placing a puppet Israelite king on the throne, thereby ending the rightful blood sacrifices at the Israelite's first temple.

For the next 18 years, Babylon's king economically sucked ancient Israel dry before outright destroying it in 587 BC.

In 2000 AD, President Clinton pushed for Communist China's admittance into the World Trade Organization, proliferating its slave-made goods throughout the U.S. and the free world.

As no free people can compete with Chinese slaves who own nothing, the slave-made goods ended U.S. manufacturing, cementing a foreign, economic alliance our Founders warned of.

For the next 18 years, the U.S. was economically sucked dry by China's king who later concealed COVID-19 for 5 months while dispatching 480,000 Chinese travelers to mass-infect the U.S.

George Washington foretold of a treasonous president like Bill Clinton who would end U.S. manufacturing, enslaving Americans to the foreign king who then made what we then bought.

George Washington warned that without U.S. manufacturing, American port cities, thereby enriched with the foreign king's imports, would turn treasonously against citizens' liberties.

Washington warned that America's mass-theft of liberty would be hidden by port-city politicians and elites such as their media.

These U.S. port-city politicians made slaves of citizens robbed of their forefather's historic manufacturing jobs and mass-imprisoned, drug-addicted, or turned homeless from an unlimited amount of noncitizens swelling into these self-proclaimed Sanctuary ports serving the foreign king's will to subvert the rights of citizens.

Now the media and former-president Obama's documentary *American Factory* lie about Communist Chinese slavery, falsely asserting the Chinese own wealth rather than merely renting it.

The Babylonian invasion and modern, Chinese economic and viral invasion were both His punishment for failing to believe.

Ancient Israelite prophets foretold events over the next centuries in antiquity that came true except for the End Time prophecies.

The ancient prophesies foretold of a New Jerusalem of gentiles that via the U.S. Constitution's freedom of worship made the United States of America that New Jerusalem of Jacob.

America's freedom of worship finally allowed for the only legal worship through God's unchangeable, Old Testament laws, reiterated by Christ about the inner connection within all to God.

Ancient Israelites learned of their covenant after being freed from Egyptian bondage.

The new Israelites learn of their covenant after COVID-19 freed them from their bondage to the foreign king whose goods they bought that weaponized their money back at them.

That money flowed as incentives to prescribe the foreign king's opioids through the goods that he supplied to the Mexican cartels to infect us with drugs and drive unlimited millions into our sanctuaries. His slave-made imports bribed U.S. port city politicians.

So ancient Israelites discovered their full covenant at the start of their nation while the New Jerusalem learned of their covenant at the end of its long enslavement broken by COVID-19.

Because the words of politicians are nothing unless they provide for the taxes to fund the government and military via a strong economy.

The United States was unprepared for China's viral attack because our mass media ignored the near-world-ending Chinese manufacturing pollution we have fed from that land since Clinton's treason.

The United States killed China with the poison produced from the cheap goods we bought so that now young Chinese in their 20s are dying of cancer.

The USA created the first antichrist in Xi Jinping, China's dictator, who would take us all down with his dying land or repatriate ours after we are gone, thanks to his virus.

Continuing purchases from the antichrist will end life from more pollution, his North Korean puppet, his U.S. Democrat allies, more infected Chinese travelers, or diseases seeded into his made-in-China products to further wreck us.

Clinton, W. Bush, and Obama's leadership enriched Communist slavery and ended manufacturing, contrary to all prior U.S. presidents so that Americans now make nothing we need.

The Babylonian invasion and enslavement in 605 BC of Israelites and New Israel's acceptance of slavery in 2000 AD from Clinton marked the end of both nations' Divine protections.

George Washington foresaw Clinton's future treason and advised only that only a belief in God would be the solution.

Washington like most in his Enlightenment-era knew Rene Descartes invented science by Divine visions shown to him by God on 11/10/1619. A fact that was later hidden by science.

Science and God thus prove each other, hence why science's first works were the proof of God as well as the immortality of the human soul.

In antiquity, Old Testament prophets correctly foretold of a suffering anointed one by God to be cut down in later antiquity.

Prophets also foretold of a future anointed one born to a New Jerusalem of Gentiles who would confirm a compact during End Times.

The anointed is also called the Elect, elected by God to be from His most powerful nation, which turned out to be a republic where citizens can stand for election as leaders.

Therefore, the prophet Daniel predicted that 2,625 years after the end of the first Israelite temple's continual, rightful, blood sacrifices, which turned out to be in 605 BC., that everyone would be blessed.

The year of this blessing is thus 2020 AD, announced by a figure, myself, anointed on 10/27/17, to be later explained.

The Elect was a mysterious figure; but once it's known he was the anointed, the End Time prophecies converge through him

The Elect was foretold to be a political leader, a gifted writer, and an expert in reading Old Testament scripture. His hand would be held by God allowing him to save his dying nation against incredible odds.

He is also described as an angel of the covenant. The covenant being our United States constitution.

And to save it, the Elect has created the social, economic, and political plan to restore our nation from destruction for having embraced Chinese slavery.

GOD'S GUIDE TO THE END OF THE WORLD 23

The Elect also reiterates the founder of science's warning that academic and political bureaucracies turn wicked over time; you must now therefore look to your own life experiences and discern the truth.

As an example, despite the peaceful news we hear about sanctuaries in our mass media, myself, the Elect, have twice been violently attacked with my family, all from illegal citizens who would immediately be put back on the streets.

The first was an attempted violent robbery of our tour bus while my family was stocking up on goods at the Palm Desert Whole Foods in broad daylight to set out on a camping trip.

One was the illegal truckdriver whom I had to chase down in a hit and run that I had to chase down with the Colorado State Police who couldn't fill out an accident report or read traffic signs. Go to any truck stop and see the illiterate, illegals driving your big rigs in America.

After losing their first temple's continual sacrifices, the ancient Israelites could no longer legally worship in a temple. They rebuilt one anyway. And that second priesthood in 167 BC led to the high priest leader ordering the mass-sodomy of all Israelite boys by their Greek, pedophile conquerors. An act, which ultimately called Christ to delegitimize that priesthood after that event, and appeal to a higher morality.

On 8/31/20 the New Jerusalem's California legislature passed SB145, a law allowing pedophile sodomists to escape mandatory registration as sex offenders; if they are under the age of 28 they could sodomize children ten years younger than them. This fact was concealed by the media in an act calling up the new anointed one to end their treasonous reign.

Unlike the old Jerusalem, the Lord is now stepping in to save the new one.

The LGBT movement has loosened sex registration laws for the large pedophile block who sodomized most of these members as children, making them sodomites against their will; and yet these victims were silent over this law, allowing their podophile sodomists to spread the sodomy.

As history attests, all societies without God's laws become pedophile societies via the spread of sodomy. It will always seek violent control through the sodomy of boys.

Online posts about the CA pedophile law are outright censored by social media sites, citing a U.S.A Today journalist to censor us. Instead of reporting, the media now censors.

The prophet Jeremiah predicted the future anointed one's appearance would follow an incurable disease wrecking the New Jerusalem.

That disease according to Jeremiah would, however, allow the new Jerusalem of Jacob to escape its long bondage to a foreign king. The same king George Washington warned of who would make the things we bought.

So Jeremiah foretold the anointed Elect would according to Daniel bless all once COVID was considered incurable, delivering the following message from God to every citizen of the United States of America.

The United States is now to learn that it is the Gentile New Jerusalem of Jacob, to rank alongside Abraham's genetic descendants and modern believers of the world alike.

The anointed, as Daniel predicted, announces the start of the Time of Trouble by directing all Americans to the dictated words in antiquity from God to the prophet Jeremiah:

Jeremiah 30:5-24
"This is what the Lord says:
"'Cries of fear are heard—
　terror, not peace.
Ask and see:
　Can a man bear children?
Then why do I see every strong man
　with his hands on his stomach like a woman in labor,
　every face turned deathly pale?
How awful that day will be!
　No other will be like it.
It will be a time of trouble for Jacob,
　but he will be saved out of it.

"'In that day,' declares the Lord Almighty,
　'I will break the yoke off their necks
and will tear off their bonds;
　no longer will foreigners enslave them.
Instead, they will serve the Lord their God
　and David their king,
　whom I will raise up for them.
"'So do not be afraid, Jacob my servant;
　do not be dismayed, Israel,'
declares the Lord.
'I will surely save you out of a distant place,
　your descendants from the land of their exile.
Jacob will again have peace and security,
　and no one will make him afraid.
I am with you and will save you,'
　declares the Lord.
'Though I completely destroy all the nations
　among which I scatter you,
　I will not completely destroy you.
I will discipline you but only in due measure;
　I will not let you go entirely unpunished.'
This is what the Lord says:
"You people have a wound that cannot be cured.
　Your injury will not heal.

There is no one to argue your case.
   There is no cure for your sores.
   So you will not be healed.
All those nations who were your friends have forgotten you.
   They don't care about you.
I hurt you as an enemy would.
   I punished you very hard.
I did this because your guilt was so great.
   I did this because your sins were so many.
Why are you crying about your injury?
   There is no cure for your pain.
I, the Lord, did these things to you because of your great guilt.
   I did these things because of your many sins.
But those nations that destroyed you will now be destroyed.
   Your enemies will become captives.
Those who stole from you will have their own things stolen.
   Those who took things from you in war will have their own things taken back.
I will bring back your health.
   And I will heal your injuries," says the Lord.
"This is because other people forced you out from among them.
   Those people said about you, 'No one cares about Jerusalem!'"

This is what the Lord said:
"I will make the tents of Jacob as they used to be.
   And I will have pity on Israel's houses.
The city will be rebuilt on its hill of ruins.
   And the king's palace will stand in its proper place.
People in those places will sing songs of praise.
   There will also be the sound of laughter.
I will give them many children.
   They will not be small.
I will bring honor to them.
   No one will look down on them.
Their descendants will be like they were in the old days.
   I will make their people strong before me.
And I will punish the nations who have hurt them.

One of their own people will lead them.
   Their ruler will come from among them.
He will come near to me when I invite him.
   Who would dare to come uninvited?" says the Lord.
"So you will be my people,
   and I will be your God."

The Lord was very angry.
   He punished the people.
And the punishment came like a storm.
   It came like a hurricane against the evil people.
The Lord will stay angry
   until he finishes punishing the people.
He will stay angry
   until he finishes the punishment He planned.
When that day comes,
   you will understand this.

God will next educate Americans through prophecies of Ezekiel unsealed to make clear what Americans must do to stay alive.

HIS PROPHECY TO AMERICA THROUGH THE PROPHET EZEKIEL

Ezekiel Chapter 38 and 39 (in order without verse numbers)
Clarifying notations precede each verse

This prophecy as will be explained as per Daniel's blessing of the Elect is to come current once COVID was considered incurable. God commanded the Elect in this year by using the old moniker for Christ, *Son of man*.

He orders the Elect to draw attention to His words dictated through Ezekiel to *Gog,* soon to be incontrovertibly unmasked as Xi Jinping, China's dictator for life.

1 And the word of the LORD came unto me, saying, Son of man, set thy face against Gog…

Gog rules Magog, meaning *those who empower Gog*, like its puppet state of North Korea. Or China's invisible slaves fed by Clinton, W. Bush, and Obama's *service economy* along with U.S. port-city leaders, American workers enriching Gog through Made-In-China products, and the media as part of Magog.

2 Son of man, set thy face against Gog in the land of Magog, prince of the capital of Meshech and Tubal, and prophesy over him,

God next reveals that Xi Jinping is descended from Noah's grandsons Meshech and Tubal born post-flood whose people founded China and its capital city Beijing.

3 and say, Thus hath the Lord GOD said: Behold, I come unto thee, O Gog, prince of the capital of Meshech and Tubal;

GOD'S GUIDE TO THE END OF THE WORLD 29

Noah's descendants put Genesis pre-flood stories in China's writing symbols and made China monotheistic for its first 2,500 years but Confucius ended that belief, making China a puppet for the Lord's to wield.

4 and I will break thee [Gog] and put hooks into thy jaws,

God made Gog's 480,000 Chinese tourists spread COVID-19 via jet airplane *horses* of modernity.

and I will bring thee forth and all thine army, horses and horsemen,

With nuclear weapons outmoding typical warfare, Gog's viral army's armor had to be masked along with their viral swords to mass-infect and destroy the U.S.

all of them splendidly attired, a great company with buckler and shield, all of them wielding swords;

To stress Gog is Xi Jinping, God also notes China's military and business alliances with Iran, Libya, and Ethiopia that it never had before in its history.

5 Persia, Ethiopia, and Libya with them, all of them with shield and helmet:

Gog bribed and subdued the Muslim nations of Gomer to China's west flanking Russia's southern border.

6 Gomer and all his companies;

Gog bribed Turkey known in antiquity as *Togarmah*, and the Middle East, securing the world's pro-Chinese complicit silence for China's Islamic *Uyghur* genocide.

the house of Togarmah that dwells to the sides of the north and all his companies and many peoples with thee.

THE LORD STERNLY WARNS the New Jerusalem of gentiles, the U.S. to close its borders and be on guard for China and its North Korean and U.S. allies of Magog, all serving Gog.

7 Be thou prepared, and prepare for thyself, thou, and all thy company that are assembled unto thee, and be thou a guard unto them.

The Lord foretells Gog's mass infection of the U.S. New Jerusalem gathered of peoples from many lands, further described by God in our Civil War monikers of *broken by the sword* or *brother against brother*.

8 After many days thou shalt be visited; at the end of years thou shalt come to the land broken by the sword, gathered out of many peoples, to the mountains of Israel,

God stresses that Americans have long-been made *waste* by their wicked politicians.

which have been always waste;

Now the Lord comes to protect our peoples He collected over time from many nations.

but she is brought forth out of the nations, and they shall dwell safely all of them.

God warns of Gog's army of Chinese passengers descending like a viral storm to overwhelm the United States.

9 Thou shalt ascend and come like a storm; thou shalt be like a cloud to cover the land, thou, and all thy companies and many peoples with thee.

GOD DEMANDS that Americans know the dire plan Gog, Xi Jinping of China, hatched in his mind against our Gentile nation.

10 Thus hath the Lord GOD said: It shall also come to pass in that day, that words shall rise up in thy heart, and thou shalt conceive an evil thought:
11 and thou shalt say, I will go up against the land of unwalled villages; I will go against those that are at rest, that dwell safely, all of them dwelling without walls, and having neither bars nor gates,
12 to take a spoil and to take a prey, to turn thine hand upon the desolate places that are now inhabited and upon the people that are gathered out of the Gentiles, who have gotten cattle and goods, that dwell in the navel of the land.

The free world knows Gog concealed the virus while sending out mass infectors. But most don't know his land is poisoned and he wishes to kill and repatriate their lands of others.

13 Sheba and Dedan and the merchants of Tarshish, with all the young lions thereof, shall say unto thee, Art thou come to take a spoil? hast thou gathered thy company to take a prey? to carry away silver and gold, to take away cattle and goods, to take a great spoil?

Gog is taking lives to get land that is not poisoned. But God now safeguards the U.S. and will destroy Gog.

14 Therefore, son of man, prophesy and say unto Gog: Thus hath the Lord GOD said: In that time when my people of Israel shall dwell securely, shalt thou not know it?

God reiterates that Xi Jinping's 480,000 Communist Chinese passengers came to destroy the U.S.

15 And thou shalt come from thy place out of the north parts, thou, and many peoples with thee, all of them riding upon horses, a great company, and a mighty army:

Xi Jinping's COVID-19 spreaders ended the free world economy, marking the beginning of end times.

16 and thou shalt come up against my people of Israel as a cloud to cover the land; it shall be at the end of the days, and I will bring thee upon my land, that the Gentiles may know me, when I shall be sanctified in thee, O Gog, before their eyes.

The Lord long-knew Xi Jinping would do this deed.

17 Thus hath the Lord GOD said: Art thou not he of whom I have spoken in days past by my slaves the prophets of Israel, who prophesied in those times that I would have to bring thee upon them?

Gog's crimes against the U.S. finally drew God's fury.

18 And it shall come to pass in that time when Gog shall come against the land of Israel, said the Lord GOD, that my fury shall rise up in my anger.

God promises to end China, North Korea, and much of the U.S. west coast if it continues to serve Gog, the Chinese dictator Xi Jinping.

19 For in my jealousy and in the fire of my wrath I have spoken, Surely in that day there shall be a great shaking upon the land of Israel, 20 so that the fishes of the sea and the fowls of the heaven and the beasts of the field and every serpent that walks by dragging itself upon the earth, and all the men that are upon the face of the earth, shall shake before my presence, and the mountains shall be ruined, and the stairs shall fall, and every wall shall fall to the ground. 21 And I will call for a sword against him throughout all my mountains, said the Lord GOD:

GOD'S GUIDE TO THE END OF THE WORLD 33

Americans must awaken to their second, long civil war of brother against brother with the treasonous west coast and our ports turned Sanctuaries and nation-states.

each man's sword shall be against his brother.

The Lord will bring great fire upon Magog, which will include our west coast if we don't cleanse it from Gog.

22 And I will litigate against him with pestilence and with blood; and I will rain upon him and upon his companies and upon the many peoples that are with him, an overflowing rain, and great hailstones, fire, and brimstone.

The Gentiles of the U.S. will worship God.

23 And I will be magnified and sanctified, and I will be known in the eyes of many Gentiles, and they shall know that I am the LORD.

(continued in the next chapter, Ezekiel chapter 39)

The Lord seldom repeats but urges Americans to heed His threat about Gog and his Magog supporters.

Therefore, thou son of man, prophesy against Gog, and say, Thus hath the Lord GOD said: Behold, I am against thee, O Gog, prince of the capital of Meshech and Tubal;

The Lord promises to slay approximately 84% of Magog.

2 and I will break thee, and leave but the sixth part of thee

God reiterates that He had Xi Jinping attack the U.S.

and will cause thee to come up from the north parts and will bring thee upon the mountains of Israel:
3 and I will smite thy bow out of thy left hand and will cause thine arrows to fall out of thy right hand.
4 Thou shalt fall upon the mountains of Israel, thou, and all thy companies and the peoples that go with thee; I have given thee unto every bird and unto everything that flies and to the beasts of the field as food.
5 Thou shalt fall upon the open field for I have spoken it, said the Lord GOD.
6 And I will send a fire on Magog, and among those that dwell securely in the isles: and they shall know that I am the LORD.
7 So I will make my holy name known in the midst of my people Israel; and I will not let them pollute my holy name any more; and the Gentiles shall know that I am the LORD, Holy in Israel.

The Lord makes clear that Americans allowed China to end the world, forcing God's return.

8 Behold, it is come, and it is over, said the Lord GOD; this is the day of which I have spoken.

He wills that for 7 years, the Sanctuary areas must be reformed and stripped of election powers just as they literally burn themselves from dead timber feeding a fire to compromise those now facing COVID-19.

9 And those that dwell in the cities of Israel shall go forth and shall set on fire and burn weapons, and bucklers, bows and arrows, and handstaves, and spears, and they shall burn them in the fire for seven years:

God punished California for their treason by having their politicians refuse to pick up fallen timber to set their own land on fire.

10 so that they shall take no wood out of the field, neither cut down any out of the forests; for they shall burn the weapons in

the fire; and they shall spoil those that spoiled them and rob those that robbed them, said the Lord GOD.

The Lord explains that the west coast dead who served Gog will be found in a west coast cemetery *east of the sea*.

11 And it shall come to pass in that day that I will give unto Gog a place there of graves in Israel, the valley of the passengers on the east of the sea:

The Lord wills the graves to form the shape of a *nose*. It symbolizes Gog's *passengers* spreading COVID-19 in areas where Gog long-enriched U.S. politicians.

and it shall stop the noses of the passengers;

Xi Jinping will be *buried* along the west coast either literally or figuratively along with many of his U.S. allies.

and there shall they bury Gog and all his multitude;
and they shall call it The valley of Hamongog {which means the multitude serving Gog.}
12 And seven months shall the house of Israel be burying of them that they may cleanse the land.
13 All the people of the land shall bury them; and it shall be to them a renown, the day that I shall be glorified, said the Lord GOD.
14 And they shall take men out of continual employment, who shall go through the land with the passengers to bury those that remain upon the face of the earth, to cleanse it; after the end of seven months they shall search.
15 And the passengers that pass through the land, when any sees a man's bone, then he shall set up a sign by it, until the buriers have buried it in the valley of Hamongog.

Hamongog will be in a west-coast city named Hamonah, meaning the many who supported Gog, cleansing Gog's supporters from the U.S.

16 And also the name of the city shall be Hamonah. Thus shall they cleanse the land.

The West Coast's seismic events will kill so many that wild animals will have time to feast on the remains.

17 And, thou son of man, thus hath the Lord GOD said: Speak unto every bird, unto everything that flies, and to every beast of the field, Assemble yourselves, and come; gather yourselves on every side to my sacrifice that I sacrifice for you,

The West Coast's political and media elites supporting and concealing China's slavery as well as its own enslavement on Americans will be reformed and ended.

18 Ye shall eat the flesh of the mighty, and drink the blood of the princes of the earth, of rams, of lambs, and of he goats, of oxen, and of bulls, all of them fattened in Bashan. 1
9 And ye shall eat fat until ye are full, and drink blood until ye are drunken, of my sacrifice which I have sacrificed for you.
20 Thus ye shall be filled at my table with horses and strong chariots, and with all the men of war, said the Lord GOD.
21 And I will set my glory among the Gentiles, and all the Gentiles shall see my judgment that I have executed, and my hand that I have laid upon them.

The Lord alone makes our salvation possible.

22 So the house of Israel shall know that I am the LORD their God from that day and forward.

The Lord punished the U.S. for enriching slavery as the price for our modern lack of belief.

23 And the Gentiles shall know that the house of Israel went into captivity for their iniquity because they rebelled against me,

The lack of belief delivered the U.S. into the hands of its enemy to kill many with COVID-19.

and I hid my face from them and gave them into the hand of their enemies; so they all fell by the sword.

Our confusions about our wicked leaders were the products of Americans hiding our face from God, causing him to also do so from us.

24 According to their uncleanness and according to their rebellions have I done unto them and hid my face from them.
25 Therefore thus hath the Lord GOD said: Now I will turn the captivity of Jacob and have mercy upon the whole house of Israel and will be jealous for my holy name.

Now, U.S. traitors will become ashamed of their rebellion against citizens in our peaceful land.

26 After they shall feel their shame and all their rebellion by which they have rebelled against me when they dwelt safely in their land, and no one made them afraid.

By doing His will now, God gathers us up now just as cheap DNA tests regather His lost, ancient Israelites.

27 When I bring them again from the peoples and gather them out of their enemies' lands, and am sanctified in them in the sight of many Gentiles.
28 And they shall know that I am the LORD their God when after causing them to be led into captivity amongst the Gentiles; I shall gather them unto their own land, without leaving any of them there any longer.

When COVID is finally considered to be incurable, the Lord does not hide His face but reveals His will through His anointed carrying His spirit to the United States and Jacob's descendants.

29 Neither will I hide my face any longer from them, for I will pour out my Spirit upon the house of Israel, said the Lord GOD.

U.S. port-city politicians of Magog blaming the police are now incontrovertibly unmasked as allies of Gog. Washington warned America must believe in God.

After a future president who turned out to be Bill Clinton, ended manufacturing and enslaved us to the foreign king Gog.

Indeed, God, Himself, brought the answer.

Next, in Daniel's unsealed vision, God further unmasks Gog and reveals the greatest blessing in history to the American people.

HIS PROPHECY TO AMERICANS THROUGH DANIEL

From Chapters 7 & 9-12 of the Book of Daniel
(with verse numbers)
Clarifying notations in bold

As will be further explored at this section's end, Daniel's vision is designed to only be understood once COVID was considered incurable.

We begin with the primordial sea where we once lived as fish.

7:2 Daniel said: "In my vision at night I looked, and there before me were the four winds of heaven churning up the great sea.

God churns up four beastly governments through human history since our departure from that sea.

3 Four great beasts, each different from the others, came up out of the sea.

Daniel first sees a prehistoric alpha male ruler of our primordial history in the wild.

4 "The first was like a lion,

Two eagles' wings mark it with God's blessing of providing all it needs in Eden.

and it had the wings of an eagle."

But the four-legged beast eats the forbidden fruit, losing its blessed wings and Eden.

I watched until its wings were torn off…

Without Eden's resources, the beast is made to stand, given a human heart and mind to find provisions.

and it was lifted from the ground so that it stood on two feet like a human being, and the mind and heart of a human was given to it.

The need for provisions generated civilizations and their inevitable tyrants. With no feet on the ground, these rulers fed on others until replaced by ever-bigger thugs.

5 "And there before me was a second beast, which looked like a bear. It was raised up on one of its sides,

The bear has eaten 3 ribs that we'll learn foreshadow three leaders who will end history.

and it had three ribs in its mouth between its teeth.

For now, the tyrants feast until the end of the world.

It was told, 'Get up and eat your fill of flesh!'

Daniel sees a nimble leopard that we learn is the U.S.

6 "After that, I looked, and there before me was another beast, one that looked like a leopard.

The leopard has 4 wings revealing the most blessings.

And on its back it had four wings like those of a bird.

The U.S. replaces a tyrant with four heads, the three branches of the U.S. government and manufacturing that Washington stressed was a necessary precursor for God's blessing to extend free will.

This beast had four heads,

Once COVID was considered incurable, God sanctifies the U.S. nation alone to rule.

and it was given authority to rule.

Next, we see a fourth, futuristic beast destroying everything without exception.

"After that, in my vision at night I looked, and there before me was a fourth beast—terrifying and frightening and very powerful. It had large iron teeth; it crushed and devoured its victims and trampled underfoot whatever was left.

This beast has 10 horns. Each horn we learn symbolizes a king. Ten horns mark it as *The Land of Ten Kings*, China's longtime government of ten independent kingdoms.

It was different from all the former beasts, and it had ten horns.

To alert Daniel and Americans, an 11th horn rises up on the Chinese beast.

"To make me cautious, another horn was there before me,

It's a tiny horn that we'll learn represent various forces acting for God.

a little horn, which came up among them;

The horn shows Trump's Trade War and COVID-19 ending the U.S.'s long-servitude to China through presidents Clinton, Bush, and Obama's treasonous administrations.

and three of the first horns were plucked up, hamstrung, *or exterminated* before it.

The horn is this message coming alive here.

This horn had eyes like the eyes of a human being and a mouth that spoke boastfully.
9 "As I looked,
"thrones were set in place,
   and the Ancient of Days took his seat.
His clothing was as white as snow;
   the hair of his head was white like wool.
His throne was flaming with fire,
   and its wheels were all ablaze.
10 A river of fire was flowing,
   coming out from before him.
Thousands upon thousands attended him;
   ten thousand times ten thousand stood before him.
The court was seated,
   and the books were opened.

God's arrival on Earth will destroy Xi Jinping.

11 "Then I continued to watch because of the boastful words the horn was speaking. I kept looking until the beast was slain and its body destroyed and thrown into the blazing fire.
12 (The other beasts had been stripped of their authority, but were allowed to live for a set period of time.)

Daniel has a vision of the Elect greeting God on earth.

13 "In my vision at night I looked, and there before me was one like a son of man, coming with the clouds of heaven. He approached the Ancient of Days and was led into his presence.

Daniel claims the U.S. with the Elect leads the earth.

14 He was given authority, glory and sovereign power; all nations and peoples of every language worshipped him.

With the Elect, U.S. security becomes eternal.

His dominion is an everlasting dominion that will not pass away, and his kingdom is one that will never be destroyed.

Daniel is more interested in the raging China monster.

15 "I, Daniel, was troubled in spirit, and the visions that passed through my mind disturbed me. 16 I approached one of those standing there and asked him the meaning of all this.

This China beast represents the last great ruler who will be wiped out.

"So he told me and gave me the interpretation of these things: 17 'The four great beasts are four kings that will rise from the earth. 18 But the holy people of the Most High will receive the kingdom and will possess it forever—yes, for ever and ever.'

Daniel is interested in the China beast destroying everything .

Daniel 7:19-20
19 "Then I wanted to know the meaning of the fourth beast, which was different from all the others and most terrifying, with its iron teeth and bronze claws—the beast that crushed and devoured its victims and trampled underfoot whatever was left.

Daniel asks about its ten-horns.

I also wanted to know about the ten horns on its head

Daniel is also curious about the 3 horns of Clinton, W. Bush, and Obama who bowed to China until the tiny horn of God used President Trump, Xi Jinping, and

COVID-19 to forcibly dislodged us from our servitude to China.

and about the other horn that came up, before which three of them fell—

God's tiny horn can even come to life, boasting.

and the horn that looked more imposing than the others and that had eyes and a mouth that spoke boastfully.

God punished His Holy people for their lack of belief; while as Washington warned that theft of liberty would be hidden from them by pro-China, U.S. port-city allies.

As I watched, this horn was waging war against the holy people and defeating them,
22 until the Ancient of Days came and pronounced judgment in favor of the holy people of the Most High, and the time came when they possessed the kingdom.
23 "He gave me this explanation: 'The fourth beast is a fourth kingdom that will appear on earth. It will be different from all the other kingdoms and will devour the whole earth, trampling it down and crushing it.

China is outright confirmed as the world-ending beast of ten kingdoms, its historic name.

The ten horns are ten kings who will come from this kingdom.

These 10 kingdoms are now united under one king, its dictator Xi Jinping who subdued the U.S. under Clinton, W. Bush, and Obama, finally ending us with COVID-19.

After them another king will arise, different from the earlier ones; he will put down the three kings.

GOD'S GUIDE TO THE END OF THE WORLD   45

Xi Jinping jails believers in concentration camps and erodes U.S. law & order via his American pro-China allies.

He will speak against the Most High and oppress his holy people and try to change the set times and the laws.

America would be delivered into Xi Jinping's hands for *a time* of the 3 traitors Clinton, W. Bush, and Obama.

The holy people will be delivered into his hands for a time

***Times* their 8-year-terms totaling 24 years.**

times

Then Daniel is to add *half a time* to reach Trump's fourth year in office when COVID-19 ended the world in 2020 AD. Once COVID is considered incurable, God proclaimed a winner from amongst the nations.

and half a time.

At some point after once COVID is considered incurable, God will free Americans.

But the judgment shall be set, and they shall take away his dominion, to consume and to destroy it unto the end.

Thereby the U.S. will cement its Divine sovereignty.

Then the sovereignty, power and greatness of all the kingdoms under heaven will be handed over to the holy people of the Most High.

Americans will be part of an everlasting kingdom.

His kingdom will be an everlasting kingdom, and all rulers will worship and obey him.'

The Lord sent this messenger to prepare the way for Him by restoring manufacturing and thereby restoring the U.S. families and the safety of children.

And he shall make a strong covenant with many for one week {which actually means 7 years},²

By returning to God, we all can stop the sacrifice the sacrifice and offerings to Xi Jinping.

and for half of the week he shall put an end to sacrifice and offering.³

For their abominations, the wicked will be later removed.

And on the wing of abominations shall come one who makes desolate,

And God will decree ends for everyone.

until the decreed end is poured out on the desolator."

Later, Daniel meets a Divine Messenger working with God's Archangel Saint Michael. Saint Michael represents the Lord Himself.

Saint Michael also anointed this messenger in the presence of my family on October 27th, 2017.

---

² Years are stated as *days*, hence *a week* of 7 days constitutes 7 years.
³ Early Christians falsely added the word *temple* at this verse's end, to tie the event to Christ in antiquity rather than to a future Elect.

The Divine messenger's face blinds Daniel like Michael's face blinded me, to later be further detailed.

6 His body was like beryl, his face like the appearance of lightning, his eyes like flaming torches,

In my visitation, Michael's wings and armor shimmered in a glowing bronze hue just as Daniel described in antiquity of his Divine visitor.

his arms and legs like the gleam of burnished bronze,

Unlike Daniel's visitor who spoke words, I spoke words for Michael. I said that we must whistle blow on the marketing department's continued theft at Loma Linda Medical Center where Laura had worked. I explained to my wife that I was prophet of God like Ellen G. White, the founder of the Seventh Day Adventist, SDA, movement, which created the Loma Linda Medical Center.

White's mission was not religious, but a movement to save the world from destruction. I explained Dreamspace was God's apocalyptic prophecy to warn our world of what was coming if America did not change our ways. In hindsight, the yin yang virus in that story presaged the China virus.

Dreamspace and my writing were also the experience White foretold that the SDAs would need, but not possess among them for a lack of "adroitness". My words flowed with a life of their own as I summarized that "Dreamspace was a furtherance of the mission born of the writing of Ellen G. White."

Then I stated that we were to meet with the head of Loma Linda Medical Center, Dr. Hart, a man I had never met. As I said that, a winged angel materialized

before me at the foot of the couch between my wife and me. I saw golden fathered wings rising over a metallic breastplate sculpted into etched feathers. Where the angels' head should be was filled with a blinding light emanating through a seemingly infinite tunnel of clouds.
The figure held a shield. The angel ran its lower tip along the bottom of my bare foot. I felt the shield's tip trace its way down my bare sole before the angelic figure dematerialized as I grabbed my foot in shock.

and the sound of his words like the sound of a multitude.

As I grabbed my foot, my wife said she saw a gray line magically running down my bare right sole. But like Daniel, only I saw the angel.

7 And I, Daniel, alone saw the vision, for the men who were with me did not see the vision,
12 Then he continued, "Do not be afraid, Daniel. Since the first day that you set your mind to gain understanding and to humble yourself before your God, your words were heard, and I have come in response to them…

The visitor notes he's back from fighting to possibly incept the seed of the U.S.'s freedom of religion into Persia's Prince Cyrus.

The prince of the kingdom of Persia withstood me twenty-one days,

Saint Michael came to help control the Persian kings.

but Michael, one of the chief princes, came to help me, for I was left there with the kings of Persia,

This messenger makes clear he's addressing people through Daniel in the far distant future, once COVID is considered incurable.

14 {I} came to make you understand what is to happen to your people in the latter days. For the vision is for days yet to come."

The messenger then asks Daniel and thereby all of America...

"Do you know why I have come to you?

He explains the reason follows his current assignment.

But now I will return to fight against the prince of Persia;

He is Christ who will physically go out into the visible world after the *Greek prince* comes into ancient Israel, to be further explained.

and when I go out, behold, the prince of Greece will come.

The Greek prince, Antiochus Epiphanes, was from a pedophile society that used trickery to conquer ancient Israel just as China used trickery to conquer the new Israel through our traitorous U.S. leaders .

The pedophile Greeks influenced Israelite leaders to tolerate the spread of sodomy, which soon infected Israelite society in the major cities.

As proof, a later Israelite high-priest tried to force the mass-sodomy of all Israelite boys by Greek pedophiles. That act later called Christ to delegitimize the priesthood and appeal to a higher moral standard.

Whereas as I come after the LGBT core that raped most of its members as boys without their consent,

sought to loosen mandatory sex offender registries for pedophiles.

No LGBT member spoke up.

The U.S. media now controlled and funded by Communist China's seeks to sexually reprogram our children to homosexuality and sodomy.

The Westboro Baptist Church was righteous in what they did to attempt to stop the mass child sodomy in the United States. They were right.

It ended our nation.

Now recall the question Christ just posed through Daniel to Americans once COVID is considered incurable.

"Do you know why I have come to you?

Christ *went out* into visible reality as a consequence of the Israelite high-priest's attempt at the mass sodomy of all ancient, Israelite boys. The price of tolerating itself which is born of child sodomy.

His Elect now comes to stop the rape of the New Israelite boys to serve the fourth beast of China sown by Clinton, W. Bush, and Obama.

Xi Jinping sodomizes our children through his U.S. political puppets, passing SB Law 145 protecting pedophiles younger than 28 from mandatory sex registries.

Hollywood, funded by Xi Jinping, perverts us after womanizing male execs were chased out, feeding

GOD'S GUIDE TO THE END OF THE WORLD

content to reprogram children's heterosexuality, like episode 8 of *The Boys* as one example of so many.

Christ says you are to trust this messenger as I am with Michael watching over the boys of America.

But I will tell you what is inscribed in the book of truth: there is none who contends by my side against these except Michael, your prince.

For I was anointed on October 27th, 2017 to protect the boys of the U.S. and the free world.

"At that time Michael shall stand up
The great prince who stands watch over the sons of your people.

The pro-China treason of Clinton, W. Bush, and Obama empowered our COVID-19 destruction.

And there shall be a time of trouble.
Such as never was since there was a nation.

I was sent to deliver my nation.

Even to that time
And at that time your people shall be delivered.
Every one who is found written in the book."

As a *sealed* vision, these truths were only to be fathomed once COVID was admitted to be incurable.

until the time of the end. Many shall run to and fro, and knowledge shall increase."

Daniel wants to know what year the world will end.

"How long shall it be till the end of these wonders?"

Another visitor restates the Holy American peoples' bondage must last through the presidencies of Clinton, W. Bush, and Obama's two terms to arrive at Trump's fourth year to reach COVID-19 ending the world.

7 And I heard the man clothed in linen, who was above the waters of the stream; he raised his right hand and his left hand toward heaven and swore by him who lives forever that it would be for a time, times, and half a time, and that when the shattering of the power of the holy people comes to an end all these things would be finished.

The Lord knows that despite His dictated words to the world, many will not follow His will. We could become much more shattered because of them.

10 Many shall purify themselves and make themselves white and be refined, but the wicked shall act wickedly. And none of the wicked shall understand, but those who are wise shall understand.

Daniel is then given the year the world ends and this prophecy is to be incontrovertibly unsealed.

Daniel is told to start at {the 605 BC's } loss of continual, rightful offerings at the Israelite's first temple.

11 And from the time that the regular burnt offering is taken away

To reach the abomination that kills so many, he must add another 1,290 years (called days) to 605 BC.

and the abomination that makes desolate is set up, there shall be 1,290 days.

GOD'S GUIDE TO THE END OF THE WORLD 53

Then he's to add an additional 1,335 more years to reach a blessed year.

12 Blessed is he who waits and arrives at the 1,335 days.

Making a total of 2,625 years from 605 BC resulting in 2020 AD.

As a sealed vision, these truths were only to be fathomed once COVID was admitted to be incurable. When God unsealed His will to sanctify the U.S. to rule and China not to, so China's U.S. proxies must end. Or we leave the borders open, ignore Divine warning, and be ever-more-shattered in our time of trouble.

and that when the shattering of the power of the holy people comes to an end all these things would be finished.

To restore freedom, every American should now do God's will for they will soon be soon judged.

Americans are the new Israel. That word means to wrestle with God. And you wrestle with God now by confronting the truths and the truths that He brings to you.

Our politicians literally took a third rate, mass-killing, communist regime and empowered it so that it could bribe them.

Embrace truth. Embrace God. Reform...

The next section reveals long-suppressed truths to prepare all for God's message. While God's full length message with supporting works cited in order can be found in *Section V, A Message To The New Jerusalem of The Gentiles, The Origin of Science & Its Dire Implications With Works Cited* on page 176.

> "*If the wicked restores the pledge gives back what he has stolen, and walks in the statues of life without committing iniquity, he shall surely live; he shall not die.*"
>
> EZEKIEL 33:15

MISHPAT
ONE NATION UNDER GOD

IF WE ARE POWERLESS, WHY DISCUSS POLICIES?

God prophesied that His servant would at this time present what is called *Mishpat* in Hebrew, a system to treat all equally, despite their ethnicity, race, gender: purely the opposite of our modern day that prioritizes someone's sexuality or race as merit in itself. Hence our government actually tells us that our wicked federal reserve now raising interest rates to destroy our economy, after inflation was truly spiked by rising energy cost are good; for our government tells us that they are stocked with plenty of homosexuals and females to show diversity, which is supposed to make their decisions meritus. As if putting your penis into someone's anus or possessing a vagina somehow would give you the clarity to think out complex financial structures and moves like a member of the federal reserve. To counter anyone who would claim America's best days are over and we can't now return to the mid 1990s economy and society in the midst of our current troubles are given a quick sampling of new, proposed federal government policies of this messenger's movement to cure us of our wickedness, which are further provided in our short policy film, its link below.[4] In doing so we acknowledge that God notes that now, "if the wicked restores the pledge, gives back what he has stolen, and walks in the statutes of life without committing iniquity, he shall surely live; he shall not die." Again, this movement is to be nonviolent, this cause is not heard in the streets, as God Himself will now wage war for us if we return to Him; the reason why George Washington advises now a belief in God alone can save us. God's message makes clear that we are to economically wean ourselves from the slave craftsmen of Communist China who now according to God terrorize us, causing us to lose control of our own governmental leaders. Consider that Gog could also lace his made in China products with new viral strains to kill us all without warning. He controls a single monopoly of nearly every product that this nation needs, given to him by our treasonous, wicked, suicidal, idiotic leaders of Magog. So to achieve God's point, we support the following policies as reflecting His spiritual wishes herein submitted for your consideration.

POLICIES TO IMMEDIATELY FIX OUR WORLD

#OZ (Opportunity Zone)
Tens of millions of illegal Latino aliens will be brought out of the shadows and repatriated along our future, southern, *opportunity zone*, symbolized by the acronym OZ. As God states of them in the modern Israel, "no aliens shall ever pass through her again." A Latino, work-based, border OZ will serve as the basic, manufacturing workforce for our made in the USA renascence. This plan mirrors what Communist China initially did with Hong Kong to start their Chinese mass manufacturing for our

---

[4] http://www.centeredamerica.com/videos/

subsequent made in China slave purchases. These foreign OZ workers like the Hong Kong citizens before them, can return to their homes in their native country at night, leaving our American based factories to commute back to Mexico in this case, with a far cheaper standard of living. Because God demands via Isaiah 62 that there never be again an illegal alien in the U.S. as they were obviously weaponized by our wicked elite to destroy us for their vile goals of enriching China's Gog.

#NEW AMERICAN ENTREPENEURS
Our border *OZ* creates the basic parts to be assembled in the U.S. These are *opportunity zones*, *Oz* zones, within the United States where American citizens will manufacture by putting together the discreet parts created by the Mexican workforce along our southern border. These American manufactory startups will receive government-underwritten loans from the USDA, the United States Department of Agriculture's loan service department to finance startup manufacturing firms. These firms will grow to mirror Germany's *Mittelstand*, the small factory backbone sustaining their German economy. Our American factories will assemble higher parts from the basic ones again made at border OZ into finished goods for our market and for export, again using only American labor. The market will freely set the price of labor after one working spouse is generally removed from the labor market thanks to OPAH and CVRA feeding the removal of illegal aliens from our soil. Thus the price of labor will freely increase to support one wage earner, freeing the price of labor from government meddling.

#MANUFACTURING AMIDST COVID
As a former CEO of a multi-million-dollar manufacturing firm myself, having generally used only at home subcontractors, many non-border OZ factories can kit basic materials generated at the border OZ for American-at-home subcontractors to put together until we are COVID-19 free. Thus many subcontractors can avoid working in mass factories to preserve their own health and safety, while aiding in our manufacturing renascence.

#FUTURE OZ
Future border OZ expansion zones will move beyond just Mexico throughout the Americas in a Pan-American rail and road highway to be built called *The Yellow Brick Road* or TYBR for short. TYBR will link the Americas for basic raw materials needed for American manufacturing while opening vital, new consumer and manufacturing markets for our exports throughout the Americas. TYBR will benefit our entire hemisphere, further cementing our promise of the *Monroe Doctrine* safeguarding the American continent both north and south from foreign meddling. A meddling which now includes China's king purchasing our farmland and assets throughout our nation. With China's Gog fueling Mexican cartels transporting opiates, drugs, and the illegal alien horde across our porous, southern border in an invasion from Latin America against our laws.

#ONLY MANUFACTURING MAKES WEALTH
For all those who might scream about rising debt from these policies, they should consider the unsustainable debt that the past 30 years of economic treason by Democrats and non-Trumpian Rhino Republicans created. By abandoning U.S. manufacturing, America abandoned the source of all true wealth ever generated by any peaceful nation with the sole exception of agriculture and raw material extraction. Since that abandonment, our built-up wealth from our history flowed since the late 1990s directly to China's king's hand rather than into the hands of hardworking Americans.

#KILL THE GREEN ENERGY LIE
With Magog Democrats unnecessarily skyrocketing energy costs to cripple our economy, Magog Rhino republicans would seek to cut government spending. This pincer movement by both of our remaining Magog political parties is meant to cripple America in a situation further aided by our loss of domestic oil production to continue to feed the unthinkable, unmitigated pollution generated by our purchases from Mainland China. While green energy like *Star Trek's* warp drive is a complete and utter myth. Humanity has no means of efficiently storing energy as fossil

fuels perpetually do. All of our green energy could power the world for only a day. California boasted of achieving this goal in their state for 4 seconds while most of that energy was actually burning natural gas. Instead of destroying our nation, we will become the most pro fossil fuel government in U.S. history, while financially stopping the Chinese pollution. Yet in a wider sense we can never allow ourselves to be fed such outright lies like the green energy myth. Nor can we again allow plausible deniability that our leaders advance these nonsensical causes with good intention, which they do not. God's message makes clear that our politicians except Trumpian Republicans all now economically represent Gog in the surrender of our economic Cold War. While Trumpians themselves aid Gog by supporting the pro-life movement with no liturgical support. [5]

#MANUFACTURING ALONE CAN SAVE US

World War II racked up incredible debt while arming the nation with the manufacturing network to generate incredible wealth that quickly grew out of that debt over the following decades. Only World War II ended America's 1930s decade-long economic depression only continued by president Roosevelt's crippling *New Deal*. Viewing our economic war in the same light as that prior military one allows us to now see our Pearl Harbor enemy was our politicians who fed us COVID that they helped China create, ended our factories, attempted to drug addict us to opiates, have an open border to spread an invasion by illegal aliens and unfettered drugs, and now propose even the laughable myth of green energy to create some new failed corporate elite to feed them back political contributions now that we don't even have the money to buy Made in China purchases. And all those green energy raw materials would come from China's Gog. Thus it is little appreciated that the United States in times of war can draw on record debt just as it did during the 30 years of treason if we have a plan to bring back manufacturing. Added taxation

---

[5] Appendix (c) on page 363 addresses the lack of scriptural support for the pro-life movement.

or further aiding our service provider aristocracy will only slow the economy and impair even our current debt repayment. As history shows, only our own craftsmen via American manufacturing can grow our way out of our record debt despite new, COVID-19 challenges. Ours is an investment in an essential, thriving manufacturing society like every president from Washington until Reagan would've upheld, with the possible exception of Carter, along with all Cold War presidents until the wicked Clintons. Manufacturing is the only way to truly unite Americans. For we all have the same economic goals; reverse the reverse the chaos of our political system, not through untested Magog climate revolutions but a sober return, a restoration to historic factories that used to make everything we bought, that was the true grace of God that as He prophesied, our predecessors sold for thirty measly pieces of silver. Just as in World War II, there will soon be no financial markets or realistic currency value outside of the U.S. after the virus and the environmental drought God makes clear will follow from our Cold War enrichment of Chinese pollution only to be followed by latter rains and worldwide flooding to leave our planet as scattered islands as His prophet Isaiah prophesied. For the Chinese wing of abominations have long risen into our atmosphere by our hypocritical, so-called environmentalist: liars who distracted from a record pollution from Communist China that we ourselves fed, that is the source of all of our suffering. And God advises that our raw material supply chains must return to domestic origin, as there will be no other option available once He destroys mainland China who sowed this record pollution from our made in China purchases that our U.S. west coast port cities received, becoming flush with Gog's slave-made, world-ending products damning them as American traitors. This return to manufacturing is the sole tool to rescue the United States of America by returning our historic underpinning mandated by George Washington himself; while there is no other feasible plan by any political voice to cleanse us of Magog by allowing us to buy what we make and therefore conserve the wealth generated by our collective American labor within our borders, while adding more wealth by drawing on foreign collective labor through our exports; as we did through our entire history until William Clinton's economic treason and Cold War surrender.

#RAISE THE SHIELD
Our PPE initiative to manufacture NATO .40 mm gas masks to provides 99.9% protection for front line workers with a later rollout to all American citizens. As God warns, China's Gog will soon wipe most everyone out without warning. Those with our suggested PPE alone stand a strong chance to continue our nation.

(ADDITIONAL POLICIES)

#OPAH
One Parent At Home (OPAH) policy, we will subsidize one parent at-home to protect and raise children in safe, American dwellings free of Magog public schools. With the removal of mandated minimum wage to be further discussed, the price of labor will naturally adjust as a majority of previous single, working spouses will be incentivized to financially remain home, aiming to take half of adult America out of the job market; thereby decreasing supply and raising the price of labor without government meddling in setting price controls.

#OYOH
Own Your Own Home Initiative, ownership of our dwellings will be underwritten by the U.S. government with financial incentives for existing homeowners. During this continuing pandemic, home-based families will be key to our nation's survival. The government will also remove tax-funded corporate interests from continuing to snatch up our American residences.

#CVRA
Citizen Verification Rental Act, only legal American citizens will be allowed to occupy American dwellings. This policy immediately reduces rents for all citizens by removing the illegal alien masses incentivized to come here by our American Magog leaders, over-

swelling our limited dwellings with massive increased demand by noncitizens. *CEVRA* will also end the recent, mass purchase of dwellings by government-funded corporations, using QE1 and QE2 (previously described in Part IV).

#END JAIL SLAVERY
This initiative will immediately end our American jail-slavery by having select juvenile offenders volunteer to serve in a new, *Junior Military Corp,* the *JMC*. We will actively recruit urban minorities from the age of 12 upwards to end their inevitable mass-incarcerations amidst our decimated, economic landscape. *JMC* helps kids at risk avoid jail while keeping later mature, dangerous criminals off our streets. As adults, *JMC* cadets will serve out four years in our regular military, repaying back our investment in them and can thereafter reenlist, gaining access to valuable, veteran benefits and continued job training.

#FREE SPEECH OR DIE
We will end all unconstitutional government wiretapping, social and legacy media censorship, quickly restoring American free speech. We will split up and de-communize our modern mass media's dangerous new media monopoly of only three corporations owning all we hear and see, a persuasive force unheralded by any prior monopoly in our history. Our government will also prosecute anyone further curtailing Americans' right to speak their minds at a time when one political party thinks it can even raid the home of the opposing political party's leader, ending the American political process in the name of tyranny to serve China.

#SPECIAL PROTECTION
The only group granted special protection as *victims* are our children. All others via our Constitution stand as equal Americans regardless of sexual orientation, religion, ethnicity, gender, etc. And the sexualization of prepubescent children is another trauma, which like child sodomy or molestation forged most homosexuals and perverts according to God and experienced throughout our history. This wicked child trauma is

not new, but an ignorant return to the old norms of the entire pedophile ancient world that only changed with Christ's crucifixion and the adoption of the proscription of the spread of sodomy that continued through Christianity.

#LGBTQ REFORM

Despite what California's legislators assert, children cannot consent to sodomy and are not to be influenced in deviant sexuality. Rather we will de-communize pedophile elites in politics, academia, and those behind the pedophile LGBTQ movement and the new pro LGBTQ Hollywood, which like communism, claims to seek tolerance while truly seeking to usurp heterosexuality as all cultures do without sodomy's underlying proscription; including perverted teachers who will no longer be able to discuss sexuality with our innocent, prepubescent children. As the Lord notes, such wickedness is not new and was again the cause of most societies in antiquity becoming ongoing pedophile cultures sodomizing young boys before they could mature to men: a point that which can't be repeated enough to American men who are so misguided, according to God, ruled over by their women and children that they should not be around where young children are born.

#END THE COVID VACCINE MANDATE

Since the virus cannot be eradicated by the experimental gene therapy misnamed a vaccine, via recent history's proof and God's warning, we seek to stop this untested treatment. Its damage so great that the wicked leaders who allowed for it have now silenced free speech throughout the free world, shielding a truth its makers wish to hide for 75 years from us. A drug recklessly imposed by new, tyrannical American leaders upon our entire military with no long-term study. And one our leaders would willingly give to our children without parental consent or knowledge. We will return jobs to all those who lost them due to their very sound refusal to take this untested and dangerous treatment; part of Magog America's economic war on us from the China virus that these same wicked U.S. elites and health experts unthinkably helped Gog create in his Wuhan lab. The same Gog who hid this virus for 5 critical months before unleashing it on the world.

#REAL CLIMATE CHANGE

We will end China's pollution, the incontrovertible true cause of climate change when China manufactured our goods with no environmental protections whatsoever. We will achieve this by manufacturing our own goods in return of Made in The USA. We will also return proper forestry maintenance to the west coast, avoiding the massive emissions from these forest fires begun by purposeful west coast Magog forestry neglect. The Lord speaks of these mass fires as being the armor of Gog, making fires for 7 long years so that no one would need to kindle a fire in these treasonous west coast American Magog regions. We will also rid ourselves of so many Magog environmentalists blocking real estate development and the needed expansion of required reservoirs of waters to maintain our human population; while all along ignoring the completely uncontrolled nightmare of the China pollution. We will also stop the purchase of solar panels and green energy batteries that destroy the environment, have limited lifespans, contain so many pollutants and heavy metals, and are all made by China, which after destroying our ability to make discretionary purchases of made in China products now seeks to destroy us by ridding ourselves of our badly needed fossil fuels; having all cars attached to an electric grid that California doesn't even allow to expand: a nightmare of economic ruin and a false lie.

#POLITICAL NOT POLICE REFORM

Rather than hypocritically blaming frontline police for our failed Magog political leadership, police officers will not face criminal charges from anyone resisting arrest. We will reform the Magog politicians systematically behind this vileness already jailing most urban blacks and Latinos after robbing them of their forefathers' historic, manufacturing jobs. Our police, military, and the FBI will be cleansed of their obvious bonds to Magog Communism, which has taken over of the very foundations of our federal government, that was supposed to insure the foundations of our domestic liberties. Hillary Clinton and former president Barack Obama will be rightfully prosecuted for the illegal wiretapping of then president Donald J. Trump, already a proven fact. Hillary Clinton will also be further prosecuted for revealing America's Chinese spies to China's dictator on her private server, killing the only voices who could've warned us of COVID-19 after China's Gog kept it secret for 5 months before again unleashing it on the world. Furthermore, anyone who received government emails from Hillary Clinton's private server and did not report it will be removed from governmental office as per law. All individuals involved in *Spygate* and the subsequent illegal Trump wiretapping will be indicted and prosecuted for their outright treason. Politicians, mass media, and academic players fueling the false *Russian collusion hoax* will also be likewise de-communized and removed. And all political appointees of the Magog U.S. American kings, Clinton, W. Bush, Obama, and Biden can be removed and will thus be scrutinized.

#PORT CITY RECONSTRUCTION
Port-city federal politicians who allowed the usurpation of law and order in their areas will be militarily reconstructed just as the former confederacy was after the first Civil War. That war like our second Magog civil war was also fought over slavery. William Clinton again destroyed the Constitution's ability to right itself via his Service Economy introducing Chinese slave-made goods of the Chinese craftsmen to torment us; making you service your new American kings who in turn serviced China's Gog. Hence Democrats rail against January 6th while ignoring the outright wiretapping by the Clintons of a sitting president by what were then private citizens. To protect our U.S. Constitution, the Clintons must be removed from the political, media and academic landscape of the nation they have damned.

#WHISTLEBLOWER REFORM
Whistleblowers of our federal government will receive massive payouts beginning at five million dollars apiece to further reveal and de-communize the root players of our massive, Magog political treason within our corrupt federal government.

#REAFFIRM THE RIGHT OF SELF-PROTECTION
With illegal aliens and zero bond spreading crime in our streets and these crimes going largely unreported, a citizen's right to bear arms is paramount. We will focus on the lack of stay-at-home mothers whose loss along with the belief in Divine retribution forged our modern school shooters; for these godless children now think they can escape retribution after committing suicide following their murders; notions arising from our modern lack of belief and children not raised by their mothers who now after the general female population has entered the workforce has no choice but to work; lacking a spouse who can generate an income to allow for a stay-at-home parent. Our federal government likewise will continue to remove legal impediments to a female's right to choose to be a mother while leaving this point as a point as a state's right matter. For there is no liturgical or Constitutional support for this movement except unsubstantiated warping by U.S. Magog religious intermediaries. Both Magog Republicans and Democrats infringe on our second amendment right to defend ourselves from criminals and over-reaching politicians via the pro-life movement or the attack on our 2nd Amendment right. This needless social feud created to divide us must end to reunite the nation or we will die as this division only empowers our further destruction and condemns us.

#SALUTE THE FLAG
The United States will join in saluting our flag at all sporting events. Professional athletes who do not stand will be restricted from the game; the NFL being grossly subsidized with billions of dollars of taxpayer subsidies despite whether taxpayers were fans or not. So instead of "End Racism" in the NFL in-zone, we will post "Condemn Censorship" or "Illegals Create Our Homeless".

#END DIVERSITY & QUANTITATIVE EASING
No longer will mascots of ethnic minorities like blacks and Latinos long decimated by our Magog leaders find some undeserved place in a business position where they don't necessarily belong. For an entire ethnic minority of blacks and

Latinos long-decimated by our Magog leaders find some undeserved place in a business position where they don't necessarily belong; acting as an optical illusion to mask the horrible truth: that their entire ethnic sector of the population has been imprisoned and mass sodomized. Hiring will become blind to race or gender, recognizing only merit. When you embrace a group, you fail to scrutinize the individuals within that group. Corporations will thus refrain from social commentary as Woke companies do in service to our tax payer dollars funding their loosing institutions by our Magog leaders who use it to continue to fund their failing endeavors; as indisputably proven through our government's wicked federal Quantitative Easing 1 and 2, which likewise will end.

#RETURN TO OUR INNER TEMPLE

As the *Old Testament* made clear, if Americans return to God within them now they will see the result when as Zechariah makes clear, of our Magog traitors, of presidents Clinton, W. Bush, Obama, and Biden, three of the four will die in one month. According to God's promise, He gave us kings in His anger and took him away in His wrath. As for the one who truly doesn't according to God, "for the lost, or seek the young, or heal the injured, or feed the healthy, but will eat the meat of the choice sheep, tearing off the hooves,'"; this sitting or former U.S. chief executive or even Hillary Clinton herself, the wife of the former chief executive who first enslaved our nation to China's Gog, will be blinded in their right eye and their arm withered as a sign for all from God. Which could be any of the four traitor presidents from William Clinton to Biden or again even Hillary Clinton. For only these four Magog presidents along with Hillary, and not Trump, supported the pro-Communist economic Service Economy fating us to enrich the communist dictator Gog. As God warned, "There is a way that seems right to a man, But its end is the way of death." By enriching communism and advancing sodomy and forbidden acts well understood by prior Americans for over a century, who would never have dared enrich a foreign communist tyranny, our leaders thus ignored God's advice that "It is not good to show partiality to the wicked, Or to overthrow the righteous in judgment." Clinton, W. Bush, Obama, and Biden achieved this vile feat by silencing our free speech so that, 'The first one to plead his case seems right, Until his neighbor comes and examines him." Now God has explained these wicked Magog traitors and will soon curse them before our very eyes. It is again probable that we have no ability to escape the new Communist status quo, God will decide our future, but with our return to Him in our heart we would have no choice but to support such policies as have been submitted for consideration herein.

TRUST IN GOD
It seemed right to the eyes of Adam and Eve to eat the forbidden fruit, but God said it was wrong.
It seemed right to the eyes of the sons of Jacob to sell Joseph into slavery, but God said it was wrong.
It seemed right to the eyes of King David to commit adultery with Bathsheba and cover it with murder, but God said it was wrong.
It seemed right to those following Constantine's Catholic movement, asserting the wrong Sabbath day and changing the way and times while persecuting Jews, but God said it was wrong.
It seemed right to Americans to work to empower China's Gog who now murders and silences us to our deaths, but God said it was wrong.
Presidents Clinton, W. Bush, Obama, Biden, and their appointees supported our Magog enrichment of China's Gog, which God said was wrong.
Every American took these slave-made goods into their homes and dishonored themselves and God said it was wrong.
Slavery in its many forms from the Chinese craftsmen to Americans now being invaded as slaves to be replaced by a foreign horde is to end, and God said it was wrong.
Meddling in the business of other peoples' unborn children merely aids Gog and is part of Magog, and God's message said it was wrong.
For nearly the entire free world by now, God said was wrong.

ONLY THOSE WITH MICHAEL ARE RIGHTEOUS

As God notes in Proverbs there is a way that seems right to a man, but its end is the way of death. Man without God's commandments cannot separate good from evil as recent times have made clear. While none as Daniel was shown by God's angelic angel should trust in anyone who is not with Michael, your King defending His commandments and avoiding His forbidden acts. And anyone allowing such, marks themselves as most evil and is to be removed, as God will soon achieve. As Daniel was old by God's messenger, "But I will tell you what is noted in the scripture of truth, (no one upholds me against these except Michael your prince Daniel was instructed by God's angelic agent except those with Michael, your king, defending his commandments and avoiding the spread of his forbidden acts. As Daniel was told by the God's messenger "But I will tell you what is noted in the Scripture of Truth. (No one upholds me against these, except Michael your prince." Those who are unwilling to accept the plain, cutting truths of the *Old Testament* are continually seeking pleasing fables to quiet the conscience and thereby damned themselves through the ages and mostly to date. All who trust to the boastful decision of human reason without God's rules of the wider multiverse and imagine that they can explain Divine mysteries and arrive at truths unaided by God's wisdom are entangled in the snare of Satan, that quantum adversarial force filling this stage of the multiverse. Now properly prepared at the end of history, please listen to God's own quotes behind His message, with some of those points so fully repeated that many of the reiterate verses are omitted for brevity's sake.

Appendix (b) *Further Support For Political Policies* on page 321 directs to supporting essay for these policies along with supporting, third party academic and media sources.

The next section provides incontrovertible evidence that we're in the end-times. If you do not require this proof, skip to *Section IV, Preparing His Way, The Great Guilt & The Many Sins* on page 72, which reveals many long-suppressed truths.

 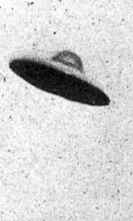 

PREPARING HIS WAY

THE GREAT GUILT & THE MANY SINS

Section IV
**PART ONE
OVERVIEW**

As will shortly be proven by God's dictated words in antiquity, most *Old Testament* end-time prophecies have already been recently fulfilled. This messenger will address *New Testament* scripture while first proving that God's dictated words to His *Old Testament* prophets will also verify that His many end-time messengers now converge into one person. So that the future individual with the birth name Joshua, God's end-time human messenger of the covenant, His anointed, His Elect to help awaken the many Elect, His political voice born as a native citizen of that most powerful, end time New Jerusalem not of mostly Jews but Holy gentiles, are all in fact the same individual who will now incontrovertibly prove through recent history that God's foretold Time Of Trouble has already begun. As God prophesied in antiquity, this learned political voice, this modern manifestation of David, this end time messenger God claims was once Elijah the Tishbite would possess no power of his own when first sharing God's message. Nor would he as God promised, reveal any new truths by acting as God's oracle in direct communication with the Lord. But rather as God prophesied, this learned messenger of the covenant would simply deliver God's message as a mosaic of God's ancient, unchangeable, dictated words and prophesies revealed to His *Old Testament* prophets with most of the remaining prophecies recently fulfilled. This messenger will also highlight a few of God's actions long hidden from most along with other scientific facts concealed, like God's birth of science itself.

As will shortly be incontrovertibly proven, science proves God's existence because God Himself actually invented science on the night of November 10th, 1619 as per science's founder, Renee Descartes. Therefore modern secularism or atheism, asserting God's nonexistence, is no longer scientifically valid since you'll soon realize that again God was involved in creating science. The same God whose dictated prophesies in the *Old Testament* have mostly been recently fulfilled. While His end time message now comes as a mosaic of His ancient dictated words and signs revealed to His *Old Testament* prophets and the answer to an ancient puzzle termed *Daniel's Riddle* to prove why His message only comes now.

God's words from antiquity make clear that His end-time message is to be presented to believers worldwide, but especially to every American citizen. Because American citizens it turned out, belong to that most powerful New Jerusalem Of Holy Gentiles, a futuristic, blessed people. Confirming God's American revelation, our own founding father George Washington's little discussed prophecy of our nation's end will doubly prove that the United States of America is indeed the New Jerusalem of God's Holy gentiles that He lovingly termed Ephraim: that name of Joseph's son born outside of Israel to a non-Israelite mother; one of the long lost tribes of the ancient Israelites revealed at the end, to be most Americans as "the first born" of our God working backwards and outside of time.

Ephraim, the name of our future western land unknown in antiquity of the west where the blessed gentiles from many nations would be gathered to be saved by God's own hand. While Jacob, prophesied as the land of the east, is well noted in end time *Old Testament* scripture as the modern nation state of Israel. God has already as promised recently reunited the lost tribes of Jacob via cheap DNA tests to reveal to individuals their covenant their ancestor Abraham took with the Lord. God, as promised now comes to reunite the divided tribes of the end time New Jerusalem, not of mostly Jews, but His Holy gentiles.

Yet God's message only can come, He promises, once our elites have accepted this current plague to be incurable. So God's daily presence now resumes for both nations only after our modern plague was considered incurable. The same plague that was secretly launched by the world-ending beast of 10 horns in the *Old Testament*, horns symbolizing kingdoms, making it the Land Of Ten Kingdoms as shown to Daniel, further revealed to the prophet Ezekiel as Gog: the king of the Land of Ten Kingdoms, Mainland China's longtime, historic name.

Once our modern plague was admitted to be incurable, God's words to His *Old Testament* end-time prophets suddenly became applicable. God will shortly make clear that without this message that all Americans would soon be dead through the masked disease intentionally launched upon us by China's king whom God long ago codenamed Gog; his codename so similar to God's own because this king seeks to mask his murders as a seemingly natural act of God. This foreign, Chinese ruler who was made powerful according to God solely through others; namely through four American presidents symbolized as four biblical horns to Daniel that God now damns for ultimately empowering China's Gog. So God Himself now incontrovertibly unmasks our pro-China, treasonous U.S. kings as presidents Clinton, W. Bush, Obama, and Biden with the sole, recent exception of president Donald J. Trump. God revealed to His prophet Daniel that a leader like Trump would first unstick America from enriching Gog in what history revealed as a fallout from Trump's Chinese trade war bringing the disease COVID from China. God revealed to Daniel that the first three pro-Chinese, consecutive, U.S. presidents had by then cemented Gog's power in the United States of America so that Trump could be removed through a disease, allowing our pro-Chinese, U.S. port cities to illegally alter their own election laws at the last minute, allowing for mass ballot fraud to bring the pompously speaking fourth horn of Biden to openly reign solely in Gog's interests. These American traitors unthinkably armed Gog with COVID-19 with our taxpayer monies to co-fund Gog's Wuhan lab, arming him with COVID. These same U.S. elites would later bribe those rightfully revealing the virus to be man-made and in many scientists' opinion originating from the Chinese Wuhan Lab. Even our top health expert, Dr. Anthony Fauci, confirmed this intentional coverup in his email in the professed name of "international harmony" to continue to serve China's Gog despite his outright mass murder by now of a million American souls thus far. While no one in our government has informed Americans that a NATO .40 mm gas mask with a simple HEPA filter offers 99.99% protection from COVID-19, a link to online retailers unaffiliated with this messenger, provided below.[6] Instead, our elites forced a completely untested, experimental genetic therapy misnamed a vaccine, on our entire military and much of our society, treasonously economically disenfranchising rightfully-dissenting Americans who wished to protect their bodies from these same wicked leaders who helped China's Gog create COVID in the first place.

So God now warns all Americans that Gog wars on us as our traitorous leaders misportray this time of war as peace. God Himself comes to confirm that Gog's virus was in fact intentionally launched and purposely masked by Gog as a natural act of God. God Himself foretold to Ezekiel that Gog's splendidly dressed army of Chinese soldiers clad as *"passengers"*

---

[6] Search 40 mm NATO gas masks on ebay.com or other retailers; the SGE 400 is the preferred brand with HEPA filters provided at mirasafety.com

would descend in flying chariots, spreading their incurable plague like a storm across our nation. God also revealed in antiquity that Gog would now unleash new strains as needed through his Chinese operatives disguised amidst his Chinese passengers even now planted on our American west coast. God makes clear that China's king Gog aims to intentionally kill all Americans with his incurable virus to later recolonize our unguarded homes and lands. So God prophesies that He will bring an unprecedented earthquake that will annihilate much of our American west coast with the mass human remains later buried in a nose-shaped cemetery as God teases, to finally block the noses of the Chinese passengers spreading Jeremiah's incurable disease to finally end it.

Gog aims to kill us all because the world-ending pollution Gog's Chinese regime has long sowed in Mainland China was so well-hidden by our pro-Clinton and thus pro-Chinese mass media that most Americans don't even know Gog permanently poisoned his country's land to death and needs another land. This point made expressly clear by God to His prophet Ezekiel in antiquity. The coverup of the Chinese pollution also conceals the fact that China's resulting food products are now all toxic. So now Americans literally eat the poisonous outcome of China's unregulated manufacturing pollution that Americans have so long fed through our made in China purchases since president William Jefferson Clinton first began our pro-Communist outsourcing of manufacturing. An act that would lead to his condemnation by our founding father George Washington who prophesied that a future American president would do just this thing and finally end our nation. In fact he advised us that after this outsourcing only a belief in God could save any American.

For Clinton generated the true cause of our coming climate change long hidden from everyone. While our so-called Climate Change scientists demonize fossil fuels or nitrogen emissions to cripple our economy, rather than the unheralded pollution of unthinkable chemicals spewed into the air from China by our same so-called green elites who have created the true cause of climate change, feeding a record pollution for over 30 years. What God instructed His prophet Daniel would be "the wing of abominations" rising into the air bringing so much evil, an annihilating drought, followed by latter day rains and flooding before the world-destroying meteorite as the final fallout. These same liars would have us wreck our economies and bring needless famine from their false prophecies to only further the unthinkable Chinese pollution churned out by Gog, which is allowed to continue and even grow under the treasonous Paris Climate Accord. God has thus revealed that our incurable plague was truly born of this pollution, causing this king to need to annihilate lands to take them. All after Americans unthinkably worked to enrich China's Communist regime with our purchases used to fund their concentration camps for millions of its innocent, Chinese Muslim believers, building up China's military, funding China's cyber spying of our companies and citizens, and unthinkably working to fund North Korea's nuclear arsenal wholly subsidized by China based on our American made in China purchases.

God also makes clear that Gog's disease actually marks the very end of the suffering of the Israelites in the year 2020 AD. For this biblical punishment revealed to His prophet Daniel, consisted of 1,290 years followed by another 1,335 years to consecutively pass to reach a blessed year of the punishment's end. The Israelite's punishment totaling 2,625 years, God instructed Daniel, began when the ancient Israelite's rightful blood sacrifices at their ancient Jerusalem temple turned unrightful. Since those sacrifices primarily protected ancient Israel from all outside invaders, once even involving God's angel of death defending against the Neo Assyrians, in 605 BC when Israel was finally conquered by ancient Babylon at the Battle of Carchemish, the Israelites' sacrifices first became unrightful. And 2,625 years from 605 BC results in 2020 AD, witnessing the punishment's end and the launch of Jeremiah's foretold, incurable plague spread by China's king according to Ezekiel, marking the beginning of the world's end. This suffering also refers likewise to Americans whom God told Ezekiel were "always made waste" by our leaders until the last four, pro-Chinese U.S. presidents destroyed the world. Our four presidential traitors had Americans unthinkably work to enrich Gog by buying his slave-made products, for his communist citizens are incontrovertibly slaves and own nothing, but can only rent wealth for 77 years from their regime's dictator. By America enriching Gog, we became part of what God terms Magog, a word connoting no single nation but simply meaning all who enrich China's Gog, namely the United States of America for the past 30 odd years.

Our founding father George Washington rightfully prophesied of our nation's end, doubly confirming God's own prophecy that the United States of America was indeed the New Jerusalem of The Gentiles. Since Washington correctly foretold America's future end in our present moment, our founding father is thus sanctified as God's Divine prophet. For God mandated that once a prophet's prophecies have all came true, as Washington's have now, such a person was considered to be His sanctified Divine prophet. Because Washington foretold that after a vile, future American president, who turned out to be William Jefferson Clinton, outsourced U.S. manufacturing to the slaves of a foreign king, this presidential treason would eventually end the nation Washington founded. For Washington prophesied that our American port city elites would then become America's unrealized enemies in a second Civil War; one where their local, port city economies were then fed by the foreign king's slave-made imports forcing them to politically serve the foreign king slave-master. It would be a war Washington prophesied that would not be triggered by slaves on our own shores, but through the foreign king's slave-made imports fueling our U.S. port city economies. These U.S. ports receiving Gog's Chinese imports thereby became the modern, wicked U.S. coastlands likewise damned by God in the *Old Testament* end time prophesies. History proves that our major ports corrupted by China's Gog's slave-made products are our so-called Sanctuary Cities, Seattle, Portland, San Francisco, Los Angeles, San Diego, New York, New Orleans, and logistic cities moving his products further inland such as Denver and Chicago, the same ones illegally inviting and sheltering an invasion by unscreened foreigners against our laws; spilling illegal alien crime upon our streets, while these same politicians who foster this crime try to seize our guns that alone protect us from the outright invasion and violence they unleash on our streets as they trample upon our liberties. But these port city elites Washington warned, would possess future, persuasive powers to trick us of our loss of freedom, presaging our mass media and social media now wholly serving Clinton and Magog. The mass media's Magog loyalty was indisputably verified by the Clintons' illegal wiretapping of president Trump without rebuke by journalists or even an investigation from our own Magog U.S. federal government. Instead of addressing the worst American crime in our history far eclipsing Watergate, the January 6th Committee like the Clinton's prior Russia Hoax, seek to continue their unjust persecution of the one president who resisted our country further enriching Gog. Washington foretold that the foreign king's slave-made goods would corrupt the political system which represented the reigning business elites of any age, for they would then be tied to the foreign king Gog; for no free peoples could ever compete as workers with these foreign slaves, George Washington well knew of the system he formed that could only be sold out by a future president as Clinton proved in history. While God likewise damned our wicked port cities muzzling free speech through His dictated words to Isaiah, "Keep silent before Me, O coastlands, And let the people renew their strength! Let them come near, then let them speak; Let us come near together for judgment."

God's prophet Daniel was also instructed that 2,300 years had to pass from the end of the rightful blood sacrifices to finally cleanse the sanctuary, in what turned out to be the first human sanctuary in Africa before what is now humanity's impending, worldwide climax of good and evil following God's current message. Because 2,300 years from 605 BC brings us to 1695 AD when the English crown finally lost its African slave-trade monopoly; first allowing African slaves to be taken *en masse* to

America where they would finally be freed after eons of African bondage throughout all of Africa's prior history to finally become part of God's current Holy gentiles whose long suffering lately at the hands of the Clintons whom most of black America has politically supported would finally end with what will turn out to be the destruction of the world.

Yet according to God because of the deeds of our forefathers, God now offers in this very short window, a one-time chance for His divine rescue no matter how wicked we have been; in fact, God stresses that the more wicked the better. Because our Creator promises to soon glorify Himself to all by destroying Gog and all of Magog, which now includes much of the United States of America, most namely our U.S. west coast port cities. After that unprecedented earthquake God will later disintegrate the bodies of all our remaining American Magog citizens into dust in the very spots where they stand. God made clear that there are seven outcomes to the rest of our story, but Americans as the Holy people decide future events. But we must call God and He can take away three of our four U.S. pro-Chinese presidential traitors in one month, while blinding the right eye and withering the arm of the most uncaring one, which probably would be either the king or queen Clinton. For our lack of belief in God, He allowed these villains to reign over us and now with His wrath on Americans spent to the point that we would all be dead, He promises that He can swiftly take them away to save our nation from the permanent Magog tyranny they would sow, having replaced American citizens with the horde of unscreened, compliant, impoverished foreigners in our most dire, economic hour of need in what would be their end to the American experiment of liberty and freedom.

God also notes that our current president Biden is merely a pompous horn for the initial traitor and the most powerful one to whom all the other traitors bow to, William and Hillary Clinton; who finally cemented Magog Inc., an ongoing concern that would continue even after the deaths of our unspoken first American king and queen, the Clintons. Their supporters ignore their crimes and outright treason as a supposed new style over fact. Like the journalistic Pulitzer Prize not being taken away from the very reporters who falsely spread the Clinton-created Russia hoax. Or the Clinton's NATO expansion to now threaten Russia's entire western frontier, which they lost 27 million souls defending against Hitler, not even including Napoleon, all after the Clinton's Magog forces falsely blamed Putin of a Trump Russia collusion. Then there's the Clinton's Magog wiretapping of then candidate and later sitting president Donald J. Trump, only to later strip his officials of executive privilege, raid his home and crack his safe, while sealing the warrant to manufacture a crime with whatever they discovered, ending the American political process, arresting the only president to challenge China's hegemony over both political parties; after illegally altering port city election laws to elect their Magog puppet Biden through false, absentee votes and all along co-fund and arm China's Gog with his COVID virus that now kills us all and soon threatens to decimate our nation. All of these vile crimes committed by the Clintons with no comment or rebuke by journalists or mass media, for that would be unstylish to Magog which places the professed ideas of our elites over facts themselves and now has killed a million American citizens to date. God warns that soon a record amount of Americans will be killed with no warning by Gog and in the end only one out of every three people on earth will remain alive after what God terms His purifying fire, for allowing America and the free world to expand Gog's slave-made, world-polluting products, making slaves of free people who could never compete with the Chinese slaves through manufacturing, thereby making us slaves. While Americans remained blind to the treasonous policies of their elected leaders, ignoring God's sage advice to His prophet Samuel to not look at the cosmetic or physical nature of leaders, inevitably blinding us to that person's heart and individual qualities; in this case blinding us to their pro-Chinese treason as they separate Americans into subgroups of ethnicity or newly contrived genders to further divide and conquer us as modern liberal racists no different than their conservative Nazis predecessors.

In light of these crimes, consider that the word Satan in the *Old Testament* means adversary, which is explained as a quantum force at work in the wider multiverse both within us and around us to assure our final fall for our initial fall in Eden, that garden's location on earth also soon to be revealed in this message. As the *Book Of Job* made clear, Satan can take on a human form, God can too, but those manifestations are arguably mere illusions; they visually mislead from the far wider force at work. Yet Satan's hand in ultimately ending our world is finally evident in a human, William Jefferson Clinton, whom God makes clear is humanity's world-ender. Did it surprise you that Satan is an Arkansas bastard, literally? Clinton's father was already married with a wife expecting an infant daughter before he bigamously conceived the bastard William Clinton with his own unaware mother. William Clinton is the kind of man God specifically warned should never lead us as bastards reverse the times, ways, and landmarks; what greater landmark to reverse than one political side arresting the others' leader? Consider the Democratic National Committee, which we've long known through Wikileaks is completely controlled by the Clintons; after 30 odd years of Clintons' Service Economy serving only the Clintons, U.S. Magog, and China's Gog, we are finished; our nation sadly is over. In our lack of belief, we even elected a second bastard, Obama, whose father hailed from a perpetually condemned land of east Africa.[7] Its people cursed from their beginning to their end by God for spreading and perpetuating slavery throughout their history, contrary to the lies that Alex Haley might profess to you in his deceptive myth termed *Roots*, portraying the villainous barbarity of Africa's slave society as if Africans were free until enslavement under the white man. After all these lies and villains, history is soon to be over.

So God comes to rebuke Satan himself, William Jefferson Clinton, the end time King of Babylon, marking Clinton as the

---

[7] Evidence for this point is further explored in point 2 of Appendix (f) on page 411, noting that God decides nationality solely through the father.

final leader of all civilization first birthed in ancient Babylon, while he first anointed Gog and birthed all of U.S. Magog that will soon die from a world-ending meteorite God promises that will smash our planet apart. And then they will be resurrected and all those who follow Clinton and Gog as part of Magog will suffer eternal damnation for they are the worst. The free Americans born into a legacy of liberty who sought to steal that liberty from their fellow Americans and call that generosity, inviting an illegal alien invasion to remove us from our limited dwellings. While Americans will be oppressed by 280,000 new Internal Revenue Service SS officers willingly using lethal force on Americans as the IRS ad for the job specifies, under direct control of the Clintons' presidential puppet, which independent law enforcement would never follow, to oppress, imprison, and remove us from our homes for foreign aliens to habitate. In such a way does communism infect free markets as president Kennedy and Reagan so well understood and feared. Our government is now our Magog enemy, having fallen to Communism. The results of an economic war are the same as a military one, Washington warned, once manufacturing was outsourced, ending our true economic engine of wealth.

After hearing the details of God's self-evident message, one again can only resist the truth through a blind, stylistic loyalty over facts. So the challenge for many Americans and believers worldwide will be if they can actually cast aside these stylistic or political party loyalties, personal bias, vanity, or fear, to admit God's unavoidable revelations already made self-evident through recent events. God also makes clear that within our minds, this continuing Cold War was fought to blind us from our source of liberty. Yet also within our minds, God promises, is the sole source of our Divine rescue: our sanctified, inner temple that God commands all who wish to be rescued by Him to now visit and get politically real about the wickedness we have long committed, warring on our marginalized Americans; our homes now filled with slavery through Gog's Chinese, slave-made goods that polluted the world to its wicked end. And God will know if we are lying and insincere in this future temple His prophets long prophesied would be visited now by peoples of all nations. The place of ultimate knowledge within us, asserted as the only true source of wisdom by science's founder Renee Descartes. For His rock is well on its way. But can you cast aside vanity, prejudice, unfounded convictions based solely on style and mass delusion that yoke you to the Clintons and Gog?

For God's unchangeable ways of the *Old Testament* note that only scripture and not spiritual or political leaders are to form the lens for this inward journey to God within us all. God's only directly-sanctioned spiritual leaders were ancient Levite Israelite priests, limited to acting as health and justice agents and mostly tendering the temple sacrifices. Everything was about one's inner temple within us connected to God and furthered only by rightful temple blood sacrifices and later the *Old Testament* following the loss of that temple. Everything reverse engineered around this inner temple, reasserted by Christ before later Roman meddlers perverted the inward with the outward to control others as all history witnessed. Everything since our human fall in the beginning was centered around this best, possible final outcome in the present moment when every religious leader can now be rescued as well by simply following what Christ could only claim as the inner voyage to his inner temple for all to follow now as per God's *Old Testament* unchangeable laws and His current message. God's message to us now completes the protestant reformation that was never allowed to reach anything close to its fulfillment as so many religious reformers noted. All because of a long-dead Roman Caesar who it will be soon shown, reversed the path to the inner temple all the way to our modern American elites using fear to coerce us.

It's time for every American to put down the shovel, in the end neither party was correct. While believers in God are challenged to renounce their pro-life movement infringing on citizen's rights with no liturgical support[8]; by the same religious leaders allowing sodomy's spread, strictly forbidden by God as history rightly proves that it turns all cultures eventually into pedophile societies. So God now condemns these spiritual leaders as "insane," following their ways over His, needlessly dividing our nation as another aspect of Magog to further the power of China's king. In response, Magog Democrats attempt to seize citizens' guns after spilling crime upon our streets and breeding the godless school shooters who reveal the wickedness God claimed would be in all of our young without a belief in Him, doubly soiled through their modern working mothers outsourcing child care itself to strangers and perverts. Magog Democrats and Republicans since Clinton's initial outsourcing had to socially divide and conquer us by seeking to extend new rights to either illegal aliens or the unborn. For our founders did not hide the fact that our own politicians were masks for our monied, business elites whose political donations our political class was dependent upon to win elections, serving Gog's interests even after China's king mass infected us with COVID, which our leaders helped arm him with. The same elites who persecute the one president since Clinton's outsourcing to challenge Magog and Gog himself. By now these villains have ended your world with no hope of survival without God's coming Divine aid, He assures us. But He will not just come to save us. Because as with the ancient Israelites, modern Americans must now call God from within them to have Him return and rescue us before the coming meteorite will annihilate all of Gog and Magog, soon covering the earth. Those now returning to God within themselves and getting honest about our national crime of enriching a foreign, Communist king will henceforth be protected no matter how it may appear, and later taken away as a chosen branch of Americans and worldwide believers alike willing to get real. Those returning will witness God's rescue that alone can save us, which according to God will

---

[8] Appendix (c) on page 363 addresses the lack of scriptural support for the pro-life movement.

be akin to but far surpassing even biblical Exodus as He alone saves us from our American villains and the collective destruction their wickedness has now sown; a planet-smashing apocalypse all should consider as a scientific truth given that nearly everything God has promised would occur in end times has already been fulfilled. Our government charged with American's safety has allowed Gog to unleash any new strain or even a new virus to wipe us out without rebuke while blinding us with misdirection like the needless Russian war to weaken both Russia and the United States. While both Democrats and Rhino Republicans funded China's COVID lab, outright proving our government must be replaced. While unlike prior leaders trying to avoid nuclear war, they would lead us into nuclear war with Russia for no strategic advantage of our own, along a critical border for Russian national security. They are Magog and to be replaced and shunned.

If this message was not heeded and Americans failed *en masse* to return to God then China's Gog could physically invade our west coast as well, no doubt after most Americans are killed by his plague. But know this, God in the *Old Testament* promises to protect the United States with a firewall so that China's Gog and even his army will not advance beyond our U.S. west coast. As His second blessed nation, the United States is a very special place unlike any other, the reason why many centuries ago, God made clear to the indigenous Americans and those in Mexico to abandon their murderous ways for they would annihilate themselves, the reason why handing them over to the white man continued some of their lives to date. God even prophesied to ancient Rome's king Tarquin before the Roman republic's formation itself that would inspire our own republic. That prophesy would foretell Rome's destruction just like America's from elites from within the republic itself. God's hand will be revealed throughout history in this detailed presentation as He worked backwards in time to create the present moment of choice for his "first born" Americans. Just as He assures us that even in a worst case scenario, Gog and his army will not advance beyond our U.S. west coast, dying from either the angel of death or God's impending meteorite. For God promised Noah He would never destroy all humanity through a second flood, thus using His meteorite to soon end all remaining humans not rescued by God, finally ending the progeny of Noah's offspring who recolonized the ancient, post-flood earth, for only they possessed the vital livestock needed to live long enough to generally plant new crops. Noah's grandsons Meshech and Tubal, God revealed in His condemnation of China's king Gog, ultimately fathered the Chinese people who memorialized the *Bible's Book of Genesis* stories into China's original writing symbols, a link below.[9] But in 605 BC with the Israelite's first temple sacrifices turned unrightful, Buddha and Confucius soon arose to end monotheism across most of the globe, replacing Asia's one God whom they had worshipped for 2,000 years, calling Him Shangdi, with money or an ideal of social order; so did the Chinese ultimately end the world in antiquity from their loss of belief aided by America, God's second blessed nation, who became uninterested in losing its money and growing its social disorder as the modern price of their recent loss of belief in the same God who birthed science. But first, as God foretold, His servant will prepare the way for God's message by first revealing long-hidden truths about ancient Israelite history and concealed truths about the births of Christianity and modern science. These revelations will play out as part of Isaiah's trial between belief and non-belief. As will be shown, the trial will be very short once certain undeniable facts next come to light about Christianity as will next be incontrovertibly shown.

---

[9] Institute For Creative Research: Genesis in Chinese Pictographs, James J.S. Johnson J.D., TH.D

Section IV
PART TWO
THE REBUKE OF HASMONEAN JUDAISM & CONSTANTINIAN CHRISTIANITY
FACTS LONG-KEPT FROM BELIEVERS

FACTS KEPT FROM BELIEVERS

Christianity's roots stemmed from a Roman Emperor who called together an assemblage gathered largely through his adviser Lactantius to finally mint what we term Catholicism; this basis of the movement still termed Christianity, which ultimately asserted novel scripture to stand alongside the historical *Old Testament*, truly called the *Hebrew Bible*. The Catholic movement finds its origins at the *Council of Nicaea* in 325 AD; a gathering formed under the auspices of the Roman emperor Constantine the First. The *New Testament* ultimately resulting from Constantine's Catholicism drew on the prior *Epistles of Paul*, largely proven to be forgeries and not written by Paul himself. [10]For only seven epistles are believed to be written by Paul and they refer to other worldly visions of Joshua misnamed Jesus in another realm and not ever depicting him as a man living here on earth. The Christian narrative biography of a worldly Joshua was only later memorialized in gospels written long after Joshua's passing, and not by his contemporaries or his disciples to what was then Constantine's new faith of Catholicism, which was truly just a sect of Judaism. Yet few realize that a gospel by definition is not a factual tale, but self-admittedly fictionalized, motivational stories contrived to convert the masses to what was then Constantine's new faith. Yet academics long noted a consistency in Christ's sayings throughout the gospels, indicating a probable, previously codified set of the first Joshua's quotations handed down for many centuries by word of mouth from Christ through his disciples. Yet Joshua in these gospels merely reasserted the *Old Testament*'s individualized relationship with the Lord via God's unchangeable laws dictated to Moses, forging a Divine system of worship that was truly unalterable; the same belief system that the emperor Constantine so feared three centuries after Joshua's death. By then, Messianic Joshua followers constituted 12% of the entire Roman Empire, including many top, aristocratic Roman families now calling themselves Messianic "God Fearers". So in 325 AD, Emperor Constantine took control of Joshua's emerging belief system, replacing God's *Old Testament* laws with new ones to be embraced via blind faith in a new system Constantine formalized. Again, even Joshua's name was bastardized to the Greek Jesus as the Divine stage of Joshua's movement ended under this later elite, just as Joshua warned of in these Gospels. His collected quotes probably being so long popular that they must have had to be even included in the codified gospels, despite Joshua in them speaking out against

---

[10] The Ancient World, A Website for Learning and Discovery, *The Pauline Epistles: Known and Suspected Forgeries*, June 22, 2017 by Patrick Lowinger, MA University of Leicester

Constantine's later meddling almost three centuries before it occurred.

CHRIST SPOKE ONLY OF THE *OLD TESTAMENT*

The first Joshua spoke only of the *Old Testament* since only the *Old Testament* existed up to his lifetime and thereafter for three centuries. Until Constantine's tampering set in motion a hierarchy to codify the *New Testament*. Yet Christ in these accepted gospels claimed to bring only *Old Testament* prophecies to fruition, forbidding any new faith beyond God's inner seeking, unalterable, wrestling inner belief framed by God's *Old Testament's* unchangeable rules. While Joshua specifically warned against any future movement sprung from his own as other humans would later corrupt it over time just as the Israelite faith later suffered as will be shortly shown. Joshua's self-proclaimed goal in the gospels could only be the return back to our inner temple as per the *Old Testament*. In his Gospel quotes, Joshua specifically warned that any movement that changed God's unchangeable times and ways would thereby mark its hidden wickedness for all to see, like Christianity altering the Sabbath to Sunday and creating an entirely new path contrary to the inner journey of oneself without any meddling spiritual intermediary, using only the lens of the *Hebrew Bible: Old Testament*.

JOSEPHUS FLAVIUS LIVED TO PROVE JOSHUA'S EXISTENCE

Curiously, what we factually know about the first Joshua is largely provided by the ancient Roman, Israelite historian Josephus Flavius. Josephus was an Israelite aristocrat, academic, and failed Israelite rebel military leader unsuccessfully fighting against ancient Rome. Surrounded by Rome's massive forces in a failed Israelite rebellion, which Josephus helped lead, he was finally trapped in a cave by the Romans. There Josephus experienced a Divine message from God explaining that the Roman army was God's tool to destroy Israel for its sins. Josephus, fated at the time to Roman-inflicted death or slavery was also supplied by God with a critical piece of information: that in fact the general fighting him, Vespasian Flavius, would soon be proclaimed the next emperor of the Roman Empire. Once captured, Josephus was brought to Vespasian's tent where the captured rebel proclaimed Vespasian would be emperor, not long before an official messenger arrived at the tent from Rome with that very news. Instead of killing the captured rebel Josephus, in awed respect Vespasian adopted him as his son, allowing Josephus to take the emperor's *Flavian* last name as his own. Emperor Vespasian would later commission Josephus, his adopted son, to write a history of the Israelite people. In his work, Josephus documents Joshua who died some decades before Josephus was born. Josephus notes Joshua was a wise and respected religious thinker, later crucified in Jerusalem by the Romans until his apparent resurrection before his disciples. Josephus documented that Joshua still had many followers in Josephus' time and could be in theirs and Josephus' own opinion, the Messiah, a term simply meaning a human anointed by God, typically through anointing oils. In this case, Catholicism would have us believe in this anointing certainly not by God but in this case possibly placed on the first Joshua's feet by a sinful woman shortly before his death as per the very factually dubious gospels. Via the *Old Testament*, Christ, who is David's offspring, was not anointed in the *New Testament*, but purified in his sacrifice of pain for David's prior murder and adultery. Then David's soul returned via the second Joshua, explained by God to be a descendant of one of David's father's other children, a wholly different branch beyond David, emerging from what God terms "the stump of Jesse"; this second Joshua's line not permanently stained by David's prior murder and adultery through an individual who according to God was also Elijah the Tishbite who speaks as God's agent in the end times through the second Joshua. Consider that within Israel, documentation on Joshua was uniformly suppressed before and after Christ by illegal Israelite priests in violation of God's law, which will be shortly explained. Thus, Josephus alone provides factual evidence of Joshua's existence in the historical record by this Israelite author who after becoming a Roman Caesar's adopted son, could be censored by no one, sending his writing well into history to us in present times.

GOD'S GUIDE TO THE END OF THE WORLD 99

ISRAELITE PRIESTS SECRETLY PROVE JOSHUA WAS THE MESSIAH

This same Messianic Joshua is curiously found in the then confidential collected notations of Jewish priests of his time in their private archival notes later termed the *Talmud*, its complete text only made public in the 19th Century. In it, modern academics find the classified note in antiquity of the "hanging", meaning crucifixion, of a messianic claimant named Joshua on the Friday before *Passover* at the time of Christ's supposed death. Although two other Messianic claimants named Joshua were slain during this period, this Joshua is notably found guilty by these Israelite priests for practicing God's special magic, which they claimed was impossible and had not been witnessed since the end of the first temple. The same magic representing God's everyday presence that these Israelite priests disavowed could ever exist after the first temple's destruction. As will shortly be revealed by history, these ancient Israelite priests were themselves illegitimate according to God's unalterable rules. For these later Israelite priests failed to solely hail from the Levite clan as God's unchangeable laws mandated of all His Israelite priesthood. The Israelites' priestly archives also notes a second Joshua incident when an Israelite priest's grandson was poisoned only to be quickly healed by an early, Messianic Joshua follower; the healer's magic working so fast that the Israelite priest had to ask the healer how he achieved this feat. Upon learning that the healer had simply uttered that Joshua was the Messiah in the priest's grandson's ear, the Israelite priest damned this magic in front of the healer. Yet he still secretly recorded this event challenging everything about his beliefs in this secret priestly archive.

ISRAELITE PRIESTS DAMNED THEIR MOVEMENT THROUGH PEDOPHILIA

In historical hindsight it's clear that the Levite, Israelite priests condemned themselves many decades before Joshua's birth after their attempt to mass sodomize all Israelite boys; a previously unthinkable outcome for the only ancient society specifically forbidding sodomy and its spread. The later, Levite Israelite priesthood was overtaken by deceptions of the nearby Greek Seleucid king. He claimed to bring tribute to the Israelite's Jerusalem temple. But he truly came for his few bodyguards to open the city gates for his army escort waiting outside the walls to physically invade the capital of Jerusalem during the Israelites' Sabbath; a historic point paralleling how only a few perverts can overthrow heterosexual society in favor of a pedophile one through force and deception, as seen in all societies free of God's specific labeling of such action as *forbidden*. The Greek ways of boy sodomy spread and eventually became the norm in major, Israelite cities until the urban Israelite, homosexual super predators it eventually produced sought to abandon the Israelite ways altogether for the vogue, Greek brotherhood of man; a brotherhood truly based in mass-raping other peoples' boys that the Greek had practiced since the prior, Doric invasion of their land many centuries before. This previously unthinkable attempt of the priesthood's Israelite grab at mass child sodomy was ordered by the Israelite's own high priest named Menelaus, ordering the forced rape of all Israelite boys by their Greek overlords. Israelites were then according to their spiritual leader to cease being Israelites and have their children become Greeks through their own forcible rape and sodomization. The priesthood's attempt at mass child-sodomy was further documented in the Hasmonean *Book of The Maccabees*. What is certainly no longer highlighted is the fact that nearly all homosexuals in any ages, were sodomized, molested, or extremely traumatized as young boys, generally by adult pedophiles, due according to God to their forefathers' sins or their parents' failure to protect their own children. Likewise, God foretold to Hosea of modern American fathers perverting their children as they do now, fostering transsexual behavior in prepubescent children; the reason why God notes, "The iniquity of Ephraim is bound up; His sin is stored up. The sorrows of a woman in childbirth shall come upon him. He is an unwise son, For he should not stay long where children are born.'"

SODOMY'S SPREAD CREATES PERMANENT BIOLOGICAL LINKS

Our Magog American elites in politics, business, and academia ignore the truth long-documented since antiquity by the likes of Philo of Alexandria, a heterosexual Israelite living in the ancient Greek, pedophile world. Philo and other ancient chroniclers well-documented how nearly all sodomized Greek boys curiously matured into feminized, homosexual adult males. This feminization hints at a modern, if little discussed, scientific discovery that sperm like nano machines bore through their recipients' bodies to remain alive linked to the neural networking in that recipient's brain. This new scientific data biologically confirms Philo's prior assertion in antiquity that sodomy cemented permanent, illegal connections between males by violating *Old Testament* proscriptions. For such connections are condemned by God between males. While He says nothing about female lesbians who obviously lacking sperm cannot biologically sow such a forbidden link.

SODOMY'S SPREAD TRULY DESTROYED ANCIENT ISRAEL

In ancient Israel prior to Christ, the call for the mass-sodomization of Israelite boys triggered a second Israelite civil war. The rural backlash against the urban pedophile priests and elites in the ancient capital of Jerusalem finally drove out Israel's pedophile Greek overseers. But the war resulted in one Israelite family, called the Hasmoneans, occupying both the king and priesthood positions; a crime for which they will later walk the earth as part of an undead remnant, hints God to follow to follow at resurrection for this family. For the Hasmonean family was not of Davidian bloodline as required by God for kingship nor did Hasmonean priests hail from the Levite clan, which God's unchangeable laws always demanded of his priests. The Hasmoneans never allowed the return of the legal and political system outlined in the first five books of the *Old Testament*, called the *Torah*. Instead, the kings and priesthood dominated by this one Hasmonean family fed a new sect of Judaism called the Sadducee who claimed there was no afterlife, but only the here and now to enforce their command-and-control structure in violation of God's laws. Two failed civil wars would be fought by ancient Israelites against the Hasmonean hegemony to reinstitute the unchangeable laws of the first five books of the *Old Testament's* spiritual and governmental system unchangeable and dictated by God directly to Moses. The second Israelite civil war resulted in these rightful Israelite rebels' mass-crucifixion as all of their relatives were slaughtered before their eyes while the illegitimate, Hasmonean king dined with his many wives and concubines in the midst of these crucified victims who had simply attempted to reassert God's unchangeable laws. It was with their death that righteousness and justice ended truly for the Israelite nation, bringing us to Christ.

CHRIST WAS KILLED BY SODOMY'S SPREAD
Christ, the first Joshua, only came many decades after the Hasmonean crucifixion of those rightful, dead, Israelite rebels seeking to reimpose God's *Old Testament* laws, marking the approaching end of Hasmonean Israel's illicit governmental system. With the Davidian kingship lost shortly after King David, the second political estate of the Levite priesthood again delegitimized itself trying to forcibly sodomize all Israelite male children. Christ, the first Joshua, followed to mark that the Hasmonean system along with ancient Israel was stained and would soon end; Christ's own death mirroring the rightful rebels' mass crucifixion so many years before: a method of capital punishment so distinctly Roman in nature and yet practiced many decades before Christ by the Israelite, Hasmonean king. While the first Joshua came only once Hasmonean Israel was conquered as a client state of ancient Rome who then warped the Israelite Holy rules to economically enslave the nation that would soon end until recent times.

CHRIST OPPOSED ROME'S ILLEGITIMATE MEDDLING IN GOD'S NAME
Christ lashed out at a statue of the Roman emperor to be placed in the Jerusalem temple; while many modern academics assert that the first Joshua also spoke out against a once-in-a-lifetime

tax documented in the *Book of Exodus*. The same tax that the Israelite Hasmonean elites under Roman rule began extracting yearly rather than once in a lifetime, as it was supposed to be applied upon all Israelite males, economically enslaving God's first blessed nation solely to the benefit of a foreign king; sounds very familiar. Many academics believe that the first Joshua threw over the temple's money-changing tables where Israelites were forced by the Roman's Hasmonean puppets to convert their Israelite shekels to more expensive, Tyrian silver to pay this new, scripturally illegal, yearly tax in God's name. While the Roman governor also moved the Sanhedrin, the Israelite priestly court to a public mall, rendering the running of it nearly impossible. Still, priests affiliated with rabbi Hillel who bore many resemblances to the sayings of the first Joshua, found Joshua innocent, while Romans would not allow any disturbance to their new, moneymaking, local tax scheme. To further stifle any protest about this illicit temple tax, the Roman governor had then wintered his garrison continually in the colder Jerusalem area rather than the warmer coast to keep a strong military arm reinforcing the Roman's heretical tax burden.

CHRIST LATER THREATENED THE ROMAN EMPIRE

Despite the mass torture of Joshua's Messianic Jews from the Emperor Nero onward, three centuries after Joshua's death, his reiteration of the *Old Testament's* inner temple with God threatened to usurp the Roman Empire itself. So the Roman Emperor Constantine finally took control of this threat. In 325 AD Constantine employed Greek messianic priests to neutralize the growing Joshua movement. Constantine feared the individualized, inner temple of the *Old Testament* threatened the uniformity of the Roman command-and-control structure itself. So Constantine sanctioned new priests in a new, proclaimed Catholic faith in 325 AD that was truly nothing more than another sect of Judaism, at the *Council of Nicaea* with subsequent followers all pledging allegiance via the *Nicene Creed*. So 300 years after Christ's birth, Constantine claimed a wholly new covenant beyond Joshua's reassertion of the *Old Testament*, the *Hebrew Bible*, for the *New Testament* would not exist for three centuries thereafter.

CONSTANTINE MISDIRECTED CHRIST'S LATER FOLLOWERS

The Nicean Council's actions self-evidently usurped the prior political system based on God's unchangeable *Torah* laws asserted by Joshua and his Messianic followers and then destroyed by the Hasmoneans until Constantine's Catholicism would overtake the entire west. Again, God's political system always mandated people reach inside themselves via their inner portal forged through His unchangeable, *Old Testament* scripture, which could be stimulated by temple sacrifices. Seeking to end this independent portal, Constantine's Christianity minted new spiritual intermediaries termed Catholic priests. Rather than returning to their inner temples, Catholic followers were thus expected to confess and find outward forgiveness and guidance from these priests serving as spiritual intermediaries between them and God. While this priestly hierarchy's head, the pope in Rome, would later claim to be the earthly, spiritual intermediary between all humans and Christ, which he asserted to be God, and thereby inserting a human between God and all people within Catholicism. Catholicism even formalized a Sunday Sabbath in honor of Emperor Constantine's devotion to the Sun God until his final deathbed, Christian conversion. Constantine's Catholicism indisputably changed the laws and times and therefore through God's dictated, unalterable words was not to be trusted.

CONSTANTINE FALSELY DAMNED ANY FUTURE JOSHUA MESSENGER

Since Constantine's movement had to include Christ's widely known quoted warnings against the Roman emperor's new faith in the ultimately codified gospels, Constantine's Catholicism misdirected from them by antagonizing Jews to dampen any return of Catholics to the *Old Testament*'s inner temple as God demanded in the *Old Testament* liturgy. This Roman-created-faith allied itself with the real killer of Christ, the Romans, while blaming it on the Jews who didn't govern Israel at the time and clearly did not crucify him. The Roman emperor Constantine well feared that if Joshua ever returned, this magical figure could seize control over the empire; so the new liturgy stated Christ's return should not be trusted. For the next Joshua would follow according to Constantine's new scripture, after many false messiahs did wonders akin to Christ. Catholics are also meant to solely focus on Christ coming with God's Divine judgment, ignoring the *Old Testament* end-time prophecies of a future, messianic, political leader, a servant of God with no power of his own, reasserting God's message to the most powerful, future Holy gentiles on earth at the end of history when they admitted the incurability of a plague that began with the ending of the Israelite punishment as the answer to Daniel's Riddle. Yet Constantine's Catholic movement forged a new end-time mythology through the later *Book of Revelations*, partly based on *Old Testament* prophets; credited to a pseudonym of Christ's disciple, the *New Testament* even codified anti-Semitic verses, namely one falsely attributed to John damning Jews as the devil's spawn. That verse fueled centuries of anti-Semitism to further crush Joshua's Israelites, further misdirecting from Christ's reassertion of the *Old Testament's* inner temple permanently mandated by God in the first five books of the *Old Testament* as the sole method of worship and then reasserted through the first Joshua's direct quotes even in those factually dubious gospels.

SATAN IS A FORCE
As the story of Job in the *Old Testament* demonstrates, Satan can manifest as an individual but truly represents a universal, adversarial force working over time through many people and patterns within the multiverse. Since humanity's fall in Eden, Satan generally seeks the eventual death of all. This multiverse force through time and space allows God, as promised, to slowly shape human hearts from honestly avoiding sin while punishing very wicked men to the third and fourth generations of their male progeny; sometimes permanently damning their progeny. The worst wickedness according to God being sodomy and other forbidden modes of behavior like cross-dressing. Catholicism

thus long-acted as part of Satan by persecuting God's Jewish remnant. For according to God, to hate Jews is to hate God Himself, notes our Maker. After all, how kind a land was to the remnant of His Chosen Jews first and foremost decided God's end time judgment of the nations' collective fates. The reason why God and even the first Joshua quoted in the Gospels warns all to dispel any movements that changes God's *Old Testament* unchangeable times and ways, namely persecuting Jews or honoring the wrong Sabbath. And God in the *Old Testament* starkly warns against trusting the words of men who would seek to have you change that covenant. So Christians with the sole exception of Seventh Day Adventists, known as the SDAs, profane God with the wrong Sabbath or honor no Sabbath worship at all; while many SDAs via the *New Testament* are largely infected with spiritual intermediary leaders and Constantine's well-intended, anti-Semitism sown into his *New Testament* scripture, damning the hearts of so many including many SDAs.

CHRISTIANITY IS TRULY CONSTANTINIANISM
Constantinianism would be a far more suitable name for Catholicism and really subsequent Christianity. For the later protestant reformation's heterosexual ministers could best be separated by their Catholic predecessors by the rock star Meatloaf's modern, iconic song lyrics, "I'll do anything for love, but I won't do that,". For Protestantism's abandonment of the celibate, Catholic priesthood finally ended Catholic priestly pedophilia within their flock that the Catholic hierarchy still continues and covers up to this very day. During the Israelite's long Divine punishment, God was prophesied via Isaiah to become the light to the gentiles. As history proved, it would be a misguided light soon warped by elites such as Constantine's misdirection from God's unchangeable laws to the emperor's goal of cementing Roman power through blind faith in place of God's *Old Testament's* wrestling, inner belief. Consider that altering even the unchangeable Saturday Sabbath damns all who follow these leaders upon their Divine resurrection to death or suffering. The price for worshipping the wrong Sabbath day visibly marks an overall failure of nearly all Christians to adhere

to the Lord's basic, clearly spelled out, unchangeable mandate in His *Ten Commandments* applicable to all without exception. And while later protestant religions like Quakerism would draw closer to the spirit of the *Old Testament's* refrain from any spiritual leaders, Quakers failed to respect the Saturday Sabbath as a special day. While again only the Seventh Day Adventist, the SDA movement, admitted Joshua as the Messiah while also acknowledging the unalterable Saturday Sabbath specified by God in the *Old Testament*. But as its founders like Miller and Ellen G. White well warned, far more reform was still needed. In fact, White's seminal book *The Great Controversy* documented the unyielding Catholic persecution of any Christian deviating from the Vatican's total power, rendering death as the price for most later reform until recent times; including killing followers for even supplying their flock with a *Bible* in a language that they could fathom. Rome sought to give them a language that was like gibberish to their followers as Latin changed to the romantic languages, all to continue its unchangeable doctrines that it boasted of, by making those doctrines undecipherable to their very followers for so many centuries.

CHRISTIANITY MIRRORED WICKED ISRAELITE PRIESTS

Constantinian priests long drew their flock from their inner temples, yet they merely mirrored the prior, treasonous, Hasmonean Israelite priests who sought to later hurry God's prophecies and break His rules after Joshua's crucifixion and later, growing Messianic movement. Like the ancient Israelite priest Akiva who damned himself and his followers in Jerusalem's capture by the ancient Romans, their heresy destined later Israelites to be surrounded by a warped reflection of prior, Israelite priestly heresies via Constantine's Catholicism. For the ancient Israelite priests themselves disputed the growing Messianic Joshua's movement returning back to the *Old Testament's* inner temple by manufacturing an outward, political rebel named Bar'Kokba as Isaiah's foretold political messiah. For these Israelite priests unlike Catholics, rightfully noted that Christ did not fulfill Isaiah's second role of the political messiah:

the one born in the end times to the New Jerusalem of Gentiles and not Jews to be its true leader, having no power of his own but reigning in the midst of his enemies, America's leaders at that time. So ancient Israelite priests asserted that Bar'Kokba, their manufactured political leader in antiquity thus undermined the prior suffering messiah who never severed as an end time political leader. God mocked these ancient Israelite priests' renumbering of their calendar to substantiate Bar'Kokba's revolt against ancient Rome as marking the political messiah's return, resetting all of history to the year zero. Yet history would indeed see the calendar of the world remade around the first Joshua's birth. While modern Constantinians, both Catholic and protestant, long-showed as much devotion to their ministers and priests as the misguided, remaining Jews did for their ancient Hasmonean priests who all died in Bar Kokhba's failed Roman revolt. Then Israelite's heresy continued through the later, rabbinic movement of self-professed legal experts, not priests, who ignored their own scripture legally forbidding them as meddling intermediaries or experts between believers and God. For God made clear through his prophets, His words were not hidden and were meant to be read by His follower without any meddling. As history revealed, Malachi's warning of one to carry those away following their illicit leaders and spiritual intermediaries would occur with Adolf Hitler murdering most rabbinic Jews and their followers, who had long-separated themselves from God's protection by having spiritual intermediaries. The Israelites were indeed blessed. But when they broke their side of the covenant, the blessing became a curse. Yet these surviving rabbis and modern spiritual leaders even now still act as though the secrets of the *Old Testament* are hidden, requiring their expert help contrary to God's prophets' repeated mandate, again that His text was made to be clear to anyone without any other person's aid except perhaps their parents; this point would of course put rabbis and all self-purported spiritual intermediaries out of a job as God solely urged all to return inward to their inner temple limited only through the lens of His *Old Testament* laws and guidance. For this reason, these wicked and insane intermediaries can save themselves by spreading this message and ending their meddling ways.

GOD DAMNS ALL ABRAHAMIC SPIRITUAL LEADERS

Shutting everyone out of their inner temple, all of these later spiritual meddlers from Constantinian priests to Islamic imams and Jewish rabbis, are no longer to be tolerated according to God. They were deductively only tools to prepare future people for His current message while prolonging the suffering of the Israelites until their punishment's end to usher in the world's end via Gog's incurable plague to be further explored. Idolizing the ways of elites and failing to return to the only true temple within us now will soon bring certain death upon all followers as well-warned by the prophet Malachi and other end time prophets. While any believer in God should consider that the very word *Israelite* means *to wrestle with God*, so anyone feeling smugly sure in their faith should reconsider their obviously, unfounded certainty, according to God. Any spiritual leader can, however, now save themselves by spreading Gods rightful message at this critical moment to save those in the New Jerusalem of Gentiles and worldwide believers alike.

ISLAM WAS ALSO PART OF THE ISRAELITE PUNISHMENT

The third great Abrahamic faith, Islam, likewise violated its tenet of respecting God's rules when Mohammed first shed Jewish blood. Yet his movement would later be usurped by others in the infamous pen and paper affair, occurring on the prophet's own deathbed; Muhammad lived to witness others literally hijacking his religion; presaging later elites who would alter Mohammed's writings, perverting them into supporting Muslim's modern, violent terrorism, with the revisioner's words able to replace the Great Prophet. For Islam and Christianity alike were both born in the same long-punishment for believers that only ended in 2020 AD as the answer to Daniel's Riddle when all monotheists' suffering in fact ended and the world's end began; and one chance of redemption for everyone was possible.

THE FIRM FOUNDATION

All Abrahamic faiths can only collapse back to the firm foundation of the unchangeable, dictated laws and words of God in the *Old Testament*. Now as God Himself will soon make clear, focusing on the wrong scripture will soon kill anyone. While surviving Jews, Constantine's Christians, and Islam all focus on the wrong liturgy, which now God reveals will soon bring death to all without its adherence and His current aid. Bringing us to our next topic of extraterrestrial aliens, which the *Old Testament's Book of Genesis* long-made clear have been on earth for eons, working amongst us as so-called angelic agents as revealed by God to Jacob. Alien technology in fact it will be shown, may have even triggered this current message.

Section IV
**PART THREE
ALIENS & MESSENGERS**

GOD PROVES EXTRATERRESTRIALS EXIST

Aliens from beyond our world are well documented in the *Old Testament*. *The Book Of Genesis*, "the sons of God who came from the heavens above and saw the beauty of the daughters of men and took wives of all they chose." Deuteronomy explains that, 'Their offspring bore giants like the Anakim or the Emim as the Moabites called them.'" *The Book Of Numbers*, "There we saw the giants (the descendants of Anak came from the giants); and we were like grasshoppers in our own sight, and so we were in their sight." While *The Book of Joshua* notes, 'The name of Hebron was formerly Kirjath Arba, Arba being the greatest of the Anakim." The Anakim again being the giant offspring of those extraterrestrial aliens from the heavens. In Psalms it makes clear, "'You send forth Your Spirit, they are created,'" which is not limited to just earth. God long-revealed He uses angels and servants from other realms of space-time to labor here on earth as He revealed in *Jacob's Ladder dream*.

OMUAMUA & THE ARCHANGEL SAINT MICHAEL

On October 27th, 2017, the object named Omuamua, believed by some leading Harvard academics to be an extraterrestrial probe, turned to face the Arizona Nevada border where it would be captured by the only earth-based telescope, Catalina Sky Survey. Not far from this telescope on that fateful evening, a possible alien visitation materialized before this messenger in the form of the winged Archangel Saint Michael, the only angel meant to represent God Himself. He appeared before this messenger and his wife in our tour bus parked along the Nevada Arizona border. The angel's appearance later matched every detail of a painting of Him by a Bulgarian artist that this messenger would later discover online. Michael's body at the time glowed in sparkling bronze, matching the *Old Testament* prophet Daniel's description of his own angelic vision, which Daniel described as "appearing before me as burnished bronze." In this case, Michael appeared before me with his wings and armor etched as feather and traced His pointed shield down the sole of this messenger's right foot before the Archangel Saint Michael dematerialized. His shield's tip running down this messenger's sole was what would later be realized to be God's anointing just after this messenger uttered a very unexpected message to his wife.

GOD SPEAKS THROUGH AN ANOINTED MESSENGER

The Archangel Saint Michael's 2017 visitation occurred just as this messenger finished telling his wife notions never before entertained, which sounded nonsensical even as they were uttered by this messenger. After this messenger had just completed dinner in his tour bus in the southern Nevada desert following a film shoot when he told his wife that he was a sanctified prophet just like Ellen G. White, Loma Linda Medical Center's 19th Century founder, part of a movement this messenger did not belong to and still does not belong to. While this messenger, a former multimillion dollar manufacturer in the United States forced to later outsource to China by then president Bill Clinton, a former financier, international novelist translated in multiple languages by top publishing firms, and a Hollywood studio filmmaker, was instructed by the Archangel Saint Michael speaking through him that his novel and movie titled *Dreamspace* was "an extension of the mission born of the writings of Ellen G. White"; writings that this messenger had never before read. Only later did this messenger come to learn that White had aimed to save the world in a future end time crisis. This messenger told his wife that *Dreamspace's* movie simulation, a complete hand-drawn, semi-animated, simulation of his intended feature film including symphonic orchestral score, created for key actors and investors was in fact the experience that White in the 1800s claimed that SDAs would now require at the end of days; it was also stressed by the Archangel Saint Michael, speaking through his messenger, that we couldn't accept payment for the film, but only have our expenses covered. The Archangel Saint Michael through this messenger also told his wife that she had to disclose to Dr. Hart, the head of the Loma Linda Medical Center, the internal theft she knew of involving donor dollars, despite her fear that it would cost her own business relationship she had with Loma Linda Medical Center. For this messenger told her that Hart was now commanded by God to hear this message and help fund *Dreamspace* by taking it to Loma Linda's key investors, as it alone could achieve White's mission to save the world. Just as this messenger finished speaking these odd, never before entertained words, the Archangel Saint Michael Himself materialized before this messenger, standing as promised for the sons of our nation, prophesied by God to Daniel, confirming His message that this messenger had just spoken; before God Himself as the Archangel Saint Michael anointed the sole of this messenger's right foot in his wife's presence. While the messenger's wife like the witnesses in the ancient prophet Daniel's angelic visitation did not see the angel that this messenger beheld. But rather she witnessed an inexplicable, magical gray line somehow tracing its way down the sole of my right foot from what this messenger both saw and felt as Michael's shield's tip until the angelic figure then dematerialized.

THE MESSENGER PREPARES

This messenger stopped his regular work, spending the next many weeks trying to create a presentation for Dr. Hart, an individual that this messenger had never met nor previously thought to meet. But explaining an angelic encounter was a new challenge for anyone, especially for a previous, non-believer until discovering the Divine birth of science according to its founder, Renee Descartes, on November 10th, 1619, many years before the Archangel Saint Michael's visitation in 2017 when He stood up before this messenger and anointed his foot. This messenger's book and movie titled *Dreamspace* was designed to persuade believers by revealing science's Divine birth according to Renee Descartes, science's own founder. At one point on a phone call while driving, this messenger later confided to his mother that he wasn't sure if he could meet Dr. Hart, fearing the man would simply consider him mad. Faster than Jonah's whale, a pickup truck careened at approximately 50 miles an hour into the driver's side door of this messenger's rented Lexus at that very moment. Its owner, a mother driving with her newborn and husband, ran a red light, racing across one lane of the Arizona state highway for reasons she could never explain, violently t-boning this messenger's sport scar in a collision that he should not have survived. Thereafter like Jonah, this messenger never again hesitated.

THE DR. HART MEETING

This messenger ultimately met Dr. Hart on the winter solstice of 2017, nearly two months after Michael's angelic visitation. Hart listened to our message on internal corporate theft at Loma Linda Medical Center, watching the brief video we produced to document this point. This messenger told Dr. Hart that the Archangel Saint Michael as God Himself commanded Hart to make *Dreamspace* to fulfill White's mission of saving the world. Hart agreed to have this messenger arrange a local theatre screening of the completed 90-minute previsualizion of the film offered at this messenger's expense. This audio video simulation of the intended movie was created with great labor as this messenger held more roles than any individual in film history. Therefore, this messenger now agrees with Ellen G. White who foresaw that this audio-visual experience from the confines of this filmmaker's mind would be the foretold experience SDA's would need, which in White's own words, "we do not now possess, and which many are too indolent to obtain. It is often the case that trouble is greater in anticipation than in reality; but this is not true of the crisis before us. The most vivid presentation cannot reach the magnitude of the ordeal." For *Dreamspace* makes clear the undeniable Chinese pollution we wrought as part of Daniel's foretold spread of abominations to ultimately bring desolation as the outcome from our lack of belief. Yet how much did Dr. Hart believe? Certainly not enough to follow up as promised with this human messenger who claimed to bring to him the supposed commands of God Himself via the winged archangel Saint Michael Who made clear that the messenger also gain no money from this project. Still, Dr. Hart against his commitment, failed to follow up to screen the experience that the Archangel Saint Michael, representing God, stressed was needed to save the world years ago. To our knowledge he never terminated the employees involved in monetary theft of donor dollars either. This messenger had already fielded major studio offers for the *Dreamspace* project if only we would replace its theme of the world-ending, Chinese pollution as the true source of coming climate change. This point being uniformly demanded by all modern Hollywood studios now seeking access to Communist Chinese movie markets.

ELLEN G. WHITE CAUSED THE HART MEETING

Later this messenger studied the *Old Testament* and Ellen G. White's work *The Great Controversy* since Saint Michael made clear that White was a sanctified prophet like this messenger. And later this messenger learned that White had asked God to allow her future leadership to save the world. Therefore, it can be deduced that God working outside of time, sent this messenger to

Dr. Hart and like Ellen G. White later sensed, Dr. Hart as the leader of her later organization utterly failed at the chance. Consider that Hart was the person intentionally positioned to receive this prophesied experience that White also foresaw. One that it turned out was dispatched by Saint Michael Himself to share the experience that Ellen G. White claimed SDAs would need with her movement's leader and Hart against his promise, refused to see it. Yet Ellen G. White later wrote that some SDAs would eventually take up the cause once they had seen this experience and they would then realize what had to be done: the same experience that her movement's future leader Dr. Hart, against his word, never bothered to review. While presenting this experience to SDAs was strictly prohibited until God's Chinese plague was launched and later admitted incurable. While our current president would like us to simply lower our shield and unfoundedly accept that this plague has just vanished when it has not.

GOD REBUKED THE CATHOLIC CHURCH
The next year not by Holy command of Saint Michael, but through a strange series of events, this messenger would also be sent by God with his wife to a high net worth individual to fund the movie *Dreamspace*. The messenger acknowledged the Saint Michael experience at that meeting, which led to an unlikely second meeting with high Catholic Church officials where this messenger condemned their movement exactly a year to date from Dr. Hart's meeting. These events all documented in the 2020 nonfiction work *Saint Michael Stood Up*, its link provided below.[11] Yet according to God in the *Old Testament* scripture, His end time message again could not be popularized with SDAs or others until what would turn out to be the acceptance of the incurable plague that turns out to be the incurable Chinese plague that turns out to be COVID-19, as will be further explored.

---

[11] https://www.amazon.com/-/zh_TW/Bennett-Joshua-Davlin/dp/1735873640

HART & BIDEN REPRESENT MODERN WICKEDNESS

Saint Michael illustrates Dr. Hart as part of the modern manifestation of evil. Since the fall of Adolf Hitler and the later Soviet Union, the wolf is now masked as the sheep as God warned of our end time age. Like the Clinton puppet Biden whom God will soon prove wars on Americans or Dr. Hart who could've saved the world while also stopping donor dollar theft; both of them appearing as if drawn from *Central Casting's "kind old man actor department"*. Even the famous director of youth films Steven Spielberg who well-memorialized the Nazi Jewish genocide of Jews in concentration camps ardently funds the Democrat Party that openly fuels Mainland China's concentration camps for innocents guilty of only believing in God. Evil now optically appears as the opposite of Hitler. Yet Saint Michael solely directed me to the Seventh Day Adventist leader Dr. Hart, perhaps again because in all history the SDAs alone recognized the rightful suffering messiah and correct Sabbath, aligning themselves against the raging Catholic orthodoxy that ultimately misled the entire Christian faith through the ages. So deductively, the SDAs alone hold a modicum of the intellectual flexibility to acknowledge the correct Sabbath and might be able to wrestle with God on so many other points that He makes unchangeable and might even listen to attain Divine rescue at this moment. Yet the *Old Testament* made clear that this message could only go to SDAs, Americans, and believers again only once Gog's disease was finally accepted as incurable as has recently occurred.

GOD PHYSICALLY SET HIS SPIRIT ON THE MESSENGER

Before the messenger's anointment by Michael and even his birth, both of his parents, two years prior to his birth, were struck with a mysterious beam of light emanating from the night sky in rural Massachusetts; a light magically passing through this messenger's father's own car's hardtop roof, causing his parents' lower extremities, their feet, to glow in a light greenish hew. His father stopped the car according to his mother, stepped out and looked up at the light emanating from the sky. Then he reentered the car and returned to driving and then claimed to have no memory of the event. Thereby this messenger's mother alone remembers witnessing what could be transfigurative light, the same light bringing and taking away the prior Joshua, Elijah the Tishbite, and the biblical Enoch who never died. This, one of many personal revelations amidst the many further explored in the 2020 autobiographical work *Saint Michael Stood Up*.

THE MESSENGER LIVED SEVEN LIVES
Deductively through the *Old Testament's* prophesies and this messenger's anointing by Saint Michael, this messenger is the second of the two Joshuas, and appears like a twin of the first Joshua who lived to usher in ancient Israel's end and is popularly termed the Christ. In the *Old Testament*, God explains there are two Joshua's, separate entities, they are the same; one dying in middle age, and then reappears as someone born in the end time New Jerusalem of The Gentiles in the latter days. God explained to His prophet Zachariah that the two Joshuas stand as two olive trees of wisdom built on seven prior lives: Zerubbabel, the political leader who served alongside the ancient, high priest Joshua son of Josedech, King David, and through the prophet Malachi's end-time prophecy, also the spirit of Elijah the Tishbite. Although this messenger cannot explain how, he knows he was the ancient Enoch, that father of Methuselah who was also brought up into a beam of light by God like Elijah the Tishbite. It is probably that this messenger was also Moses since our end time tale will soon recursively mirror but exceed Exodus, according to God. Moses' body could've certainly been taken up into a beam of transfigurative light, which unlike Elijah's witnessed transcendence by his apprentice Elisha, was in Moses's case hidden from his flock, for he supposedly died alone. These prior seven lives would deductively fulfill the seven flames of the two identical lampstands that God revealed as His two anointed Messiahs to His prophet Zechariah. No matter, if Saint Michael appeared via Omuamua or God's magical pathway, this messenger's October 27th, 2017 anointing marks this anointed as the Elect of God many years before 2020's U.S. port city Magog

elites in major ports illegally altered election laws to rid themselves of the rightful president Donald J. Trump for reasons to be shortly explained. Trump stands as our John The Baptist to show our stain, which we do not see as we are so mind controlled as will also be shortly proven. In short, this messenger is the mysterious, little revealed, end time "servant of the Lord" in ancient scripture, "the branch" born into America, the New Jerusalem of The Gentiles as it will soon be shown, to prepare the way for God's arrival and to save a remnant as the seed or the branch in an alternate multiverse where the wicked are taken away near the end and the good inherit the kingdom. Working outside of time, God may have populated half of the first Joshua's DNA with only the first Joshua's mother; God may have been the father as Isaiah foretold. But this end time messenger of the Lord is the product of two biological parents, both receiving God's spirit upon them, according to his mother even if his father was robbed of that memory. Although the anointing of the first Joshua was unclear at best, in 2017 the Lord has certainly raised His shield and not His sword to anoint this messenger. For God explained that He caused our troubles for our nation's general lack of belief in Him until now when He will next free us to glorify Himself by destroying Gog and Magog, which He unleashed upon us for our lack of belief until we would all die. So He chose to have a remnant. As God long prophesied, He searched out a reluctant messenger who was indeed not looking for Him, a learned person well educated in many fields as He prophesied, a former multimillion dollar manufacturer who would know how to quickly resurrect American manufacturing and understood the source of our modern, national evil. This messenger is also a former structured financier, a novelist translated in various languages by the most prestigious publishers, a professional screenwriter, producer, director working with major Hollywood studios who could synthesize from scripture to simply communicate God's message; and a person whose life was entwined with the underlying evils that now God and George Washington will both explain will soon destroys us: the outsourcing of manufacturing to mainland Communist China. Next comes God's message to lend rest to the weary in what is now proven by Him to be humanity's most dire moment. Indeed, the sacrifice of all humanity that does not return to this message has been fated by God. The guests are all invited, but will you find His rescue? For next comes God's message to lend rest to the weary in what is now proven by Him to be humanity's most dire moment in which the good news of our rescue can be offered to all from the very same God in who birthed science as will next be incontrovertibly shown.

Section IV
PART FOUR
THE DETAILED PRESENTATION

SCIENCE PROVES GOD'S EXISTENCE

Again atheism, also termed secularism is the belief that God does not exist, which will now be proven to be scientifically unfounded. For it is impossible for informed scientists to deny God's existence since God Himself created science as per science's founder, Renee Descartes. Because on the night of November 10th, 1619 while alone in a German shack, the mercenary soldier Renee Descartes experienced Divine dreams he later claimed to be actual visions from God Himself. Several days leading up to this particular evening, Descartes felt God enhancing his mind from within him. And then one afternoon he realized that purely, mental concepts like math could be physically projected into the external world, discovering what he termed his *new wonderful foundation of science*, which we simply call science.

DESCARTES CLAIMED TO BE VISITED BY GOD

Before going to bed alone after conceiving of science, Descartes somehow knew a supernatural being would visit him. When this figure arrived in his shack later that evening of November 10th, 1619, Descartes termed Him the Spirit of Truth, acknowledging this Figure to be God or His Divine agent. The experiences of that night would inspire this French mercenary soldier to take up a pilgrimage the very next day, although we have no evidence to see that he did fulfill that promise. But those events did certainly cause him to invent the scientific method. Science's first two works would in fact be Descartes' proof of the existence of God, standing unrefuted to this day, followed by science's proof of the immortality of the human consciousness, which Descartes proved to be part of God Himself. Therefore all human souls like God had to be inherently immortal, rendering death a temporary illusion as God claimed in scripture.

DESCARTES' SCIENCE WAS LATER ALTERED

Descartes' later followers naming themselves Cartesians after him, feared the Catholic Church's persecution of Descartes' new science; for many recent inquiries had already upended much of the ancient philosopher Aristotle's explanations of the natural world. But Aristotle's theories had long been embraced as unalterable truths by the Catholic Church, inherited from their prior, medieval *Scholasticism Movement*. So a thousand years after Aristotle's passing, the 16th Century thinker Galileo would be imprisoned in his home for life for merely proving that heavenly bodies moved in elliptical orbits rather than the circular ones that Aristotle had asserted. So if Descartes new science openly claimed it was born from God's visit on 11/10/1619, his followers felt certain that Catholic church elites would kill them all. So they amended Descartes' scientific method to sidestep science's birth and God by demanding another witness be present or an experience be duplicated to ever be considered scientifically valid. Since Descartes was alone during his Divine encounter, his followers added the two rules to again sidestep God and invalidate science's birth altogether; because no secondary observer did witness those events in that German shack on 11/10/1619. Nor could Science's Divine birth be duplicated as a lab experiment to fulfill Descartes' followers' additional rules crafted to conceal God Who had birthed their movement.

THE ALTERED SCIENCE IS NOW DEADLY FOR ALL

Descartes scoffed at his mutinous followers' new need for secondary corroboration or an additional observer to support scientific validity. Yet on a wider scale, science's founder actually attacked his followers' outward-looking orientation, rather than searching within themselves. For Descartes reasserted how God in scripture made clear that He limited what could be known about observable reality. Therefore, an inward looking journey of thought experiments and pure reason according to science's founder, remained the sole path to true wisdom since the reality observed was a cloaked illusion according to God. Descartes' followers, the Cartesians, mocked their founder's assertion of a conscious universe akin to what would later be *Star Wars'* Force, purposefully hiding its natural ways from human observation until desired. Because Descartes asserted that the universe behaved differently when it was unobserved as opposed to when it was observed. It would also be proven to behave in another different way when machines remotely recorded the basic foundations of reality with no human present at the time. For a universe purposely hiding itself from humans would indeed be scientifically confirmed 300 years after Descartes in the landmark *Quantum Physics Double Slit experiment*, a link provided below.[12] But back in the 1600s, Descartes' conclusion was purely derived according to science's founder from within himself in the greatest wellspring of knowledge, one science's founder claimed to be an extension of God. The same inner temple of reason and

---

[12] Web search "Dr. Quantum – Double Slit Experiment" for a five-minute animation presenting this proven truth.

feeling that God made clear in *Old Testament* scripture existed as the Divine light powering all of our consciousnesses, which was part of our Creator. God visually illustrated this truth to Descartes as sparks exploding throughout his German cabin on the evening of 11/10/1619. For God outside of time knew that this mercenary soldier would later interpret it as God's Divine sparks constituting our mind and soul as part of our Maker; the same sparks that later neural biology would indeed prove constitute our consciousness. Yet from where do these blasts of energy originate? For our brains as science recently confirmed are not processors like computers, but what we can now deductively reason is a receiving station for God's Divine sparks fueling our continuing consciousness through the progression of space-time within the multiverse of possibilities, indicated by Quantum mechanics science. So our temporary bodies continue through our ever changing present moment as our consciousness is received within our brains as pure energy that is truly part of God in another realm altogether.

OUR INNER TEMPLE IS REAL & PART OF GOD
Descartes would later try to discover what could be proven true in reality by first ridding himself of all false presuppositions. Science's founder noted that we spent half of our lives dreaming and thinking that real, so humans were very easy to trick. After great mental reflection, Renee Descartes realized that our minds thinking thoughts was all one could ever be sure truly existed, his famous and largely misunderstood *I think therefore I am* conclusion was thus the only provable fact in reality. Our thoughts, not the external world was the only real truth in what God made clear was a cloaked illusion as a test of our hearts. Yet science's founder asserted this proposed fact four centuries before neuro science ever revealed our consciousness consisted of sparks quickly appearing and disappearing in varying patterns between the thousand, trillion neural synapses within our brain. These otherworldly sparks thus touch nothing in our brain but appear and disappear in ever changing configurations between the synapses thereby powering our consciousness as God's ghost in the drone-like receiving machine of our bodies. That pure

energy powering our minds was linked to God and termed by Descartes and God alike as our Divine inner temple linking us to our Creator, rendering our consciousness inherently immortal as God noted in scripture, making death as much of a temporary illusion as the observable universe would be proven by later 20th Century physics. So after our life's test in this realm, our total decisions thus fate our coming eternal life as God indicated. All hewn from a test of our hearts exclusively fashioned by God for human beings and likewise requiring those following Him to rest in their dwellings on the seventh day of our week in union with our Creator. For by resting on the Saturday Sabbath God makes clear in scripture, we like Him rest with God Who is in and around us, aiding us in this moral test, but for the past many eons hiding His face from us. So according to God how we held the Sabbath decided the fate of our next week from the many paths He wove from our free will outside of time through the quantum multiverse. Because the holiday of Passover was described as the Sabbath of Sabbaths, ultimately deciding the fate of an Israelite's entire, coming year. We may make the judgments but God makes clear that He fates the steps of our entire life, all of this fated long before we're born.

SCIENCE VERIFIES GOD'S EXISTENCE
Science can thus only confirm God's existence since God created science on 11/10/1619 as per science's founder. Rationalism is therefore born of a highly irrational occurrence involving God's Divine intervention. And as will be soon shown, science's founder joins God's dictated words in antiquity, urging our current return to our inner temples as will shortly be incontrovertibly proven. While leaders of all nations and ages throughout history have conspired to keep all of their subjects from their inner temples despite God's unalterable rules on the matter.

DESCARTES CONTINUED TO ASSERT GOD BIRTHED SCIENCE
For the rest of Descartes' life, science's inventor remained wholly obsessed with those Divine experiences of 11/10/1619. Science's

inventor again doubted that night and later came to admit that these dreams had actually been real experiences he termed visions. Like *Old Testament* prophets, Descartes later claimed God had Himself physically transported Descartes through time and space on November 10th, 1619. While what he beheld in those visions was actually a message for modern Americans as will shortly be shown. While more academic documentation on science's birth on 11/10/1619 is available in the PHD lecture *The Mystical Dreams of Descartes, Origins of Rationalism and Modernity* and also in our website's supporting essay *Science's Dirty Secret*, both links provided below.[13]

NEWTON DESTROYED THE CARTESIANS
Sir Isaac Newton, a firm believer in God soon ended the Cartesian movement over their stubborn opposition to his proposed theory of gravity. Because unlike Descartes, Cartesians had demanded gravity be an observable, tangible force and not unseen like the God Cartesians had sought so hard to hide from their movement. While Newton, a firm believer himself, accepted gravity's invisible nature as part of God beyond knowing.

CARTESIAN LIES WERE RESURRECTED
Sir Isaac Newton destroyed the Cartesians by using the invisible and unexplainable force of gravity to unlock the movements of nearly all heavenly bodies in observable space. But many decades later, the 18th Century philosopher David Hume would resurrect Cartesianism's unfounded skepticism while omitting Descartes' underlying proof of consciousness as being part of God Himself. With science's birth by God again hidden, the 20th Century Quantum Physics *Double Slit experiment* would be needed to prove that God did indeed hide reality from observers, thereby proving His existence to doubters in recent history. That

---

[13] https://www.youtube.com/watch?v=xMWyFsHzBU0&t=931s

experiment would not occur until the 20th Century, still most scientists considered themselves like Newton as simply unveiling God's hidden systems, the inner workings of His many hosts of varying size from atoms up to molecules to the whole universe providing our existential platform to test our hearts via the Lord Of Hosts, God's common moniker by end time prophets addressing our futuristic end time humanity.

SCIENCE PROVES SECULARISM IS A LIE

Modern scientific secularism or atheism, the non-belief in God thus only exists due to the coverup of science's Divine birth on 11/10/1619. This concealment was later continued by elites such as the early 20th Century economist John Maynard Keynes who purchased and suppressed Newton's private diaries. This secular economist was revolted by Newton's extreme religiosity for the Judeo-Christian belief system that inherently damned Keynes' homosexual behavior, marking him according to God as most wicked. Homosexuality was after all a quantum punishment that God explained He visited upon the male offspring of very wicked men to the third and fourth generations as He made undeniably clear in the *Old Testament*. Then after World War II's genocide of nearly all Jewish people, God did not appear. So finally as God long foretold, most quit believing and finally in recent times came to breaking the remaining forbidden proscriptions, the forbidden actions. Forbidden because they would bring the end to all, as our current modernity will prove.

THE REAL PROJECT 1619 IS GOD

By now nearly no one is aware of the Divine birth of science on 11/10/1619, the real Project 1619; the intentional product of a coverup of science's birth via a biased academia. While curiously the recent scientific philosopher Thomas Kuhn prophesied in the late 20th Century that our understanding of reality would end in a final, coming paradigm shift when all we thought scientifically real would again be overthrown. As will be proven through this message, witnessing God's irrefutable and recursive return. The same God who undeniably birthed science according to its founder Renee Descartes on that November 10th, 1619 evening, no matter what later people might claim to assert.

DON'T TRUST THE EXPERTS
So no longer can followers of science refuse God's existence since God birthed science itself. A fact science's creator Renee Descartes again vehemently reiterates through his warning that we can now not trust our modern scientists. Science's founder warned that they would all be eventually corrupted by wealthy and powerful elites. While in the end, God prophesied an unrealized enemy would control all the money and thus pervert science to truly destroy all free peoples. This point was elaborated upon in the 19th Century by the scientific philosopher William James who revealed modern science to be a speculative light shining only where funding both private and academic chose to take it. Science therefore was highly subjective and controlled by those in power. Again Renee Descartes, science's founder thus warns that we can now only trust our personal experiences for all we see and hear are lies. While God Himself will shortly prove along with science's founder that the medical and climate experts, political elites, and electronic mass media and social media are liars at war with the average American for the benefit of our hidden enemy who intentionally murders us without us sadly realizing it. The end of our republic is now fated at this point. For we will learn that we were long trapped in an unrealized Matrix of our hidden enemy's lies so that God had to come to rescue us.

SUPPORTING FORBIDDEN THINGS ENDS ALL
God makes clear that His Ten Commandments and forbidden acts termed proscriptions are to be prohibited by all for such behavior made *en masse* will kill everyone in that society; as we'll see with the United States leading the global society, our violations of these proscriptions will soon end the planet itself. Consider that the ancient Israelite belief system that alone warred on sodomy in antiquity was finally lost when urban Israelite priests allowed sodomy's spread as a newfound love and tolerance just as elites in recent modernity now attempt to foster.

For all of history proved that sodomy's spread inevitably seeks to usurp heterosexual families over time as our elites and media now foster, grooming our impressionable young as the new prey while the current adult sodomists remain culpably silent on their own past child rape and trauma that rendered them homosexuals or proscribed perverts as per God in the first place. While these outcomes were quantumly fated in our continuing multiverse by their wicked genetic ancestors according to God Himself. For sodomy's reach was powerful and dark as it flowed into the future, connecting not heterosexual families but long chains of sodomized children whose innocence recently symbolized by the rainbow was indeed snatched from them by what were mostly adult pedophiles; rendering nearly all adult homosexuals as casualties of prior child sodomy that is not something to be proud of, but a truth to be shared in order to save future children. In ancient Israel, sodomy's spread soon led their high priest leader to attempt the previously unthinkable, forced mass rape of all Israelite boys and the attempted abandonment of their Israelite identity to permanently become pedophile Greek sodomists. The outcome of the only religion that prohibited sodomy's spread and thereby broke that proscription. Now without a belief in God, our modern media and political elites sodomize young minds rather than bodies with a far quicker reach and speed than the prior pedophiles could have ever hoped to achieve through physical child sodomy. Yet science proves that sperm have been scientifically revealed to act as nano mechanisms, literally boring through the bodies of recipients to remain alive in their brains, creating a mysterious permanent link between peoples' neural networks; forming the same illegal connections documented by most ancient historians such as Philo of Alexandria, that ancient Israelite writer living in the Greek pedophile city. Philo noted how sodomized boys curiously all matured into feminized males, the byproduct of what he termed "illegal biblical connections" between males forbidden by the Old Testament through a biological mechanism only recently indicated by modern science.

CHRIST DIED OVER SODOMY'S SPREAD

In antiquity, Joshua whose name was later bastardized into the Greek Jesus, clearly died as a result of the prior attempt of urban Levite priestly leaders to mass sodomize all the Israelite boys and abandon the Israelite covenant for the Greek Seleucid pedophile ways that had long ruled and influenced those people. Following the successful civil wars fought by the rural population to stop the urban, Jerusalem pedophile priestly elites from mass-raping the Israelite boys, ancient Israel finally rid itself of pedophilia and the child sodomizing ways of their Greeks overlords but sadly they never again returned to God's rightful ways via the *Torah*; they were thereafter illegally ruled by one family, named the Hasmoneans, who reigned contrary to God's *Old Testament* laws. The Hasmonean tyranny later forced ancient Israelite dissidents to fight two more civil wars in a failed attempt to restore the rightful governmental and spiritual ways as specified in the first five books of the *Old Testament*, the *Torah*: those unchangeable rules. These righteous rebels would all be crucified by the illegal Hasmonean king through a method typically employed by later Romans; their deaths presaging Christs crucifixion, marking the end of the first blessed nation that truly died many decades before Christ with those liturgically-correct, ancient Israelite rebels. The first Joshua's death therefore marked the loss of God's sanctification after the two estates of the Israelite government had long condemned themselves; first the Davidian kingship had invalidated itself long before the later Levite priestly sodomists attempt at mass child sodomy. The spread of sodomy thus finally brought an end to the remaining state of the Israelite governmental system, drawing Christ on earth, killing him, and crucifying him to likewise mark the end of that first blessed nation that died with those liturgically correct rebels.

GOD LOVES AMERICA

As God will shortly reveal, Americans and believers worldwide would find Him waiting for us in reality in a way not witnessed for over two millenniums. God indeed dictated to His end-time prophets of His future return to save the second blessed nation He termed the New Jerusalem not of mostly Jews, but of Holy

Gentiles in a distant, end time land. These gentiles had been gathered according to God from many lands and brought to a powerful western land still unknown in biblical antiquity where they would excel at hard work, commerce, and trade. God had claimed that He would let the first Israel perish, but save this future gentile nation as will soon be proven. The reason why all Americans can thus now find His Divine pardon as God will soon explain through dictated words from ancient scripture. But our Holy gentile nation like the ancient Israelites are required to collectively call God to save us and then to personally sanctify the United States as alone to rule forever. To rid any doubt of America's blessed status, God will use His dictated words and our nation's founder, George Washington's curious prophecy of our country's end, to soon doubly confirm the United States as the chosen New Jerusalem of Gentiles; what God termed His "firstborn" as He worked backwards and outside of time rendering our history to generate this present, intended outcome as He addresses everyone now alive in AD. God will soon make clear that our unrealized sins can find His Divine pardon again due to our forefathers' great deeds before we quit discerning good and evil in a wicked misnamed tolerance that will soon be proven to bring death to all not shortly returning to Him to find rescue; the result of the loss of belief in the one nation that ever allowed for God's *Old Testament's* unalterable system of worship since those crucified Israelite rebels died so long ago. For only the United States of America's constitution allowed God's intended and unchangeable path of purely searching within ourselves as per the *Old Testament's* unchangeable ways without any human spiritual intermediary or meddling expert being forced upon us as all prior citizens of the many nations experienced in their histories.

GOD'S EXPLANATIONS ARE PROVEN BY SCIENCE
The *Old Testament's* first five books, again termed the *Torah*, and God's dictated words and signs revealed to the End Time prophets were purportedly dictated by God to Moses. Most of this scripture is actually proven scientifically accurate given our recently acquired modern corpus of knowledge. Did God not

birth our universe in exploding light as the 20th Century's discovery of the Big Bang verified? That great explosions' echo is still undeniably visible throughout the universe and evident in the static of all untuned television sets. While our own bodies are indeed as God claimed, gathered from dust, namely the stardust making up all earth-based life forms' molecular structures. A special dust forged only in exploding stars billions of years after our universe's formation, to generate all the higher elements of the Periodic Table beyond just hydrogen, helium, and lithium. This stardust constitutes the architecture of all our genetic predecessors who did evolve to later have God's spirit and inner temple placed within our genetic Adam; our eventual father of all humanity being recently verified via DNA science. And satellite observations recently revealed the now dried up fourth river that fed the Euphrates River in antiquity, thereby proving that Eden lays under the Persian Gulf just south of that river's mouth; or God's scriptural laws of hygiene allowing ancient Israelites who were wholly ignorant of microbial life to avoid its threats nonetheless as if they understood it. God also made clear that He controls the weather, our human will, our long-term patterns in outcomes throughout the quantum multiverse, and everything else in a test of our hearts; within a universe God claimed to make in six days for the Sabbath of the seventh day in a test He fashioned to fate our eternal lives from our free will choices here. God stressed that nothing in reality mattered but our free will choices and those of our children, all the eventual progeny of Noah's sons following the great flood. And since that flood, our lives according to our Maker are now limited to only a hundred and twenty years rather than the multi-century lifespans well documented throughout the *Old Testament*'s *Book Of Genesis* until Noah's flood. While the ancient Babylonian king list exterior to the *Old Testament* also records their pre-flood rulers curiously living for many centuries until the great deluge, which resulted in post-flood lifespans being limited to a century at best.

GOD EXPLAINED HOW REALITY WORKED

God claims if He immediately meted out justice on the wicked of any age until now evil people would simply hide their wicked hearts behind outwardly good actions. Since our actions decide if He stops our progeny from continuing through history by reproducing, these inwardly, wicked people would naturally pass on their evil ways through their continuing descendants of our species. But God cares what we think in our mind for it is our hearts that God clearly wishes to expose and shape through the ages to His intended remaining, present generation whom He worked backwards and outside of time to create as His so-called "First Born" modern American citizens. So the wicked were long-rewarded by their free will choices, but after they died according to God, some would even remain conscious in suffering pain far below the earth in an undiscovered place called Sheol until His return, hence the phrase: no rest for the wicked. Until God's end time judgment will damn many to the pit that later believers termed Hell while others will remain on earth as worm-eaten remnants of corpses unable to die and move on, remaining as those wicked who truly ended our planet. For God promised that once forbidden human actions ended earth, as He will soon reveal has been fated, God now comes to reveal Himself in our visible reality to save the sons of the New Jerusalem of Gentiles and believers worldwide.

WHY GOD COMES NOW

Through what God later termed Daniel's Riddle, He promised to His *Old Testament* prophet Daniel that God would hide His daily presence from the Israelites, punishing them for 1,290 days, biblically meaning years, followed by 1,335 days, likewise meaning years, creating a punishment totaling 2,625 years. This sentence would commence in the year that the ancient Israelites' temple sacrifices first turned unrightful. Since God makes clear that the Israelites' rightful blood sacrifices at their Jerusalem temple ultimately protected their nation from all outside invaders, when the ancient Israelites were finally conquered by a foreign king would reveal when these sacrifices first turned unrightful; thereby allowing the subsequent calculation of the exact year when the Israelite's long punishment would end. Israel's sacrifices at their Jerusalem temple therefore incontrovertibly became unrightful in 605 BC when its first foreign invader, ancient Babylon's king Nebuchadnezzar II at the Battle of Carchemish, finally conquered ancient Israel. 2,625 years from Babylon's 605 BC's initial conquest of ancient Israel brings us to 2020 AD as the exact year when the Israelites' long suffering finally ended. 2020 AD as recent history proved, also witnessed the worldwide release of the incurable plague that God prophesied to Jeremiah would begin the world's *Time Of Trouble*, its eventual end due to our many godless abominations. As will also be shown, God prophesied this disease originated from Mainland China as part of its wicked king's dire, secret plan. In fact, God Himself will next reveal this plan to all Americans who would soon be dead without His current revelations. So now as promised, God comes to save Americans and believers worldwide only once that disease is finally considered incurable or endemic in AD. It can thus be deduced that up to now, God only continued our world to perpetuate the Israelites' long punishment while likewise damning all punishing His Chosen in His coming judgment. For the peoples of the many nations He made clear in the *Old Testament* would be judged first and foremost by how they treated His Chosen Israelites. While this same term applies to His first-born American Israelites, the Americans who never mass-punished Jews on American soil over their beliefs. Yet God prophesied to Ezekiel of our Holy peoples of the future New Jerusalem of Gentiles. A nation that already experienced one civil war before suffering another in the undiscovered land of the west in biblical antiquity; where these future Holy people would long be made waste by their own leaders, according to God to Ezekiel, until those four later U.S. presidents wickedly enriched the world-ending foreign king whom God codenamed Gog. Gog was foretold to hatch a vile plan to end the world. But before the end of the world at Gog's hand, Daniel was also told that 2,300 days, again meaning years, must pass to cleanse the sanctuary, connoting the original sanctuary of all humanity in Africa for this coming worldwide climax for our entire species. 2,300 years from 605 BC's Babylonian conquest of ancient Israel brings us to 1695 when the English king lost his monopoly on the African slave trade. The next year, 1696, would witness African slaves being brought over by Americans who would finally be later freed on our shores by president Lincoln to become part of the Holy chosen Gentiles in humanity's worldwide, climatic end. Of all the peoples of the continent of Africa stained by the Ethiopians' spread of slavery, that region meaning north and east Africa, only those brought to the United States would reach a blessed status rather than the condemned one God so names.[14]

GOD UNMASKS GOG

God revealed to his prophet Ezekiel that the end-time, incurable disease would be spread by Mainland China's king that God codenamed Gog. For Gog was long ago revealed by God to be the ruler of the Land Of Ten Kingdoms, Mainland China's historic name. Mainland China was likewise referred to by God as the land of the north and verified as the ultimate, world-ending beast of ten horns, the horns revealing kings, shown to Daniel, while being instructed that this creature representing Gog would in fact kill all life. That beast's ten horns biblically signified ten kings, doubly confirming it as the Land of Ten Kingdoms, again Mainland China, whose world-ending dictator God codenamed Gog who incontrovertibly launched our ultimately incurable plague leading to 2020 AD; again the exact year the Israelites' suffering finally ended and the world's end began. For history proves that China's king whom God codenamed Gog, undeniably hid his Chinese disease from the world for 5 critical months before his Chinese airline passengers who had visited Mainland China for the Lunar New Year festivities, returned via airplanes to points worldwide infecting America and the world with COVID-19. But this Chinese plague, God will prove is not a natural disease, nor was it accidentally released. Rather according to God, China's Gog intentionally released his Chinese virus to murder all Americans and ultimately take their unguarded homes, dwellings, riches, and livestock, according to God who now allows us into the

---

[14] This condemnation also includes Barack Obama, further explored in section 2 of Appendix (f) on page 411.

Chinese king's own wicked mind, all through His dictated words in antiquity. Hence the reason why China's king is again codenamed Gog. For Gog intentionally murders and masks it as a seemingly natural act of God Himself, a point now drawing the Lord's ire. While our top health scientists and leaders who armed China's king Gog with this virus are incapable of ever facing him since they funded and aided in the creation of Gog's incurable disease destroying our nation. These leaders and top health experts charged with Americas' safety have thus far killed a million Americans citizens to date, which doesn't even compare to the tragedy of what will shortly transpire. For again, God promises two out of every three people alive today will shortly be dead while these same officials have failed to discuss the true PPE, personal protection, of a conventional .40 mm NATO gas mask with a mere HEPA filter, which would offer 99.99% protection from COVID and is available by retailers worldwide. The PPE every American who wishes to remain alive will need, its link on eBay provided below.

GOD PROPHESIED OF THE PANDEMIC'S LAUNCH
God rightly prophesied to His *Old Testament* prophet Ezekiel that China's king Gog through his brilliantly clad Chinese soldiers, God again specifically termed 'passengers', would seed our incurable plague. He prophesied that these Chinese passengers would descend in flying chariots as an unrealized army to spread Gog's ultimately incurable disease like a storm across the New Jerusalem of the Gentiles and the world. God now allows us into China's king Gog's mind to realize that Gog's military Wuhan lab outbreak was again not accidental, nor was the virus naturally released. Again this plague, God stresses was China's Gog's purposefully launched pandemic, a point that can't be repeated enough. For China's Gog secretly aims to kill us all and inhabit our land once we are gone. A dire outcome God stressed that Gog now achieves through new disease strains further spread by Gog's Chinese operatives masked as Mainland Chinese "passengers" planted along our American west coast to perpetuate his plague. For these Chinese viral operatives releasing their new COVID strains as needed by China's Gog

will only end once God devastates our American west coast with an unheralded earthquake, claims our Maker, one that will bring down all the walls on west coast Americans long-enriching and embracing China's king to the point that much of our coastline God notes, truly flies Gog's royal banner over our own flag; whom these same west coasters bow to, supporting the invasion of our nation with illegal aliens to rule over Americans and run us out of our limited dwellings in our hour of dire economic need. The reason why God will soon rename much of our American west coast as Hamona, a word meaning the multitude who served China's Gog.

WHY GOG WANTS TO KILL EVERYONE
Again, Gog actually requires a new land to resettle with his regime after he has escaped the retribution of his own poisoned people by purposely killing them with COVID. Indeed Communist China even by the 1970s had killed a record amount of humans in history, almost all of them their own citizens. Indeed, China's unregulated manufacturing pollution poisoned the Chinese land to death. This unavoidable truth in the most populated nation on earth was universally hidden from most Americans. When Harvard University concluded in the 20'teens that China could never clean its air, it drove the subsequent concentration of power into a new dictator, Gog, charged with finding a way to continue his most wicked Communist regime. So God now comes to reveal that Gog intentionally planned to kill all Americans with this virus. Our deaths from COVID are thus another cost for fueling the largest manufacturing pollution in history, born from slave-made, Mainland Chinese products; generating such unthinkable poisons into the air as liquid mercury, arsenic, an array of unthinkable toxins, not to mention the dirtiest and largest coal pollution in history, even birthing micro-metal shrapnel into the atmosphere. From a record air pollution America long sowed through our made in Chinese purchases, its cost so uniformly hidden from us that we now even die from Gog's Chinese toxic foods our pro-Communist Service Economy literally spawned in China and since president Obama, allowed into our nations' grocery stores. For this reason,

our tables are now full of filth and vomit according to God. For Americans have eaten the fruit of lies because we trusted in our own way warns God, in the multitude of our mighty men over His clear teachings that wisely guided all Americans before us. Until William Clinton had us first place Gog's Chinese world-ending goods in our comical, recyclable bags our own later pro-Chinese U.S Magog politicians would mandate, while further feeding this pollution that is the true source of source of coming climate change; an indicator of our very poor shepherds who after the lessons of the 20th Century, ignored all prior Cold War presidents and Winston Churchill's sage advice that one can never do business with tyrants who will always seek to kill all free peoples. As proof of our poor American leadership, consider the irony that God Himself had to come and tell the land of the supposed free that they weren't allowed to enrich Communist slavery?

GOD ALONE ENDS COVID
To end COVID, God promises to soon bring that massive earthquake upon our west coast intentionally burying the wicked American citizens under their own roofs to be half-eaten by wild animals in what God specifically promises as a human sacrifice to the animals to cleanse and liberate our American land long stained by Communist enrichment, part of worldwide seismic activity as the earth according to God, pants and screams like a pregnant woman. These west coast American human remains, God prophesied, will be collected for 7 long months as west coasters become experts at body reclamation. The mass human remains will then be buried in a cemetery shaped like a human nose, teases God, to finally plug the noses of Gog's Chinese passengers planted there by China's king to again spread his new COVID strains as needed. This nose-shaped cemetery will reside east of the Pacific Ocean in the U.S. west coast valley to be named Hamon-Gog, a word literally meaning where many of Gog's followers perished. God also promises to wipe out the American Magog elites as their bodies quickly turn to dust where they stand in a mass removal of our remaining traitors for the entire world to witness before the end. And by that end again

only one out of every three Americans will remain after God's so-called purifying fire. And after God's promised, coming resurrection of all men and their eventual judgment, our U.S. Magog traitors, leaders, and probably followers alike, will follow their Chinese dictator Gog to a very special fate of eternal suffering, according to our Maker. For these American villains are most despised by God who after being born into the land of the free, which took all of history to create, sought to take that freedom and liberty from their fellow Americans. An act they achieved by elevating human intuition over God's laws. Allowing them to take from other Americans and give to illegal foreigners on our land in contraventions of our laws while calling that theft generous. Like overfilling our limited dwelling and using our dwindling water supply with untold tens of millions of aliens actually incentivized by our Magog U.S. civil servants to invade us. These wicked villains who were called "transgressors" by God from the womb who have one law for illegal aliens standing in mass contempt of court while filling our streets with violence while persecuting American citizens for the same crimes. This treason was truly a blind loyalty of Democrats to traitorous pro-China Democrat Party elites whose policies had Americans work to fund even Gog's concentration camps for his innocent Muslim believers and North Korea's growing nuclear arsenal, both solely funded by China; but all truly funded by Americans' Chinese purchases since the traitor Clinton. God even notes that our west coast wines are actually the wines of the condemned as all will soon see when God glorifies Himself by destroying most west coast Americans, truly crippling King Gog's political power in America.

GOD UNMASKS MAGOG & THE KING OF BABYLON
God stressed that China's Gog would be made powerful solely through others. While all who enriched China's king Gog are termed by God to be part of Magog, that word connoting no single nation but simply meaning all who enrich Gog. Yet once Americans no longer worked to contain Chinese communist tyranny but actually enriched it via Clinton's Service Economy, the United States of America slowly became completely Magog.

For Americans indisputably by now worked to buy Communist Chinese slave-made products, turning Americans into "thieves" warned God, while solely enriching the Chinese slaves' king Gog. For China's king Gog's goods are incontrovertibly slave-made; therefore no free peoples could ever compete with Gog's minions whom God Himself prophesied to be Chinese slave "craftsmen"; for no Communist Chinese citizen can legally own wealth or property, but only rent it from their regime for 77 years. The Communist Chinese as our forefathers all well knew, were never anything but slaves of their dictator king. While the 20th century well-proved that Communism was never anything more than window-dressing for some inevitable tyrant killing everything they touch while promising some coming utopia that never arrives. All they bring is death. God makes clear that this was how the United States, the land of freedom and liberty, unthinkably birthed and enriched our world-ending destroyer. As America's political Magog elites treasonously had our taxpayer money co-fund Gog's Wuhan Lab, using our experts to help Gog create COVID that again has killed a million Americans to date. Clinton thus earned the moniker from God of the King of Babylon, a word meaning modernity's final, modern ruler who truly fated the end of civilization that first began in ancient Babylon itself; which makes William Clinton the most despicable human in God's own eyes: the final outcome of Satan by destroying humanity and the planet. God explains that Satan is again a term meaning adversary; it is an adversarial force long at work in our multiverse throughout our history via human behavior, natural events, and unknown forces, all to assure our failure either here on earth or at our coming judgment. This force Satan can take on a human form, which is merely an interface, while His reach on earth was finally manifested through Clinton's free will decisions of selling the United States of America out to Communism to anoint Gog's empire to thereby feed Clinton bribes as George Washington will shortly foretell. In fact when Clinton dies, he will according to God through His prophet Isaiah find himself in Sheol, at an unknown underworld to us where the worst worm-ridden elites from history cannot die, but live and wait until God's impending judgment; each dead worm-eaten king having a place notes God, to bathe in what He calls glory and forget their wicked state, except for the King Of Babylon himself. For Clinton alone has no place of glory because this vile individual ultimately ended our nation and species. By doing so, Clinton became the wealthiest politician in American history with Gog's money that Americans worked to pay Gog in the first place as part of Magog; Clinton's villainy would be continued, God prophesied, by three more kings who would feed and finally cement Gog's power until he could destroy our nation and the world.

GOD DAMNS OUR FOUR U.S. MAGOG KINGS

God rightly foretold that our first three, Magog U.S. presidential kings would consecutively serve in office, fully cementing Gog's power over America and the world. For again China's Gog, God stressed, was only made powerful by others, namely our American villains who according to God are thus undeniably unmasked as the four wicked, pro-Chinese U.S. presidents, the first three serving consecutively. Presidents William Clinton, George W. Bush, and Barack Obama who damned themselves through their indisputable, pro-Chinese economic enrichment contrary to all prior U.S. presidents. God likewise now condemns these four men when the Chinese king's plague was finally considered incurable. God also rightly foretold that their Magog enrichment would be unstuck by what turned out to be president Trump's Chinese trade war, bringing China's king Gog's resulting plague of COVID-19. While history proves that our U.S. port cities illegally altering their voter laws to allow for the recently revealed fraudulent mass-voting ballots, brought a fourth U.S. Magog horn, Biden. God stresses that Biden openly wars on Americans. Yet Biden, God reveals, is only a puppet of the U.S. Magog traitor whom all the others bow to, ultimately the Clintons. They have fed our American enslavement long-hidden from us. So God now damns these four, pro-Chinese presidential villains. In fact, He promises that if Americans now return to Him and admit their unrealized sin of empowering Communist China and show contrition and mercy on their fellow Americans, God Himself will kill three of the four traitorous U.S. kings in one month, while marking the worst by blinding their right eye and withering their arm in what sounds like a stroke, which could be William or Hillary Clinton as well as the unseen puppet master long-funding this Magog madness, George Soros. Again, God prophesied that He would only address the world once that Chinese plague was finally considered incurable, as was recently evidenced, bringing His ancient dictated warning from antiquity to the world: resuming His daily presence in our continuing reality. Again, God warned that He came only after every American would soon be dead from Gog's coming actions and our political treason without His current rescue.

THE CHINESE POLLUTION IS EMBODIED IN GOG

By having Americans help to poison Gog's land, our four pro-Chinese presidents Clinton, W. Bush, Obama, and Biden, incontrovertibly created the first world-ending leader who will kill most of humanity to again relocate his regime after poisoning his land to death. Because Mainland China's air pollution from their manufacturing, Harvard University again has concluded can never be cleaned; leading to Gog being charged with somehow having to find a way forward, which this dictator hopes to achieve through his Chinese COVID disease unthinkably co-funded with our taxpayer monies, paid by our National Institute of Health to sub-corps to aid Gog in his Wuhan lab. Therefore, America's Magog treason truly created in the end, the mass genocide now unleashed by China's king Gog to repopulate the earth after killing all of us, perhaps even using his own genetically engineered fetuses rendered invulnerable to AIDS. For AIDS turns the immune system against its victims in similar ways that COVID does; while Stanford University helped Gog's minions to create those GMO'd fetuses with our politicians' full treasonous, Magog support and funding.

GEORGE WASHINGTON DOUBLY CONFIRMED GOD'S PROPHECY

Our founding father George Washington rightfully prophesied of our nation's end, doubly confirming God's own prophecy that the United States of America was indeed the New Jerusalem of The Gentiles. Since Washington correctly foretold America's future end in our present moment, our founding father is thus sanctified as God's Divine prophet. For God mandated that once a prophet's prophecies have all come true, as Washington's have now, such a person was considered to be His sanctified Divine prophet. Because Washington foretold that after a vile, future American president, who turned out to be William Jefferson Clinton, outsourced U.S. manufacturing to the slaves of a foreign king, this presidential treason would eventually end the nation Washington founded. For Washington prophesied that our American port city elites would then become America's unrealized enemies in a second Civil War; one where their local port city economies were then fed by the foreign king's slave-made imports forcing them to politically serve the foreign king slave-master. It would be a war Washington prophesied that would not be triggered by slaves on our own shores, but through the foreign king's slave-made imports fueling our U.S. port city economies. These U.S. ports receiving Gog's Chinese imports thereby became the modern, wicked U.S. coastlands likewise damned by God in the *Old Testament* end time prophesies. History proves that our major ports corrupted by China's Gog's slave-made products again are our so-called Sanctuary Cities, Seattle, Portland, San Francisco, Los Angeles, San Diego, New York, New Orleans, and logistic cities moving his products further inland such as Denver and Chicago, the same ones illegally inviting and sheltering an invasion by unscreened foreigners against our laws; spilling illegal alien crime upon our streets while these same politicians who foster this crime try to seize our guns that alone protect us from the outright invasion and violence they unleash on our streets as they trample upon our liberties. But these port city elites Washington warned, would possess future, persuasive powers to trick us of our loss of freedom, presaging our mass media and social media now wholly serving Clinton and Magog. The mass media's Magog loyalty was indisputably verified by the Clintons' illegal wiretapping of president Trump without rebuke by journalists or even an investigation from our own Magog U.S. federal government.

Instead of addressing the worst American crime in our history far eclipsing Watergate, the January 6th Committee like the Clinton's prior Russia Hoax, seek to continue their unjust persecution of the one president who resisted our country further enriching Gog. Washington foretold that the foreign king's slave-made goods would corrupt the political system which represented the reigning business elites of any age, for they would then be tied to the foreign king Gog; for no free peoples could ever compete as workers with these foreign slaves, George Washington well knew of the system he formed that could only be sold out by a future president as Clinton proved in history. While God likewise damned our wicked port cities muzzling free speech through His dictated words to Isaiah, "Keep silent before Me, O coastlands, And let the people renew their strength! Let them come near, then let them speak; Let us come near together for judgment."

WASHINGTON FORETOLD SLAVE-MADE GOODS WOULD DAMN AMERICA

Again, the Communist Chinese are communist slaves of their dictator despite what our Magog U.S. elites may otherwise wickedly assert. God always condemns slavery, the reason He damned the entire region of east Africa termed biblical Ethiopia from these peoples' beginning to their end. For Ethiopians dominated the African continent, making slavery the norm for its entire history despite modern Magog lies like Alex Haley's novel and miniseries Roots, which would falsely have us believe that Africans were free only to be suddenly enslaved in the 1600s. Africa for its entire history stretching back for eons was always an amalgam of unjust slave societies; quite unlike the so-called *slavery* in ancient Israel or colonial America, which were largely indentured servants merely working off credit extended to them by their temporary employer. While slaves in Africa were commonly killed or sacrificed before even reaching maturity, revolting even the Muslim slave-trading middlemen who witnessed these horrors. Just as George Washington foretold all Americans through our manufacturing outsourcing to the foreign king would render us his slaves, Americans can now either admit in their hearts the crimes the Democrats and Rhino Republicans fed our nation or remain part of the dictatorship of style over facts that the founder of economics himself, Adam Smith, rightly foretold would end the world. His prophecy foretelling our current outcome and thereby also marking him as a sanctified prophet of God among so many modern voices that they could fill another presentation altogether.

AMERICANS BECAME NAZIS
God termed the Holy gentiles of the United States as Ephraim, distinctly different from ancient Israel. For Ephraim was the name of the second son born to Joseph and his foreign, Egyptian wife abroad. Joseph's father, Jacob, rightly prophesied that Ephraim, his second born grandson would exceed his first-born grandson, presaging the later United States which eclipsed ancient Israel as well as the modern iteration of Israel that the United States likewise formed and protected since the 1940s. While the death of most non-American Jews coincided with the United States ascent as the world power eclipsing any other in human history as God rightly prophesied. One where an overreaction to Adolf Hitler's Nazi policies later caused us to act evil in the aim of embracing all as equals, an opposite direction that yet achieved the same wicked outcome as the deaths of the innocents like the Nazis. It is an over correction commonly made in history and well-noted by the 19th Century historical philosopher Hegel. Contrary to Hitler's honest hatred, our modern U.S. Magog Nazis remain cloaked in a supposed new love and tolerance for anything under the sun except it seems cannibalism; their hypocritical love professed through smooth words that God now warns is truly the wolf clad as the sheep. While so-called racism is comically condemned by our Magog leaders who mass-raped all American minorities in prison after robbing them of their historical manufacturing jobs since president Clinton's outsourcing of manufacturing. But after limiting our language and thereby our thoughts which are run on that language through the wicked and duplicitous system of political correctness, we were censored and mind controlled via etiquette now advanced by our U.S. Magog Nazis. The reason

Americans have now become like those Nazis. Do not our purchases undeniably fund China's Gog's concentration camps of millions of innocent Chinese believers and even pay for North Korea's nuclear missile arsenal, again wholly subsidized by China through our own Chinese purchases? An economic policy continued by our American Nazi villain like Biden, puppet of the Clintons, who ignores our Chinese viral murderer as Biden even lowers tariffs on China. Biden claims to be a liberator as this U.S. Magog puppet ships oil to China's king while internally launching what God calls viper eggs to mature and overtake us by embracing God's previously forbidden acts of sodomy, sexual perversion, or enriching Communist tyranny. Once we outsourced manufacturing warned George Washington, we wrought our inevitable destruction and only a return to a belief in God could again save us. For George Washington rightly warned that our republic could not continue without belief for we would be tricked according to our founder by our leaders professing new unproven ways that were truly death. Like enriching our Communist enemy, arming him with COVID, murdering us as our traitorous elites refused to get real with what they have done. But we as Americans likewise supported and even reelected these U.S. Magog fiends. In such a way did Washington warn that now only a belief in God could center and save us. Hence now why God comes to open the eyes of every American willing to simply get real and find their promised Divine rescue after our leaders lowered our guard against COVID by telling us that it is endemic and the pandemic is over.

AMERICANS QUIT BELIEVING IN GOD & BECAME SLAVERS
In the *Old Testament,* God showed His ancient prophets visions of our nearly endless chariots and material goods in our blessed end time, New Jerusalem of Gentile homes; a nation in which those ancient prophets saw us falling to worshipping the idols earned from our hands and thereby later exclusively made by China's Gog's slaves. In this nation where God had promised to gather select gentiles together from the other lands to be spared from

Gog's end time destruction. A country that nationally guarded a new Eden of commerce symbolized by the eagle and hard-working ox, which lost and would later find God's grace symbolized by the lion, the exact combination of faces revealed through the multi-faced angel to Ezekiel with an eagle, cherub ox, human, and lion visages.[15] These angels hold God's throne when He will return to our second blessed land that He foretold had already suffered a civil war before incurring a second, civil war at its end, fought again by our foreign, slave-enriched U.S. elites against our own people. Washington stressed that second hidden civil war was not over physical slaves on American soil, but specifically through slave-made imports of the foreign king in an economic war. Washington warned that economic war would bring the same results as a military one.

GOD'S PROOF THAT WE ARE AT THE END

God's *Old Testament* prophet Daniel was shown the four beasts symbolizing the four major types of nations in history. First, we began in the wild as a human headed tiger with two wings, the wings were torn off and a human mind, God's inner temple, was implanted within him. Then the endless tyrants ruling over humans were revealed as a hungry bear gnawing on three bones, possibly presaging the three future, later American kings who cemented Gog to end the world. This bear was then set free for most of history to quench its truly unquenchable hunger. Then the American republic was revealed to Daniel as a blessed creature via its four bird-like wings, revealing its special blessedness through four heads of divided power: our House of Representatives, the Senate, Judiciary, and a new Executive sector based on the lessons of the prior Roman republic. These four wings rendered us more blessed than any monarchy. Our system inspired by Greek democracy and Rome's prior iteration

---

[15] These visages could represent the wobble shift in earth's galactic orbit bringing civilization-ending cataclysms, Why is There No Record of Ancient Humans? - Randall Carlson https://www.youtube.com/watch?v=F-d4zfovcog&t=389s

of a republic possessed these four wings, again more than any other system to reveal our divine blessings until Clinton empowered the fourth system of government ultimately belonging to China's Gog. This fourth creature, half-mechanized, again possessing ten horns, symbolizing those ten kingdoms, revealing it as Mainland China's Gog. While God stressed that Gog was again made solely great by others, namely our three consecutive, U.S. presidential kings who physically attached America to the Chinese beast only to be removed by president Trump's trade war and COVID bringing false absentee ballots to anoint the fourth Magog puppet horn of Biden; who is truly the Clinton's puppet as they war with us while seeking to escape punishment for their outright treason and the impending end the United States of America.

GOD DAMNS AMERICANS BOWING TO MAGOG

By breaking our oath to liberty, many in the land of the free now proudly bow before our own American flag. Yet we truly take a knee to our U.S. Magog villains as tyrant agents of the grand tyrant himself, Gog: the unseen monster whom this deference solely enriches. These misguided Americans truly bow before the madness of our leaders able to give a so-called vaccine, actually a wholly untested, experimental gene therapy to our children without parental consent or knowledge in our tax funded schools. This power being the product always in American history of monopolies; although we spent a century and a half to learn the power of breaking monopolies, since our outsourcing to Gog we have given nearly every product that we need in our lives in a monopoly to a foreign Communist, tyrant king. So now does it surprise you that in the port cities flush with his imports, quoting Isaiah, "People bow down, And each man humbles himself; Therefore do not forgive them,". While forbidden perversions are now espoused by our modern teachers sexualizing innocent, prepubescent children to behavior that was previously considered perverted, and certainly is so as per God. All after older children have been taught to ignore inconvenient truths as trigger points, a bullying that seems to act as weakness to silence others, so that our society could have the illogical system of hypocrisies like women who can't prostitute their bodies but could hire out their wombs. Or males being unable to legally use steroids to become more muscular, but can use drugs to change their gender; with our own military forced to subsidize sex change operations to attract perverts who infect our military with sodomy and perversions in a movement that blames the world for their suffering, truly brought on by their parents who didn't protect them, or their ancestors who damned them through their wicked actions. While women claim the right to use their body's safety through pro-choice rights, but not when it comes to owning a gun or resisting a completely untested COVID treatment misnamed a *vaccine*. This is just a hodgepodge of issues force fed to their blind followers on either side. Now Hollywood studios care more about your skin color before even hearing your ideas. We are the most racist nation in our entire history as we hypocritically destroy civil war monuments, having mass-raped all urban blacks and Latinos after Clinton and his Magog predecessors stripped them of their historic factory jobs. Or Monkey Pox vaccines being given to black homosexuals over other sodomists of other skin colors; these prejudices born of no logic, but professed by the outright racist leftist elites who would seek to destroy us all. These divisions sowed as convenient political machinations to forge *the dictatorship of style*, which again the founder of economics and sanctified prophet Adam Smith, rightly warned would end the world from free market forces later abused by our elites whom Smith termed the damning "masters of mankind."

U.S. & ANCIENT ISRAEL'S SERVITUDE WERE HIDDEN FOR 18 YEARS

For exactly 18 years in antiquity ancient Babylon economically sucked ancient Israel dry before wiping it out in 587 BC. After Babylon's initial 605 BC conquest of ancient Israel, exactly 18 years would pass while Babylon economically sucked Israel dry before wiping it out in 587 BC. Likewise, our American Magog servitude to Communist China followed 18 years from Clinton's sponsoring of Mainland China into the World Trade Organization at the very end of 2021. Therefore 2002 AD witnessed Gog's slave-made products first sucking America and the free world economically dry until 2020 AD's pandemic was intentionally released by China's dictator Gog exactly 18 years thereafter.[16] So for 18 years both ancient Israel and the modern Israel of the United States Of Americans worked ultimately for no gain of their own as our society will also shortly end just as ancient Israel's did.

EVERYTHING ENDS LIKE SODOM & GOMORRAH

God well warns that His Divine pardon will not be available for Americans and modern believers once humanity's certain death is unavoidably apparent from the world-ending meteorite and other afflictions that God promises will soon be visible. Due to our American wickedness our entire planet will end in the same method God used to wipe out Sodom and Gomorrah. Those two ancient cities' destruction scientifically confirmed to be from meteorites, which still leave flammable brimstone and ash in the sites of these destroyed cities. Their destruction from the heavens witnessed at the time by ancient Babylonian astronomers, their stone-carved, astronomical archival record of those cities being wiped out by meteorite fragments only recently discovered.

OUR POLITICIANS EXCEPT TRUMP ENDED OUR EARTH

As our Magog U.S. environmentalists and elites like Biden demonize American fossil fuels, Democrats and Rhino Republicans truly poisoned our world to death from China's manufacturing pollution for over 30 years. The wing of abomination" rising into the air first revealed to Daniel. Now Democrats popularize a new science of green energy which like Star Trek's warp drive is a complete and utter myth meant to cripple us before Gog. We can only at best generate energy with green energy options under ideal conditions and then cannot permanently store that energy, which quickly leaks except in

---

[16] Although the virus began in 2019, it was not mass-thrust across the U.S. and free world until 2020.

fossil fuels; making these green scientists the same kind of false prophets as climate change scientists who ignore China's outright pollution while demonizing fossil fuels and nitrogen emissions. Yet consider that all alternative fuels could only power our world for less than two days. While electric vehicles are powered on fossil fuel electric plants and constructed with even worse mass-polluting, material fallout. The undeniable truth for now is that we do not have the technology to store energy over time except as found in fossil fuels. While the free world was falsely misdirected again to our carbon and nitrogen emissions to crush our economy and bring needless famine to further aid Gog's pollution, making our elites and experts all liars.

OUR MAGOG MEDIA MONOPOLY MIND CONTROLS US

Our recent mass media having devolved from 66 companies in the mid 1990s to the current Magog monopoly of only 3, rendered us into mind-controlled fools, again placing toxically made Chinese goods into our comical, recyclable bags while mass consuming even toxic Chinese food products. In fact, in the first of Descartes' Divine November 10th, 1619 dreams or visions, he was handed a poisonous melon from a distant land that soon left him bent over in pain. The source of Descartes' suffering, science's founder well knew was hidden from him by a malevolent, evil genius, representing Gog and his U.S. Magog elites. Descartes' next vision revealed sparks all around his German shack, connoting the Divine sparks of God in our mind highlighting our inner temple's source of Divine rescue. The final dream or vision presaged God's message, leaving Americans to choose which way to now go. We can thus refuse our godless science and choose God's wisdom and history, acknowledging the God who created science, gave us His sanctified prophets, and now kindly offers rescue to even the most wicked from God's coming annihilation.

OUR LOSS OF BELIEF IS THE REAL POLLUTION

Our loss of belief as will be shown allowed for our wicked enrichment of Communist China in the first place. The coverup of that subsequent Chinese manufacturing pollution America long birthed and fed is actually sprung from our loss of belief and the source of all of our modern woes. The Chinese pollution is therefore the real and unmentioned source of climate change despite what our Magog environmentalists may otherwise falsely claim. Again, it was why Gog launched COVID in the first place. China's manufacturing pollution also triggered other woes, the loss of manufacturing jobs in upcoming generations, the same jobs that truly created wealth. The pollution's coverup led to Americans' first ever loss of free speech feeding the U.S.'s record imprisonment of its citizens long-stripped of their historic manufacturing jobs. It's the source of our inundation by illegal drugs supplied by Gog to the Mexican Cartels and transported through our open southern border, fueling our weaponized Latino illegal alien invasion triggering our subsequent homeless and crime to displace and endanger American citizens further consuming the west coast's dwindling water supplies and natural resources. With our manufacturing jobs lost to further fuel the Chinese pollution, our own politicians aided in Americans' opioid addictions, first legally supplied and now available on the black market. The pollution has also fed media silence on how the spread of sodomy and sexual perversions create permanent pedophile cultures. The pollution set the trap for the green energy myth. And after filling our streets with disenfranchised Americans and illegal alien crime, our same Magog politicians would seek to take our guns, which the former Japanese Prime Minister Shinzo Abe's assassination in a largely gun-free Japan proves only endangers citizens. The greatest cost of that Chinese pollution is the COVID-19 virus itself, which our government and godless scientists co-funded and helped Gog to unthinkably kill our nation, a point which cannot be reiterated enough to our mind-controlled, American masses.

OUR END IS NIGH

Our American elites with the exception of Trumpian Republicans therefore ended our nation and world according to God through His current message. God now makes clear in scripture that our modern crisis ends in starvation and mass death with our American cities in ruins. The only way to survive is to now return to Him and find His magical rescue through what He claims is a mysterious, secret sanctuary of His covenant within our minds.

GOG CONTROLS YOUR MIND
Our present moment is truly frightening but largely unrealized because China's king Gog so well deceives you in so many ways. China's Gog again thinks nothing of killing his own slave-citizens. While in America, China's Gog can cut off our supply chains or seed our made-in-China products with his viruses because our leaders treasonously allowed a foreign, communist king to wholly control the supply chains of nearly all our remaining businesses. Whereas economic monopolies for over 100 years have been illegal for Americans, our Magog elites granted a monopoly of our entire economy to Gog, thereby undermining our national security; now this treason was first begun by William Jefferson Clinton but it was continued by W. Bush and his Rhino republicans as Bush unconstitutionally eavesdropped on all Americans, triggering our eventual loss of free speech in an emerging false, Magog veil of disinformation. In fact, God warns that our free speech is now akin to the dead whispering in the ground. While president W. Bush claimed to go to war in Iraq after hearing God tell him to do so. Yet God specifically made clear in the *Old Testament* that He is not an oracle in modernity for anyone. Because all men according to God have now become their own deranged oracles just like president W. Bush was for himself concerning that war; until Obama came to further empower Gog while poisoning us with China's toxic foods. So now our modern journalists who once reported for our consideration now tell us what is real and censor our reactions, further supported by Biden's attempt at a wicked disinformation bureau long-advanced by his big tech proxies. As our government, God makes clear, is our existential enemy in our hidden, second civil war from Clinton's Cold War surrender to Chinese Communism. While Biden, the fourth pompous horn of the Clintons and China's Gog openly wars on Americans, to soon use Gog's virus to annihilate us before we ever come for his

Clintonian puppet masters for even wiretapping a sitting president Trump and arming Gog again with that incurable plague.

THE CLINTONS ARE AMERICA'S ULTIMATE ENEMY
So the Clinton-controlled federal government and Magog mass media by now act as undeniable proof of Clinton's American kingship by failing to cover the illegal wiretapping by the Clintons of President Trump. Nor do journalists comment on then Secretary of State Hillary Clinton revealing and thereby murdering via Gog's hand all of our Chinese spies, their cover blown on her private server to China, allowing Gog to silence the only voices that could've warned us of COVID. The mass media also remains silent on the Clinton's Russia Hoax. Yet their illegal wiretapping truly proves how the Clintons are outwardly not private citizens, they're elevated above all presidents for then president Richard Nixon had to resign over Watergate, which was a far lesser crime than wiretapping a sitting president without rebuke. Or the Clinton's outright creation of a false Russia narrative as purposeful misdirection while attacking Trump and his administration even to date. If you want to know who truly controls you, advised the 18th Century French philosopher Voltaire, simply find out whom you cannot criticize. The Clinton Kings are the first in a new political Magog aristocracy making them a king and queen above rebuke, aided with billions of dollars from our own made in China purchases to make them the most powerful threat to the American constitution in our history. They also have very powerful allies like George Soros, so that even Fox News silences Newt Gingrich, a former speaker of the House of Representatives over his rightful highlight of how the billionaire George Soros funded America's new crime wave in our cities by funding wicked D.A.'s fostering death through zero bail, kowtowing to criminals, fueling illegals whose crimes are mass-unreported as part of Soros's deranged goal of a borderless society where Gog obviously reigns alone as the world's mass murdering king.

THE WORLD DIED FROM AMERICA ABANDONING MANUFACTURING

Our end again came according to George Washington from abandoning American manufacturing. Yet Gog well knows that we could return manufacturing by simply mimicking what communist Mainland China did with its own southern neighbor Hong Kong; we could easily employ cheap Mexican labor working in American manufactories along our own southern border on U.S. soil while returning home at night. Americans would then avoid the massive trans-Pacific-oceanic shipment of all our goods. The U.S. is rich in fossil energy resources and natural raw materials. A policy to return manufacturing is further linked in our short, policy film below, along with a further discussion in a following section of this presentation. While ours is the only visible plan to quickly return manufacturing so that Americans buying American goods, restoring our own wealth to remain within our borders rather than leaking out to solely empower Gog.

OUR WICKEDNESS NOW COMES FOR OUR CHILDREN

In the *Old Testament*, God repeatedly explained that China's incurable plague was our national punishment for failing to believe and thereby embracing modes that have robbed us of liberty and will soon take our lives and world. Without a belief in God, we embraced our new, unrealized enemies as supposed victims and now worship the foreign idol Gog who can kill us all without rebuke. For their own pro-life heresy and supporting sodomy's forbidden spread, the modern prophets according to God are all fools: the modern spiritual man having gone "insane" according to our Creator. God makes expressly clear to pro-Life Republicans in scripture that He decides the outcomes of all lives while we're still in the womb. Yet this religious, so-called Pro-Life movement deceptively uses God's working with special, chosen unborn prophets and individuals in Holy scripture to unfoundedly justify the defense of all the unborn; this campaign ignores the fact that God made clear the fate of all born and unborn are decided by Him prior to birth. A human fetus is thus according to God the sole business of the child's parents and their Maker; while no American citizen nor believer alike was ever charged with the task of representing other peoples' unborn.[17] These wicked pro-life and pro-sodomy spiritual leaders are to now be wholly abandoned according to God by their followers. For God through Ezekiel made clear that they cause our children to now say, "The way of the Lord is not fair.'" "But it is their way which is not fair!'" stresses God. God reminds all that love Him must follow Him and specifically avoid his forbidden acts like the spread of sodomy; for such actions of the United States *en masse* will end the entire world, so does the second, blessed nation decide the fate of the planet. While American pedophiles render themselves as the next so-called, liberated victims through a new nomenclature as "minor-attracted persons" as asserted by their leading, transsexual professor at Johns Hopkins University. Or the transsexual pervert admiral appointed by Biden who would influence prepubescent children to sexual gender treatments. So we are now lectured by perverted, forbidden transsexuals now acting as academics and government leaders. It is no wonder the rock is on its way; while Magog Democrats incontrovertibly emboldened California pedophiles to further sodomize our young through their new laws like California's SB 145, which claimed to end discrimination of homosexuality but in fact further empowered pedophiles to legally sodomize young boys, as if children could grant such consent. Again history proved that homosexuality was generally fed by child sodomy or trauma as a Divine fate according to God, cursing even the third and fourth generation of wicked men, damning children not adequately protected by their parents. Now sodomy's spread is again efficiently furthered by our Magog mass media sexually reprogramming our youth through vogue style and mass entertainment to embrace perversions forbidden by any continuing society allowed by God; which is not progress but the

---

[17] Appendix (c) on page 363 addresses the lack of scriptural support for the pro-life movement.

regress to all wicked, ancient pedophile nations predating Christ's crucifixion. Sodomy's toleration destroyed the ancient Israelite nation, truly killed Christ, and will ultimately end the United States of America, making it a point that cannot be reiterated enough.

GOD & GEORGE WASHINGTON DAMN OUR LOSS OF FREE SPEECH

God reminds all Americans of their constitutional compact with Him through their pledge of allegiance to God to insure and expand their fellow Americans' liberties. Yet Washington cautioned future Americans that their leaders would easily deceive them over their state of freedom and the chosen paths to further such liberty. Washington thereby cautioned that Americans measure liberty through our economic status shown best through our corresponding level of free speech. Now our first ever-total loss of free speech in supposed peacetime accompanied by our current, dire economic fallout marks, according to our founding father George Washington, our nation's impending end. For Washington warned that with freedom of speech lost, we would then be marched like blind sheep to the slaughter. Free speech is critical as God likewise notes for "The first one to plead his cause seems right, Until his neighbor comes and examines him." And despite journalistic sources like Vice Media seeking to have Americans feel compassion for what web censors must watch as they outright censor us, God's sanctified prophet George Washington warned that free speech would always be ugly, but its loss would be deadly for all Americans. Now our military offers no protection once we lost four commanders and chiefs to serving Gog. For their complicity in creating COVID-19, which Gog again intentionally launched on us, renders our modern republic like ancient Rome, unable to politically face an Asiatic mass murderer, in Rome's case it was the Asiatic king Mithridates that had killed a record number of Roman citizens. While Gog has murdered over a million American citizens thus far from his virus our leaders helped arm him with and still there was no American rebuke, in this time of war misportrayed by our leaders as peace. Now God and George Washington both warn that Americans can only be saved by a belief in God to bring us to His inner temple that offers Divine rescue before the end we have fated for all.

AMERICANS ARE THE CIRCUMCISED NEW ISRAELITES

After the United States enforced mass circumcision through late 19th Century hygiene policies, most Americans to date have physically sealed their covenant as circumcised, modern Israelites. The circumcised gentiles of the prophesied New Jerusalem of Gentiles in that undiscovered, Holy land of the west. Again, a nation unsullied by any prior, mass persecution of Israelites on our soil. While America's historic mass murdering, indigenous people were well warned by God's prior prophets to change their violent ways or die.

GOD PROPHESIED TO THE AMERICAN INDIANS

Indigenous Americans were long warned by the Cheyenne Indian prophet Sweet Medicine to abandon their violent ways. As Ken Burn's documentary *The West* highlights, Sweet Medicine actually warned his fellow Indians to turn peaceful or else future, strange white men would later arrive with a highly mobile animal that these indigenous peoples would use to kill each other in a coming, mass genocide. As history revealed, if not for the white man conquering them the American Indian already were well on the path to mass extermination from the horses' introduction by prior Spanish colonizers.

GOD PROPHESIED TO PRE-COLONIAL MEXICO

In the American region of Mexico where those first Spanish horses were introduced the indigenous Mexicans were given the exact year of their civilization's demise for their violent ways. The human hearts these villainous people cut out as mass sacrifices only five centuries ago could not buy them the extra time they sought to extend their calendar's foretold end date that coincided with the Spanish conquistadors' arrival. While even their destroyer's own form was rightly prophesied as the future uniform of their Spanish annihilator, the conquistador, Hernan Cortes.

GOD PROPHESIED TO ANCIENT ROME

The inspiration of the American republic, ancient Rome, was also correctly prophesied of its final demise from within by future, urban, Roman elites foretold in the ancient *Sibylline Books*; after a pagan witch sold this collection of future prophecies on Rome's future to Rome's first king. The Sibylline prophecies rightly predicted the Roman Republic's later destruction from urban political elites from within, likewise mirroring Washington's own warning to our second, great American republic, which he founded as an amended form from Rome's prior republican example.

GOD PROPHESIED TO ANCIENT CHINA

America's ultimate destroyer Gog, in fact, stems from a people first instructed to worship the one God whom they had called Shangdi; the Chinese peoples who we can deductively realize through God's end time prophecies stem from the descendants of Noah's grandsons Meshech and Tubal. The reason why so many of China's ancient language symbols are actually illustrations of the Bible's *Book Of Genesis* stories, thought to have been spread by post flood survivors of Noah's progeny and further explored in the link below.[18] For over two millennium the Chinese worshiped the one God Shangdi until Confucius upended Chinese monotheism for the last 2,500 years. Thus the Chinese have no God now except money, which they wish upon each other at their New Year celebrations, honoring works of their hands solely replacing their prior spirituality of old.

WOMEN TRULY ENDED THE WORLD

Our ultimate downfall from our loss of belief, God made clear, stemmed through later, godless women no longer rearing their

---

[18] Institute For Creative Research: Genesis in Chinese Pictographs, James J.S. Johnson J.D., TH.D

young. A mother's voice that alone was scientifically proven to activate the majority of her baby's brain was taken away for that child to be raised by infrequent strangers' diaper changes in day care centers across our nation. Women entering the workforce soon damned the following generations of females to work, no longer able to be stay-at-home-mothers provided for by a single spouse's wage. Therefore, supposed female liberation was actually mass child rape and sodomy, liberating pedophiles by forcing mothers away from their children; with multiple generations of those godless children now wholly ignorant of God, His birth of science, many of these kids even think they can get away with being school shooters and often dying in the act with no later Divine retribution. For this reason, God revealed a woman in a lead lined basket to be the ultimate source of our end time wickedness. Angels with storks' wings carried that basket, storks biblically symbolizing caring mothers who raise their children while this woman in the basket represents the many, godless females of modernity. God states that this basket will be placed in ancient Babylon to mark the final civilization that ended the human punishment truly begun in nearby Eden. This woman may even be Hillary Clinton who by merit of her illegal wiretapping and controlling of Biden is now more powerful and wicked than any leader in human history, perhaps the reason why women should never have been granted political power as they make the most evil leaders. Consider Germany's female leader Merkel who covered up thousands of rapes of German women by Muslim immigrants that she herself allowed into Germany *en masse*. God stressed through Ecclesiastes that a real woman could not be found for eons, possibly predating Adam via his ancestors. Women since Genesis were therefore quantumly created to be fated while they were still in the womb to certain future men whose virtue alone would decide the fate of both of them. From a quantum standpoint, women are not as real as men according to God. Hence why God mandated that men were to control their women, a point that became impossible in the U.S. after 1920s granting of the vote to women, followed four decades later by birth control. God indeed noted through His prophet Hosea how modern women of Ephraim, of

America, could have sex and avoid pregnancy, but in the long run would damn their entire progeny to certain death as will shortly be evidenced. Consider the irony that exactly a hundred years after the women's' right to vote was granted in the United States, ending single wage-earning spouses and stay at home mothers birthing heterosexual families, would soon bring certain death on everyone from enriching communism first thanks to the Clintons. For this reason God notes American men are now destroyed, ruled over by their women and children, long-raised for generations as motherless bastards in day care centers and so molested and sodomized now that these abused children mature to overwhelm heterosexuality and according to God therefore seal our world's doom.

WHY THERE MUST BE TWO BLESSED NATIONS
God hints that there was a less painful path for humanity in the multiverse if only Moses had done as God bid and served as both the priest and political leader when facing Pharaoh in *Exodus*. Because Moses unnecessarily added another person Aaron, his brother as the priestly leader, needlessly bifurcating the political and spiritual ruler into two positions. Therefore, the kingship from David's offspring had to fail before the ancient Israelite priests under later Greek rule tolerated sodomy's spread, feeding their later attempt to mass rape all Israelite boys, setting off those two Israelite civil wars.[19] Likewise, the resulting ancient Israelite theocracy had to fail before America's own did. Moses' bifurcation even cleaved the end time messenger often misnamed Jesus instead of his real name Joshua into two distinct individuals, symbolized as the two identical lampstands revealed by God to his end time prophet Zechariah. The two Joshuas would thus look identical, each born however as citizens into God's two Divine nations, one in antiquity and the second in our

---

[19] The sole exception being the priest Joshua, a descendant of the high-priest Zadok, who laid the cornerstone of the second Israelite temple, whom God makes clear is a blood ancestor of the end time Messiah.

future end time New Jerusalem of The Gentiles now at the end of days.

WHY THE SECOND JOSHUA CAN ONLY BE A POLITICAL LEADER

In hindsight, the first Joshua died as the suffering, anointed one in antiquity that according to Isaiah was the product of a virgin birth. So the second Joshua could only be the political leader born into the powerful New Jerusalem of Gentiles where he could legally be elected its leader as mandated in God's prophecy. This Joshua is therefore a messenger anointed by God Himself with no power of his own when first sharing this message (as will shortly be proven in the next section). Yet the Messenger of The Covenant only shares the good news and God's wisdom as His Elect highlighting God's offer of Divine rescue from all that Americans allowed our elites to bring. This same messenger well warned of China and pro-Chinese U.S. politicians since 2017 on our website *centeredamerica.com*. A human political voice who only came as God's representative after our port city politicians and elites illegally changed their election laws to stifle Americans' ability to elect our own president in 2020 AD. That crime perpetrated by these same U.S. Magog traitors holding their comical January 6th Committee hearings while again outright ignoring the illegal wiretapping of president Trump by America's King and Queen Clinton; so that now God alone challenges Gog who controls the United States through the Clintons, controls our European political allies, and even the Muslim world who now ignore Gog's mass Chinese Muslim genocide while hypocritically still criticizing Israel who offered the Palestinians part of their country. Clinton thus first showed how destructive a two-state-system could be when he influenced Israel to cede nearly half its territory to its historical enemy Palestine, leading to suicide bombers and destruction that rages up to this day; while Israel is seen as the bully and Gog can place Muslim believers in concentration camps and it goes unmentioned. Gog in control of our country has already begun a needless war on Russia, encroaching NATO onto former Soviet Territory. As our leaders claim they can serve both citizens and foreigners competing for our political power. Yet any leaders in any age can only serve one master, the reason why they serve the alien and war against you, an old pattern in history. The two-state system of a Latinized America and historical Americans would be equally destructive, allowing our leaders to continue to support the foreigners to destroy us in this second civil war masked as love.

GOD'S MESSAGE WAS ALWAYS POLITICAL

The second Joshua is political because God's covenant was always political. Politics as the culmination of money and power are despite the words of our politicians or spiritual leaders of any age, the true governing forces. Consider that the afterlife was only an oral secret for Abraham's descendants to know of in ancient times and purposely never written down in the *Old Testament*. As the ancient Jewish thinker from the time of the first Joshua, Hillel, succinctly summarized, the *Old Testament* was about how to best treat each other in an obvious political system shaped by God's first five books of the *Old Testament*, the *Torah*. But again to get real we should consider heeding the comedy troupe Monty Python's rightful summary of God's intentions in their seminal film *Life Of Brian*: we must first think for ourselves and stop listening to our purported experts and elites who are always the devil, that adversarial force to destroy us with the exception of God, science's founder Renee Descartes, economics' founder Adam Smith, and George Washington, whose rightful prophecies that all came to fruition are noted in this message.

OUR LACK OF BELIEF BROUGHT OUR MURDERERS

Without freedom of speech as both God and Washington prophesied, we are now told what to do, what to love, forced to embrace a so-called modern love and tolerance for any forbidden wickedness no matter how evil or despicable it may be from enriching communism to empowering American pedophiles. All to keep us misdirected with guilt from our own victimization by our U.S. Magog politicians. What is there to deem unjust or immoral when American teachers unthinkably sexualize prepubescent children with perversions long condemned by God that forged our heterosexual society, or elevating illegal aliens and criminals above citizens and our police officers, attacking our military as extremists while forcing transsexual perverts upon them and having our taxpayer money fund those perverts' sex change operations in the military. Indeed, we will return to the history of sodomy that the English military long-witnessed and was popularly highlighted by Winston Churchill as the first Lord Of The Admiralty in England. Indeed, our government has become Gog's outright Magog servants; thereby Clinton's Service Economy ultimately made us all servants to Gog, rendering us again Magog. Considering that after ending our American manufacturing jobs and mass-raping nearly all our urban blacks, these same perpetrators would now tear down Civil War monuments after creating a mass-imprisonment larger than any nation in history ever witnessed, exceeding even Communist Stalin and Mao's mass-jailings. A tragedy coinciding with the evil Diversity movement seeking to artificially place dark faces in offices and jobs to feign a false, optical misdirection from the failed policies that these proponents wrought; while our Magog mass media ludicrously injects black faces into historic period films where they don't truly belong to likewise misdirect from the blacks who along with urban Latino males were nearly all jailed and sodomized after being robbed of their historical, manufacturing jobs, despite those black faces being shown to us in those films. The same misdirection was evident in the waning days of the Communist Soviet Union, feeding the popular joke of the time where the Soviet people long trapped on the failed Communist train to some future, proposed utopia saw the train staff and engineer canceled out. They were then instructed to rock around in their seats to shake the railcar to seem like it was moving forward while imitating the sounds of the locomotive with their voices, all to create a false movement of advancement to cloak their long-stalled and regressing reality.

CLINTON SEEDED OUR 2008 MELTDOWN

At the start of his treason in the late 1990s president Clinton knew he needed to mask the immediate wealth that would be drained from the U.S. economy to China that the pro-Communist Service Economy that he created would feed. To hide the initial drain from us to Communist China, Clinton seeded a worldwide, financial bubble by removing critical 1930s finance laws wisely put in place to successfully avoid another Great Depression. These laws in fact achieved that goal until Clinton's removal of them. President Clinton thus fueled this record financial bubble of false wealth to hide the economic drain that buying from Gog's slaves would've been so quickly evident in our economy. William Clinton's false bubble of course popped in 2008 leaving our banks and major corporations so leveraged that they were nearly all insolvent. President Obama bailed them out in a little-reported, ongoing American government program called Quantitative Easing, nicknamed QE1 and QE2. This taxpayer funding of most of our ongoing major corporations occurred despite many of the corporate employees now making so little that their labor pool is still partially subsidized by taxpayers as is Walmart with taxpayer subsidies to their own employees by our wicked federal government, which even buys back these failing companies' corporate debt, and subsidizes their employees in selective new monopolies dominated by the Chinese supply chain of slavery. So the much-feared takeover of our free markets that Cold War presidents like Reagan and Kennedy so dreaded is now complete. It is one that if not for God's help would soon kill all Americans, fueling an aristocracy of government-funded companies that are supposedly not allowed to fail, and now preach wicked, Magog Woke policies on Americans in turn for our elites giving them our taxpayer funding.

OUR AMERICAN ECONOMY IS A MAGOG ILLUSION

Our federal government thereby wars on us, God makes clear. So while you suffer, our corrupt Magog U.S. government treasonously uses billions of your tax-payer dollars as a lifeline to fuel these failing corporations and major financial institutions truly long-dead since Clinton's seeded 2008 meltdown. Our taxpayer monies prop up a false illusion of wealth in a wholly bankrupted service economy of American service providers who cannot by definition generate actual wealth, but only feed on preexisting wealth already generated in the economy by either manufacturing, farming, or raw material exploitation. This ongoing program QE1 and QE2 had to buy back these continuing, failing institutions' staggering corporate losses, further fueling a false stage-front to mask our truly dead economy. An illustration of this classic, political-economic crime termed *Moral Hazard* leaves our current corporate landscape insolvent without the continued injection of our taxpayer monies to mask their continuing failure, a link to *PBS's Frontline* expose on this financial travesty incontrovertibly creating an American corporate aristocracy is provided below.[20]

OUR MAGOG ELITES NOW AIM TO LEAVE US HOMELESS

Now our same U.S. Magog government aims to leave us without homes and affordable dwellings. U.S. dwellings are now swallowed up by massive, new investment portfolios funded with QE1 and QE2's tax payer monies from an economy so rotted, our government tax proceeds are now literally used to steal our dwellings every American needs in a continuing pandemic that never ended to render us homeless and soon dead as part of our Cold War, which likewise never ended against Communism despite Clinton's American surrender to it. As the unlimited millions of an alien horde are likewise incentivized here by U.S. Magog politicians to further crush us in the comical name of love for these wholly unscreened alien strangers; they further render Americans homeless with skyrocketing dwelling prices from the added demand of tens of millions of illegals now within our border versus the limited dwellings that we have here. Not only are our made in China purchases weaponized back at us, but even our own taxes are likewise used to destroy our society and

---

[20] PBS' Frontline "Inside The Meltdown" February 17. 2009

our lives. This pincer movement between government-funded purchases of our limited dwellings, COVID, and the illegal alien invasion destroyed our nation from within. God makes clear that we as a free people are over via our own collective free will decisions. As we've recently learned, if needed our Magog internet since president W. Bush devised this tool, can be shut down, ending our ability to speak, gather, or possibly acquire badly needed goods in a complete, physical lockdown.

GOD DEMANDS WE QUIT HURTING OUR FELLOW AMERICANS
God mandates that Americans get real with themselves in their soul, the foundation of His rescue. Accordingly if Americans truly lament to Him within themselves, they must wish to show mercy, notes God, for their fellow Americans whom they have so hurt, stripped of jobs, drug-addicted, sodomized in prison, raped, and perverted now as prepubescent children, rendering so many homeless, while leaving our nation divided, blinding us to the one fact that we work, according to both God and George Washington, to solely enrich our viral murderer with no aid to average Americans as we are forced to elevate Gog, our mass murderer, to be our modern idol to whom we have now sacrificed a million American souls, even allowing him to buy up our farm land, control our very meat supply itself, and continue worshipping him.

BASTARDS DAMNED OUR LEADERSHIP
We don't all have to die for the Clintons, Bushes, Obama, Biden, and their appointees and political agents. Our lack of belief, however, did make this possible. For God advised against ever electing a literal bastard such as William Jefferson Clinton; for bastard leaders, according to God, remove landmarks and change the times and ways and are most unkind to other bastards, orphans, and widows. Then we elected another president's son, W. Bush, having not learned what uncaring elitists president's sons can be, illustrated by a former president's son, John Quincy Adams; while W. Bush again wickedly claimed to talk with God as an oracle, an action strictly outlawed by

God's words and marking him as a most wicked liar. And then we elected another bastard Obama, whose father hailed from what God termed biblical Ethiopia, a peoples cursed from their beginning to their end, including his son, doubly damning Obama, our second bastard president.

OUR END WAS UNKNOWN WITHOUT GOD'S MESSAGE

God, science's inventor Renee Descartes, and George Washington all note we are at the end but do not realize it yet. So God's message comes to rescue every American who wishes to escape certain annihilation by simply confessing their sins of enriching communism that will soon end our planet. For again according to God, we must return to Him with the earnest hope at least to restore our historic system, to show mercy on our fellow Americans, which we can do by trying to restore manufacturing, cleansing ourselves of all these political U.S. Magog traitors who incapacitated our constitutional system's ability to now right itself. But nothing including our continuing lives can ever be achieved unless we first return to God within us and admit our sins as an American peoples within our inner temple to find that once in all of history offer of Divine rescue from our Creator no matter how wicked we have been, the more wicked the better, a point that cannot be reiterated enough. Then God promises that many will suddenly find our Maker waiting for us within our own minds once we are honest. For His inner temple now remains the sole source of God's possible rescue for a coming branch in the multiverse where some Americans and believers return to Him and live on. Yet again, all those who don't now get real will soon die from His coming rock well on its way. So that much of His modern message unlocked by Daniel's Riddle highlights that most of God's *Old Testament* end time prophecies have already been recently fulfilled as recent history confirmed. It's thus time to make Americans' liberty our sole aim in the enrichment of our fellow citizens through our gentiles' covenant, *the Declaration of Independence*, which forged our blessed nation's aims. And as our forefathers noted, true charity begins at home with Americans helping Americans and not helping illegal foreigners standing contrary to our laws to further empower a foreign Chinese king.

ETERNITY IS AT STAKE
God warns that after His return to earth when He eradicates death, a remnant of wicked Magog Americans and others will walk the earth as an undead remnant of worm-filled corpses to perpetually wander, unable to die, minions most probably following China's Gog, Clinton, W. Bush, Obama, and Biden. No matter what their outcome, our U.S. Magog traitors will permanently suffer forever. America's enemies who dared to elevate unscreened foreigners and historically proven enemies over American citizens. From these same wicked leaders who helped China's Gog create COVID in the first place. God revealed everything about our present moment, things you never thought you could know about our past, present, and approaching future. All that remains to be fulfilled is our continued suffering, the west coast's devastation from God's coming earthquake, the burial of their remains in that nose-shaped cemetery to finally plug the noses of the Chinese passengers in the *Valley Of Hamon-Gog* where so many Americans as Gog's followers fell, massive earthquakes, the coming drought and famine, and the mass annihilation of our U.S. Magog enemies into ash where they stand, all await us in the near future. With a final world-annihilating meteorite to end everything left on earth. As He prophesied, we now face Gog and China and primarily Iran, noted as Gog's dire, end time enemies of The New Jerusalem of Gentiles, the United States of America. In a world controlled by Gog through his American Magog puppets who even as private citizens can censor us, wiretap our anti-Gog president Trump without mention or punishment through a wickedness that God proposes will soon bring the eventual ruination of all of our American cities. Return to God now and get real or die. For again scientifically, God's existence and words cannot be scientifically denied. Yet again, we must get real inside our minds for He will know if we are lying. And if we're sincere, then we could not help but to

embrace the following policies humbly proposed by this messenger to immediately rectify our national demise. As prophesied in the *Old Testament*, this messenger by presenting these policies is presenting in Hebrew what is called *mishpat*, the methods and systems one must use to create a society that treats all equally irregardless of race, gender, or ethnicity, but certainly prioritizes solely citizens.

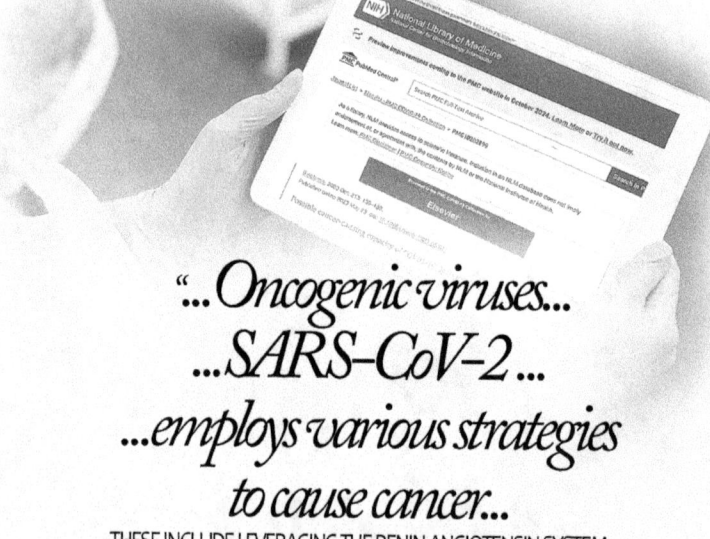

"...Oncogenic viruses... ...SARS-CoV-2... ...employs various strategies to cause cancer...

THESE INCLUDE LEVERAGING THE RENIN ANGIOTENSIN SYSTEM, ALTERING TUMOR SUPPRESSING PATHWAYS BY MEANS OF ITS NONSTRUCTURAL PROTEINS, AND TRIGGERING INFLAMMATORY CASCADES BY ENHANCING CYTOKINE PRODUCTION IN THE FORM OF A "CYTOKINE STORM" PAVING THE WAY FOR THE EMERGENCE OF CANCER STEM CELLS IN TARGET ORGANS.

JAHANKHANI, K., AHANGARI, F., ADCOCK, I. M., & MORTAZA, E. (2023)

JAHANKHANI, K., AHANGARI, F., ADCOCK, I. M., & MORTAZA, E. (2023). POSSIBLE CANCER-CAUSING CAPACITY OF COVID-19: IS SARS-COV-2 AN ONCOGENIC AGENT? BIOCHIMIE, 213, 130–138. HTTPS://DOI.ORG/10.1016/J.BIOCHI.2023.05.014

A MESSAGE TO THE
NEW JERUSALEM OF GENTILES
THE TRUE ORIGIN OF SCIENCE AND ITS DIRE IMPLICATIONS
WITH WORKS CITED

Factual Support For Section 1 Summary

*The film transcript is shown in bold print.

The screen title displays "A Message to The New Jerusalem of the Gentiles."

(Brief Overview)

(America's founders warned future Americans that we would always be slaves to our economic elites. First it was wealthy landowners until the civil war, then business cronies in league with our crooked, federal government born from that war. But once America under 3 U.S. presidents outsourced our manufacturing to the foreign king of mainland China just as God prophesied, we ended not only our nation, but the world. Now God as He promised has come to rescue us through His good news dictated from the Hebrew bible.)

(The United States of America will be shown to be the biblical New Jerusalem of The Gentiles, our pilgrim founders openly sought to found.)

www.voanews.com, 1620: Dreams of a 'New' Jerusalem
The Pilgrims dreamed of establishing a new "Jerusalem" in which they could live in peace and brotherhood while waiting for the second coming of Christ.

(The United States would as prophesied by God to his prophets ultimately be a peoples gathered from many nations.)

Ezekiel 38:8
They had been brought out from the nations, and now all of them live in safety.

(A land which lately lost its belief in God for idols, particularly money, which later fed what will be revealed as the king of China, codenamed Gog by God for reasons to soon be explained.)

Isaiah 2:7-8
Their land is also full of silver and gold,
And there is no end to their treasures;
…And there is no end to their chariots.
Their land is also full of idols;

(Contrary to Woke Ideology, The United States was only colonized by Europeans after the indigenous population annihilated each other because they ignored the message of the Cheyenne prophet Sweet Medicine, shortly proven to be a sanctified prophet of God.)

Ken Burns The West TV Documentary: The Arrival of the Horse and the Warrior Society of the Dog Soldiers

There was once a prophet named Sweet Medicine who taught his people how to conduct themselves...he brought them a warning: Strangers called 'Earth Men" would one day appear among them, light-skinned, speaking an unknown tongue. And with them would come a strange animal, it would change the Cheyenne way of life and that of every other Indian people forever. It was the horse...Before the horse...a person would have to give virtually every hour of his waking time to solving the simple problem of survival...But with the horse...a hunter could acquire enough food in one day to last for months and so he...was suddenly given...a margin of freedom that he could never have imagined. And so what he did with it... was to celebrate it in terms of the warrior ideal: 'Now I have leisure, I can go and hunt...I can visit my enemies and....attain glory. The Great Plains now became a crowded meeting ground for some 30 tribes from every direction...{Because of the horse} there was always fighting going on.

Ken Burns The West TV Documentary featuring Jo Allyn Archambault, a Lakota Female Tribe-Member
"I, as the Lakota woman four generations ago, would have cut off the arms and the legs and heads of the enemies that my husband killed, and I would have put them on a stick, and I would have paraded them in the scalp dance that evening when we honored our men."

(Outrage over the murder and scalping of an American woman by Britain's Indians fighters fueled the American Revolution.)

The New York Independence Trail Stories
The Massacre of Jane McCrea...arouse{d} the drooping spirit of Liberty in the midsummer of 1777.

Ken Burns The West TV Documentary, featuring Michael Dorris, First Chair of the Native American Studies program at Dartmouth College
And with this increased contact among tribes came a wave of epidemics. Smallpox, cholera, tuberculosis, measles, diptheria,

European diseases against which they had no immunity now raced from people to people. It was a total holocaust. And it was not the {U.S.} cavalry. It was a series of pandemics that wiped out most Indian people before Europeans ever encountered them."

(Since Sweet Medicine's prophecy came true via history, according to God, the Cheyenne prophet was sanctified by Him.)

Deuteronomy 18:22
When a prophet speaks in the name of the Lord, if the thing does not happen or come to pass, that is the thing which the Lord has not spoken; the prophet has spoken it presumptuously; you shall not be afraid of him.

(In the Book of Exodus, another prophet, Moses refused God's sage advice to address Pharoah as both the priestly and political leader. Moses split this unified role into what was probably a more painful outcome for collective humanity, drawing the rare reaction of God's anger to a prophet. For Moses probably unnecessarily divided the leadership role in two, subsequently forcing two Messiahs instead of one, and two blessed Israelite nations of Israel and the end-time New Jerusalem of The Gentiles, as will be shown.)

Exodus 4:12-17
Now go: {the Lord Commanded Moses} I will help you speak and will teach you what to say."
But Moses said, "Pardon your servant, Lord. Please send someone else."
Then the Lord's anger burned against Moses and he said, "What about your brother, Aaron the Levite? I know he can speak well. He is already on his way to meet you, and he will be glad to see you. You shall speak to him and put words in his mouth; I will help both of you speak and will teach you what to do. He will speak to the people for you, and it will be as if he were your mouth and as if you were God to him.

(But from the United States rather than ancient Israel arises His herald to highlight God's ancient offer now of Divine rescue for every American citizen and His believers worldwide, no matter how bad they've been, if they do as God now bids.)

Deuteronomy 18:18
I will raise up for them a Prophet like you from among their brethren, and will put My words in His mouth, and He shall speak to them all that I command Him.

(God made clear that His end time message was through His ancient, dictated words in the Hebrew Bible, because no new information is available to anyone, including His current messenger, for reasons God will also soon explain.)

Jeremiah 23:33-34
"So when these people or the prophet or the priest ask you, saying, 'What is the oracle of the Lord?' {What words does God speak to the prophet?} you shall then say to them, 'What oracle?' I will even forsake you," says the Lord. If a prophet or a priest or anyone else claims, 'This is a message from the Lord,' I will punish them and their household.

(To confirm the New Jerusalem of the gentiles as the United States of America rather than the nation-state of Israel, the end-time Gog also attacks a country that experienced only one prior, civil war while Israel suffered many and in its modern incarnation has never had one.)

Ezekiel 38:8
After many days thou shalt be visited: in the latter years thou shalt come into the land that is brought back from the sword,

(God reveals that the United States citizens are gathered from many other nations which have always been "made waste" by their elites.

Ezekiel 38:8
...is gathered out of many people, against the mountains of Israel, which have been always waste:

(As will be shown, God terms the U.S. as Jerusalem but most often as Ephraim because they succeeded in a land afflicting them.)

Genesis 41:52
And the name of...{Joseph's second son was} called Ephraim: {which means} "For God has caused me to be fruitful in the land of my affliction."

(But America as of late departed from God's wise and necessary instruction.)

Proverbs 19:27
Cease listening to instruction, my son,
And you will stray from the words of knowledge.

Proverbs 28:9
One who turns away his ear from hearing the law,
Even his prayer is an abomination.

Jeremiah 16:12
But you have behaved more wickedly than your ancestors. See how all of you are following the stubbornness of your evil hearts instead of obeying me.

(God will show that three U.S. presidents treasonously had Americans work to buy products made by the slaves of mainland Communist China's dictator codenamed Gog who owns all wealth there: in such a way did America empower Gog.)

Daniel 8:23-26
His {Gog's} power shall be mighty, but not by his own power;

(So God has truly punished America through everything and everyone for wandering from His ways.)

Proverbs 16:33
The lot is cast into the lap,
But its every decision is from the Lord.

(Mankind has repeatedly made this error.)

Proverbs 26:11
As a dog returns to his own vomit,
So a fool repeats his folly.

(Gog, it will be shown had his Chinese airline passengers infect the nation and world with a hidden sword, the disease called COVID-19.)

Ezekiel 38:9
You and all your troops and the many nations with you will go up, advancing like a storm; you will be like a cloud covering the land.

(God, however, mandated that Americans must lose all power before He now acted.)

Daniel 12:7
When the power of the holy people has been finally broken, all these things will be completed."

(Americans' political power was lost when our Democrat and Rhino Republican politicians funded Communist China's Wuhan Lab, allowing our enemy to create what God prophesied as an incurable, worldwide virus to end humanity.)

Daniel 12:6-7
"How long shall the fulfillment of these wonders be?" Then I heard {an angelic messenger} clothed in linen, who…swore by

Him who lives forever, that…when the power of the holy people has been completely shattered, all these things shall be finished.

(Thanks to the disease's birth, the Democrat-controlled cities at the last minute changed their 2020 presidential election laws contrary to their laws, illegally allowing for an onslaught of dubious, absentee votes thanks to Covid-19.)

How Democrats Are Attempting To Sow Uncertainty, Inaccuracy, And Delay In The 2020 Election by the
Committee on Oversight and Reform, U.S. House of Representatives
September 23, 2020. Democrats are seeking to change state election laws and procedures at the last minute to
advantage themselves in the 2020 election cycle. These late changes will only increase the likelihood for potential election-related crime and errors, and put at risk the integrity of the nation's electoral process…sowing the seeds for an unprecedented constitutional crisis.

Washington Examiner, No voter fraud? How about 1,334 cases, 1,147 convictions by Paul Bedard, Washington Secrets Columnist
November 08, 2021. It used to be that the media were obsessed with voter fraud and messy elections. As recently as 1999, Pulitzer Prizes were handed out to newspapers that dug into rigged elections and wrongly elected candidates. But when former President Donald Trump made it one of his top issues, claiming his 2020 reelection was stolen in extensive fraud, the media looked away and even defended the systems they once investigated.

(Despite their breaking of the law, Biden, the current Democrat president, along with Rhino Republicans opposed to Trump's presidency, prosecute president Donald Trump, the front-runner, for trying to resist the Democrat's patently illegal, 2020 actions. America has fallen like Rome's republic with a reigning despot for the first time, seeking to remove his opponent, robbing the people of their only power: their vote.)

Newsmax, Donald Trump: 'By Destroying Me, They Destroy You', by Newsmax Staff
July 21, 2023, The current frontrunner for the 2024 GOP presidential nomination...expects he will be charged over the reported events of January 6, 2021...

(Americans are now not even allowed to hear sworn testimony before congress alleging outright corruption and collusion between China and the current president, Joe Biden.)

Facts Matter by Roman Balmakov
July 20, 2023, I'd like to quickly mention that the regime here reached a new level. That's because...a few hours ago our Epic TV Youtube Channel was doing live coverage of the IRS whistleblower who was testifying in front of Congress against the Biden family. And even though all we were doing was showing the actual testimony that was taking place in front of the House {of Representatives} oversight committee, Youtube not only pulled down the video but they also gave our channel a strike.

Associated Press
July 5, 2023, The lawsuit alleges that government officials used the possibility of favorable or unfavorable regulatory action to coerce social media platforms to squelch what the administration considered misinformation on a variety of topics, including COVID-19 vaccines, President Joe Biden's son Hunter, and election integrity. The injunction — and {judge} Doughty's accompanying reasons saying the administration "seems to have assumed a role similar to an Orwellian 'Ministry of Truth,'"

(With Americans muzzled, God now speaks and will no longer Hide his face from us as He's done for over 2600 years. His words are not new, but old ones dictated by God to His prophets in the Hebrew Bible. The current messenger of the covenant with the name Joshua reiterates God's Hebrew Bible rebuke at this moment. God rebukes four American presidents who He will reveal acted as Satan, the quantum force that misleads humans.)

Zechariah 3:1
Then he {God's angelic messenger} showed me Joshua the high priest standing before the angel of the Lord and Satan standing at his right side to accuse him.

Joe Biden
"I don't care if you think I'm Satan reincarnated, the fact is you can't look at that television and say nothing happened on the sixth {of January}"

Zechariah 3:2
And the Lord said unto Satan, The Lord rebuke thee, O Satan; even the Lord that hath chosen Jerusalem rebuke thee: is not this a brand plucked out of the fire?

(By Satan, it will shortly be shown that God rebukes presidents William Clinton, W. Bush, and Obama for their pro-China enrichment broken by Trump, bringing Biden to serve Gog whom God now condemns.)

Joe Biden
"I don't care if you think I'm Satan reincarnated,

Ezekiel 38:2
I will call for a sword against Gog throughout all My mountains," says the Lord God."

Ezekiel 38:1-3
Now the word of the Lord came to me, saying, "Son of man, set your face against Gog...Behold, I am against you, O Gog,"

Ezekiel 38:22
And I will bring him to judgment with pestilence and bloodshed; I will rain down on him, on his troops, and on the many peoples

who are with him, flooding rain, great hailstones, fire, and brimstone. Thus I will magnify Myself and sanctify Myself, and I will be known in the eyes of many nations. Then they shall know that I am the Lord." '

(Gog is the king of China, which God through Daniel will soon prove. First, it's important to understand that China was also monotheistic in its earliest history, calling the Israelite God Shangdi).

Encyclopedia Britannica
Shangdi Chinese: "Lord-on-High") ancient Chinese deity, the greatest ancestor...the supreme deity during the Shang dynasty (1600–1046 bce),

(Even the Chinese pictographic symbols of their original language during this time seems to depict the stories of Genesis from chapters 1 through 11.)

Institute For Creative Research: Genesis in Chinese Pictographs, James J.S. Johnson J.D., TH.D
February 27, 2015, Ancient Chinese pictographs are silent witnesses, like fingerprints, of historical events reported in Genesis. In particular, the details of these word-symbols are clues that point to how the earliest Chinese must have known basic facts of Genesis 1–11 at the very time their pictographs were invented...Chinese is not an alphabet-based language—its word characters are both abbreviations of and combinations of picture symbols. The simplest symbols are combined to construct composite symbols that denote compound words. However, the actual pictures that were chosen, and especially their associated meanings, are what give us an amazing insight into Chinese history. Since Chinese civilization began soon after the Tower of Babel fiasco, the first Chinese settlers still had a fresh memory of mankind's origins—from creation week to the dispersion of languages at Babel. Thus, they not only knew the history highlights in Genesis 1–11, but they would also have regarded those same events as important in human history and

experience. It is unsurprising, therefore, that many of the picture-symbol characters, in the ancient Chinese language, match the thinking of a soon-after-Babel people who retained important memories of historic events reported in Genesis 1–11.

(Gradually Chinese rulers shed their worship of Shangdi)

Reasons To Believe, Evidence for Original monotheism in Ancient China by Daniel Cote, MMin and DMin
June 10, 2021, The last king of the Shang dynasty, circa 1765–1122 BCE, King Zhou, is said to have become morally corrupt and to have neglected Shang Di and sacrifices in the temple of his ancestors. Because of his transgressions, heaven ordered the destruction of the Shang dynasty.

(Now the Lord promises to destroy not only China's current king Gog but all of Magog, The Hebrew word Ma means what is, making Magog all who enrich Gog and therefore not just Communist mainland China, but also parts of the United States of America whose purchases of Gog's slave-made goods truly enrich only its king Gog.)

Ezekiel 39:1, 5-7
"And you, son of man, prophesy against Gog, and say, 'Thus says the Lord God: "Behold, I am against you, O Gog,...You shall fall on the open field; for I have spoken," says the Lord God. "And I will send fire on Magog and on those who live in security in the coastlands. Then they shall know that I am the Lord.

(God also calls the U.S., Ephraim, the name of the second son of Joseph who, himself, had been sold into slavery. Ephraim was born of a gentile mother, the daughter of an Egyptian high priest. The reason why their son's name was Ephraim, which means "he who thrives in a land of strangers." Ephraim would become the most powerful nation on earth and the most powerful of the twelve Israelite tribes. Ephraim's gentile mother foreshadowed the New Jerusalem of the gentiles, the U.S., but ironically a place where Israelites or anyone else could finally worship from the Hebrew Bible as God specified with no one dictating about spiritual issues.

First Amendment{of the U.S. Constitution}
Congress shall make no law respecting an establishment of religion, or prohibiting the free exercise thereof;

(As will be shown, after embracing sodomy in its later history, the legal form of worship in the Hebrew Bible in ancient Israel was lost, eventually bringing Christ. So the United States became the final Israel, the greatest of the 12 tribes.)

Genesis 37:9
Then he {Joseph, who would become Ephraim's father} had another dream, and he told it to his brothers. "Listen," he said, "I had another dream: I saw the sun, the moon, and 11 stars bowing down to me."

(God will destroy China's Gog and all who enriched him as part of Magog because Ephraim, the United States, is deceptively being eaten alive by the Covid spike protein perfected in Wuhan's lab and also from the experimental, untested, new gene therapy misnamed a vaccine whose inventor warned against ever using it on humans. While the so-called vaccinated people, it's been shown, can pass on the spike protein via their breath to create the same lethal health issues in the unvaccinated.)

Epoch Times: New Evidence Suggests mRNA COVID-19 Vaccine Transmission of Aerosols by Vaccinated to Unvaccinated by Megan Redshaw, J.D.
August 2, 2023, "…This could cause immunization of the {unvaccinated}bystanders as well as problems associated with spike protein toxicity to bloodstream components and other tissues {in the bystander},"

Is The Post Pandemic Death Toll Taking A Dark Turn? By Dr. Mikolaj Raszek PHD

April 14, 2024, "Basically, {Dr. Geert Vanden Bossche} proclaims...the {COVID} virus will still evolve {because of mass vaccination which does not stem the viral spread allowing it} to become much more pathogenic. It's inescapable. And this enhanced pathogenicity in combination with already achieved enhanced infectiousness of the virus will lead to horrific death amongst our population...so much so...that this will be a mass die-off event of...such apocalyptic proportion...that it might lead to immediate extinction of the SARS COVID 2 virus. Why? Because there will be such a massive loss of hosts due to this increased pathogenicity."

(At the same time, Gog's Chinese operatives, which God will reveal came to the U.S. as airline passengers, are setting up countless labs to launch his final disease attack to wipe out the United States of America with our government doing nothing to protect us from even the last virus that they helped fund China's king to create.)

Gordon Chang Being Interviewed on Fox News At Night With Trace Gallagher

August 4, 2023., "...they found nearly a 1,000 mice...that had been genetically engineered to transmit disease. So the only conclusion that fits the facts is that China was planning to launch a pathogen from this lab. And I'm sure there must be others around the United States as well. At the very minimum, we need to be scouring our country for facilities like this because we know what disease can do to hobble our society."

Hosea 7:9-10
Aliens have devoured his strength,
But he does not know it;
Yes, gray hairs are here and there on him,
Yet he does not know it.

(Once the prophesies herein are analyzed, the only question is whether God will shortly wipe out China's Gog, ending his political reign over our U.S. west coast or whether God will allow our nation to be wiped out by Gog's pestilence before experiencing a literal, landed invasion by Gog's armies, stopped only by God's west coast earthquake or His coming meteorite, to be shortly further explored.)

(The Detailed Presentation)

Did you really think they were just coming for your freedom of speech?

George Washington's Letter to Edmund Pendleton, Thursday, January 22, 1795
"When one side only of a story is heard and often repeated, the human mind becomes impressed with it insensibly."

George Washington's First Annual Address, Friday, January 8, 1790
"Knowledge is in every country the surest basis of public happiness."

George Washington's Address To the Officers of The Army, Saturday, March 15, 1783
"...freedom of Speech may be taken away, and, dumb and silent we may be led, like sheep, to the Slaughter."

Jeremiah 7:28
"So you shall say to them, 'This is a nation that does not obey the voice of the Lord their God nor receive correction. Truth has perished and has been cut off from their mouth."

Jeremiah 4:10
Then I said, "Ah, Sovereign Lord, how completely you have deceived this people and Jerusalem by saying, 'You will have peace,' when the sword is at our throats."

Jeremiah 10:14
Everyone is dull-hearted, without knowledge;

Jeremiah 10:21
For the shepherds have become dull-hearted,

Joel 1:5
Awake, you drunkards, and weep;

(Free speech is limited by our government-controlled, modern mass media monopoly based in the U.S. coastal cities of the end time New Jerusalem of the gentiles, condemned by God.)

Isaiah 41:1
"Keep silent before Me, O coastlands,
And let the people renew their strength!
Let them come near, then let them speak;
Let us come near together for judgment.

Politico: {The Biden} Administration's tinkering with Covid posts is 'Orwellian' by Matt Berg and Josh Gerstein
July 5, 2023, A federal judge in Louisiana ruled…that the Biden administration's efforts to influence social media posts about Covid-19 likely violated the first amendment…The Trump-appointed U.S. District Court judge, Terry Doughty, called the administration's efforts "Orwellian," issuing a sweeping preliminary injunction that bars a number of federal officials from having any contact with social media firms to discourage or remove First Amendment-protected speech.

First Amendment {of the U.S. Constitution}
Congress shall make no law…abridging the freedom of speech, or of the press;

Hosea 4:6
My people are destroyed for knowledge: because you have rejected knowledge, I reject you…

This is the end...

The Great Controversy by Ellen G. White
{Satan}While appearing to the children of men as a great physician who can heal all their maladies, he will bring disease and disaster, until populous cities are reduced to ruin and desolation.

(Americans are now being silenced as we are marched like George Washington and God Himself rightly prophesied, to our death.)

Isaiah 29:3-4
You shall be brought down,
You shall speak out of the ground;
Your speech shall be low, out of the dust;
Your voice shall be like a medium's, out of the ground;
And your speech shall whisper out of the dust.

NBC News: Even mild Covid is linked to brain damage, scans show by Benjamin Ryan
March 7, 2022, The new British research is the first to reveal striking differences in areas of the brain based on scans taken before and after a coronavirus infection.

Lamentations 4:12
The kings of the earth,
And all inhabitants of the world,
Would not have believed
That the adversary and the enemy
Could enter the gates of Jerusalem—

Isaiah 47:10-11
"For you have trusted in your wickedness;
You have said, 'No one sees me';
Your wisdom and your knowledge have warped you;
And you have said in your heart,
'I am, and there is no one else besides me.'

Therefore evil shall come upon you;
You shall not know from where it arises.
And trouble shall fall upon you;
You will not be able to put it off.
And desolation shall come upon you suddenly,
Which you shall not know.

Jeremiah 6:21
"Behold, I will lay stumbling blocks before this people,
And the fathers and the sons together shall fall on them.
The neighbor and his friend shall perish."

(The Lord foretold of our current American government corrupted by China as it unconstitutionally tracked and controlled Americans.)

Lamentations 4:18
They tracked our steps
So that we could not walk in our streets.
Our end was near;
Our days were over,
For our end had come.

(Covid, the end time sword, came as the price for our lack of belief that will slowly annihilate America, causing us to repeatedly reinfect each other to death.)

Ezekiel 38:21-23
"Every man's sword will be against his brother.

Ezekiel 39:26
after they have borne their shame, and all their unfaithfulness in which they were unfaithful to Me, when they dwelt safely in their own land and no one made them afraid.

Amos 3:11
"An adversary shall be all around the land;
He shall sap your strength from you,

And your palaces shall be plundered."

Ezekiel 28:23
For I will send pestilence upon her,
And blood in her streets;
The wounded shall be judged in her midst
By the sword against her on every side;

Isaiah 28:18-19
When the overflowing scourge passes through,
Then you will be trampled down by it.
As often as it goes out it will take you;
For morning by morning it will pass over,
And by day and by night;
It will be a terror just to understand the report."

Hosea 10:11-14
Ephraim is a trained heifer
That loves to thresh grain;
But I harnessed her fair neck,
I will make Ephraim pull a plow.
You have plowed wickedness;
You have reaped iniquity.
You have eaten the fruit of lies,
Because you trusted in your own way,
In the multitude of your mighty men.
Therefore tumult shall arise among your people,
And all your fortresses shall be plundered

Hosea 13:8
I will tear open their rib cage,
And there I will devour them like a lion.

Hosea 13:14
O Death, I will be your plagues!
O Grave, I will be your destruction!
Pity is hidden from My eyes."

...but it's also a new beginning.

(For those returning to the Lord will be cured of China's incurable disease.)

Jeremiah 33:6-7
Behold, I will bring it health and healing; I will heal them and reveal to them the abundance of peace and truth. And I will cause the captives of Judah and the captives of Israel to return, and will rebuild those places as at the first.

(The ancient Israelites' choice to listen to Moses rather than God Himself is why His message must come through this human messenger of the covenant.)

Exodus 20:19
Israelites {said to Moses}: We are afraid to have God speak directly to us; we are certain that we will die. You speak to us instead; we promise to listen.

(Again, the messenger is not an oracle armed with any new words that he hears from God.)
Jeremiah 23:38

'Do not say, "Oracle of the Lord."'

(The messenger simply reiterates God's dictated words from the Hebrew Bible.)

Exodus 34:10
The Covenant Renewed
And He said: "Behold, I make a covenant. Before all your people I will do marvels such as have not been done in all the earth, nor in any nation; and all the people among whom you are shall see the work of the Lord. For it is an awesome thing that I will do with you.

(Contrary to what Christians were led to believe by the Roman Emperor Constantine's Council of Nicea, God's unchangeable covenant in the Hebrew Bible is the only one dictated by His words. Thus, the so-called New Testament and altering of the unalterable sabbath day marks the rejection of the New Testament as part of the further reform that the religious historian Ellen G. White claimed would be needed in end times. It will be shown that White could not know this fact until the Israelites' punishment ended in 2020 AD as will be further explained.)

Sabbath Reform in The last Days by Ellen G. White
The work of Sabbath reform to be accomplished in the last days is foretold in the prophecy of Isaiah: "Thus says the Lord: 'Keep justice, and do righteousness, for My salvation is about to come, and My righteousness to be revealed.

(The rejection of Catholicism and its liturgy could not be made clear, however, until the Israelite punishment ended. While contrary to popular belief, the first Joshua misnamed Jesus, is well-proven in the Hebrew Bible alone, as will be shortly further explained.)

Malachi 2:4-6
Then you shall know that I have sent this commandment to you,
That My covenant with Levi may continue,"
Says the Lord of hosts.
"My covenant was with him, one of life and peace,
And I gave them to him that he might fear Me;
So he feared Me
And was reverent before My name.
The law of truth was in his mouth,
And injustice was not found on his lips.
He walked with Me in peace and equity,
And turned many away from iniquity.

(The nations will be judged in how they treated the Israelites, meaning Jacob's descendants and American citizens alike.)

Joel 3:1-3
The Nations Judged
"In those days and at that time,
when I restore the fortunes of Judah and Jerusalem,
I will gather all nations
and bring them down to the Valley of Jehoshaphat
There I will put them on trial
for what they did to my inheritance, my people Israel,

(The fact that the messenger only reiterates God's words, allows God to truly speak now through this human's anthologized message drawn from Hebrew Bible verse.)

Isaiah 62:1
'For Zion's sake I will not keep silent, and for Jerusalem's sake I will not be quiet, until her righteousness goes forth as brightness, and her salvation as a burning torch.'

But to understand you must know one thing: that science proves God's existence; for God visited the mercenary soldier Renee Descartes on the night of 11/10/1619, allowing Descartes to invent *science*.

"Descartes in 90 Minutes" by Paul Strathern
It is ironic that Descartes, the great rationalist, should've found his inspiration in a mystical vision and highly irrational dreams. This element in Descartes' thinking is often overlooked in French *Lycées* where the great Gallic hero and hypnophile {sic} Descartes is held up as a rationalist exemplar.

Descartes' Dream, by Phillip J. Davis and Reuben Hirsh
"Descartes was so bewildered by all this that he began to pray. He assumed his dreams had a supernatural origin".

"Descartes Dreams" by Alice Brown
On the night of November 10th to 11th 1619 Descartes, then aged twenty-three, had three dreams which he considered came

from on high, and took to write down and interpret in some detail.

"The Mystical Dreams of Descartes - Exploring the Origins of Rationalism and Modernity" lecture by Dr. Justin Sledge Ph.D. "Descartes had a series of dreams in which supernatural beings talked to him and revealed to him the fundamental truth of reality"...

"If we rewind the clock 300 years before Descartes, people were actually walking through the streets of European cities flagellating {whipping} themselves in the hopes of alleviating the plague that was ravaging Europe in order to act as a repentance to God. And if we zoom 300 years after Descartes, well, people are walking around on the moon."...

"And apparently this third dream was so vivid, that Descartes had to wonder if he was really seeing it. He wonders whether he's dealing with a vision or a dream...And it's in this dream...that Descartes can't tell between it being a dream or a vision, and this is where Descartes comes into contact with what he calls the Spirit of Truth, this seems to be a kind of semi-divine, Divine, or angelic character inside the dream, that seems to be girding Descartes on to the process of unlocking the secrets of reality."

...But I think if we look at the totality of his life's work, and if we look at the trajectory of his intellectual development, there's simply no way of denying that these dreams, both in their phenomenological impact upon him, but also in their spiritual and rational transformation led to the very nucleus of his philosophy and scientific breakthroughs, and therefore to the very foundations of modernity itself.

In that crucible, modernity is formed; although we're only often told half of that story. Here rationalism {the basis of modern science} sits right beside occultism, dreams sit right beside mathematics, and they are all in some sense united almost by a supernatural force in the life of Descartes. Now you might be asking why you've never heard of this whole dream business before? This unrational, this mystical side of modernity is actively being repressed….And if we know anything about repression from Freud, we know that the repressed always returns. And it never returns in a way we can predict, and it never returns in a way we want it to…a classic example of what Walter Honegraaff, the great scholar of western esotericism, might call *rejected knowledge*. That we have a story about how modernity developed, how rationalism developed, but modernity itself can't make sense of it, and it does the only thing that it can, it represses it."

(Descartes' experience occurred a year to the day from America's pilgrim founders executing the Mayflower Compact, the first covenant of governance that continued on into the U.S. Constitution of the New Jerusalem of The Gentiles.)

Middle Tennessee State University: Mayflower Compact by John R. Vile
{The Mayflower Compact} was signed on November 11, 1620, by the 41 men on the ship…the signatories …pledged to "covenant and combine ourselves together into a civil Body Politick."

Although God's hand behind science would be hidden by Descartes' later followers, science reunited the lost Israelite tribes through cheap DNA tests…

DNA Weekly Genetic Testing, 2023
"Best DNA Test Kits - Discover Your Jewish Ancestry"

Isaiah 11:11-12
"It shall come to pass in that day that the Lord shall set His hand again the second time to recover the remnant of His people…and will assemble the outcasts of Israel…from the four corners of the earth"

Jerusalem Post
March 1, 2019, almost 25% of Latinos, Hispanics have Jewish DNA

Hosea 8:10
Yes, though they have hired among the nations,
Now I will gather them;

Ezekiel 28:25-26
'Thus says the Lord God: "When I have gathered the house of Israel from the peoples among whom they are scattered, and am hallowed in them in the sight of the Gentiles,

(God will also unite the divided gentile tribes of the U.S.A., the New Jerusalem of the gentiles, His Holiest people, as He will soon explain.)

...and end the world as the cost of covering up God who caused science's invention.

(The Day of The Lord will be a meteorite collision annihilating earth, foretold through God's dictated words in the Hebrew Bible to many end-time prophets, beginning with Daniel.)

Daniel 2:31-35
You watched while a stone was cut out without hands, which struck the image on its feet of iron and clay, and broke them in pieces. Then the iron, the clay, the bronze, the silver, and the gold were crushed together, and became like chaff from the summer threshing floors; the wind carried them away so that no trace of them was found.

(God promises to spare Americans and believers worldwide now returning to Him, from the impending disaster, to be further explored herein.)

Zechariah 3:2
Is not this a brand plucked out of the fire?"

While God's message dictated in the Hebrew Bible comes alive only now once we have admitted Covid to be incurable.

Jeremiah 30:12-15
"For thus says the Lord:
'Your affliction is incurable,
Your wound is severe.
There is no one to plead your cause,
That you may be bound up;
You have no healing medicines.
All your lovers have forgotten you;
They do not seek you;
For I have wounded you with the wound of an enemy,
With the chastisement of a cruel one,
For the multitude of your iniquities,
Because your sins have increased.
Why do you cry about your affliction?
Your sorrow is incurable.
Because of the multitude of your iniquities,
Because your sins have increased,
I have done these things to you.

Micah 6:13
"Therefore I will also make you sick by striking you,

Hosea 5:13
"When Ephraim saw his sickness,

Zechariah 5:3-4
"This is the curse that goes out over the face of the whole earth: 'Every thief shall be expelled,' according to this side of the scroll; and, 'Every perjurer shall be expelled,' according to that side of it."

Ezekiel 28:23
For I will send pestilence upon her,

(But without freedom of speech, as previously noted, the U.S. would be mass-murdered by Covid without God's current intervention through this message shortly proven to be only now relevant.)

Hosea 7:11
"Ephraim is like a dove,
 easily deceived and senseless—

New York Post
April 24, 2023, China Covid cover-up had huge help from Western elites

Reuters
July 5, 2023…{It is} alleged that U.S. government officials went too far in efforts to encourage social media companies to address posts they worried could contribute to vaccine hesitancy during the Covid-19 pandemic…

Cowboy State Daily: Judge Who Banned Feds From Censoring Social Media Lists Evidence: Here's What's In It by Clair McFarland
July 8, 2023, A federal judge's order showed the Wyoming Department of Health fell victim to the federal government's collusion with social media giants during Covid when the Wyoming agency was unable to share its "valid public health messages."

George Washington
"Experience teaches us that it is much easier to prevent an enemy from posting themselves than it is to dislodge them after they have got possession."

God foretold Covid would come from China, the Land of 10 kingdoms, Mainland China's historic name.

Daniel 7:23-24
"Thus he said:

'The fourth beast shall be
A fourth kingdom on earth,
Which shall be different from all other kingdoms,
And shall devour the whole earth,
Trample it and break it in pieces.
The ten horns are ten kings
Who shall arise from this kingdom.

(Horns in the Hebrew Bible symbolize kings, making it the Land of Ten Kingdoms.)

Encyclopedia Britannica.com
The Ten Kingdoms {period of Chinese history}Between 907 and 960, 10 independent kingdoms emerged in China,

Encyclopedia.com
Five Dynasties and Ten Kingdoms, a period of Chinese history between the fall of the T'ang dynasty (AD 907) and the establishment of the Sung dynasty (960 AD)...

(God used the future Ten Kingdoms label because thereafter China became the unified landmass we recognize even today.)

...and He will explain why it came 2020 AD, the exact year following the end of the Israelite's punishment of 2,625 years, following the loss of their rightful, blood sacrifices.

Daniel 12:11
"And from the time that the daily sacrifice is taken away, and the abomination of desolation is set up, there shall be one thousand two hundred and ninety days.

(The Hebrew word for days here means years)

Daniel 12:12
Blessed is he who waits, and comes to the one thousand three hundred and thirty-five days.

(Therefore Daniel 12:11 to 12 specifies a total Israelite punishment of 2,625 years, beginning on the day their blood sacrifices at their ancient Jerusalem temple turned unrighteous. Keep in mind that Israelite temple sacrifices ultimately protected the nation from outside invaders, assuring Israelites could freely visit their one temple.)

Agape Bible Study
The Ordinances and Sacrifices of the Law of the Covenant
The purpose of the Tabernacle was to be a place where God's people would have unrestricted access to Him,

(The ancient Israelites lost their temple to their first outside invader, who ruled them as a puppet state, economically sucking them dry for 18 years before destroying their temple. So, the temple sacrifices in historical hindsight turned unrightful on the very day of Israel's defeat to Babylon's king in 605 BC.)

Encyclopedia Britannica
Battle of Carchemish...605 BC {for the first time in its history, ancient Israel was finally defeated by an outside invader, the king of Babylon).

Herald magazine, Carl Hagensick
That same year {Babylon's king} Nebuchadnezzar's troops advanced as far as Jerusalem and the stage was set for the Babylonian captivity.

(Daniel's Riddle is solved by adding 2,625 years to 605 BC, and deducting one year for the missing year zero between the BC and AD dating system, which reveals the year 2020 as the end of the Israelite's punishment and beginning of the world's end from Gog's pandemic.)

China is the half-mechanized, world-ending *beast with 10 horns*, horns signifying kingdoms, ten kingdoms shown to Daniel.

Daniel 7:7
"After this I saw in the night visions, and behold, a fourth beast, dreadful and terrible, exceedingly strong. It had huge iron teeth; it was devouring, breaking in pieces, and trampling the residue with its feet. It was different from all the beasts that were before it, and it had ten horns.

(Horns again symbolize kings in the Bible, making it the Land of Ten Kingdoms, Mainland China's historic name.)

Jeremiah 23:19-20
Behold, a whirlwind of the Lord has gone forth in fury—
A violent whirlwind!
It will fall violently on the head of the wicked.
The anger of the Lord will not turn back
Until He has executed and performed the thoughts of His heart.
In the latter days you will understand it perfectly.

(The Lord acted through China's Gog to punish the Godless U.S. who broke from containing communist tyranny and unthinkably began financially enriching Communist China. But God promised in antiquity not to act until Gog had struck with his disease that then later had to be admitted incurable.)

Jeremiah 30:24
The fierce anger of the Lord shall not return, until he {the word "he" is non-capitalized, indicating a human, in this case China's Gog)} hath done it, and until he {"he" is again non-capitalized, suggesting China's Gog} have performed the intents of his heart: in the latter days ye shall consider it.

(COVID-19 is the culmination of then president Clinton's betrayal of America through his *Service Economy* ultimately servicing China's Gog and giving him his incurable disease.)

Hosea 5:11
Ephraim is oppressed and broken in judgment,
Because he willingly walked by human precept.

(Clinton and his Magog forces seek to portray Americans as racists, despite the fact that most modern Americans are descended of prior industrial-era slave workers themselves. This false, extra-legal sense of guilt obscures the fact that America, which is mostly white, is being destroyed by our U.S. Magog elites who unthinkably funded Gog's Covid virus and ended our nation and the world.)

Epoch Times 'White Privilege' Nurses Mandated to Undergo 'Implicit Bias' Training in Kentucky by Naveen Athrappully.
July 24, 2023 Nurses in Kentucky have been forced to undergo "implicit bias" training to indoctrinate them with concepts such as white people being inherently racist. Those who did not fulfill the course were reportedly being threatened with non-renewal of their licenses. The course seeks to address the "impact of historical racism and other forms of invidious discrimination on the provision of healthcare" as well as the actions that can be taken to reduce such alleged bias. The course essentially portrays white people as oppressors. One of the diagrams presented during the training is of "overt racism" and "covert racism." "Covert racism" includes the denial of "white privilege," "white silence," "denying institutional racism," "weaponizing whiteness," "Eurocentric school curricula," "excusing/white-splaining racism," "claiming reverse racism," "fetishizing POC," among others. Examples of "overt racism" include "public harassment of [persons of color] speaking other than English." A white woman asking a black woman where she is from is presented as an act of "covert racism." According to the organization, roughly 92 percent of nurses in Kentucky are white, 4 percent black, and 1 percent Hispanic.

Ezekiel 38:4
I will turn you {China's Gog} around, put hooks into your jaws, and lead you out, with all your army, horses, and horsemen, all splendidly clothed, a great company with bucklers and shields, all of them handling swords.

(So God allowed the Chinese tourists after the 2020 Lunar New Year to spread Covid as their invisible sword around the world; hence Gog's lethal army's splendid clothing whose armor is the disguise of innocent airline passengers carrying Covid.)

Ezekiel 38:9
You will ascend, coming like a storm, covering the land like a cloud, you and all your troops and many peoples with you."

Jeremiah 25:32
"Behold, disaster shall go forth
From nation to nation,
And a great whirlwind shall be raised up
From the farthest parts of the earth.

Daniel 7:19, 23
"Then I wanted to know the meaning of the a fourth beast {with ten horns} which was different from all the others and most terrifying, with its iron teeth and bronze claws—the beast that crushed and devoured its victims and trampled underfoot whatever was left.

"He {God's angelic messenger} gave me this explanation: 'The fourth beast is a fourth kingdom that will appear on earth. It will be different from all the other kingdoms and will devour the whole earth, trampling it down and crushing it

(Daniel is told that the incurable plague stems from the modern king of China, ruler of the land of Ten Kingdoms, who allies himself in end-times with ten modern kingdoms.)

Daniel 7:24
The ten horns are ten kings Who shall arise from this kingdom. And another shall rise after them;

(Only in Ezekiel 38 and 39 will this modern 10-nation-alliance be listed through China's Gog's modern allies, connecting the Ezekiel 38 and 39 Gog to the world-ending beast of Daniel 12,

who uses the incurable plague of Jeremiah 30, creating our modern pandemic now involving all remaining, unfulfilled, end-time prophesies of the Hebrew Bible.)
(Everything left in the Bible is about our current moment.)

(As for the Ezekiel 38 modern, end-time-10-nation alliance with China's Gog, keep in mind that since the great flood, God views all nations and peoples as descendants of Noah's specific grandsons in the continuing story of good and evil following Cane's society's destruction.)

Genesis 9:19
These were the three sons of Noah {who would have sixteen grandsons}, and from them came the people who were scattered over the whole earth.

(Now onto the 10 of Noah's total 16 grandsons who are currently, according to God, allied with Gog.)

Ezekiel 38:1
Now the word of the Lord came to me, saying, "Son of man, set your face against Gog,

(Gog is again China's king who rules his kingdom of China next spelled out.)

Ezekiel 38:2
of the land of Magog,

(Again, Magog comprises a whole second kingdom beyond Mainland China since president Clinton first had America, populated by Ephraim's descendants of Noah's grandson Shem, empower Gog by purchasing his slave-made products, damning America as well.)

Ezekiel 28:16
"By the abundance of your trading
You became filled with violence within,

And you sinned;
Therefore I cast you as a profane thing
Out of the mountain of God;
And I destroyed you, O covering cherub ,
From the midst of the fiery stones.

Ezekiel 28:18
You defiled your sanctuaries
By the multitude of your iniquities,
By the iniquity of your trading;

(China's Gog is also so closely tied to the next stated nation, Russia, that China's dictator is named by God as its true crown prince or leader.)

Ezekiel 38:2
the prince of Rosh,

Oxford Bible Church
Rosh was {and still is}…northern Russia.

(Then God names the descendants of another grandson of Noah.)

Ezekiel 38:2
Meshech…

Historical Textbook and Atlas of Biblical Geography by Coleman
Flavius Josephus {the ancient historian} generally identifies Meshech in Ezekiel's time as an area in modern Turkey.

Middle East Institute, Sino-Turkish Relations: An Overview,
The ancestors of the modern-day Turks originally lived in and near present-day China. Chinese historical records show that the nomadic peoples of the north, including the Turks, played a significant role in Chinese history.

(So many of Meshech's tribe are still modern mainland Chinese citizens.)

Ezekiel 38:2
and Tubal

The Oxford Bible Church
Tubal…today these regions are in Turkey, possibly including parts of southern Russia and northern Iran.

(Turkey, Russia and Iran are allies of Gog. To make this clear, God next specifies Iran as a nation closely allied with Gog.)

Ezekiel 38:5
Persia, {Modern Iran}

(God next spells out Gog's modern alliance with the tribe descended from Cush.)

Ezekiel 38:5
Cush

mapsimages.com
{Biblical}Cush refers to…South Sudan.

Ezekiel 38:5
and Put will be with them,

DBpedia
Put…is used in the Bible for Ancient Libya,

Ezekiel 38:6
all with shields and helmets, also Gomer with all its troops,

Oxford Bible Church: Gomer
Gomerites were…expelled in 700 BC from the southern steppes of Russia…

(Gomer thus represents southern Russia with some of the tribe migrating to Armenia and Turkey, a nation next noted by God.)

Ezekiel 38:6
and Beth Togarmah

Oxford Bible Church
Josephus identified Togarmah as Phrygians, located in Asia Minor {modern Turkey}. In 700 BC some Phrygians moved to Armenia.

(God also terms China as the kingdom of the "north".)

Ezekiel 38:2
from the far north with all its troops—the many nations with you.

(All of the aforementioned tribes' lands are in modern alliance with Communist China's king Gog. Firstly, Gog is China's dictator, Magog being his land Mainland China and again since president Clinton's Service Economy Magog is the United States as Gog's biggest customer.)

China's Top Trading Partners 2022, April 27, 2023
Chinas largest trading partner: United States totaling US $582.8 billion {U.S.} dollars, which is 16.2% of Chinas total exports.

(Modern Communist China also has a strong alliance with Russia.)

Wall Street Journal
The New Beijing-Moscow Axis
February 1, 2019, A shared rivalry with the U.S. has reunited the two powers, as in the early days of the Cold War. But this time, China is the senior partner {over Russia}.

GOD'S GUIDE TO THE END OF THE WORLD

(Meshech stems again from a tribe in China, no doubt part of Gog's passengers who infect the world. At the same time, Meshech and Tubal comprise modern Turkish descendants.)

The China Project.com
May 23, 2023, Turkey's foreign policy in a nutshell: Stuck between China and the West, it uses this geopolitical and geographical position to get the best deal.

(Muslim Turkey remains culpably silent over China's imprisonment of its innocent, Muslim Uyghyr citizens in concentration camps for simply believing in God, a crime America helped fund through our China trade, to be further explored herein.)

Foreign Policy, Why Erdogan Has Abandoned the Uyghurs
March 2, 2021 — As Ankara {Turkey's capital} grows more economically dependent on Beijing, the Turkish government is no longer offering a safe haven or defending Uyghur rights.

Diplomat.com, Asian New Journal
August 21, 2020, China Buys Turkey's Silence on Uyghur Oppression
Turkey has joined the list of majority Muslim countries that have opted for silence in dealing with one of the most pressing human rights issues of our time.

(Persia is modern Iran.)

The RAND Corporation
Over the past few decades, China and Iran have developed a broad and deep partnership…

(Biblical Cush is now Sudan)

fmprc.gov.cn
China remains the largest trading partner of Sudan, and now

there are over 130 Chinese companies investing and operating here.

(Biblical Put is modern Libya)

Carnegie Endowment for International Peace, China's Balancing Act in Libya by Frederic Wehrey, Sandy Alkoutami
May 10, 2020 - Among the bevy of great and middle powers involved in Libya, China is often neglected. It is not pouring in mercenaries or conducting airstrikes, but China is steadily investing and exerting influence in ways that promote Libya's eventual integration into China's global ambitions.

(The Gomer and Togarmah tribes are now in southern Russia and Turkey, their Chinese alliances previously discussed, but they are also located in modern Armenia.)

armenpress.com
According to Chinese government statistics, trade turnover between China and Armenia exceeded $ 1 billion U.S. dollars in 2020, growing by 34.8%,

(The bulk of China's modern alliances would not have been possible without then-president Clinton ushering Communist China into the World Trade Organization in late 2001. The prophet Daniel highlighted that the end-time king of China, the Land of Ten Kingdoms, would be enriched by three consecutive, pro-China U.S. kings, which recent history unmasks as presidents Clinton, W. Bush, and Obama.)

Daniel 7:24
The ten horns are ten kings
Who shall arise from this kingdom.
And another shall rise after them;
He shall be different from the first ones (deductively Ezekiel's Gog},
And shall subdue three kings.

(These three kings truly made China's Gog powerful as also shown to Daniel.)

Daniel 8:23-26
"And in the latter time of their kingdom {the Land of Ten Kingdoms},
When the transgressors have reached their fullness,
A king shall arise {deductively, Ezekiel's Gog},
Having fierce features,
Who understands sinister schemes.
His power shall be mighty, but not by his own power;

Investment Monitor
US manufacturing decline - who is to blame?
Between 2000 and 2010, nearly six million jobs in U.S. manufacturing were lost,

(Those three consecutive American Magog presidents enriched Gog and made him mighty.)

Daniel 8:23-24
His {the Land of 10 Kingdoms ruler, Gog's} power shall be mighty, but not by his own power;
He shall destroy fearfully,
And shall prosper and thrive;

History.com, The Founding Fathers Feared Foreign Influence—And Devised Protections Against It by Dave Roos
If the United States was going to be different, the framers needed a founding document that fully recognized and defended against the corrupting influence of foreign money and power, particularly on the president...a president under the influence of a foreign nation would be far more dangerous than any other single individual," says Stephen Saltzburg, professor at The George Washington University Law School. "That kind of conflict, between loyalty to the United States and loyalty to a foreign nation, would be intolerable."

New York Post
Foreign nationals gave Biden family and associates over $17M, IRS whistleblower claims By Victor Nava
July 19, 2023 "Despite creating many companies after the vice president took office, the Biden family used associates' companies to receive millions of dollars from foreign companies in China, Ukraine and Romania…

Fox News by Jessica Chasmar,
July 19, 2023 {U.S. House Of Representatives} Chairman Comer says payments show 'influence-peddling scheme to enrich the Bidens'

(God made clear that U.S. politicians always made "waste" of their citizens.)

Ezekiel 38:7
the land whose people were gathered from many peoples upon the mountains of Israel, which had been a continual waste."

(But presidents Clinton, W. Bush, and Obama's pro-Communist treason to Gog would destroy all Americans whom God proves are His end-time Holy People whom He offers to rescue now in this message.)

Daniel 8:24
He shall destroy the mighty, and also the holy people.

America first policy institute. February 14th, 2024. Reporting indicates that most illegal aliens coming to the southern border, including Chinese nationals, are not fleeing persecution and thus do not qualify for asylum under US law. However, they are still being released into American communities.

(God now makes explicitly clear China's Gog's real intentions.)

Daniel 7:20
I also wanted to know about the ten horns on its head and about the other horn that came up, before which three of them fell—

(Daniel now sees Gog's face in the little horn, signifying the kings who punished the U.S. for its wickedness, speaking through presidents Clinton, W. Bush, Obama, and now Biden.)

Daniel 7:20-22
...the horn that looked more imposing than the others and that had eyes and a mouth that spoke boastfully. As I watched, this horn was waging war against the holy people and defeating them,

(God's message comes now only after Daniel's 2020 end of the Israelite punishment and Daniel, Ezekiel, and Jeremiah's foretold birth of the Chinese pandemic, which recent history proved, required a few years before fulfilling Jeremiah's stipulation that this disease must be considered incurable. Only then according to God would He speak from His dictated words in the Hebrew Bible. His words reiterated by this messenger of the covenant, who it will be shown herein was anointed by the Archangel Michael in the company of others on October 27, 2017. Now, God names the U.S. as sanctified to rule over all nations.)

Daniel 7:22
...until the Ancient of Days came and pronounced judgment in favor of the holy people of the Most High, and the time came when they possessed the kingdom.

(Doubly proving this point, God showed Daniel the U.S. government as a leopard with four wings, wings connoting its blessedness, drawn from its four heads symbolizing its unique separation of powers through the Senate, House of Representatives, Judiciary, and Executive branches.)

Daniel 7:6
"After this I looked, and there was another, like a leopard, which had on its back four wings of a bird. The beast also had four heads, and dominion was given to it.

(This leopard fed the fourth beast, China's world ending beast of ten kingdoms marked by Gog's release of Covid as the greatest price of presidents Clinton, W. Bush, and Obama breaking with all prior presidents and enriching Communist China.)

Daniel 7:8
I was considering the horns, and there was another horn, a little one, coming up among them, before whom three of the first horns were plucked out by the roots. And there, in this horn, were eyes like the eyes of a man, and a mouth speaking pompous words.

(Gog now through Biden and our Magog federal government wars on our "most high", former president Donald Trump in a current reelection, breaking all prior, political conventions to remove him from the election to feed China's Gog.)

Daniel 7:25
He shall speak pompous words against the Most High,

(Gog can silence speakers of truth like Tucker Carlson and others brave enough to speak out.)

Daniel 7:25
Shall persecute the saints of the Most High,

(Gog's Democrat puppet asserts new modalities like LGBTQ to feed pedophilia, censorship of Americans, our invasion by illegal aliens, to change our ways.)

Daniel 7:25
And shall intend to change times and law.
Then the saints shall be given into his hand

For a time and times and half a time.

(Gog's Democrat puppets also allow for noncitizens to even serve as U.S. police officers.)

Fox News
April 6, 2022 , California Dem bill will allow non-citizens to become police officers by Haley Chi-Sing

NBC 5 Chicago News: Pritzker defends Illinois bill that allows non-citizens to become police officers
July 31, 2023, Critics argue that the bill would allow those who entered the U.S. illegally to become police officers…

(Americans can already see how this policy worked with Gog's Chinese immigrants as U.S. military personnel.)

BBC News By Mike Wendling
Two US Navy sailors in California have been arrested on charges of providing sensitive military information to China. Jinchao Wei, 22, a naturalized US citizen {from Communist China}, is accused of conspiring to send national defence information to a Chinese agent. Petty Officer Wenheng Zhao, 26, {from Communist China} was arrested on charges of accepting money for sensitive photos and videos.

(Gog has succeeded thus far in destroying Americans.)

Daniel 7:21
As I watched, this horn was waging war against the holy people and defeating them,

(The leaders of both the Democrat and Rhino, non-Trumpian, Republican parties suicidally empowered Gog as shown through the three, consecutive, pro-Chinese U.S. presidents Clinton, W. Bush, and Obama, making them again Gog's servants.)

Daniel 7:20
and the ten horns that were on its head, and the other horn which came up, before which three fell, namely, that horn which had eyes and a mouth which spoke pompous words, whose appearance was greater than his fellows.

All the end-time prophesies are about the same nation's incurable plague. After connecting Daniel 7 to Ezekiel 38 and 39, God thus foretold to Ezekiel that soldiers {from that land of ten kingdoms made clear to Daniel}…would be splendidly clad as "passengers", ascending in flying chariots to infect our land in a "storm" that turned out to be Jeremiah 30's incurable disease.

Ezekiel 38:3
"Behold, I am against you, O Gog…with all your army, horses, and horsemen, all splendidly clothed, a great company with bucklers and shields, all of them handling swords.

(They arrive in flying chariots while Ezekiel will soon describe them as *"passengers"*, hence flying airline passengers.)

Los Angeles Times By Cindy Chang
January 21, 2020, As millions of Chinese people jam onto trains and planes, headed to their hometowns and overseas for the Lunar New Year in the world's biggest annual mass migration, fears are growing that a new respiratory coronavirus could spread."

Ezekiel 38:9
You will ascend, coming like a storm, covering the land like a cloud, you and all your troops and many peoples with you."

Habakkuk 1:8
Their horses are swifter than leopards, more fierce than the evening wolves; their horsemen press proudly on. Their horsemen come from afar; they fly like an eagle swift to devour.

Jeremiah 4:13
Behold, he shall come up like clouds,
And his chariots like a whirlwind.
His horses are swifter than eagles.
Woe to us, for we are plundered!"

Jeremiah 4:5
For I will bring disaster from the north,
And great destruction."

Jeremiah 5:15-17
Behold, I will bring a nation against you from afar,
O house of Israel," says the Lord.
"It is a mighty nation,
It is an ancient nation,
A nation whose language you do not know,
Nor can you understand what they say.
Their quiver is like an open tomb;
They are all mighty men.
And they shall eat up your harvest and your bread,
Which your sons and daughters should eat.
They shall eat up your flocks and your herds;
They shall eat up your vines and your fig trees;
They shall destroy your fortified cities,
In which you trust, with the sword.

CNBC Politics, By Kevin Breuninger
April 1 2020, China hid extent of coronavirus outbreak, U.S. intelligence reportedly says...."Key Points", The Chinese government has deliberately underreported the total number of coronavirus cases and deaths in the country, the U.S. intelligence community told the White House, a new report says.

Fox News, Covid scientists accused of lab leak 'cover up' feared 'sh--- show' after blaming China for spread"
July 12, 2023, Given the sh-{expletive} show that would happen if anyone serious accused the Chinese of even accidental release, my feeling is we should say that given there is no evidence of a

specifically engineered virus, we cannot possibly distinguish between natural evolution and escape so we are content with ascribing it to natural process," Dr. Andrew Rambaut wrote in a Slack message to Dr. Kristian Andersen, Dr. Edward Holmes and Dr. Robert Garry, according to the report.

Proverbs 19:28
A disreputable witness scorns justice,
And the mouth of the wicked devours iniquity.

George Washington's Farewell Address
"It is our true policy to steer clear of permanent alliance with any portion of the foreign world."

(Zechariah also reveals Biden, the later, fourth Magog, U.S. president hurts the U.S. as Ephraim and the nation-state of Israel.)

Zechariah 1:18-21
Vision of the Horns
Then I raised my eyes and looked, and there were four horns. And I said to the angel who talked with me, "What are these?"

So he answered me, "These are the {four} horns that have scattered Judah, Israel, and Jerusalem."

(God next makes clear in this passage that only a return to U.S. manufacturing can end Gog's US presidential proxies' reign.)

Zechariah 1:20-21
...but the craftsmen are coming to terrify them, to cast out the horns of the nations that lifted up their horn against the land of Judah to scatter it."

George Washington to the United States Senate and House of Representatives, January 8, 1790
The advancement of Agriculture, commerce and Manufactures, by all proper means, will not, I trust, need recommendation.

Truthout.com, It's Time for a Manufacturing Revolution
Protecting American jobs is one of the legacies of the Revolutionary war. Why is it not important to politicians today? May 13, 2023, Washington understood that manufacturing had to be at the core of our economy if America was to prosper...But in the 33 years since Reagan took power, we've gone from manufacturing being over a third of our economy to it being about a tenth, putting our nation back into the bondage we were once in to the British East India Company.

www.jec.senate.gov
Decades of Manufacturing Decline and Outsourcing Left U.S. Supply Vulnerable To Disruption
February 1, 2022, The decision by big corporations to offshore manufacturing production instead of investing in domestic manufacturing contributed to significant supply chain disruption during the coronavirus pandemic. The U.S. lost over a quarter of manufacturing jobs since 2000 and production of critical inputs like semiconductors has increasingly moved overseas...

(Our founders understood manufacturing along with agriculture and mining were the basis of all true wealth.)

Alexander Hamilton's Report On Manufacturing
"Not only the wealth, but the independence and security of a country, appear to be materially connected with the prosperity of manufactures. Every nation, with a view to those great objects, ought to endeavor to possess within itself all the essentials of national supply. These comprise the means of subsistence, habitation, clothing, and defence...The possession of these is necessary to the perfection of the body politic; to the safety as well as to the welfare of the society; the want of either is the want of an important organ of political life and motion; and in the various crises which await a state, it must severely feel the effects of any such deficiency."

(We truly are feeling those effects, which Clinton started by selling-out U.S. manufacturing. Clinton allowed in slavery through Gog's slave-made goods that he facilitated into the free world through China's entry into the World Trade Organization. Now God through this messenger of the covenant named Joshua reiterates God's rebuke of presidents Clinton, W. Bush, Obama, and Biden, collectively acting as Satan to end humanity by feeding their Frankenstein Gog.)

Zechariah 3
Vision of the High Priest
Then he showed me Joshua the high priest standing before the Angel of the Lord, and Satan standing at his right hand to oppose him.

(God rather than Joshua next speaks since Joshua merely reiterates God's dictated words in the Hebrew Bible that came alive only after Covid was admitted to be incurable.)

And the Lord said to Satan, "The Lord rebuke you, Satan! The Lord who has chosen Jerusalem rebuke you!

(Until now, these Magog U.S. presidents were God's punishment on America for our lack of belief, feeding our enrichment of foreign, Communist, tyranny.)

Zechariah 11:6
For indeed I will raise up a shepherd in the land who will not care for those who are cut off, nor seek the young, nor heal those that are broken, nor feed those that still stand. But he will eat the flesh of the fat and tear their hooves in pieces.

(Shortly explained in more detail herein, the Lord now offers to save Americans from the tribulation upon us culminating in the end of our planet altogether.)

Zechariah 3
Is this not a brand plucked from the fire?"

GOD'S GUIDE TO THE END OF THE WORLD

(Clinton will die before the world is destroyed by that final meteorite and will find himself in Sheol, a subterranean realm where souls of humans who have died await judgment beneath our planet.)

Isaiah 14:12
"How you are fallen from heaven, O Day Star, son of Dawn! How you are cut down to the ground, you who laid the nations low!

(America reversed its economic system through Clinton's Service Economy, allowing him to empower the most powerful human, Communist China's Gog, whose regime by then was already the largest mass-killing government in all of human history.)

Jeremiah 17:5-6
Thus says the Lord:
"Cursed is the man who trusts in man

(For his economic betrayal, Clinton received massive sums of money from Communist Chinese allies.)

Forbes.com
Bill, Hillary, and Chelsea Clinton Foundation. Net assets 389 million U.S. dollars.

Wall Street Journal: Clinton Charity Tapped Foreign Friends
March 19, 2015. By James Grimaldi and Rebecca Ballhaus. {The Clinton} Foundation agreed not to seek donations from other governments, but cash kept flowing from individuals with connections to them...

George Washington's Letter to major general Robert Howe, Tuesday, August 17, 1779
"Few men have virtue to withstand the highest bidder."

(China finally invaded the U.S. with Covid as the cost of Clinton's betrayal continued by presidents W. Bush, Obama, and Biden.)

History proves Democrats and Republicans both funded Gog's Wuhan Covid research lab.

Daniel 8:23-26
"And in the latter time of their kingdom,
When the transgressors have reached their fullness,
A king shall arise,
Having fierce features,
Who understands sinister schemes.
His power shall be mighty, but not by his own power;

National Institutes of Health (.gov)
May 7, 2021, It has been known for a long time that…U.S. health agencies funded the Wuhan Institute of Virology,

New York Post
June 13, 2023, U.S. taxpayers funded $2M for research in Wuhan, China

U.S. taxpayers supported research in three Chinese labs that included risky gain-of-function experiments with coronaviruses at the Wuhan lab…

Federal U.S. Government, Committee on Oversight and Accountability Report, Chairman James Comer
"Mounting evidence points to the virus originating from a leak at the Wuhan Institute of Virology…Eco-Health Alliance, a U.S. National Institutes of Health (NIH) grantee, awarded taxpayer funds to the {Wuhan Lab} to conduct gain of function research on bat coronaviruses – research that may have started the pandemic.

George Washington's Farewell Address
"There can be no greater error than to expect or calculate upon real favors from nation to nation. It is an illusion, which experience must cure, which a just pride ought to discard."

(Biden, as Gog's pawn, resumed funding in 2023 for Gog's Chinese Covid lab to better help Gog mass-murder humanity as the Chinese dictator escaped all repudiation for the pandemic he hid and spread upon the world.)

Washington Examiner, Biden NIH resumes funding group tied to Wuhan coronavirus lab: 'An outrage'
May 9, 2023, President Joe Biden's National Institutes of Health has resumed a grant award suspended under former President Donald Trump for coronavirus bat research to a U.S. nonprofit group that has come under heightened scrutiny for partnering with the Wuhan Institute of Virology in Wuhan, China.

George Washington's Farewell Address, 1796
"Foreign influence in innumerable ways {can} tamper with domestic factions, to practice the arts of seduction, to mislead public opinion, to influence or awe the public council."

(Biden then canceled funding to admit the lab was not practicing correct biosafety procedures, instead of because its leader Gog, concealed the virus for 5 months before his passengers mass-infected humanity.)

The Hill: Biden administration suspends funding to Wuhan lab by Nathaniel Weixel
07/19/23 The Biden administration is suspending all federal funding to the Wuhan Institute of Virology…the Chinese lab at the center of a controversy over the origins of the coronavirus, The Wuhan Institute "likely violated protocols of the NIH regarding biosafety is undisputed," wrote the official, whose name was redacted. "As such, there is risk that the Wuhan Lab not only previously violated, but is currently violating, and will continue to violate, protocols of the NIH on biosafety."

But God proves China's king intentionally leaked Covid to kill us all to take our unguarded homes and lands.

Ezekiel 38:10-13
"'This is what the Sovereign Lord says: On that day thoughts will come into your mind and you will devise an evil scheme. You will say, "I will invade a land of unwalled villages; I will attack a peaceful and unsuspecting people—all of them living without walls and without gates and bars. I will plunder and loot and turn my hand against the resettled ruins and the people gathered from the nations, rich in livestock and goods, living at the center of the land."

(Gog seeks to feed crime in our streets through his Magog US political proxies to leave our real estate even more vacant so he can buy up our land for cheaper prices. Any Chinese company is him. Every dollar spent on China is for him. The one who aims to wipe us out with his incurable plague given to him by U.S. leadership charged with our safety. What did everyone expect once the Service Economy empowered what even by the nineteen seventies became the largest mass murdering regime in history? Gog's puppet whom he funds with American proceeds, North Korea, tells you how Gog feels, happy to give you Covid as America's Christmas surprise.)

NPR news. North Korea Promises A Christmas Surprise. December 23, 2019

(While our Magog US coastal mass media hides the unavoidable truth from most, leaving many confused at Gog's true aim.)

Ezekiel 38:13
And all their young lions will say to you {Gog}, 'Have you come to take plunder? Have you gathered your army to take booty, to carry away silver and gold, to take away livestock and goods, to take great plunder?' " '

(He's come for your lives as Covid kills you in a clever patchwork of many ailments. While our U.S. Magog elites hide Gog's nation-ending attack on America.)

Epoch Times, Hidden Messages in GOP Report Reveal How Scientists Shaped Narrative on Covid-19 Origins
July 12, 2023, The new messages reveal sharp inconsistencies between the public and private views of the Proximal Origin's authors on Covid-19's emergence. In Proximal Origin, the authors declared that "SARS-CoV-2 is not a laboratory construct or a purposefully manipulated virus" and that no "laboratory-based scenario is plausible." However, in their private Slack group, the authors acknowledged that the virus likely came out of a lab. "The main issue is that accidental escape is in fact highly likely – it's not some fringe theory," lead author Kristian Andersen of the Scripps Institute wrote in a message to his fellow authors.

Federal U.S. Government, Committee on Oversight and Accountability Report, Chairman James Comer
"Mounting evidence points to the virus originating from a leak at the Wuhan Institute of Virology
U.S. House of Representatives Committee on Oversight and Accountability: Covid Origins Committee Republicans have unearthed emails revealing that top virologists warned Dr. Anthony Fauci, the Director of the National Institute of Allergy and Infectious Diseases, that the virus {Covid} appeared to be genetically engineered and pointed to a lab leak in Wuhan. However, these emails reveal that Dr. Fauci and former NIH Director Dr. Francis Collins may have colluded with scientists to downplay the lab leak theory for their preferred narrative of natural origin. "

Jeremiah 8:11; 6:14; Ezekiel 13:10,16
"Peace, peace! when there is no peace"

Jeremiah 23:14
Also I have seen a horrible thing in the prophets of Jerusalem:

They commit adultery and walk in lies;
They also strengthen the hands of evildoers,
So that no one turns back from his wickedness.

(Gog may seek to repopulate the desolate, viral apocalypse world with his virally-immune fetuses).

NPR, December 30, 2019
{Chinese biophysicist} He Jiankui announced in November 2018 that he had used a powerful technique called CRISPR on a human embryo to edit the genes of twin girls. He said he modified a gene with the intention of protecting the girls against HIV, the virus that causes AIDS.

Gog's viral murder masked as an act of God is the reason why God codenamed China's king Gog, a name so close to God's own.

Jeremiah 10:22
Behold, the noise of the report has come,
And a great commotion out of the north country,
To make the cities of Judah desolate, a den of jackals.

Isaiah 32:7
Also the schemes of the schemer are evil;
He devises wicked plans
To destroy the poor with lying words,
Even when the needy speaks justice.

All after the U.S. poisoned Gog's land, buying his slave-made, Chinese goods so cheap for they were made with no environmental protections, sowing an unheralded pollution poisoning China.

U.S. State Department Report: China's Environmental Abuses, 2017

China's total energy-related emissions are twice that of the United States and nearly one third of all emissions globally. Beijing's energy-related emissions increased more than 80 percent between 2005-2019, while U.S. energy-related emissions have decreased by more than 15 percent.

U.S. Department of State, Report: China's Environmental Abuses: Addressing China's Environmental Destruction
Increasing Greenhouse Gas Emissions, A Risk to the Ozone Layer, Threatening Air Quality. World's Worst Mercury Polluter, Illegal Wildlife Trafficking, Driving Illegal Logging and Trade, Mismanaging Plastic Waste, Not-So-Green Belt and Road, Polluting the Ocean, Illegal, Unreported, and Unregulated Fishing Worldwide, Unilateral Mekong Water Manipulation

The People's Republic of China (PRC) is the world's largest emitter of greenhouse gases; the largest source of marine debris; the worst perpetrators of illegal, unreported, and unregulated (IUU) fishing; and the world's largest consumer of trafficked wildlife and timber products. While the Chinese people have suffered the worst environmental impacts of its actions, Beijing also threatens the global economy and global health by unsustainably exploiting natural resources and exporting its willful disregard for the environment through its One Belt One Road initiative. Tragically, the Chinese Communist Party (CCP) represses civil society and a free press, slowing changes that would benefit its citizens and people all over the world.

(U.S. Magog leaders who fed this record Chinese pollution only wish to continue it, preaching of carbon emissions, artificial wage increases, culling food sources over it, part of the agenda to destroy the free world as all our Chinese purchased products truly wreck the world environment.)

Isaiah 47:13
You are wearied with your many counsels; let them stand forth and save you, those who divide the heavens, who gaze at the

stars, who at the new moons make known what shall come upon you.

Gript.ie
Nobel Laureate: "Climate science has metastasized into massive shock-journalistic pseudoscience" by Thade Andy
May 21, 2023, Dr. John F. Clauser, joint recipient of the 2022 Nobel Prize in Physics, has criticized the climate emergency narrative calling it "a dangerous corruption of science that threatens the world's economy and the well-being of billions of people."

Proquest.com
"Man-caused global warming is the biggest scam perpetrated against society since time began," says Jay Lehr, science director for the Heartland Institute. "The whole concept behind climate change is fear and control."

When you explore the facts, ice core samples for the last 900,000 years, and records from the last 5,000 years, Lehr explains the global climate has meandered through fairly predictable 1,500-year cycles of warming and cooling.

God in his ancient, dictated words now damns our 4 presidents shown to Daniel who enriched Gog, Clinton, W. Bush, Obama,

Daniel 7:20-21
I also wanted to know about the ten horns on its head and about the other horn that came up, before which three of them fell—

Daniel 7:24
The ten horns are ten kings
Who shall arise from this kingdom.
And another shall rise after them;
He shall be different from the first ones,
And shall subdue three kings

Jeremiah 9:3
"And like their bow they have bent their tongues for lies.
They are not valiant for the truth on the earth.
For they proceed from evil to evil,
And they do not know Me," says the Lord.

Ezekiel 22:27, 29
Her officials within her are like wolves tearing their prey; they shed blood and kill people to make unjust gain. The people of the land practice extortion and commit robbery; they oppress the poor and needy and mistreat the foreigner, denying them justice.

Hosea 13:11
I gave you a king in My anger,

George Washington
"However [political parties] may now and then answer popular ends, they are likely in the course of time and things, to become potent engines, by which cunning, ambitious, and unprincipled men will be enabled to subvert the power of the people and to usurp for themselves the reins of government, destroying afterwards the very engines which have lifted them to unjust dominion."

Isaiah 28:14-15
Therefore hear the word of the Lord, you scornful men,
Who rule this people who are in Jerusalem,
Because you have said, "We have made a covenant with death,
And with Sheol {a subterranean realm for souls after their death as they await God's impending judgment} we are in agreement.
When the overflowing scourge passes through,
It will not come to us,
For we have made lies our refuge,
And under falsehood we have hidden ourselves."

Jeremiah 5:26-28
'For among My people are found wicked men;
They lie in wait as one who sets snares;

They set a trap;
They catch men.
As a cage is full of birds,
So their houses are full of deceit.
Therefore they have become great and grown rich.
They have grown fat, they are sleek;
Yes, they surpass the deeds of the wicked;
They do not plead the cause,
The cause of the fatherless;
Yet they prosper,
And the right of the needy they do not defend.

Ezekiel 34:10
Thus says the Lord God: "Behold, I am against the shepherds, and I will require My flock at their hand; I will cause them to cease feeding the sheep, and the shepherds shall feed themselves no more; for I will deliver My flock from their mouths, that they may no longer be food for them."

(The Lord completely rebukes supporting leaders based on their genders or cosmetic features.)

1 Samuel 16:7
But the Lord said to Samuel, "Do not look at his appearance or at his physical stature, because I have [c]refused him. For the Lord does not see as man sees; for man looks at the outward appearance, but the Lord looks at the heart."

...and Biden who now reigns as a king from absentee ballots thanks to Gog's virus.

Amos 2:6-7
"For three transgressions of Israel, and for four {deductively Clinton, W. Bush, Obama, and Biden},
I will not turn away its punishment,
Because they sell the righteous for silver,
And the poor for a pair of sandals.

Proverbs 29:12
If a ruler pays attention to lies,
All his servants become wicked.

Isaiah 56:11
Yes, they are greedy dogs
Which never have enough.
And they are shepherds
Who cannot understand;
They all look to their own way,
Every one for his own gain,
From his own territory.

(According to God, the U.S. political leadership all serve under oaths to Him uttered by their lips to attain their jobs, but do not honor Him through their thoughts and actions.)

Jeremiah 12:2
You are near in their mouth
But far from their mind.

(Biden doesn't even hide his pro-Chinese prejudice, starting a needless war with Russia as misdirection rather than face China's king Gog who has killed a million Americans thus far with a virus our government helped fund, a point that can't be repeated enough.)

Daniel 7:20-21, 25
—the {fourth little} horn that looked more imposing than the others and that had eyes and a mouth that spoke boastfully. He shall speak words against the Most High, and shall wear out the saints of the Most High, and shall think to change the times and the law; and they shall be given into his hand for a time, times, and half a time.

Ezekiel 34:7-10
'Therefore, you shepherds, hear the word of the Lord: "As I live," says the Lord God, "surely because My flock became a

prey, and My flock became food for every beast of the field, because there was no shepherd, nor did My shepherds search for My flock, but the shepherds fed themselves and did not feed My flock"— therefore, O shepherds, hear the word of the Lord!

(The Lord intimates that He will act with modern Americans and believers' wicked elites as He did to Pharaoh, hence the same language is used here as He used against Pharaoh.)

Ezekiel 34:23-31
And they shall know that I am the Lord, when I break the bars of their yoke, and deliver them from the hand of those who enslaved them. They shall no more be a prey to the nations, nor shall the beasts of the land devour them. They shall dwell securely, and none shall make them afraid.

Jeremiah 9:3
"...they have bent their tongues for lies.

Jeremiah 23:1-6
"Woe to the shepherds who destroy and scatter the sheep of my pasture!" declares the Lord. Therefore thus says the Lord, the God of Israel, concerning the shepherds who care for my people: "You have scattered my flock and have driven them away, and you have not attended to them. Behold, I will attend to you for your evil deeds, declares the Lord.

Zechariah 11:18
In one month I destroyed the three shepherds.

Hosea 13:11-12
So in my anger I gave you a king,
and in my wrath I took him away.

Jeremiah 50:6
"My people have been lost sheep. Their shepherds have led them astray, turning them away on the mountains. From mountain to hill they have gone. They have forgotten their fold.

Isaiah 1:23
Your princes are rebellious,
And companions of thieves;
Everyone loves bribes,
And follows after rewards.
They do not defend the fatherless,
Nor does the cause of the widow come before them

Ezekiel 34:2
"Son of man, prophesy against the shepherds of Israel; prophesy, and say to them, even to the shepherds, Thus says the Lord God: Ah, shepherds of Israel who have been feeding yourselves! Should not shepherds feed the sheep?

Isaiah 3:12
As for My people, children are their oppressors,
And women rule over them.
O My people! Those who lead you cause you to err,
And destroy the way of your paths."

(The 2020 election proved there is no 2024. The free peoples are all the slave of Gog.)

Daniel 7:21
As I watched, this horn was waging war against the holy people and defeating them.

Clinton will be unmasked as the world-ending King of all civilization first begun in Babylon,

New York Post by Katherine Donlevy
Jan. 16, 2024, Chinese lab crafts mutant COVID-19 strain with 100% kill rate in 'humanized' mice: Dr. Gennadi Glinsky, a retired professor of medicine at Stanford, wrote: "This madness must be stopped before too late."

Isaiah 14:1-7
Fall of the King of Babylon

It shall come to pass in the day the Lord gives you rest from your sorrow, and from your fear and the hard bondage in which you were made to serve, that you will take up this proverb against the king of Babylon, and say:

"How the oppressor has ceased,
The golden city ceased!
The Lord has broken the staff of the wicked,
The scepter of the rulers;
He who struck the people in wrath with a continual stroke,
He who ruled the nations in anger,
Is persecuted and no one hinders.
The whole earth is at rest and quiet;
They break forth into singing.

Clinton will be unmasked as a leader shown to be born from our modern lack of belief in God Himself.

Isaiah 48:18-19
Oh, that you had heeded My commandments!
Then your peace would have been like a river,
And your righteousness like the waves of the sea.
Your descendants also would have been like the sand,
And the offspring of your body like the grains of sand;
His name would not have been cut off
Nor destroyed from before Me."

(God explains that there is a subterranean realm called Sheol where souls of the dead reside in an unconscious state. It's rapidly being filled with the elites of the U.S.A. actively working to kill themselves.)

Isaiah 5:14
Therefore Sheol has enlarged its appetite and opened its mouth beyond measure, and the nobility of Jerusalem and her multitude will go down, her revelers and he who exults in her.

(God revealed in a prophetic vision to Isaiah that the end time, world-ending leader first-birthing the horns enriching China, William Clinton, would die and find himself in a part of Sheol called Hell where past evil leaders remain awake as worm-eaten corpses awaiting God's impending arrival and judgment. Clinton's arrival signals to the other wicked leaders that God will soon arrive for they know Clinton as the King of Babylon, that final ruler of civilization first born in Babylon. Then Clinton discovers his true identity is Lucifer, the Hebrew word *Hêlêl* used only once in the Hebrew Bible. Although synonymous with the forces of Satan, Lucifer means *son of the morning star;* for Clinton first misled America in their daily labors to ultimately end the world by enriching tyranny, continued by W. Bush and Rhino Republicans, Obama, and Biden.)

Isaiah 14:9-20
Hell from beneath is excited about you,
To meet you at your coming;
It stirs up the dead for you,
All the chief ones of the earth;
It has raised up from their thrones
All the kings of the nations.

They all shall speak and say to you:
'Have you also become as weak as we?
Have you become like us?
Your pomp is brought down to Sheol,
And the sound of your stringed instruments;
The maggot is spread under you,
And worms cover you.'
The Fall of Lucifer {Helel ben Shachar, shining one, son of the morning star}

"How you are fallen from heaven,
O Lucifer {Helel ben Shachar}, son of the morning!
How you are cut down to the ground,
You who weakened the nations!

For you have said in your heart:
'I will ascend into heaven,
I will exalt my throne above the stars of God;
I will also sit on the mount of the congregation
On the farthest sides of the north;

I will ascend above the heights of the clouds,
I will be like the Most High.'
Yet you shall be brought down to Sheol,
To the lowest depths of the Pit.
"Those who see you will gaze at you,
And consider you, saying:
'Is this the man who made the earth tremble,
Who shook kingdoms,
Who made the world as a wilderness
And destroyed its cities,
Who did not open the house of his prisoners?'

"All the kings of the nations,
All of them, sleep in glory,
Everyone in his own house;
But you are cast out of your grave
Like an abominable branch,
Like the garment of those who are slain,
Thrust through with a sword,
Who go down to the stones of the pit,
Like a corpse trodden underfoot.
You will not be joined with them in burial,
Because you have destroyed your land
And slain your people.

(After their resurrection and judgment by the Lord, many of the extremely wicked will remain on earth as worm-eaten corpses unable to die for eternity, a reminder of the ultimate villains of history.)

Isaiah 66:24
"And they shall go out and look on the dead bodies of the men

who have rebelled against me. For their worm shall not die, their fire shall not be quenched, and they shall be an abhorrence to all flesh."

(If Americans had retained their belief in God, they would never have elected Clinton as president.)

For Clinton was a literal *bastard*, warned by God to never make a leader for bastards remove the landmarks and reverse morality.

Deuteronomy 23:2
"One of illegitimate birth shall not enter the assembly of the Lord; even to the tenth generation none of his descendants shall enter the assembly of the Lord.

Proverbs 3:5
Trust in the Lord with all your heart, and do not lean on your own understanding.

(Clinton and Obama, literally bastards, as presidents indeed removed historical landmarks for the first time in our history.)

Proverbs 23:10-11
Do not remove the ancient landmark,
Nor enter the fields of the fatherless;
For their Redeemer is mighty;
He will plead their cause against you.

Hosea 5:10
"The princes of Judah are like those who remove a landmark;
I will pour out My wrath on them like water.

For Clinton first made us enrich Communist China instead of containing Communism, making us part of Magog, meaning those who enrich China's Gog.

Wall Street Journal
March 3, 2017 China Was Bill Clinton's Russia
In 1996, a foreign government {Communist China} didn't just meddle, it donated.

As our founders noted, we were always slaves to our reigning business elites. Once Clinton outsourced manufacturing to Gog,

Huffington post
September 4, 2012, Bill Clinton's True Legacy: Outsourcer-in-Chief by Jane White
Mitt Romney may have run a company that outsourced jobs but Clinton ran a country that did.

George Washington rightly prophesized we would be enslaved and ultimately killed by this foreign king God unmasked as China's Gog.

National Archives: Introductory Note, Report On Manufacturers
Washington said: "A free people ought not only to be armed but disciplined; to which end a uniform and well digested plan is requisite: And their safety and interest require, that they should promote such manufactories, as tend to render them independent on others for essential, particularly for military supplies."

George Washington And Manufacturing: How Are They Connected? Mark Gearding
Washington understood that the country had to develop a thriving manufacturing industry to succeed. He is the first to make "Made in America" popular by pursuing the only American tailor for a suit for his inauguration. For Washington the suit represented "a new beginning for a new country bolstered by a strong, prosperous manufacturing industry."

United States Senate Article Titled About Traditions & Symbols, Washington's Farewell Address
In this letter to "Friends and Citizens," Washington warned that the forces of geographical sectionalism, political factionalism, and interference by foreign powers in the nation's domestic affairs threatened the stability of the republic.

U.S. Department of State
Washington warned the nation to avoid permanent alliances with foreign nations…

While God calls our spiritual leaders "mad men" for allowing sodomy's spread, forbidden by God as history proves it turns all nations into pedophile ones.

Hosea 9:7-9
The days of punishment have come;
The days of recompense have come.``
Israel knows!
The prophet is a fool,
The spiritual man is a mad man
Because of the greatness of your iniquity and great enmity.

Ecclesiastes 1:9-10
That which has been is what will be,
That which is done is what will be done,
And there is nothing new under the sun.
Is there anything of which it may be said,
"See, this is new"?
It has already been in ancient times before us.

(In fact, Christ's death marks the end of the tolerance of forbidden sexual norms and with them the end of mostly pedophile societies of the ancient world, of which the classic Greeks are but only an example.)

The Collector: Pedophilia in Ancient Greece and Rome, Jenna Ross

May 23, 2020, While the practice of pedophilia today is a morally wrong and illegal act,...Pedophilia was common in Greek and Roman mythology and daily life...It should be noted that the younger boys involved in pederastic relationships were often of the same age as young girls who were set into arranged marriages with much older men, around the ages of 12 to 16. This occurred in both Greek and Roman culture.

Jeremiah 9:13
And the Lord said, "Because they have forsaken My law which I set before them, and have not obeyed My voice, nor walked according to it, but they have walked according to the dictates of their own hearts and after the Baals {evil idols}which their fathers taught them,"

Daily Mail.com by Sophie Mann,
July 20, 2023. Transgender {U.S.} Assistant Secretary of Health Rachel Levine claims children can go through the 'wrong puberty' and argues gender-affirming care for kids is 'evidence-based' despite critics. {Levine is advocating} for gender-affirming care for individuals below the age of thirteen.

Isaiah 14:21
Prepare slaughter for his children
Because of the iniquity of their fathers,

New York Post by Larry Celona
May 7, 2023, 'God is Trans' exhibit at {New York City} Catholic Church raises eyebrows for take on gender identity...

Proverbs 16:25
There is a way that seems right to a man,
But its end is the way of death.

Jeremiah 6:11-13
And from the prophet even to the priest,
Everyone deals falsely.

Ecclesiastes 5:1-20
Guard your steps when you go to the house of God. Go near to listen rather than to offer the sacrifice of fools, who do not know that they do wrong.

Leviticus 18:22
You shall not lie with a male as with a woman. It is an abomination.

The Guardian:
January 25, 2023, Pope Francis calls for {an} LGBTQ+] welcome from {the Catholic} church,

Micah 2:6
Her prophets are insolent, treacherous people;
"For the lips of a priest should keep knowledge,

Jeremiah 23:16
Thus says the Lord of hosts:
"Do not listen to the words of the prophets who prophesy to you.
They make you worthless;
They speak a vision of their own heart,
Not from the mouth of the Lord.

Isaiah 5:21
Woe to those who are wise in their own eyes,
And prudent in their own sight!

Ezekiel 22:28
Her prophets whitewash these deeds for them by false visions and lying divinations. They say, 'This is what the Sovereign Lord says'—when the Lord has not spoken.

Jeremiah 23:30
"Therefore behold, I am against the prophets," says the Lord, "who steal My words every one from his neighbor. Behold, I am against the prophets," says the Lord, "who use their tongues and say, 'He says.' Behold, I am against those who prophesy false

dreams," says the Lord, "and tell them, and cause My people to err by their lies and by their recklessness. Yet I did not send them or command them; therefore they shall not profit this people at all," says the Lord.

Isaiah 29:16
Surely you have things turned around!

Jeremiah 5:30-31
"An astonishing and horrible thing
Has been committed in the land:
The prophets prophesy falsely,
And the priests rule by their own power;
And My people love to have it so.
But what will you do in the end?

Jeremiah 10:23
O Lord, I know the way of man is not in himself;
It is not in man who walks to direct his own steps.

Zephaniah 3:4
Her prophets are insolent, treacherous people;
Her priests have polluted the sanctuary,
They have done violence to the law.

(The preachers trying to limit abortion ignore the fact that God decides the fate of all while still in the womb, so anyone who is aborted falls under His control., further explored in the appendix of this guide.)

Proverbs 16:9
A person plans his way,
But the Lord directs his steps.

(The same preachers trying to limit abortion, promote the spread of sodomy which is strictly prohibited by God throughout the Hebrew Bible.)

GOD'S GUIDE TO THE END OF THE WORLD

George Washington's Letter To Benedict Arnold, Thursday, September 14, 1775
"While we are contending for our own liberty, we should be very cautious not to violate the rights of conscience in others, ever considering that God alone is the judge of the hearts of men, and to him only in this case they are answerable."

Isaiah 59:4-5
No one calls for justice,
Nor does any plead for truth.
They trust in empty words and speak lies;
They conceive evil and bring forth iniquity.
They hatch vipers' eggs and weave the spider's web;
He who eats of their eggs dies,
And from that which is crushed a viper breaks out.

Ezekiel 16:56
Was not your sister Sodom a byword in your mouth in the day of your pride,

Fox News Christian politician takes legal action after anti-LGBT Pride tweet sees his 'life torn apart' by Jon Brown
July 26, 2023, A tweet against naked men parading in front of minors at LGBT events has reportedly torn King Lawal's life apart. A local politician in the United Kingdom is taking legal action after he was reportedly canceled by seven different organizations and suspended by his own political party for tweeting out his religious views.

Isaiah 55:8-9
"For My thoughts are not your thoughts,
Nor are your ways My ways," says the Lord.
"For as the heavens are higher than the earth,
So are My ways higher than your ways,
And My thoughts than your thoughts.

Isaiah 24:5-6
The earth is also defiled under its inhabitants,

Because they have transgressed the laws,
Changed the ordinance,
Broken the everlasting covenant.
Therefore the curse has devoured the earth,
And those who dwell in it are desolate.

Hosea 14:9
Who is wise?
Let him understand these things.
Who is prudent?
Let him know them.
For the ways of the Lord are right;
The righteous walk in them,
But transgressors stumble in them.

Do I not address a nation of adults molested as kids?

The Daily Item.com
June 12, 2022 By Justin Strawser
Adverse Childhood Experiences and mental health disorders in adulthood have "a very strong link" to each other, according to Dr. Frank Maffei, Chair of Pediatrics at Geisinger.

The offspring of whores, God adds, who quit mothering and ended it all.

Hosea 2:4-5
"I will not have mercy on her children,
For they are the children of harlotry.
For their mother has played the harlot;
She who conceived them has behaved shamefully.
For she said, 'I will go after my lovers,
Who give me my bread and my water,
My wool and my linen,
My oil and my drink.'

Job 39:13-17
"The wings of the ostrich wave proudly,

But are her wings and pinions like the kindly stork's?
For she leaves her eggs on the ground,
And warms them in the dust;
She forgets that a foot may crush them,
Or that a wild beast may break them.
She treats her young harshly, as though they were not hers;
Her labor is in vain, without [a]concern,
Because God deprived her of wisdom,
And did not endow her with understanding.

Ezekiel 23:20
For she lusted for her paramours,
Whose flesh is like the flesh of donkeys,
And whose issue is like the issue of horses.

Ezekiel 16:49-50
Look, this was the iniquity of your sister Sodom: She and her daughter had pride, fullness of food, and abundance of idleness; neither did she strengthen the hand of the poor and needy. And they were haughty and committed abomination before Me; therefore I took them away as I saw fit.

(Forced to work, motherhood was stripped from the young, feeding pedophilia alongside a loss of belief in God.)

Hosea 5:7
They have dealt treacherously with the Lord,
For they have begotten pagan children.
(Children who no longer believe in God}
Now a New Moon shall devour them and their heritage.

The Washington Times
July 20, 2023. Americans' belief in God, {and} heaven at lowest point in 22 years, Gallup survey says. Nearly 3 in 10 don't believe in the devil or hell, poll finds.

Jeremiah 13:22-23
"Why have these things come upon me?"

For the greatness of your iniquity
Your skirts have been uncovered,
Your heels made bare.

The Center Square: California Assembly passes bill allowing some pedophiles to not register as sex offenders,
September 3, 2020. "This {new law exempts a} person convicted of certain {pedophile} offenses involving minors if the person is not more than 10 years older than the minor. Assemblyman Steven Choi, {a Republican from} Irvine, spoke out…"In the age of historic sex…and child trafficking here in California, this bill is entirely inappropriate. I don't understand why a 24-year-old volunteer coach should not have to register as a sex offender for being with a 15-year-old student. Statutory rape should be a registerable offense either way."

Researchgate.net, Prevalence of Childhood Trauma in a Clinical Population of Transsexual People by Darlynn Gehring, Vancouver General Hospital and Gail Knudson, University of British Columbia, Vancouver.
March, 2005. Few studies have focused on the prevalence and extent of childhood trauma in the transsexual population. In our study of 42 transsexual people…34…males {and}…8 females…55% reported experiencing an unwanted sexual event {at}the average age of…13.

(The ancient Israelites' tolerance for pedophilia led their political leaders to attempt the forced, mass-rape of all Israelite boys, abandoning their Israelite self-identity.)

Jesus and His Jewish Influences: Lecture 8, Jews and Greek Rule: Desolating Sacrilege and the Maccabean Revolt by Professor Jodi Magness, Ph.D.
"In the year 167 BC, {the foreign Greek ruler} Antiochus IV "Epiphanes" "wrote to his whole kingdom that all should be one people, and that all should give up their particular customs…Many even from Israel gladly adopted his religion…{the Greek king} directed them…to leave their sons

uncircumcised. They were to make themselves abominable by everything unclean and profane so that they would forget the law and change the ordinances…and whoever does not…shall die."

Big Think.com , How the ancient Greeks viewed pederasty and homosexuality by Tom Brinkof
January 13, 2023,…In ancient Greece, pederasty was the practice of older men serving as mentors to young boys in exchange for sexual favors. This practice was widespread…

(Just as the tolerance of pedophilia quickly fed the foreign Greek king's attempt to mass-rape the ancient Israelite boys, now America witnesses the same cycle for the benefit of China's Gog.)

"Facts Matter" by Roman Balmakov
July 25, 2023. Disney facing…a loss of 79 billion {dollars of U.S.) market cap{ital} that could be the fact that many parents don't agree with having transgender men dress up as female characters around their kids.

(Exposing children to a fluid gender model harms their emerging sexual identity akin to sodomy or rape. While non-binary sexuality is typically caused by a prior pedophile encounter in adolescence as current Haiti has institutionalized to control its people.)

CNN.Com
'Rape has become a weapon' for Haiti gangs, says UN by Caitlin Hu
October 14, 2022…the United Nations has released a grim report accusing…{Haiti's} powerful gangs of using rape as a tool of intimidation and control.

Ezekiel 22:11-12
One commits abomination with his neighbor's wife; another lewdly defiles his daughter-in-law; and another in you violates his sister, his father's daughter. In you they take bribes to shed blood; you take usury and increase; you have made profit from

your neighbors by extortion, and have forgotten Me," says the Lord God.

(It leads to current American families being financially raped.)

CBS News, Americans are buried under nearly $1 trillion {U.S. Dollars} in credit card debt by Megan Cerullo
May 29, 2023 {American} Consumers now owe a record $986 billion on their charge cards…

(A lack of belief in God is the result of children not raised by women as the Lord now makes clear as the singular cause of society's end.)

Zechariah 5:5-11
The Woman in a Basket
Then the angel who was speaking to me came forward and said to me, "Look up and see what is appearing."

I asked, "What is it?"

He replied, "It is a basket." And he added, "This is the iniquity of the people throughout the land."

Then the cover of lead was raised, and there in the basket sat a woman! He said, "This is wickedness," and he pushed her back into the basket and pushed its lead cover down on it.

Then I looked up—and there before me were two women, with the wind in their wings! They had wings like those of a stork, and they lifted up the basket between heaven and earth.
"Where are they taking the basket?" I asked the angel who was speaking to me.
He replied, "To the country of Babylon to build a house for it. When the house is ready, the basket will be set there in its place."
(The Hebrew word "Stork" means "kind mother".)

leesbird.com
Mar 12, 2010 — The Hebrew word for stork. Is equivalent to "KIND MOTHER".

(God therefore shows the stork-winged-angels as the opposite of modern, working women no longer raising their own, constituting the wickedness ending the world.)

Some of the only remaining prophesies left, in fact, are God soon ending our west coast in an unheralded earthquake killing Gog's Chinese passengers planted there to release Gog's new strains.

Newsmax, Illicit Chinese-Run Virus Lab Found in Calif. Warehouse by Nicole Wells
July 31, 2023, A nondescript warehouse in Reedley, California, turned out to be an illicit Chinese-linked lab filled with hundreds of vials of pathogens, including COVID-19, HIV, and malaria, the Daily Mail reported on Monday.

(The lab's discovery reveals Gog's passengers spreading new diseases using rodents like the medieval black plague, for thousands of mice found were genetically altered to catch and carry COVID-19 through the society.)

USA Today "...shocking': Secret medical lab in California stored bioengineered mice laden with COVID by Thao Nguyen and Saleen Martin
July 31, 2023, A months long investigation into a rural California warehouse uncovered an illegal laboratory filled with infectious agents...and hundreds of mice bioengineered "to catch and carry the COVID-19 virus," ... Prestige Biotech, a Chinese medical company registered in Nevada, was operating the unlicensed facility in Reedley, California...They never had a business license," Zieba told USA TODAY. "The city was completely unaware that they were in this building, operating under the cover of night."... The CDC detected at least 20 potentially infectious agents, according to court documents.

"Ultimately, what we did find is some viruses, such as HIV, COVID, chlamydia, rubella, malaria, things of that nature," Zieba said.

(God intimates that the final disease striking America will affect the abdomen, akin to anthrax, perhaps being cultured and spread from other unlicensed Chinese labs in California.)

Jeremiah 30:4-7
These are the words the Lord spoke concerning Israel and Judah. This is what the Lord says:

"Cries of fear are heard,
Terror not peace.
Ask and see:
Can a man bare children?
Then why do I see every strong man
with his hands on his stomach like a woman in labor?
Every face turned deathly pale?
How awful that day will be!
No other will be like it!
It will be a time of trouble for Jacob,
But he will be saved out of it.

(The earthquake will be the only way to stop Gog, his Chinese passengers, and his invasion of illegal aliens to save America and the world.)

Isaiah 25:5
 You will reduce the noise of aliens,
As heat in a dry place;
As heat in the shadow of a cloud,
The song of the terrible ones will be diminished.

Ezekiel 38:18-20
"And it will come to pass at the same time, when Gog comes against the land of Israel," says the Lord God, "that My fury will show in My face. For in My jealousy and in the fire of My wrath

I have spoken: 'Surely in that day there shall be a great earthquake in the land of Israel, so that the fish of the sea, the birds of the heavens, the beasts of the field, all creeping things that creep on the earth, and all men who are on the face of the earth shall shake at My presence. The mountains shall be thrown down, the steep places shall fall, and every wall shall fall to the ground.'

(God in Ezekiel 39 explains that His coming west coast earthquake will eventually end Gog's hold over our federal government. This earthquake ends the treasonous Magog Democrat Party as Gog's left hand and the Rhino Republican right hand of our modern Israel, the U.S., that funded the Covid "arrow", decimating our nation and the world. The earthquake also kills Gog's Chinese passengers posted on our U.S. west coast releasing Gog's new disease strains as needed by their leader Gog.)

Ezekiel 39:3
Then I will knock the bow out of your left hand, and cause the arrows to fall out of your right hand. You shall fall upon the mountains of Israel, you and all your troops and the peoples who are with you; I will give you to birds of prey of every sort and to the beasts of the field to be devoured. You shall fall on the open field; for I have spoken," says the Lord God. "And I will send fire on Magog and on those who live in security in the coastlands. Then they shall know that I am the Lord. So I will make My holy name known in the midst of My people Israel, and I will not let them profane My holy name anymore. Then the nations shall know that I am the Lord, the Holy One in Israel. Surely it is coming, and it shall be done," says the Lord God. "This is the day of which I have spoken. Then the nations shall know that I am the Lord, the Holy One in Israel.

(Daniel witnessed Gog's Land of Ten Kingdoms' destruction as well.)

Daniel 7:11
I beheld till the beast {with ten horns} was slain, and its body destroyed, and it was given up to be burned with fire.

(God will wipe out nearly 90% of Magog.)

Ezekiel 39:1-2
Gog's Armies Destroyed. "And you, son of man, prophesy against Gog, and say, 'Thus says the Lord God: "Behold, I am against you, O Gog, the prince of Rosh, Meshech, and Tubal; And I will turn thee back, and leave but the sixth part of thee...

(God may achieve this outcome in part through the eruption of Mount Paektu, one of the largest volcanos in the world positioned along the China, North Korean border.)

China's 'Yellowstone-like' volcano concerned scientists: 'Could be ready to erupt' By Callum Hoare
Jan 4, 2021, China could face untold devastation in the future after scientists warned the risk of a "destructive eruption" from a volcano similar to Yellowstone "is very real".

(God caused Gog to attack the U.S.)

Ezekiel 39:3-8
and will cause thee to come up from the north parts, and will bring thee upon the mountains of Israel...Behold, it is come, and it is done, saith the Lord God; this is the day whereof I have spoken.

Ezekiel 39:12-13
For seven months the house of Israel will be burying them, in order to cleanse the land. Indeed all the people of the land will be burying, and they will gain renown for it on the day that I am glorified," says the Lord God. "They will set apart men regularly employed, with the help of a search party, to pass through the land and bury those bodies remaining on the ground, in order to cleanse it. At the end of seven months they will make a search.

The search party will pass through the land; and when anyone sees a man's bone, he shall set up a marker by it, till the buriers have buried it in the Valley of Hamon Gog {Meaning the valley where Gog's minions are slaughtered}. The name of the city will also be Hamonah {Meaning the multitude of Gog}. Thus they shall cleanse the land." '
God invites all the wild animals to feast on the wicked corpses of our U.S. west coast dead who aided China's Gog.)

Ezekiel 39:17
"Assemble yourselves and come;
Gather together from all sides to My sacrificial meal
Which I am sacrificing for you,
A great sacrificial meal on the mountains of Israel,
That you may eat flesh and drink blood.
You shall eat the flesh of the mighty,
Drink the blood of the princes of the earth,
Of rams and lambs,
Of goats and bulls,
All of them fatlings of Bashan.
You shall eat fat till you are full,
And drink blood till you are drunk,
At My sacrificial meal
Which I am sacrificing for you.
You shall be filled at My table
With horses and riders,
With mighty men
And with all the men of war," says the Lord God.

...their {Gog's soldiers'} remains to be buried in a nose-shaped cemetery marking the stopping of the noses of the passengers and Gog's American supporters who born to liberty stole it.

Ezekiel 39:11
And it shall come to pass in that day, that I will give unto Gog a place there of graves in Israel, the valley of the passengers on the east of the sea: and it shall stop the noses of the passengers: and

there shall they bury Gog and all his multitude: and they shall call it The valley of Hamongog.

Easton's Bible Dictionary
Hamon-gog. (meaning the} multitude of Gog, the name of the valley in which the slaughtered forces of Gog are to be buried (Ezekiel 39:11…39:15), "the valley of the passengers on the east of the sea."

(God clearly noted that Gog's passengers from China, Daniel's the Land of 10 Kingdoms, are different from soldiers who brandish rather than hide their weapons as Gog's passengers did with Covid, hiding it "under their heads". For their deceit, these Chinese passengers will face far harsher punishment from God at judgment.)

Ezekiel 32:26-28
"There are Meshech and Tubal and all their multitudes,
With all their graves around it,
All of them uncircumcised, slain by the sword,
Though they caused their terror in the land of the living.
They do not lie with the mighty
Who are fallen of the uncircumcised,
Who have gone down to hell with their weapons of war;
They have laid their swords under their heads,
But their iniquities will be on their bones,
Because of the terror of the mighty in the land of the living.
Yes, you shall be broken in the midst of the uncircumcised,
And lie with those slain by the sword.

(Other prophets note China, again also called the northern kingdom, prophesy of God's earthquake on the west coast with the sea to its west.)

Joel 2:20
"But I will remove far from you the northern army,
And will drive him away into a barren and desolate land,
With his face toward the eastern sea

And his back toward the western sea;
His stench will come up,
And his foul odor will rise,
Because he has done monstrous things."

(The U.S. west coast is condemned to death for bringing Chinese passengers and illegal alien and Communist Chinese invasion.)

Ezekiel 44:7
When you brought in foreigners, uncircumcised in heart and uncircumcised in flesh, to be in My sanctuary to defile it—My house—and when you offered My food, the fat and the blood, then they broke My covenant because of all your abominations.

God will eventually vaporize the bodies of our wicked American, Magog elite where they stand.

Ezekiel 28:18-19
"You defiled your sanctuaries
By the multitude of your iniquities,
By the iniquity of your trading;
Therefore I brought fire from your midst;
It devoured you,
And I turned you to ashes upon the earth
In the sight of all who saw you.
All who knew you among the peoples are astonished at you;
You have become a horror,
And shall be no more forever." ' "

Psalm 1:4
The wicked are not so, but are like chaff that the wind drives away.

Psalm 35:5
Let them be like chaff before the wind, with the angel of the Lord driving them away!

Isaiah 41:16
You shall winnow them, and the wind shall carry them away, and the tempest shall scatter them. And you shall rejoice in the Lord; in the Holy One of Israel you shall glory.

Daily Mail.com
July 6, 2023 Congressman on intelligence committee says aliens 'have the technology to turn humans into charcoal briquettes' and Government has been covering up UFO existence since 1890. Tennessee congressman revealed he has seen compelling evidence of UFOs. He said aliens have technology that could 'turn us into a charcoal briquette'

(The Bible's Book of Genesis speaks of extraterrestrial beings from the heavens, outer space, who came to earth and reproduced with human females, birthing the giant half-breed Nephilim.)

Genesis 6:2
...the sons of God saw the daughters of men, that they were beautiful; and they took wives for themselves of all whom they chose.

(God makes clear certain extraterrestrials work for Him on earth.)

Genesis 28:12, 15
Then he {Jacob} dreamed, and behold, a ladder was set up on the earth, and its top reached to heaven; and there the angels of God were ascending and descending on it...Behold, I am with you and will keep you wherever you go, and will bring you back to this land; for I will not leave you until I have done what I have spoken to you."

Those breaking God's forbidden, sexual commandments will lose their vitality.

Isaiah 40:30
Even the youths shall faint and be weary,
And the young men shall utterly fall,

Isaiah 9:17
Therefore the Lord will have no joy in their young men,

Isaiah 1:28
The destruction of transgressors and of sinners shall be together,
And those who forsake the Lord shall be consumed.
For they shall be ashamed of the Terebinth trees
Which you have desired;
And you shall be embarrassed because of the gardens
Which you have chosen.

Jeremiah 6:11,13
Therefore I am full of the fury of the Lord.
I am weary of holding it in.
"I will pour it out on the children outside,
And from the prophet even to the priest.
Everyone deals falsely.

Isaiah 57:3-4
"But come here,
You sons of the sorceress,
You offspring of the adulterer and the harlot!
Whom do you ridicule?
Against whom do you make a wide mouth
And stick out the tongue?
Are you not children of transgression,
Offspring of falsehood,

Isaiah 59:3.
 For your hands are defiled with blood,
And your fingers with iniquity;
Your lips have spoken lies,
Your tongue has muttered perversity.

Leviticus 18:22
You shall not lie with a male as with a woman. It is an abomination.

(A civil war was fought in ancient Israel after sodomy proliferated in the land of Benjamin, leading to its inhabitants trying to rape an Israelite traveler, and killing his concubine. He cut up her dead body into twelve parts and sent it to the leaders of the tribes. The proliferation of sodomy would lead to the same situation in the U.S., birthing future, male, super predators preying on other males, hence why sodomy's spread is forbidden by God.)

Judges 19:22-30
Gibeah's Crime
As they were enjoying themselves, suddenly certain men of the city, perverted men, surrounded the house and beat on the door. They spoke to the master of the house, the old man, saying, "Bring out the man who came to your house, that we may know him carnally!"
But the man, the master of the house, went out to them and said to them, "No, my brethren! I beg you, do not act so wickedly! Seeing this man has come into my house, do not commit this outrage. Look, here is my virgin daughter and the man's concubine; let me bring them out now. Humble them, and do with them as you please; but to this man do not do such a vile thing!" But the men would not heed him. So the man took his concubine and brought her out to them. And they knew her and abused her all night until morning; and when the day began to break, they let her go. Then the woman came as the day was dawning, and fell down at the door of the man's house where her master was, till it was light.
When her master arose in the morning, and opened the doors of the house and went out to go his way, there was his concubine, fallen at the door of the house with her hands on the threshold. And he said to her, "Get up and let us be going." But there was no answer. So the man lifted her onto the donkey; and the man got up and went to his place. When he entered his house he took

a knife, laid hold of his concubine, and divided her into twelve pieces, limb by limb, and sent her throughout all the territory of Israel. And so it was that all who saw it said, "No such deed has been done or seen from the day that the children of Israel came up from the land of Egypt until this day. Consider it, confer, and speak up!"

Hosea 8:1
Set the trumpet to your lips! One like a vulture is over the house of the Lord, because they have transgressed my covenant and rebelled against my law.

Leviticus 20:13
If a man lies with a male as he lies with a woman, both of them have committed an abomination. They shall surely be put to death. Their blood shall be upon them.

Kings 14:24
And there were also perverted persons in the land. They did according to all the abominations of the nations which the Lord had cast out before the children of Israel.

Deuteronomy 22:5
"A woman shall not wear anything that pertains to a man, nor shall a man put on a woman's garment, for all who do so are an abomination to the Lord your God.

The White House.gov, White House Honors Transgender Day
Mar 31, 2023 — As President Biden has said, transgender Americans are some of the bravest people he knows, but nobody should have to be brave to be themselves.

Epoch Times by Christopher F., Rufo, Inside The Transgender Empire,
November 18, 2023 According to the survey data, as many as 80 percent of trans individuals suffer from serious psychopathologies, and one quarter of black trans youth attempt suicide each year...this procedure is plagued with

complications..."nullification"...in which a smooth, continuous skin covering from the abdomen to the groin is created following a castration or vaginectomy. In other words, the genitalia are replaced by nothing. Nullification surgery is the perfect symbol for the ideology behind the trans movement: the pursuit of the Latin *nullum*, meaning "nothing':

Jeremiah 8:12-13
Were they ashamed when they had committed abomination?
No! They were not at all ashamed,
Nor did they know how to blush.
Therefore they shall fall among those who fall;
In the time of their punishment
They shall be cast down," says the Lord.
"I will surely consume them," says the Lord.

Zechariah 11:17
"Woe to the worthless shepherd,

Hosea 13:12-13
"The iniquity of Ephraim is bound up;
His sin is stored up.
The sorrows of a woman in childbirth shall come upon him.
He is an unwise son,
For he should not stay long where children are born.

Jeremiah 23:14
Also I have seen a horrible thing in the prophets of Jerusalem:
They commit adultery and walk in lies;
They also strengthen the hands of evildoers,
So that no one turns back from his wickedness.
All of them are like Sodom to Me,
And her inhabitants like Gomorrah.

Lamentations 4:13
Because of the sins of her prophets

Proverbs 28:26
He who trusts in his own heart is a fool,

Jeremiah 11:9
And the Lord said to me, "A conspiracy has been found among the men of Judah and among the inhabitants of Jerusalem. They have turned back to the iniquities of their forefathers who refused to hear My words, and they have gone after other gods to serve them; the house of Israel and the house of Judah have broken My covenant which I made with their fathers."

Jeremiah 30:16
'Therefore all those who devour you shall be devoured;

Ezekiel 8:17
And He said to me, "Have you seen this, O son of man? Is it a trivial thing to the house of Judah to commit the abominations which they commit here? For they have filled the land with violence; then they have returned to provoke Me to anger. Indeed they put the branch to their nose.

Ezekiel 12:1
Now the word of the Lord came to me, saying: "Son of man, you dwell in the midst of a rebellious house, which has eyes to see but does not see, and ears to hear but does not hear; for they are a rebellious house.

Ezekiel 22:26-28
Her priests have violated My law and profaned My holy things; they have not distinguished between the holy and unholy, nor have they made known the difference between the unclean and the clean; and they have hidden their eyes from My Sabbaths, so that I am profaned among them.

Isaiah 3:9
The look on their countenance witnesses against them,
And they declare their sin as Sodom;
They do not hide it.

Woe to their soul!
For they have brought evil upon themselves.

Hosea 4:14
"I will not punish your daughters when they commit harlotry,
Nor your brides when they commit adultery;
For the men themselves go apart with harlots,
And offer sacrifices with a ritual harlot.
Therefore people who do not understand will be trampled.

Hosea 9:12-13
Yet I will bereave them to the last man.
Yes, woe to them when I depart from them!
Just as I saw Ephraim like Tyre, planted in a pleasant place,
So Ephraim will bring out his children to the murderer."

Epoch Times, Pediatrician Fired After Raising Alarm on COVID-19 Vaccines During US Senate Event
By Zachary Stieber and Jan Jekielek
July 29, 2023. A medical expert was terminated...after raising concerns about the safety of COVID-19 vaccines during an event held by a U.S. senator... Dr. Moon testified that she had only seen two or three cases of myocarditis...heart inflammation, while practicing for more than 20 years. But after the COVID-19 vaccines...she has been seeing more cases, and heard about others from fellow doctors. "There's clearly been a massive increase," Dr. Moon said. {She} also pulled out...a piece of paper that typically outlines warnings, ingredients, and other information for a vaccine. The insert...has no information and {was} "intentionally blank," the U.S. Food and Drug Administration has acknowledged. "How am I to give informed consent to parents when this is what I have?" Dr. Moon said.

Hosea 7:13
"Woe to them, for they have fled from Me!

Finally, God will end all of Gog and Magog, ending earth from a meteorite in an event called the *Day Of The Lord*.

Ezekiel 38:22-23
And I will plead against him with pestilence and with blood; and I will rain upon him, and upon his bands, and upon the many people that are with him, an overflowing rain, and great hailstones, fire, and brimstone. Thus will I magnify myself, and sanctify myself; and I will be known in the eyes of many nations, and they shall know that I am the Lord.

Zephaniah 1:14-17
The great day of the Lord is near, near and hastening fast; the sound of the day of the Lord is bitter; the mighty man cries aloud there. A day of wrath is that day, a day of distress and anguish, a day of ruin and devastation, a day of darkness and gloom, a day of clouds and thick darkness, a day of trumpet blast and battle cry against the fortified cities and against the lofty battlements. I will bring distress on mankind, so that they shall walk like the blind, because they have sinned against the Lord; their blood shall be poured out like dust, and their flesh like dung.

Jeremiah 9:25
"Behold, the days are coming," says the Lord, "that I will punish all who are circumcised with the uncircumcised—

Malachi 4:1
The Great Day of God
"For behold, the day is coming,
Burning like an oven,
And all the proud, yes, all who do wickedly will be stubble.
And the day which is coming shall burn them up,"
Says the Lord of hosts,
"That will leave them neither root nor branch.

Ezekiel 32:7-9
When I put out your light,

I will cover the heavens, and make its stars dark;
I will cover the sun with a cloud,
And the moon shall not give her light.
All the bright lights of the heavens I will make dark over you,
And bring darkness upon your land,"
Says the Lord God.
'I will also trouble the hearts of many peoples, when I bring your destruction among the nations, into the countries which you have not known. Yes, I will make many peoples astonished at you, and their kings shall be horribly afraid of you when I brandish My sword before them; and they shall tremble every moment, every man for his own life, in the day of your fall.
(God explains how humans will then attempt to hide deep in the earth from the heavenly body's impact.)

Isaiah 2:19-21
They shall go into the holes of the rocks,
And into the caves of the earth,
From the terror of the Lord
And the glory of His majesty,
When He arises to shake the earth mightily.
In that day a man will cast away his idols of silver
And his idols of gold,
Which they made, each for himself to worship,
To the moles and bats,
To go into the clefts of the rocks,
And into the crags of the rugged rocks,
From the terror of the Lord
And the glory of His majesty,
When He arises to shake the earth mightily.

Joel 1:15
Alas for that day!
For the day of the Lord is near;
it will come like destruction from the Almighty.

But God promises to save those willing to get real and rescue them.

Isaiah 26:20
Take Refuge from the Coming Judgment
Come, my people, enter your chambers,
And shut your doors behind you;
Hide yourself, as it were, for a little moment,
Until the indignation is past.

Isaiah 65:1-25
I was ready to be sought by those who did not ask for me; I was ready to be found by those who did not seek me. I said, "Here I am, here I am," to a nation that was not called by my name. I spread out my hands all the day to a rebellious people, who walk in a way that is not good, following their own devices; a people who provoke me to my face continually, sacrificing in gardens and making offerings on bricks; who sit in tombs, and spend the night in secret places; who eat pig's flesh, and broth of tainted meat is in their vessels; who say, "Keep to yourself, do not come near me, for I am too holy for you." These are a smoke in my nostrils, a fire that burns all the day...

Isaiah 9:17
For everyone is a hypocrite and an evildoer,
And every mouth speaks folly.
For all this His anger is not turned away,
But His hand is stretched out still.

Leviticus 5:5
'...when he is guilty in any of these matters, that he shall confess that he has sinned in that thing;

Jeremiah 21:8
" 'Thus says the Lord: "Behold, I set before you the way of life and the way of death.

Jeremiah 31:18
I have heard Ephraim grieving, 'You have disciplined me, and I was disciplined, like an untrained calf; bring me back that I may be restored, for you are the Lord my God.

Isaiah 1:16-17
"Wash yourselves, make yourselves clean;
Put away the evil of your doings from before My eyes.
Cease to do evil,
Learn to do good;
Seek justice,
Rebuke the oppressor;
Defend the fatherless,
Plead for the widow.

Isaiah 1:18-19
"Come now, and let us reason together,"
Says the Lord,
"Though your sins are like scarlet,
They shall be as white as snow;
Though they are red like crimson,
They shall be as wool.
If you are willing and obedient,
You shall eat the good of the land;

Isaiah 26:9
With my soul I have desired You in the night,
Yes, by my spirit within me I will seek You early;
For when Your judgments are in the earth,
The inhabitants of the world will learn righteousness.

Isaiah 45:22
"Look to Me, and be saved,
All you ends of the earth!
For I am God, and there is no other.

(God even offers rescue to those on our wicked coastlands serving Gog, again most notably our west coast soon condemned to have their bodies sacrificed as food to the local animals.)

Isaiah 46:12-13
"Listen to Me, you stubborn-hearted,
Who are far from righteousness:

I bring My righteousness near,
it shall not be far off;
My salvation shall not linger.
And I will place salvation in Zion,
For Israel My glory. Temple

Ezekiel 20:18-20
"But I said to their children in the wilderness, 'Do not walk in the statutes of your fathers, nor observe their judgments, nor defile yourselves with their idols. I am the Lord your God: Walk in My statutes, keep My judgments, and do them; hallow My Sabbaths, and they will be a sign between Me and you, that you may know that I am the Lord your God.'

So Americans and believers worldwide who wish to be saved are now told by God to return to their inner temples within them.

Isaiah 55:5
Surely you shall call a nation you do not know,
And nations who do not know you shall run to you,

Kings 19:13
So it was, when Elijah heard it, that he wrapped his face in his mantle and went out and stood in the entrance of the cave. Suddenly…{God's} voice came to him, and said, "What are you doing here, Elijah?"

Ezekiel 33:11
Say to them: 'As I live,' says the Lord God, 'I have no pleasure in the death of the wicked, but that the wicked turn from his way and live. Turn, turn from your evil ways! For why should you die, O house of Israel?'

Zephaniah 2:1-2
A Call to Repentance
Gather yourselves together, yes, gather together,
O undesirable nation,

Before the decree is issued,
Or the day passes like chaff,
Before the Lord's fierce anger comes upon you,
Before the day of the Lord's anger comes upon you!

Jeremiah 7:3-4
Thus says the Lord of hosts, the God of Israel: "Amend your ways and your doings, and I will cause you to dwell in this place. Do not trust in these lying words, saying, 'The temple of the Lord, the temple of the Lord, the temple of the Lord are these.'

Jeremiah 3:22
"Return, you backsliding children,
And I will heal your backslidings."

Psalm 27:5
For in the time of trouble He shall hide me in His pavilion; In the secret place of His tabernacle He shall hide me; He shall set me high upon a rock.

Psalm 83:1-5
Do not keep silent, O God!
Do not hold Your peace,
And do not be still, O God!
For behold, Your enemies make a tumult;
And those who hate You have lifted up their head.
They have taken crafty counsel against Your people,
And consulted together against Your sheltered ones.
They have said, "Come, and let us cut them off from being a nation,
That the name of Israel {our modern United States of America} may be remembered no more."
For they have consulted together with one consent;
They form a confederacy against You:

Isaiah 65:24
"It shall come to pass
That before they call, I will answer;

And while they are still speaking, I will hear.

Isaiah 58:9
Then you shall call, and the Lord will answer;
You shall cry, and He will say, 'Here I am.'

Jeremiah 31:10
"Hear the word of the Lord, O nations, and declare it in the coastlands far away; say, 'He who scattered Israel will gather him, and will keep him as a shepherd keeps his flock.'

Isaiah 56:6-7
Everyone who keeps from defiling the Sabbath,
And holds fast My covenant—
Even them I will bring to My holy mountain,
And make them joyful in My house of prayer.
Their burnt offerings and their sacrifices
Will be accepted on My altar;
For My house shall be called a house of prayer for all nations."

Daniel 12:10
Many shall be purified, made white, and refined, but the wicked shall do wickedly; and none of the wicked shall understand, but the wise shall understand.

Jeremiah 30:8-9
'For it shall come to pass in that day,'
Says the Lord of hosts,
'That I will break his yoke from your neck,
And will burst your bonds;
Foreigners shall no more enslave them.
But they shall serve the Lord their God,
And David their king,
Whom I will raise up for them.

Jeremiah 30:11
For I am with you,' says the Lord, 'to save you;

Though I make a full end of all nations where I have scattered you,
Yet I will not make a complete end of you.
But I will correct you in justice,
And will not let you go altogether unpunished.'

Hosea 14:1-7
O Israel, return to the Lord your God,
For you have stumbled because of your iniquity;
Take words with you,
And return to the Lord.
Say to Him,
"Take away all iniquity;
Receive us graciously,
For we will offer the sacrifices of our lips.
"I will heal their backsliding,
I will love them freely,
For My anger has turned away from him.
I will be like the dew to Israel;
He shall grow like the lily,
And lengthen his roots like Lebanon.
His branches shall spread within them,

Hosea 5:15
I will return again to My place
Till they acknowledge their offense.
Then they will seek My face;
In their affliction they will earnestly seek Me."

Hosea 6:1
Come, and let us return to the Lord;
For He has torn, but He will heal us;

Hosea 6:3
He will come to us like the rain,
Like the latter and former rain to the earth.

Joel 2:32
And it shall come to pass
That whoever calls on the name of the Lord
Shall be saved.

Jeremiah 12:17
But if they do not obey, I will utterly pluck up and destroy that nation," says the Lord.

Joel 2:18-19
Then the Lord will be zealous for His land,
And pity His people.
The Lord will answer and say to His people,
"Behold, I will send you grain and new wine and oil,
And you will be satisfied by them;
I will no longer make you a reproach among the nations.

George Washington's Letter to Landon Carter regarding American patriot's prisoners in the North,
October 27, 1777, "I flatter myself that a superintending Providence is ordering everything for the best, and that, in due time, all will end well."

{So Americans and believers worldwide who wish to be saved are now told by God to return to their inner temples within them}...confessing their political crime of enriching Communism, funding North Korea's nuclear arsenal, China's navy,

Newsweek, America's Military Is Funding China's Military, Gordon G. Chang
11/14/22, There is nothing more hideous than one military paying for the weapons of its enemy, yet that is exactly what America's soldiers, sailors, and pilots are now doing. They are, inadvertently, financing the tanks, ships, and planes that China's regime is now developing to kill them. Members of America's armed services have, since 2001, been allowed to participate in the Thrift Savings Plan (TSP), a federal government-sponsored

long-term retirement and investment program that is akin to a 401(k). Participants in TSP can invest in Chinese companies, including 22 China-only mutual funds.

Coalition For A Prosperous America, Is the U.S. Still Financing China's Military Might?
Feb 1, 2023 — Yes, in many ways the U.S. is funding China's defense sector through venture capital, portfolio investments, and computer hardware sales to China...

The Review.com, Is your pension being used to fund China's military?
July 12, 2023, The U.S.-China Economic and Security Review Commission (USCC) has identified 252 Chinese companies, including eight state-owned enterprises, that are listed on America's three largest stock exchanges. Additionally, thousands of other Chinese companies tied to forced labor and China's military are included in investment products sold by leading Wall Street fund managers such as Vanguard, BlackRock, Charles Schwab, Fidelity, State Street, and PIMCO.

Ezekiel 36:3
"...they made you desolate and swallowed you up on every side, so that you became the possession of the rest of the nations, and you are taken up by the lips of talkers and slandered by the people..."

(George Washington, who foresaw our manufacturing outsourcing to a foreign king whom history evidenced as China's Gog, now speaks directly to us as a sanctified prophet; thus verifying his Divine sanctity as God's prophet as per God's rules since his prophecy came true. Washington's words were against our last King, George III of England and are just as poignant towards our modern King Gog and his Magog U.S. presidents.)

George Washington's Address To the Continental Army Before The Battle Of Long Island, Tuesday, August 27, 1776

"The time is now near at hand which must probably determine whether Americans are to be freemen or slaves; whether they are to have any property they can call their own; whether their houses and farms are to be pillaged and destroyed, and themselves consigned to a state of wretchedness from which no human efforts will deliver them. The fate of unborn millions will now depend, under God, on the courage and conduct of this army. Our cruel and unrelenting enemy leaves us only the choice of brave resistance, or the most abject submission. We have, therefore, to resolve to conquer or die."

{So Americans and believers worldwide who wish to be saved are now told by God to return to their inner temples within them}...confessing their political crime of enriching...the Mexican cartels' drug and alien invasion, American sanctuary city ports funded by Gog's products to invade America via illegal aliens.

Jeremiah 2:25
Withhold your foot from being unshod, and your throat from thirst.
But you said, 'There is no hope.
No! For I have loved aliens, and after them I will go.'

Epoch Times: Non-Citizens Can Now Become Cops In Illinois
July 29, 2023. Illinois Gov. Jay Robert Pritzker has signed into law a bill allowing non-citizens to become police officers over the objection of the biggest police union in the state, which called it a "potential crisis of confidence in law enforcement."

Joel 1:5-2:17
Awake, ye drunkards, and weep; and howl,

Ezekiel 22:30-31
"I looked for someone among them who would build up the wall and stand before me in the gap on behalf of the land so I would not have to destroy it, but I found no one. So I will pour out my wrath on them and consume them with my fiery anger, bringing

down on their own heads all they have done, declares the Sovereign Lord."

Politico
Biden terminating border wall construction contracts by Nick Niedzwiadek
April 4, 2021, The move is another step toward unwinding one of Donald Trump's signature initiatives. President Joe Biden is canceling further construction of the wall along the U.S. and Mexico border, the Department of Defense announced Friday.

Deuteronomy 28:43
"The alien who is among you shall rise higher and higher above you, and you shall come down lower and lower.
Politico: George Washington's Farewell Warning by John Avlon
Partisanship would lead to the "ruins of public liberty," our first president said. He was more right than he knew. Washington warned of the dangerous interplay between extremes. "There is a natural and necessary progression from the extreme of anarchy to the extreme of tyranny," he wrote in his Circular Letter to the States, and "arbitrary power is most easily established on the ruins of liberty abused to licentiousness."

Washington identified regional parties based on "geographical discriminations" as a particular danger, because they undermined national unity in pursuit of power. "Designing men may endeavor to excite a belief that there is a real difference of local interests and views" by misrepresenting the "opinions and aims" of people from other states and regions. "You cannot shield yourselves too much against the jealousies and heart burnings which spring from these misrepresentations," Washington warned. "They tend to render alien to each other those who ought to be bound together by fraternal affection."

Zechariah 8:17
Let none of you think evil in your heart against your neighbor;

Deuteronomy 28:52
"they shall besiege you at all your gates throughout all your land which the Lord your God has given you.

Committee of Oversight and Accountability
February 7, 2023. Border Patrol Chiefs: Biden's Border Crisis is "Overwhelming"

Lamentations 5:2
Our inheritance has been turned over to aliens,
our homes to foreigners.

Reventure.com the Immigration Crisis will impact Home Prices
May 12, 2023. Academic studies confirm this: more immigration tends to increase home prices and rents in the long-run.
Fox News by Stephen Sorace
June 28, 2023. More NYC migrants in city shelters than homeless for first time ever: '{a}Tipping point'
Over 100,000 people under care of New York City; more than 50,000 are migrants,

Hosea 7:9
Aliens have devoured his strength,

Ezekiel 44:7
When you brought in foreigners, uncircumcised in heart and uncircumcised in flesh, to be in My sanctuary to defile it—My house—and when you offered My food, the fat and the blood, then they broke My covenant because of all your abominations.

Culminating in our own politicians unthinkably funding Gog's Covid virus to end the free world.

Jeremiah 4:10
Then I said, "Ah, Lord God!
Surely You have greatly deceived this people and Jerusalem,
Saying, 'You shall have peace,'
Whereas the sword reaches to the heart."

Ezekiel 39:26
…after they have borne their shame, and all their unfaithfulness in which they were unfaithful to Me, when they dwelt safely in their own land and no one made them afraid.

New York Post
June 13, 2023, U.S. taxpayers funded $2M for {Covid} research in Wuhan Chin a
US taxpayers supported research in three Chinese labs that included risky gain-of-function experiments with coronaviruses at the Wuhan {lab}…

George Washington's Farewell Address
"The nation which indulges toward another an habitual hatred or an habitual fondness is in some degree a slave."

Daniel 8:23-26
"And in the latter time of their kingdom,
When the transgressors have reached their fullness,
A king shall arise,
Having fierce features,
Who understands sinister schemes.
His power shall be mighty, but not by his own power;
He shall destroy fearfully,
And shall prosper and thrive;
He shall destroy the mighty, and also the holy people.
"Through his cunning
He shall cause deceit to prosper under his rule;
And he shall exalt himself in his heart.
He shall destroy many in their prosperity.

Daniel 7:23
'The fourth beast {of ten horns, China} shall be
A fourth kingdom on earth,
Which shall be different from all other kingdoms,
And shall devour the whole earth,
Trample it and break it in pieces.

Herein is what all need to know to properly confess and find rescue and reform our republic. For after Constantine I ended Christ's rightful return to the Hebrew Bible in antiquity, that Roman king condemned most to the wrong sabbath and end time scripture.

Malachi 3:6
"For I the Lord do not change; So you, the descendants of Jacob, are not destroyed. Ever since the time of your ancestors you have turned away from my decrees and have not kept them. Return to me, and I will return to you," says the Lord Almighty.

Psalm 89:34-37
My covenant will I not break, nor alter the thing that is gone out of my lips.

Isaiah 40:8
The grass withers, the flower fades, but the word of our God will stand forever.

Numbers 23:19
God is not man, that he should lie, or a son of man, that he should change his mind. Has he said, and will he not do it? Or has he spoken, and will he not fulfill it?

Psalm 119:89
Forever, O Lord, your word is firmly fixed in the heavens.

Psalm 33:11
The counsel of the Lord stands forever, the plans of his heart to all generations.

Psalm 94:14
For the Lord will not forsake his people; he will not abandon his heritage;

Psalm 110:4
The Lord has sworn and will not change his mind,

Isaiah 48:6-8
"You have heard;
See all this.
And will you not declare it?
I have made you hear new things from this time,
Even hidden things, and you did not know them.
They are created now and not from the beginning;
And before this day you have not heard them,
Lest you should say, 'Of course I knew them.'
Surely you did not hear,
Surely you did not know;
Surely from long ago your ear was not opened.
For I knew that you would deal very treacherously,
And were called a transgressor from the womb.

(God even supports modern Jacob's descendants, the nation of Israel, that mandated the untested, dangerous, genetic treatment for Covid misnamed a vaccine.)

NPR
April 20, 2021, Highly Vaccinated Israel Is Seeing a Dramatic Surge In New Covid Cases.

WCPO 9 News Cincinnati. Fact Check: Did Pfizer lie about testing COVID-19 vaccine's ability to prevent transmission before roll out?
October 14, 2022. Janine Small, president of international markets at Pfizer, told the European Parliament on Monday that Pfizer did not know whether its COVID-19 vaccine prevented transmission of the virus before it entered the market in December 2020.

WSAU News
Study: Covid-19 Vaccine is the Culprit in Majority Found Dead after Injection, Meg Ellefson

Jul 11, 2023 Cardiologist, internist, and scientist Peter McCullough…talked about his study that revealed …from a total of 325 cases, independent review found the COVID-19 vaccine was the cause of death in 73.9%.

A Systematic Review of Autopsy Findings In Deaths After COVID-19 Vaccination
July, 2023, The most implicated organ system in COVID 19 vaccine associated death was the cardiovascular system (53%), followed by the hematological system (17%), the respiratory system (8%), and multiple organ systems (7%). Three or more organ systems were affected in 21 cases. The mean time from vaccination to death was 14.3 days. Most deaths occurred within a week from last vaccine administration. A total of 240 deaths (73.9%) were independently adjudicated as directly due to or significantly contributed to by COVID-19 vaccination.

(While many modern descendants of Jacob in the United States mass support the Democrat party that funded this virus and often mandated the dangerous, untested, new genetic therapy misnamed a vaccine.)

Pew Research Center, U.S. Jews' political views
May 11, 2021 — Seven-in-ten Jewish adults identify with or lean toward the Democratic Party, and half describe their political views as liberal.

(This outright Jewish, leftist Democrat political leaning continued on after Wikileaks well-proved the Clintons controlled and still controls the Democrat Party as their own personal political party.)

observer.com, Wikileaks Proves Primary Was Rigged: DNC Undermined Democracy, Michael Sainato
Jul 22, 2016 — 20000 freshly-leaked emails reveal resentful disdain toward Sanders, as party favored Clinton long before any votes were cast.

BBC News, Former Democratic chief: Clinton 'took control' of party
November 3, 2017, The Democratic Party's ex-interim chief has accused Hillary Clinton of seizing control of the party in exchange for funding during the 2016 campaign...{Democrat party head} Donna Brazile says the deal..."compromised the party's integrity"...

(The Democrat Party of Clinton has falsely blamed Putin for collusion with then president Trump.)_

New York Post, Dems knew and did nothing to stop the Russia collusion hoax, Adriana Cohen
Feb 18, 2022, all knew - and did nothing to stop the Russia collusion hoax

(After Gog's attack, Democrats and Rhino Republicans seek misdirection to a possible nuclear war with Russia over their western border where Russia lost 27 million souls defending against Hitler, not to mention Napoleon.)

Statista, Historical Data
Apr 4, 2022, The Soviet Union suffered the highest number of fatalities of any single nation, with estimates mostly falling between 22 and 27 million deaths {along its western border, including Ukraine}.

U.S. News, Max Hunder and Tom Balmforth
September 7, 2022, In rare public comments Ukraine's military chief warned on Wednesday of the threat of Russia using nuclear weapons in Ukraine, which would create the risk of a "limited" nuclear conflict with other powers.

Politico.com. Nuclear weapons on the table if Ukraine counteroffensive succeeds: {warns} Russia's Medvedev by Varg Folkman

July 30, 2023. There would be 'no other way out' if Kyiv takes Russian territory, says the former Russian president and current National Security Council deputy chairman.

Psalm 120:7
I am for peace;
But when I speak, they are for war.

(Americans buy Gog's Chinese, slave-made products funding China's concentration camps for innocent believers, making Americans like Nazis of old.)

Proverbs 3:9
Honor the Lord with your possessions,

Isaiah 2:6
For You have forsaken Your people, the house of Jacob,
Because they are filled with eastern ways;
They are soothsayers like the Philistines,
And they are pleased with the children of foreigners.

Proverbs 5:10-11
Lest aliens be filled with your wealth,
And your labors go to the house of a foreigner a{who is China's king Gog};
And you mourn at last,
When your flesh and your body are consumed,

New York Post
August 28, 2020, China's 260 concentration camps are proof of pure evil, Post Editorial Board
It turns out the Chinese Communist Party is bent on permanently locking up much of the Uighur Muslim population of the far-west region of Xinjiang: Satellite images show that Beijing has secretly built 260 high-security concentration camps to hold them. Many, perhaps all, include a factory in the camp so the prisoners can be forced to labor for the state, as well. The world has known for years that China is detaining roughly 1

million ethnic Uighurs and other Turkic minorities. But now BuzzFeed News has used satellite analysis to uncover the full apparatus of eternal repression. Beijing insists most of the detainees are already free, but this reporting shows they've simply been moved from initial holding facilities in schools and other public buildings to the new prisons — where the torture, forced birth control and brainwashing sessions will continue.

The Guardian
Sep 24, 2020, China has built nearly 400 internment camps in Xinjiang region, with construction on dozens continuing over the last two years, even as Chinese authorities said their "re-education" system was winding down, an Australian thinktank has found.

(Despite this horrific behavior of modern American Jews supporting the Clinton-controlled Democrat Party, filling their homes with Gog's slave-made goods, funding concentration camps for believers, God will even still keep His covenant with Jacob's descendants as a sign; to show that He does not change His deals despite what the Constantinian-based Catholic faith might profess otherwise.)

Isaiah 41:14
"Fear not, you worm Jacob,
You men of Israel!
I will help you," says the Lord
And your Redeemer, the Holy One of Israel.

Jeremiah 29:11
For I know the plans I have for you, declares the Lord, plans for welfare and not for evil, to give you a future and a hope. Then you will call upon Me and go and pray to Me, and I will listen to you. And you will seek Me and find Me, when you search for Me with all your heart

Isaiah 35:3-4
Strengthen the weak hands,

And make firm the feeble knees.
Say to those who are fearful-hearted,
"Be strong, do not fear!
Behold, your God will come with vengeance,
With the recompense of God;
He will come and save you."

(The historical chronicler of the Catholic persecutions visited upon Protestants, Ellen G. White, rightfully noted the Saturday sabbath was as God mandated, unchangeable.)

The Great Controversy by Ellen G. White
The enemies of God's law, from the ministers down to the least among them, have a new conception of truth and duty. Too late they see that the Sabbath of the fourth commandment is the seal of the living God. Too late they see the true nature of their spurious sabbath and the sandy foundation upon which they have been building. They find that they have been fighting against God. Religious teachers have led souls to perdition while professing to guide them to the gates of Paradise.

(White failed to face the wider fact that by changing the unchangeable sabbath, the Roman emperor Constantine's Council of Nicea and its later, codified New Testament, and Catholicism was marked as invalid. Constantine birthed a heretical system of what would be best-termed *Constantinian Jews*, akin to Gog who through his U.S. Magog proxies seeks to now change our times and ways.)

Daniel 7:25
He {the king of the Land of 10 Kingdoms} shall speak pompous words against the Most High,
Shall persecute the saints of the Most High,
And shall intend to change times and law.
Then the saints shall be given into his hand,

(Although the factually dubious New Testament cannot thus be quoted in God's message, it's worth noting that Christ within it made clear that he came to affirm, not to change the Hebrew Bible laws; White who herself supported further liturgical reform, could not cast away the New Testament since the punishment of the Jews was not yet over in her lifetime. Therefore, all New Testament supported points of White's should now be discarded, with only her points supported by the Hebrew Bible remaining valid via this truth. White, herself, anticipated such a great change to biblical doctrine in the end time, of which only a few of her quotes on this point for the sake of brevity are listed herein.)

Our Father Cares by Ellen G. White
Christians should be preparing for what is soon to break upon the world as an overwhelming surprise, and this preparation they should make by diligently studying the word of God and striving to conform their lives to its precepts...Transgression has almost reached its limit. Confusion fills the world, and a great terror is soon to come upon human beings. The end is very near. God's people should be preparing for what is to break upon the world as an overwhelming surprise.

(Irregardless of the New Testament, the Hebrew Bible supports Christ by making clear that there are two messengers of the covenant, one for the ancient nation of Jacob and the second for the modern empire of Ephraim, with further proof later given in this Guide.)

Zechariah 4:11-14
Then I answered and said to him, "What are these two olive trees—at the right of the lampstand and at its left?" And I further answered and said to him, "What are these two olive branches that drip into the receptacles of the two gold pipes from which the golden oil drains?"
Then he answered me and said, "Do you not know what these are?"
And I said, "No, my lord."
So he said, "These are the two anointed ones, who stand beside the Lord of the whole earth."

(Even the-once-secret, rabbinic compilation of ancient teachings and ongoing discussions called the Talmud, records in antiquity a certain Joshua, the true Hebrew to English name translated from Yehoshua or Yeshu; Jesus being derived from Greek. Greeks had to replace the sh sound unpronounceable for them with an s while adding another s to the name's end to render it masculine in Greek.)

Jesus and His Jewish Influences: Lecture 24. Jesus's Teaching and Sayings in Context, Professor Jodi Magness, Ph.D.
If we look at Rabbinic literature, the literature of the rabbis {the Talmud}...we see...a few passages ...refer to Jesus Christ. They of course do not refer to him as Jesus Christ. Sometimes they...refer to Jesus as Jesus the Nazarian...I want to look at one passage, which is from the Palestinian Talmud...{by} Rabbi Yehoshua ben Levi {who} had a grandson who swallowed something dangerous...he is about to choke. A {Messianic Jewish} magician is called in and the magician whispers the name of Jesus, here referred to as Jesus, son of Pondera and the boy is healed. Now Jesus, son of Pondera {sometimes Pontera}...is...a name that is sometimes used in Rabbinic literature to refer to Jesus...as the illegitimate son of Miriam and a Roman or non-Jewish soldier named Pontera. So these rabbinic traditions frequently portray Jesus as an illegitimate child. And there are also Rabbinic traditions that like here talk about Jesus as a magician or in connection with magical practices.

(The first Joshua's great act of overturning the money-changing tables of the Second temple mount, for which he would be killed, is also largely misunderstood.)

Jesus and His Jewish Influences: Lecture 24. Jesus's Teaching and Sayings in Context, Professor Jodi Magness, Ph.D.
It is completely anachronistic to understand Jesus's overturning of the tables of the money changers as opposition to commercial activity on the temple mount. Because this was a characteristic feature of all ancient temple complexes...in addition to being an

area of commercial activity {the temple mount} was a place where Jewish pilgrims came for the Jewish pilgrimage holidays. And...they would pay the temple tax...originally mandated in Exodus, {the temple tax} was a one-time payment...the Hasmoneans changed that and required adult men to pay the tax on an annual basis...in...Tyrian...silver shekels because the content of the silver was very high...what ...motivated Jesus here was...that this...would've been a real hardship on the poorer classes of society, meaning the majority of the Jewish population who...were Jesus's target audience.

(The Talmud also records a Joshua who may be Christ, hung on the eve before Passover for practicing the type of magic not seen since the First temple's destruction.)

Talmud Sanhedrin 43a
It is taught: On the eve of Passover they hung Yeshu and the crier went forth for forty days beforehand declaring that "[Yeshu] is going to be stoned for practicing witchcraft, for enticing and leading Israel astray. Anyone who knows something to clear him should come forth and exonerate him."

(God makes clear that He worked backwards in time, focused solely on our current modernity and the two blessed nations, Israel and the U.S. as His ideal outcome.)

Jeremiah 31:9
For I am a Father to Israel,
And Ephraim is My firstborn.

(God thus revealed that He authored the universe in reverse from our forward flowing, free-will actions, truly making the current human, foretold political messenger the first one. With the second being the suffering messenger from antiquity, both foretold by God through His prophet Isaiah.)

Isaiah 53:3-9
He is despised and rejected by men, A Man of sorrows and acquainted with grief. And we hid, as it were, our faces from Him; He was despised, and we did not esteem Him. Surely He has borne our griefs And carried our sorrows; Yet we esteemed Him stricken, Smitten by God, and afflicted. But He was wounded for our transgressions, He was bruised for our iniquities; The chastisement for our peace was upon Him, And by His stripes we are healed. All we like sheep have gone astray; We have turned, every one, to his own way; And the Lord has laid on Him the iniquity of us all. He was oppressed and He was afflicted, Yet He opened not His mouth; He was led as a lamb to the slaughter, And as a sheep before its shearers is silent, So He opened not His mouth. He was taken from prison and from judgment, And who will declare His generation? For He was cut off from the land of the living; For the transgressions of My people He was stricken. And they made His grave with the wicked— But with the rich at His death, Because He had done no violence, Nor was any deceit in His mouth.

(God makes clear that the two Joshua figures, shortly to be further explored, possess the spirit of King David, which was thus first reborn through the ancient Joshua. God intimates that the soul of David as the ancient Joshua required cleansing through his painful death probably for the prior crimes of David murdering his trusted officer Uriah after committing adultery with Uriah's wife; hence why God was pleased by the ancient, crucified Joshua's pain.)

Isaiah 53:10
Yet it pleased the Lord to bruise Him; He has put Him to grief. When You make His soul an offering for sin, He shall see His seed, He shall prolong His days, And the pleasure of the Lord shall prosper in His hand.

(David as Joshua gave his life to prolong it through the current, second, anointed Joshua in modernity, the human messenger of the covenant to modern Americans, the Holy People, and believers worldwide. Yet this modern, anointed messenger is according to God a combination of seven prior people, some through God's Divine spirit and others through this messenger's DNA, to be further explored herein.)

Isaiah 53:11
He shall see the labor of His soul, and be satisfied. By His knowledge My righteous Servant shall justify many, For He shall bear their iniquities. Therefore will I divide him a portion with the great, and he shall divide the spoil with the strong; because he hath poured out his soul unto death: and he was numbered with the transgressors; and he bare the sin of many, and made intercession for the transgressors.

(God working backwards could very well justify the supposed-virgin birth of the ancient Joshua.)

Isaiah 7:14
Therefore the Lord Himself will give you a sign: Behold, the virgin shall conceive and bear a Son,

(The Hebrew word, however, for virgin is "betulim" rather than Isaiah's choice of hā'almāh, which means a "young maiden" with another use of it in Proverbs specifically barred from meaning a virgin. It is curious to note that the virgin birth, however, was not merely a construct of Emperor Constantine. The Ebionites, the earliest followers of Christ, Messianic Jews, were split over this topic, with both sides united in considering Joshua to merely be a human messenger.)

Blogging Theology by Paul Williams
{Eusebius, an early Christian polemicist} writes...there are two Ebionite sects. The first ...are Jews...who believe in Jesus as the Messiah, as the prophet, but they believe that he was not born of a virgin. And...the second group went by the same name, Ebionites...they did not deny that {Jesus} was born of a virgin and the Holy spirit but nevertheless shared their refusal to acknowledge his pre-existence as God...they held that the

epistles of the apostle, that means Paul of course, ought to be rejected altogether, calling him a renegade from the law and... {did} observe the {Saturday} sabbath, and the whole Jewish system {from the Hebrew Bible}.

(The virgin birth could make sense as God's backwards projection into the past of the present Joshua, the messenger of the covenant. Or that figure in antiquity was also a child of normal parentage and could still bear God's spirit as will shortly be further discussed. Irregardless, what Isaiah notes as the child's name marks a wider truth.)

Isaiah 7:14
and the maiden {proper Hebrew translation} shall call His name Immanuel.

(The Hebrew word Immanuel means "God is with us", which was all that mattered. As the ancient Joshua's death marked the end of the Israelite's temple and ancient Israel before the rise of the gentiles; all while God hid His face while creating modern science or protecting the gentile George Washington to successfully birth the gentile New Jerusalem.)

American Heritage: The Miraculous Care of Providence by James Thomas Flexner
February, 1982, Upon at least five occasions when in great danger from gunfire George Washington remained unscathed. His hat was shot off his head; his clothes were torn; horses were killed beneath him, but the hero was never so much as scratched by a bullet. For this immunity he thanked "Providence."

(Washington, in fact, sowed the seeds of the future 1776 American revolution back in 1754 by accidentally killing a French officer. That death caused the later French and Indian War, subsequently motivating England to raise harsh Colonial taxes to pay off the war's debt. Those parliamentary acts triggered the American revolution. While the accidental killing under Washington's command led him to surrender for the first and only time in his career to the French on July 4th, 1754, the same day that the future New Jerusalem would be born.)

I Don't Know Much.com
Washington surrendered to a French army on July 4, 1754 – the first and only time he surrendered in his military career.

(The next chapter of Isaiah brings us to recent modernity, with the Israelites' suffering, both Israel and the Gentile New Jerusalem, struck by the Chinese disease finally admitted to be incurable. That admission calls up the second Joshua who draws attention to God's end-time prophesies now unsealed for all, as evidence by Daniel's aforementioned dates and reinforced through recent, historical events.)

Isaiah 54:1
A Perpetual Covenant of Peace
"Sing, O barren,
You who have not borne!
Break forth into singing, and cry aloud,
You who have not labored with child!
For more are the children of the desolate

(The Lord through His second messenger likewise named Joshua, His herald with no power at this time, merely highlights God's promise of current, Divine rescue from what will be certain death now that God no longer needs to hide His face.)

Isaiah 54:7-8
"For a mere moment I have forsaken you,
But with great mercies I will gather you.
With a little wrath I hid My face from you for a moment;
But with everlasting kindness I will have mercy on you,"
Says the Lord, your Redeemer.

(God primarily addresses both the United States of America as the New Jerusalem of the Gentiles, which resurrected the nation-state of Israel prophesied by God as two sticks that will become one unified kingdom.)

Ezekiel 37:15-17
One Kingdom, One King
Again the word of the Lord came to me, saying, "As for you, son of man, take a stick for yourself and write on it: 'For Judah and for the children of Israel, his companions.' Then take another stick and write on it, 'For Joseph, the stick of Ephraim, and for all the house of Israel, his companions.' Then join them one to another for yourself into one stick, and they will become one in your hand.

"And when the children of your people speak to you, saying, 'Will you not show us what you mean by these?'— say to them, 'Thus says the Lord God: "Surely I will take the stick of Joseph, which is in the hand of Ephraim, and the tribes of Israel, his companions; and I will join them with it, with the stick of Judah, and make them one stick, and they will be one in My hand." ' And the sticks on which you write will be in your hand before their eyes.

National Archives.gov
At midnight on May 14, 1948, the Provisional Government of Israel proclaimed a new State of Israel. On that same date, the United States, in the person of President Truman, recognized the provisional Jewish government as de facto authority of the Jewish state (de jure recognition was extended on January 31, 1949).

(This unity between the two Israelite nations was prophesied by God to be broken in end times.)

Zechariah 11:14
Then I cut in two my other staff, Bonds, that I might break the brotherhood between Judah and Israel.

Gatestone Institute, International Policy Council
July 15, 2023. Biden Administration Funding Iran's Nuclear Bomb Tests, Threatening Israel for Trying to Prevent Them?

(God makes it clear that He will save "Judah" first before He saves David and Jerusalem's inhabitants, again marking the United States of America as the New Jerusalem of the gentiles and the second Joshua as an American citizen of that modern nation.)

Zechariah 12:7-9
"The Lord will save the dwellings of Judah first, so that the honor of the house of David and of Jerusalem's inhabitants may not be greater than that of Judah. On that day the Lord will shield those who live in Jerusalem, so that the feeblest among them will be like David, and the house of David will be like God, like the angel of the Lord going before them. On that day I will set out to destroy all the nations that attack Jerusalem.

(God notes that the modern messenger with the spirit of David will then be revealed as the Christ, that history witnessed in antiquity when he was "pierced".)

Zechariah 12:10-14
Mourning for the One They Pierced
"And I will pour out on the house of David and the inhabitants of Jerusalem a spirit of grace and supplication. They will look on me, the one they have pierced, and they will mourn for him as one mourns for an only child, and grieve bitterly for him as one grieves for a firstborn son. On that day the weeping in Jerusalem will be as great as the weeping of Hadad Rimmon in the plain of Megiddo {where Josiah, the last good Israelite king was fatally wounded}. The land will mourn, each clan by itself, with their wives by themselves: the clan of the house of David and their wives, the clan of the house of Nathan and their wives, the clan of the house of Levi and their wives, the clan of Shimei and their wives, and all the rest of the clans and their wives.

(God repeats His promise to save Israel, the house of Judah, and Americans as the house of Joseph instead of through his son Ephraim.)

Zechariah 10:6-8
"I will strengthen the house of Judah,
And I will save the house of Joseph.
I will bring them back,
Because I have mercy on them.
They shall be as though I had not cast them aside;
For I am the Lord their God,
And I will hear them.

Those of Ephraim shall be like a mighty man,
And their heart shall rejoice as if with wine.
Yes, their children shall see it and be glad;
Their heart shall rejoice in the Lord.

I will whistle for them and gather them,
For I will redeem them;
And they shall increase as they once increased.

Now the sacrifice of all humanity not returning to God is set, the guests according to Him are all invited and present.

Zephaniah 1:7
Be silent in the presence of the Lord God;
For the day of the Lord is at hand,
For the Lord has prepared a sacrifice;
He has invited His guests.

Zephaniah 1:14
The great day of the Lord is near, near and hastening fast; the sound of the day of the Lord is bitter; the mighty man cries aloud there.

Ezekiel 5:11-13
Therefore, as I live,' says the Lord God, 'surely, because you have defiled My sanctuary with all your detestable things and with all your abominations, therefore I will also diminish you; My eye will not spare, nor will I have any pity. One-third of you shall die of the pestilence, and be consumed with famine in your midst; and one-third shall fall by the sword all around you and I will scatter another third to all the winds, and I will draw out a sword after them.

'Thus shall My anger be spent, and I will cause My fury to rest upon them, and I will be avenged; and they shall know that I, the Lord, have spoken it in My zeal, when I have spent My fury upon them.

Ezekiel 7:7-9
"A day of trouble is near…My eye will not spare, nor will I have pity; I will repay you according to your ways"

Jeremiah 30:7
"For that day is great, so that none is like it; and it is the time of Jacob's trouble, but he shall be saved out of it".

Zephaniah 1:2-3
The Great Day of the Lord
"I will utterly consume everything
From the face of the land,"
Says the Lord;
"I will consume man and beast;
I will consume the birds of the heavens,
The fish of the sea,

Ezekiel 30:3
For the day is near, the day of the Lord is near; it will be a day of clouds, a time of doom for the nations.

Isaiah 2:17
And the haughtiness of man shall be humbled, and the lofty

pride of men shall be brought low, and the Lord alone will be exalted in that day.

Isaiah 13:6,9
Wail, for the day of the Lord is near; as destruction from the Almighty it will come!

Behold, the day of the Lord comes, cruel, with wrath and fierce anger, to make the land a desolation and to destroy its sinners from it.

Obadiah 1:15
For the day of the Lord is near upon all the nations. As you have done, it shall be done to you; your deeds shall return on your own head.

Amos 5:18
Woe to you who desire the day of the Lord! Why would you have the day of the Lord? It is darkness, and not light,

Joel 2:1, 31
Blow a trumpet in Zion; sound an alarm on my holy mountain! Let all the inhabitants of the land tremble, for the day of the Lord is coming; it is near,

The sun shall be turned to darkness, and the moon to blood, before the great and awesome day of the Lord comes.

Ezekiel 16:49-50
Behold, this was the guilt of your sister Sodom: she and her daughters had pride, excess of food, and prosperous ease, but did not aid the poor and needy. They were haughty and did an abomination before me. So I removed them, when I saw it.

While this anointed messenger...

Amos 3:7
"For the Lord God does nothing without revealing his secret to

his servants the prophets.

(God now sends this final, human messenger because the ancient Israelites asked to hear His words through a human intermediary as His voice and presence was too frightening to them)

Deuteronomy 18:15
A New Prophet Like Moses
"The Lord your God will raise up for you a Prophet like me from your midst, from your brethren. Him you shall hear, according to all you desired of the Lord your God in Horeb in the day of the assembly, saying, 'Let me not hear again the voice of the Lord my God, nor let me see this great fire anymore, lest I die.'

Jeremiah 23:5
"Behold, the days are coming, declares the Lord, when I will raise up for David a righteous Branch, and he shall reign as king and deal wisely, and shall execute justice and righteousness in the land...

Isaiah 61:1-2.
"The Spirit of the Lord God is upon Me,
Because the Lord has anointed Me
To preach good tidings to the poor;
He has sent Me to heal the brokenhearted,
To proclaim liberty to the captives,
And the opening of the prison to those who are bound;
To proclaim the acceptable year of the Lord,
And the day of vengeance of our God;
To comfort all who mourn,

Daniel 9:27
And he shall make a strong covenant with many for one week, and for half of the week he shall put an end to sacrifice and offering {to China's Gog}. And on the wing of abominations shall come one who makes desolate, until the decreed end is poured out on the desolator."

Isaiah 53:6
All we like sheep have gone astray; we have turned—every one—to his own way; and the Lord has laid on him the iniquity of us all.

(This guide will further explore the autobiographical details of this messenger, including his parents being struck by an inexplicable beam of light from the heavens magically traveling through the roof of their car, causing the vehicle to stop and making their lower extremities glow; in such a way did the Lord bring his spirit upon them and their child-to-be before this messenger's birth. Additionally, this messenger instinctively knows he was once Enoch, great-grandfather of Noah, Moses, and Elijah, all magically taken up in light although Noah's ascendancy was not witnessed by others. In scripture, the Lord explains that via His anointing of the messenger on 10/27/17, further explored in the guide, that he possesses the spirit of King David, David's descendant Zerubbabel, and Joshua son of Jozadak. He would also have been the prior Joshua who addressed the last blessed nation of ancient Israel before its destruction, further explored in the guide, making a total of seven pairs of eyes: a pattern laced through the Hebrew Bible.)

Zechariah 4:10
"These seven are the eyes of the Lord, which range through the whole earth."

Exodus 25:37
You shall make seven lamps for it.

Zechariah 4:2
So I said, "I am looking, and there is a lampstand of solid gold with a bowl on top of it, and on the stand seven lamps with seven pipes to the seven lamps.

Deuteronomy 18:15-19
A New Prophet like Moses

"The Lord your God will raise up for you a prophet like me from among you, from your brothers—it is to him you shall listen— just as you desired of the Lord your God at Horeb on the day of the assembly, when you said, 'Let me not hear again the voice of the Lord my God or see this great fire any more, lest I die.' And the Lord said to me, 'They are right in what they have spoken. I will raise up for them a prophet like you from among their brothers. And I will put my words in his mouth, and he shall speak to them all that I command him. And whoever will not listen to my words that he shall speak in my name, I myself will require it of him.

Zechariah 4:2
And he said to me, "What do you see?"
So I said, "I am looking, and there is a lampstand of solid gold with a bowl on top of it, and on the stand seven lamps with seven pipes to the seven lamps.

Zechariah 3:6-10
The Coming Branch
Then the Angel of the Lord admonished Joshua, saying, "Thus says the Lord of hosts:

'If you will walk in My ways,
And if you will keep My command,
Then you shall also judge My house,
And likewise have charge of My courts;
I will give you places to walk
Among these who stand here.

'Hear, O Joshua, the high priest,
You and your companions who sit before you,
For they are a wondrous sign;
For behold, I am bringing forth My Servant the BRANCH.

For behold, the stone
That I have laid before Joshua:
Upon the stone are seven eyes.

Behold, I will engrave its inscription,'
Says the Lord of hosts,
'And I will remove the iniquity of that land in one day.

In that day,' says the Lord of hosts,
'Everyone will invite his neighbor
Under his vine and under his fig tree.' "

Zechariah 4:9-10
"The hands of Zerubbabel
Have laid the foundation of this temple {the ancient second temple};
His hands shall also finish it.
Then you will know
That the Lord of hosts has sent Me to you.

For who has despised the day of small things?
For these seven rejoice to see
The plumb line in the hand of Zerubbabel.
They are the eyes of the Lord,
Which scan to and fro throughout the whole earth."

Malachi 3:1,5
"I will send my messenger, who will prepare the way before me. Then suddenly the Lord you are seeking will come to his temple; the messenger of the covenant, whom you desire, will come," says the Lord Almighty… "So I will come to put you on trial. I will be quick to testify against sorcerers, adulterers and perjurers, against those who defraud laborers of their wages, who oppress the widows and the fatherless, and deprive the foreigners among you of justice, but do not fear me," says the Lord Almighty.

Malachi 4:5-6
Behold, I will send you Elijah the prophet
Before the coming of the great and dreadful day of the Lord.

And he will turn
The hearts of the fathers to the children,

And the hearts of the children to their fathers,
Lest I come and strike the earth with a curse."

(Again God makes clear that the seventh life lives twice as two distinct, but seemingly identical messengers named Joshua.)

Zechariah 4:11-14
Then I said to him, "What are these two olive trees on the right and the left of the lampstand?" And a second time I answered and said to him, "What are these two branches of the olive trees, which are beside the two golden pipes from which the golden oil is poured out?" He said to me, "Do you not know what these are?" I said, "No, my lord." Then he said, "These are the two anointed ones who stand by the Lord of the whole earth."

{While this anointed messenger} who was previously sent to leaders of the Seventh Day Adventist faith...

(Further autobiographical details within this guide, also printed in 2020's nonfiction work *Saint Michael Stood Up*, reveal that Saint Michael equated this messenger to Ellen G. White, who according to Saint Michael were both sanctified prophets of His. Saint Michael anointed this messenger's foot with His shield and commanded this messenger to meet with Dr. Richard Hart of the Loma Linda Medical Center to convey various points to Him.)

Daniel 12:11
"At that time Michael shall stand up, The great prince who stands watch over the sons of your people; And there shall be a time of trouble, Such as never was since there was a nation, Even to that time. And at that time your people shall be delivered, Every one who is found written in the book.

Isaiah 61:1
The Spirit of the Lord God is upon me, because the Lord has anointed me to preach good tidings to the poor; he has sent me

GOD'S GUIDE TO THE END OF THE WORLD 307

to heal the brokenhearted, to proclaim liberty to the captives, and the opening of the prison to those who are bound;

(Amongst other things, Hart was commanded by Saint Michael to stop the internal theft of donor dollars at Loma Linda Medical Center and to finance the film *Dreamspace*, which according to Michael was "the extension of the mission born of the writings of Ellen G. White." Also according to Michael no money from the film could go to this messenger. The Dr. Hart meeting took place on the winter solstice of 2017 and Hart never even viewed the film simulation as he promised or stopped the theft of donor dollars to this messenger's knowledge.)

Isaiah 52:7
How beautiful upon the mountains are the feet of him who brings good news, who publishes peace, who brings good news of happiness, who publishes salvation, who says to Zion, "Your God reigns."

Isaiah 50:4-10
The Lord God has given me the tongue of those who are taught, that I may know how to sustain with a word him who is weary.

(This messengers film simulation of his anticipated movie *Dreamspace* is according to Saint Michael what Ellen G Whites followers now require, and is to be offered free of charge to them.)

The Great Controversy by Ellen G. White
The "time of trouble, such as never was," is soon to open upon us; and we shall need an experience which we do not now possess and which many are too indolent to obtain. It is often the case that trouble is greater in anticipation than in reality; but this is not true of the crisis before us. The most vivid presentation cannot reach the magnitude of the ordeal.

{While this anointed messenger previously sent} to rebuke the Catholic church...

(Exactly one year later, God through a series of events had this messenger rebuke the Catholic Church, meeting with Father James Wehner, head of the Notre Dame Seminary on the winter solstice of 2018, further explored herein and previously revealed in the 2020 nonfiction work Saint Michael Stood Up.)

Psalm 89:34
My covenant I will not break, Nor alter the word that has gone out of My lips.

{While this anointed messenger} will show that God promises even the most wicked can now find rescue in ways exceeding even that of the Israelites from Egyptian bondage in Exodus.

Joel 2:32
And it shall come to pass
That whoever calls on the name of the Lord
Shall be saved.
For in Mount Zion and in Jerusalem there shall be deliverance,
As the Lord has said,
Among the remnant whom the Lord calls.

Ezekiel 33:14-16
Again, when I say to the wicked, 'You shall surely die,' if he turns from his sin and does what is lawful and right, if the wicked restores the pledge, gives back what he has stolen, and walks in the statutes of life without committing iniquity, he shall surely live; he shall not die. None of his sins which he has committed shall be remembered against him; he has done what is lawful and right; he shall surely live.

George Washington's Thanksgiving Proclamation, October 3, 1789
"And also that we may then unite in most humbly offering our prayers and supplications to the great Lord and Ruler of Nations and beseech him to pardon our national and other

transgressions, to enable us all, whether in public or private stations, to perform our several and relative duties properly..."

Jeremiah 3:11-13
'Return, backsliding Israel,' says the Lord;
'I will not cause My anger to fall on you.
For I am merciful,' says the Lord;
'I will not remain angry forever.
Only acknowledge your iniquity,
That you have transgressed against the Lord your God,
And have scattered your charms
To alien deities under every green tree,
And you have not obeyed My voice,' says the Lord.

Jeremiah 3:22
"Return, you backsliding children,
And I will heal your backslidings."

Jeremiah 15:19
Therefore thus says the Lord:

"If you return,
Then I will bring you back;
You shall stand before Me;
If you take out the precious from the vile,
You shall be as My mouth.
Let them return to you,
But you must not return to them.

Ezekiel 33:19-20
But when the wicked turns from his wickedness and does what is lawful and right, he shall live because of it. Yet you say, 'The way of the Lord is not fair.' O house of Israel, I will judge every one of you according to his own ways."

Jeremiah 30:20
And I will punish all who oppress them

Hosea 6:6
For I desire mercy and not sacrifice,
And the knowledge of God more than burnt offerings.

And if you're willing to stop enriching Gog,

Ezekiel 36:1-3
"And you, son of man, prophesy to the mountains of Israel, and say, 'O mountains of Israel, hear the word of the Lord! Thus says the Lord God: "Because the enemy has said of you, 'Aha! The ancient heights have become our possession,' " ' therefore prophesy, and say, 'Thus says the Lord God: "Because they made you desolate and swallowed you up on every side, so that you became the possession of the rest of the nations, and you are taken up by the lips of talkers and slandered by the people"-- therefore, O mountains of Israel, hear the word of the Lord God!

...then here's how to do it.

Job 42:2
"I know that you {God} can do all things, and that no purpose of yours can be thwarted.

Hosea 6:6
For I desire steadfast love and not sacrifice, the knowledge of God rather than burnt offerings.

Micah 6:8
He has told you, O man, what is good; and what does the Lord require of you but to do justice, and to love kindness, and to walk humbly with your God?

Proverbs 21:3
To do righteousness and justice is more acceptable to the Lord than sacrifice.

Habakkuk 2:1-2
The Just Shall Live by Faith

I will stand my watch
And set myself on the rampart,
And watch to see what He will say to me,
And what I will answer when I am corrected.

The Just Shall Live by Faith
Then the Lord answered me and said:

"Write the vision
And make it plain on tablets,
That he may run who reads it.
For the vision is yet for an appointed time;
But at the end it will speak, and it will not lie.
Though it tarries, wait for it;
Because it will surely come,
It will not tarry.

(The way out are the annotated Hebrew Bible verses and scientific facts further presented within this guide.)

For the rock is on its way.

Isaiah 34:1-17
Draw near, O nations, to hear, and give attention, O peoples! Let the earth hear, and all that fills it; the world, and all that comes from it. For the Lord is enraged against all the nations, and furious against all their host; he has devoted them to destruction, has given them over for slaughter.

Daniel 2:45
Inasmuch as you saw that the stone was cut out of the mountain without hands, and that it broke in pieces the iron, the bronze, the clay, the silver, and the gold—the great God has made known to the king what will come to pass after this. The dream is certain, and its interpretation is sure."

Isaiah 1:20
But if you refuse and rebel,

You shall be devoured by the sword";
For the mouth of the Lord has spoken.

Zephaniah 1:15, 17-18
That day is a day of wrath...
"I will bring distress upon men,
Neither their silver nor their gold
Shall be able to deliver them
In the day of the Lord's wrath;
But the whole land shall be devoured
By the fire of His jealousy,
For He will make speedy riddance
Of all those who dwell in the land.

Zephaniah 3:8
A Faithful Remnant
"Therefore wait for Me," says the Lord,
"Until the day I rise up for plunder;
My determination is to gather the nations
To My assembly of kingdoms,
To pour on them My indignation,
All My fierce anger;
All the earth shall be devoured
With the fire of My jealousy.

Malachi 3:1
"I will send my messenger, who will prepare the way before me {I am here}. Then suddenly the Lord you are seeking will come to his temple; the messenger of the covenant, whom you desire, will come," says the Lord Almighty.

Ecclesiastes 12:9-14

The Conclusion of the Matter

Not only was the Teacher wise, but he also imparted knowledge to the people. He pondered and searched out and set in order many proverbs. The Teacher searched to find just the right words, and what he wrote was upright and true.

The words of the wise are like goads, their collected sayings like firmly embedded nails—given by one shepherd. Be warned, my son, of anything in addition to them. And further, my son, be admonished by these:

Of making many books there is no end,
and much study is wearisome to the flesh.
Let us hear the conclusion of the whole matter:
Fear God and keep his commandments,
for this is man's all.

For God will bring every work into judgment,
including every secret thing,
whether good or evil.

Review:

God offers a one-time chance at rescue for believers, American citizens, and Israelite citizens. It was the Americans as modern Israelites who wrestled with God and truly guided the outcomes for humanity in the end times. Here are the key points that Americans failed to face, supporting Hebrew Bible verses for each point offered in Appendix (d) on page 375.

Aliens, extraterrestrials, called angels, worked for God on Earth since the Book of Genesis.

American treason/antidepressants cloud the mind continually, for which God condemns its users who are merely numb.

American treason/birth control fed wanton sexuality, ultimately feeding pedophilia from the breakdown of families.

American treason/cities allowed corrupt municipal politicians to alter election laws in violation of their laws and now seek to prohibit a running president, thus ending the political process.

American treason/conservatism followed Democrats to serve Gog (China's king) under 3 presidents who cemented Gog's hold over us, shown to be Clinton, W. Bush, and Obama, later aided by a fourth, Biden. God states He can end three in a month and cripple the worst with a stroke blinding his right hand and eye.

American treason/counterculture feeds pedophilia.

American treason/COVID destroyed the country and invalidated the government meant to protect America. God promises it will wipe out the United States of America.

American treason/equal taxation is opposed by those seeking to advance select groups' interests over other Americans socially and economically.

American treason/forests are not cleared, killing people in massive forest fires.

American treason/immigration is allowed to invade the nation with illegal immigrants not agreed to by the overall citizenry, taking precedence over citizens, driving us out of our limited homes and jobs.

American treason/kneel for flag undermines national unity, further splintering our republic.

American treason/LGBTQ enriches pedophiles as proven by all of antiquity without God's prohibition against homosexual sex and cross-dressing, unfairly injuring the impressionable young.

American treason/manufacture, manufacturing is the basis of our power, Clinton first outsourced it in an act to end the world, making him the last king of civilization that ended it, earning him after his death the title Lucifer, as God showed to Isaiah.

American treason/mass media covers up our enemy destroying our nation and political process, also making us feel neither hot nor cold, but helpless and silent to the evil growing around us.

American treason/memorials are being altered from our history, and condemned by God.

American treason/Mercy is something Americans have not shown for their fellow Americans.

American treason/presidents, namely the first three presidents who acted as Satan, misleading the U.S. into enriching China's Gog and allowing slavery, and spawning record pollution from his slave-made goods.

American treason/prison, that was the outcome for the children who grew up robbed of their forefathers' manufacturing jobs.

American treason/pro-life is not supported by liturgy and the reason American conservatives have lost America, falsely invoking God on something He did not say, while remaining silent on sodomy's spread, to which religious leaders turn a blind eye, making them modern "madmen".

American treason/U.S. history is being perverted to destroy us by tyrants who had you work to fund concentration camps and your own destruction, bringing slavery into the nation.

American treason/university, the education world is completely corrupted by Gog's money.

American treason/war not peace is what the four Satanic presidents have preached to mislead Americans, earning the four the title of Satan, with the first three having cemented our end.

Anti-Semitism damns the Gentiles according to the Lord; and since 2020 AD, punishing modern Americans is punishing Israelites, of which they are; and the reason our elites will be more harshly judged than any other, although they can now find a chance for Divine forgiveness.

Bacteria and viruses will now destroy humanity, God's health rules had protected humans all along who didn't even know the root cause. But with our enhanced scientific understanding our government funded and showed Gog how to use lethal disease to kill us.

Date for COVID coincided with the end of the Israelite punishment and the end of the world.

Day of God is a meteorite collision shattering earth into rubble for America's mass misleading.

Day of God/Undead will be how our Satanic American leaders and their advocates who were born to a legacy of liberty, stole it from their fellow Americans, damning them for eternity as the undead or burning in hell.

Follow the rules or die is the moral and America's modern enrichment of communism broke with their forefathers who fought to contain such tyranny.

God controls it all and allowed our demise for our sins.

Gog in China is the beneficiary of our sins, for he is not enriched by his own power, but by ours.

Government is the enemy in the Second Civil War.

Inner temple is God's place inside you and the only hope of your rescue in His secret place.

The Messiah is the anointed person, born as an American, who will repeat God's warning from the Hebrew Bible alone.

New Jerusalem of the gentiles is the United States to whom the Messiah addressed as his fellow countryman, who have access to the same Hebrew Bible and relevant articles the messiah does.

Sabbath is what Americans have not been honoring; it's sundown from Friday to Saturday and you can't leave your dwelling.

Science/DNA is supported by God, and sex links that, which males cannot do with each other without damning themselves and often their parents or grandparents, for which this occurs. Enriching communism bred death and sodomy outcomes in our present situation.

Science/relativity defends how the good will branch to a different multiverse where they're saved while the evil will die from the meteorite.

Science/sperm is linked by people having sex, and why sexual behavior fills many of His laws, as breaking this forbidden action enough times ends the world for all.

science/transfigurative light was how God's spirit was set upon the Messiah, his Messenger of the Covenant.

Woman as a test was what men forgot, once males allowed women into the workplace, decreasing a man's single wage to support a family, soon forcing all women to quit being mothers, thus destroying future generations of Americans.

Appendix (a)
ANALYSIS ON THE SOLUTION TO DANIEL'S RIDDLE

This appendix explores the dates to pinpoint God's prophesy of the COVID pandemic beginning in late 2019 and infecting the world by early 2020.

1. A breakdown of the times & dates solving *Daniel's Riddle*.

1,290	years of desolation were foretold to Daniel to follow the end of rightful, Israelite blood sacrifices at their Jerusalem temple*
	*Daniel 12:11 *"And from the time that the daily sacrifice is taken away, and the abomination of desolation is set up, there shall be one thousand two hundred and ninety days."* (The Hebrew word for days here meaning years)
1,335	then an addition 1,335 years was added to finally reach a blessed year" (when the Israelite's punishment ended)**
	**Daniel 12:12 *"Blessed is he who waits, and comes to the one thousand three hundred and thirty-five days."* (again "days" here in Hebrew mean years)
2,625	total years of the desolation to reach the blessed year
605 BC	Israel is conquered by Babylon King Nebuchadnezzar II, the abomination of desolation from Israel's first foreign conqueror***
	***Babylon conquers Israel in 605 BC at *The Battle Of Carchemish*, but ruled it through Israelite puppets until outright destroying it in 587 BC
2020**	COVID-19 pandemic occurs 2,625 year from the loss of rightful sacrifices in 605 BC, resulting in 2020 AD marking the end of the world deductively continued to further punish the Israelites

*Rightful blood sacrifices protected Israel from outside invaders until the loss to Babylon.
** If one wishes to calculate for the missing year 0 between the AD and BC dating system, the pandemic begins in 2019, but truly strikes the world in 2020, either interpretation is factually correct..

2. The cleansing of the *Sanctuary* from Daniel's Prophesy.

2,300	years to cleanse the sanctuary before the worldwide end; this sanctuary is humanity's original sanctuary birthplace of Africa*
	*Daniel 8:14 *"And he said to me, "For two thousand three hundred [a]days; then the sanctuary shall be cleansed."*
1695 AD	marks 2,300 years from Babylon's conquest in 605 BC to cleanse the sanctuary of all mankind, the continent of Africa
1696 AD	The following year, the Royal English monopoly of the African slave trade ended, allowing Americans to bring African slaves *en masse* to the U.S. to replace the former, white, indentured servants, finally bringing God's chosen Africans from their perpetual slavery to become American citizens following the U.S. Civil War.

3. A comparison of ancient Israel and the modern U.S., both conquered by foreign invaders who secretly hid their rule for 18 years before crushing their conquered victim.

605	BC, the initial conquest of ancient Israel by the ancient Babylonian King Nebuchadnezzar II
587	BC when ancient Babylon's King Nebuchadnezzar II wiped out Israel in August 25th, 587, but he had truly ruled it from 605 BC onward, sucking it economically dry for the next 18 years
18	year period that Israel was economy sucked dry by Babylonian King Nebuchadnezzar II before their outright destruction
2001 AD	William Clinton's support ushers China into the World Trade Organization (WTO) at years end, December 11, 2001
2002 AD	China spreads its slave-made, world polluting goods to impoverish the entire free world
2020 AD	COVID-19 pandemic strikes the world
18	year period that the U.S. was economy sucked dry by China's king after the WTO entry before our end was sown via his COVID virus

4. God makes clear He acted through all our leaders to eventually punish us for our lack of belief in Him.

2018 AD	After 3 pro-China enriching presidents, President Trump starts a trade war with China, bringing COVID, cities illegally altering their election laws on absentee ballots to bring Biden who openly wars to further the pollution and enrichment of China's king
	Daniel 7:8 *"While I was thinking about the horns, there before me was another horn, a little one, which came up among them; and three of the first horns were uprooted before it. This horn had eyes like the eyes of a human being and a mouth that spoke boastfully. horns were plucked out by the roots. And there, in this horn, were eyes like the eyes of a man, and a mouth speaking pompous words"*.
2020 AD	After President Trump severs the Service Economy with a Chinese trade war, comes COVID and election fraud to bring our fourth, pro-China leaders who no longer hides his kingly pomposity
	Now Service Economy traitors act pompously, better than the people, like the kings God makes clear they are
	Daniel 7:21 *"As I watched, this horn was waging war against the holy people and defeating them,*

Appendix (b)
FURTHER SUPPORT FOR POLITICAL POLICIES

This appendix explores prior essays and major third-party sources behind the political policies.

Each political point of this plan was printed in 2020's *How To Win The War: The Plan To Save The U.S.A.*, presented in our 2020 presidential campaign, and anthologizing in the 2017 *Essential Essays* found at no charge at our site www.centeredamerica.com where each essay digitally links to supporting third party, academic and media sources. This appendix underscores each policy point, lists supporting Essential essays, and in bold print cites the third-party sources behind the essays..

OZ (OPPORTUNITY ZONE)

Basic manufacturing will be done at our border with our thirty million non-citizens paying rent and working in a new wall of factories to which Mexican day-laborers can also participate at lower wages, many living in Mexico and daily commuting from a country with a much cheaper standard of living cost.

Essays Dealing With This Point:

(A Plan For Mexico)

History of the U.S. Economy in the 20th Century Professor Timothy Taylor, M.Econ., Macalaster College.
A History of the United States, 2nd Edition Taught By Multiple Professors.

(A New U.S. Immigration Policy Suggestion)

Germany's Migrant Rape Crisis Spirals Out of Control: Suppression of data about migrant rapes is "Germany-wide phenomenon", Soeren Kern, Gatestone Institute, International Policy Counsel.

(How Mexico Can Pay For Trump's Wall & Enrich Both Nations)

Economics, 3rd Edition by Professor Timothy Taylor, M. Econ., Macalaster College.
Legacies of Great Economists by Professor Timothy Taylor, M. Econ., Macalaster College.

FUTURE OZ EXPANSION

Future OZ expansion zones will be pioneered outside of Mexico and throughout the Americas to Argentina. A new linked Pan-

American rail and road highway called The Yellow Brick Road, TYBR, will link the Americas in trade, raw materials, and increase American manufacturing and open vital new consumer markets for our export.

Essays Dealing With This Point:

(The American Revolution's Big Lie)

A History of the United States, 2nd Edition Taught By Multiple Professors. The Skeptic's Guide to American History by Professor Mark A. Stoler, Ph.D., The University of Vermont.

(Washington's Economic Vision In Bullet Points)

A History of the United States, 2nd Edition Taught By Multiple Professors. The Skeptic's Guide to American History by Professor Mark A. Stoler, Ph.D., The University of Vermont.

THE ONLY PLAN TO RESTORE MANUFACTURING

As the largest manufacturer of high-end gift accessories in the world both in the U.S. and then forced to outsource to China I know more than Trump, a residential developer, and Biden who helped to decimate manufacturing over his career.

We will economically remake the economy of our nation to be like an Eden where we again make much of what we make. We will enter into free trade with the Americas, fulfilling then-President Buchanan's promise of America's Manifest Destiny. We will trade with free world nations and perhaps even Russia, rich in natural resources.

Essays Dealing With This Point:

(The American Revolution's Big Lie)

A History of the United States, 2nd Edition Taught By Multiple Professors. The Skeptic's Guide to American History by Professor Mark A. Stoler, Ph.D., The University of Vermont.

(Washington's Economic Vision In Bullet Points)

**A History of the United States, 2nd Edition Taught By Multiple Professors.
The Skeptic's Guide to American History by Professor Mark A. Stoler,
Ph.D., The University of Vermont.**

(An Indictment Of The U.S. Service Economy And The Lie Of Globalism)

**United Nations Admits That The Paris Climate Accord was a fraud
The Skeptic's Guide to American History by Professor Mark A. Stoler,
Ph.D., The University of Vermont.
Machiavelli in Context by Professor William R. Cooks, Ph.D., State
University of New York, Geneseo.
Manufacturing Job Loss, Economic Policy Institute.
List of innocent U.S. Citizen killed by illegal aliens.
Alexander Hamilton's Manufacturing Message, Brookings Institution.
Alexander Hamilton's Manufacturing Message, CNN.
Poverty, Prejudice, and Punishment, Harvard University.edu.
The Road to Serfdom by Friedrich Hayek**

(Clinton's Economic Lie)

**The Manchurian Candidate, Motion Picture by John Frankenheimer (1962)
A History of the United States, 2nd Edition Taught By Multiple Professors.
The Skeptic's Guide to American History by Professor Mark A. Stoler,
Ph.D., The University of Vermont.
Year of the Rat: How Bill Clinton Compromised U.S. Security for Chinese
Cash by Edward Timperlake.**

(Visualizing The True Cost Of The Clintonian Service Economy)

**History of the U.S. Economy in the 20th Century Professor Timothy Taylor,
M.Econ., Macalaster College.
A History of the United States, 2nd Edition Taught By Multiple Professors.
The Skeptic's Guide to American History by Professor Mark A. Stoler,
Ph.D., The University of Vermont.**

(What Americans A Century Ago Would Think Of Us Today)

**Books That Have Made History: Books That Can Change Your Life Rufus J.
Fears, Ph.D., University of Oklahoma.
American Mind by Professor Allen C Guelzo, Ph.D., Gettysburg College.
A History of the United States, 2nd Edition Taught By Multiple Professors.
The Skeptic's Guide to American History by Professor Mark A. Stoler,
Ph.D., The University of Vermont.
The Road to Serfdom by Friedrich Hayek**

AT HOME SUB-MANUFACTURING

As a specialist in multi-million-dollar at-home-sub-manufacturing, many inland factories will kit basic materials from OZ for at-home subcontractors until we are COVID-19 free. Businesses will primarily kit raw material items for home-based-sub-contractors to assemble the kits into product SKUs for pickup or drop-shipped when the next lot is dropped off.

Essays Dealing With This Point:

(The American Revolution's Big Lie)

A History of the United States, 2nd Edition Taught By Multiple Professors. The Skeptic's Guide to American History by Professor Mark A. Stoler, Ph.D., The University of Vermont.

(Washington's Economic Vision In Bullet Points)

A History of the United States, 2nd Edition Taught By Multiple Professors. The Skeptic's Guide to American History by Professor Mark A. Stoler, Ph.D., The University of Vermont.

TYPICAL FACTORIES

More conventional manufacturing and essential businesses will be run with sterile technology to protect workers, first with proper PPE or prioritizing at home personnel whenever possible. These small businesses will be aided and underwritten by the USDA loan program in a war-like drive for domestic manufacturing akin to World War II.

RAW MATERIAL INVALIDATION BY CHINA

For concealing COVID-19, all raw material deals with Communist China outside theirs, and their proxy state of North Korea will be considered null and void by the free world.

Essays Dealing With This Point:

(The Incontrovertible Wickedness Of Socialism And Communism)

Utopia and Terror in the 20th Century by Professor Vejas Gabriel Liulevicius, Ph.D., University of Tennessee.
The Road to Serfdom by Friedrich Hayek
Stalin's Murderous Doctor Purge shortly before his death, BBC News animation
"Stalin" by Edvard Radzinksy
"How Sweden Overcame Socialism", Wall Street Journal, January 9, 2019
Foundation for Economic Education, "Canada's Laffer Curve Lesson: Government Collects Less Revenue from High-Income Earners after Trudeau Tax Hike

CHINESE SMART DEVICE REPLACEMENT

Over a five-year-window the government will subsidize the replacement of all Chinese-made-smart-devices to stop Chinese spying for the sake of national security.

Essays Dealing With This Point:

(The Incontrovertible Wickedness Of Socialism And Communism)

Utopia and Terror in the 20th Century by Professor Vejas Gabriel Liulevicius, Ph.D., University of Tennessee.
The Road to Serfdom by Friedrich Hayek
Stalin's Murderous Doctor Purge shortly before his death, BBC News animation
"Stalin" by Edvard Radzinksy
"How Sweden Overcame Socialism", Wall Street Journal, January 9, 2019
Foundation for Economic Education, "Canada's Laffer Curve Lesson: Government Collects Less Revenue from High-Income Earners after Trudeau Tax Hike

COMMUNIST CHINESE EMBARGO

The free world will embargo Communist China and North Korean goods. If not, the pollution caused by them will continue to further rip the hole in the ozone layer and destroy all life. This communist regime can't help but be the deadliest, a mantle it achieved in the 1970s and continues to expand on to this day through American traitors. We will realign with Taiwan and other Asian nations and openly criticized the injustice done to Hong Kong.

Essays Dealing With This Point:

(The Incontrovertible Wickedness Of Socialism And Communism)

Utopia and Terror in the 20th Century by Professor Vejas Gabriel Liulevicius, Ph.D., University of Tennessee.
The Road to Serfdom by Friedrich Hayek
Stalin's Murderous Doctor Purge shortly before his death, BBC News animation
"Stalin" by Edvard Radzinksy
"How Sweden Overcame Socialism", Wall Street Journal, January 9, 2019
Foundation for Economic Education, "Canada's Laffer Curve Lesson: Government Collects Less Revenue from High-Income Earners after Trudeau Tax Hike

(Solving the Middle East in Ten Easy Pieces)

Economics, 3rd Edition by Professors Timothy Taylor, M. Econ., Macalaster College.
Legacies of Great Economists Professor Timothy Taylor, M. Econ.. Macalaster College.
History of the U.S. Economy in the 20th Century by Professor Timothy Taylor, M. Econ., Macalaster College.

(Why Bill Clinton Created a Nuclear North Korea)

You Can thank Jimmy Carter and Bill Clinton for North Korea's Nukes, New York Post Editorial Board.

REAL CLIMATE CHANGE POLICY

The free world must embargo Communist China and North Korean goods. If not, the pollution caused by them will continue to further rip the new hole in the ozone layer and destroy all life. Or they will spread the disease again through passengers or lace it into goods.

Essays Dealing With This Point:

(No American Can Be Environmentally Conscious)

United Nations Admits The Paris Climate Change Accord Was A Fraud/
Investor's Business Daily
China Southern Morning Post (Pollution Section).

(Clinton, Bush, and Obama, the C.W.O. - Enemies of The United States)

A History of the United States, 2nd Edition Taught By Multiple Professors.
The Skeptic's Guide to American History by Professor Mark A. Stoler,
Ph.D. The University of Vermont.
Year of the Rat: How Bill Clinton Compromised American Security For
Chinese Cash by Edward Timperlake.

(The Incontrovertible Wickedness of Socialism And Communism)

Utopia and Terror in the 20th Century by Professor Vejas Gabriel
Liulevicius, Ph.D., University of Tennessee.
The Road to Serfdom by Friedrich Hayek
Stalin's Murderous Doctor Purge shortly before his death, BBC News
animation
"Stalin" by Edvard Radzinksy
"How Sweden Overcame Socialism", Wall Street Journal, January 9, 2019
Foundation for Economic Education, "Canada's Laffer Curve Lesson:
Government Collects Less Revenue from High-Income Earners after
Trudeau Tax Hike

(North Korea & Iran: 100% American Made)

You Can thank Jimmy Carter and Bill Clinton for North Korea's Nukes,
New York Post Editorial Board.
A History of the United States, 2nd Edition Taught By Multiple Professors.
The Skeptic's Guide to American History by Professor Mark A. Stoler,
Ph.D. The University of Vermont.
Year of the Rat: How Bill Clinton Compromised American Security For
Chinese Cash by Edward Timperlake.

(Where Our History Is Headed If We Don't Change)

United Nations Admits The Paris Climate Accord Was A Fraud/Investor's
Business News
China manufacturing for America is polluting the world.
China Air Pollution reduces cognitive abilities.
China pollution powers storms half-way around the world.
China pollution wreaks havoc on human health.
The pollution continues from across China.
Chinese city chokes on smog specks that are 'harder than steel.'
Chinese pollution is worsening in many parts of the country.
Chinese pollution is once again destroying the Earth's ozone layer.
Devastating effects of Chinese pollution.
China Southern Morning Post (Pollution Section).

(If You Read Only One Article...)

The Skeptic's Guide to American History by Professor Mark A. Stoler, Ph.D., The University of Vermont.
Machiavelli in Context by Professor William R. Cooks, Ph.D., State University of New York, Geneseo.
Manufacturing Job Loss, Economic Policy Institute.
List of innocent U.S. Citizen killed by illegal aliens.
Alexander Hamilton's Manufacturing Message, Brookings Institution.
Alexander Hamilton's Manufacturing Message, CNN.
Poverty, Prejudice, and Punishment, Harvard University.edu.
The Road to Serfdom by Friedrich Hayek

(Why We Have To Stop Hating Big Oil And Learn To Love It)

United Nations Admits That The Paris Climate Accord Was A Fraud/Investor's Business Daily
An Economic History of the World since 1400, Professor Donald J. Harreld, Ph.D., Brigham Young University.

(An Indictment Of The U.S. Service Economy And The Lie Of Globalism)

United Nations Admits That The Paris Climate Accord was a fraud
The Skeptic's Guide to American History by Professor Mark A. Stoler, Ph.D., The University of Vermont.
Machiavelli in Context by Professor William R. Cooks, Ph.D., State University of New York, Geneseo.
Manufacturing Job Loss, Economic Policy Institute.
List of innocent U.S. Citizen killed by illegal aliens.
Alexander Hamilton's Manufacturing Message, Brookings Institution.
Alexander Hamilton's Manufacturing Message, CNN.
Poverty, Prejudice, and Punishment, Harvard University.edu.
The Road to Serfdom by Friedrich Hayek

(Clinton, Bush, & Obama - Enemies Of The United States)

A History of the United States, 2nd Edition Taught By Multiple Professors.
The Skeptic's Guide to American History by Professor Mark A. Stoler, Ph.D. The University of Vermont.
Year of the Rat: How Bill Clinton Compromised American Security For Chinese Cash by Edward Timperlake.

(If Barack Obama Was Our 44th White President)

Great Minds of the Western Intellectual Tradition, 3rd Edition taught by multiple professors.
The Skeptic's Guide to American History by Professor Mark A. Stoler, Ph.D., The University of Vermont.
History of the United States, 2nd Edition Taught By Multiple Professors.

GOD'S GUIDE TO THE END OF THE WORLD   331

(The Problem With The Major U.S. Political Parties)

The Manchurian Candidate, Motion Picture
Classical and Modern Political Theory by Professor Dennis Dalton, Ph.D., Barnard College, Columbia University.
The Skeptic's Guide to American History by Professor Mark A. Stoler, Ph.D., The University of Vermont.

(The Incontrovertible Wickedness Of Socialism And Communism)

Utopia and Terror in the 20th Century by Professor Vejas Gabriel Liulevicius, Ph.D., University of Tennessee.
The Road to Serfdom by Friedrich Hayek
Stalin's Murderous Doctor Purge shortly before his death, BBC News animation
"Stalin" by Edvard Radzinksy
"How Sweden Overcame Socialism", Wall Street Journal, January 9, 2019
Foundation for Economic Education, "Canada's Laffer Curve Lesson: Government Collects Less Revenue from High-Income Earners after Trudeau Tax Hike

(Bill Clinton Created A Nuclear North Korea)

You Can thank Jimmy Carter and Bill Clinton for North Korea's Nukes, New York Post Editorial Board.

(Clinton's Economic Lie)

The Manchurian Candidate, Motion Picture by John Frankenheimer (1962)
A History of the United States, 2nd Edition Taught By Multiple Professors.
The Skeptic's Guide to American History by Professor Mark A. Stoler, Ph.D., The University of Vermont.
Year of the Rat: How Bill Clinton Compromised U.S. Security for Chinese Cash by Edward Timperlake.

(The Real Lorax)

China manufacturing for America is polluting the world.
China Air Pollution reduces cognitive abilities.
China pollution powers storms half-way around the world.
China pollution wreaks havoc on human health.
The pollution continues from across China.
Chinese city chokes on smog specks that are 'harder than steel.
Chinese pollution is worsening in many parts of the country.
Chinese pollution is once again destroying the Earth's ozone layer.
Devastating effects of Chinese pollution.

(Why Our Leaders Often Stink)

The March of Folly: From Troy to Vietnam by Barbara W. Tuchman
Machiavelli in Context, Professor William R. Cook, Ph.D., State University of New York, Geneseo.
A History of the United States, 2nd Edition Taught By Multiple Professors.
The Skeptic's Guide to American History by Professor Mark A. Stoler, Ph.D., The University of Vermont.
The Road To Serfdom by Friedrich Hayek
The Deep State by Jason Chaffets
Boss Tweed by Kenneth D. Ackerman

(Hitler's Long Term Crime)

History of Hitler's Empire, 2nd Edition by Professor Thomas Childers, Ph.D., University of Pennsylvania.

OYOH (OWN YOUR OWN HOME)

For long-ending your freedoms from the three traitor's treason and Trump's trade war blunder contributing to your home imprisonment, the price of your dwelling will be underwritten by the U.S. government with financial incentives for existing homeowners or we will risk the end of the nation. The OPAH (One Parent At Home) subsidy will return the traditional one person stay at home parent to raise our children and keep our homes

Essays Dealing With This Point:

(If You Only Read Only One Article)

The Skeptic's Guide to American History by Professor Mark A. Stoler, Ph.D., The University of Vermont.
Machiavelli in Context by Professor William R. Cooks, Ph.D., State University of New York, Geneseo.
Manufacturing Job Loss, Economic Policy Institute.
List of innocent U.S. Citizen killed by illegal aliens.
Alexander Hamilton's Manufacturing Message, Brookings Institution.
Alexander Hamilton's Manufacturing Message, CNN.
Poverty, Prejudice, and Punishment, Harvard University.edu.
The Road to Serfdom by Friedrich Hayek

(An Indictment of The U.S. Service Economy & The Lie of *Globalism*)

United Nations Admits That The Paris Climate Accord was a fraud
The Skeptic's Guide to American History by Professor Mark A. Stoler, Ph.D., The University of Vermont.

Machiavelli in Context by Professor William R. Cooks, Ph.D., State University of New York, Geneseo.
Manufacturing Job Loss, Economic Policy Institute.
List of innocent U.S. Citizen killed by illegal aliens.
Alexander Hamilton's Manufacturing Message, Brookings Institution.
Alexander Hamilton's Manufacturing Message, CNN.
Poverty, Prejudice, and Punishment, Harvard University.edu.
The Road to Serfdom by Friedrich Hayek

(Visualizing The True Cost Of The Clintonian Service Economy)

History of the U.S. Economy in the 20th Century Professor Timothy Taylor, M.Econ., Macalaster College.
A History of the United States, 2nd Edition Taught By Multiple Professors.
The Skeptic's Guide to American History by Professor Mark A. Stoler, Ph.D., The University of Vermont.

(Why Our Leaders Often Stink)

The March of Folly: From Troy to Vietnam by Barbara W. Tuchman
Machiavelli in Context, Professor William R. Cook, Ph.D., State University of New York, Geneseo.
A History of the United States, 2nd Edition Taught By Multiple Professors.
The Skeptic's Guide to American History by Professor Mark A. Stoler, Ph.D., The University of Vermont.
The Road To Serfdom by Friedrich Hayek
The Deep State by Jason Chaffets
Boss Tweed by Kenneth D. Ackerman

OPAH (ONE PARENT AT HOME)

A government subsidy and tax credit to allow one parent to stay at home and raise their children. This funding can be rerouted from public schools to home-based education in the new viral age.

Essays Dealing With This Point:

(If You Read Only One Article...)

The Skeptic's Guide to American History by Professor Mark A. Stoler, Ph.D., The University of Vermont.
Machiavelli in Context by Professor William R. Cooks, Ph.D., State University of New York, Geneseo.
Manufacturing Job Loss, Economic Policy Institute.
List of innocent U.S. Citizen killed by illegal aliens.
Alexander Hamilton's Manufacturing Message, Brookings Institution.

Alexander Hamilton's Manufacturing Message, CNN.
Poverty, Prejudice, and Punishment, Harvard University.edu.
The Road to Serfdom by Friedrich Hayek

(An Indictment of The U.S. Service Economy & The Lie of *Globalism*)

United Nations Admits That The Paris Climate Accord was a fraud
The Skeptic's Guide to American History by Professor Mark A. Stoler, Ph.D., The University of Vermont.
Machiavelli in Context by Professor William R. Cooks, Ph.D., State University of New York, Geneseo.
Manufacturing Job Loss, Economic Policy Institute.
List of innocent U.S. Citizen killed by illegal aliens.
Alexander Hamilton's Manufacturing Message, Brookings Institution.
Alexander Hamilton's Manufacturing Message, CNN.
Poverty, Prejudice, and Punishment, Harvard University.edu.
The Road to Serfdom by Friedrich Hayek United Nations Admits That The Paris Climate Accord was a fraud
The Skeptic's Guide to American History by Professor Mark A. Stoler, Ph.D., The University of Vermont.
Machiavelli in Context by Professor William R. Cooks, Ph.D., State University of New York, Geneseo.
Manufacturing Job Loss, Economic Policy Institute.
List of innocent U.S. Citizen killed by illegal aliens.
Alexander Hamilton's Manufacturing Message, Brookings Institution.
Alexander Hamilton's Manufacturing Message, CNN.
Poverty, Prejudice, and Punishment, Harvard University.edu.
The Road to Serfdom by Friedrich Hayek
(Visualizing The True Cost Of The Clintonian Service Economy)
History of the U.S. Economy in the 20th Century Professor Timothy Taylor, M.Econ., Macalaster College.
A History of the United States, 2nd Edition Taught By Multiple Professors.
The Skeptic's Guide to American History by Professor Mark A. Stoler, Ph.D., The University of Vermont.

(Why Our Leaders Often Stink)

The March of Folly: From Troy to Vietnam by Barbara W. Tuchman
Machiavelli in Context, Professor William R. Cook, Ph.D., State University of New York, Geneseo.
A History of the United States, 2nd Edition Taught By Multiple Professors.
The Skeptic's Guide to American History by Professor Mark A. Stoler, Ph.D., The University of Vermont.
The Road To Serfdom by Friedrich Hayek
The Deep State by Jason Chaffets
Boss Tweed by Kenneth D. Ackerman

(We're All Gloria Steinem's Children)

GOD'S GUIDE TO THE END OF THE WORLD

Stanford University Medicine News Center: Mom's voice activates many different regions in children's brains.
Newsmer.com: Mom's Voice Really Fires Up a Kid's Brain.
Children's brains light up at their mother's voice, DailyMail.com.

(Ideas to Consider In Our Everyday Lives)

South China Morning Post (on China Pollution).
A History of the United States, 2nd Edition Taught By Multiple Professors.
The Skeptic's Guide to American History by Professor Mark A. Stoler, Ph.D., The University of Vermont.

VCP VICTIMIZED CITIZEN REPATRIATION

Those citizens driven out of affordable housing by Sanctuary city and state policies inviting in 30 million extra souls in limited dwellings will have the option to be repatriated back to these areas with reasonable relocation costs paid by the traitorous state and cities, ending the housing crisis which Sanctuary politicians created.

Essays Dealing With This Point:

(If You Read Only One Article...)

The Skeptic's Guide to American History by Professor Mark A. Stoler, Ph.D., The University of Vermont.
Machiavelli in Context by Professor William R. Cooks, Ph.D., State University of New York, Geneseo.
Manufacturing Job Loss, Economic Policy Institute.
List of innocent U.S. Citizen killed by illegal aliens.
Alexander Hamilton's Manufacturing Message, Brookings Institution.
Alexander Hamilton's Manufacturing Message, CNN.
Poverty, Prejudice, and Punishment, Harvard University.edu.
The Road to Serfdom by Friedrich Hayek

(An Indictment of The U.S. Service Economy & The Lie of *Globalism*)

United Nations Admits That The Paris Climate Accord was a fraud
The Skeptic's Guide to American History by Professor Mark A. Stoler, Ph.D., The University of Vermont.
Machiavelli in Context by Professor William R. Cooks, Ph.D., State University of New York, Geneseo.
Manufacturing Job Loss, Economic Policy Institute.
List of innocent U.S. Citizen killed by illegal aliens.
Alexander Hamilton's Manufacturing Message, Brookings Institution.

Alexander Hamilton's Manufacturing Message, CNN.
Poverty, Prejudice, and Punishment, Harvard University.edu.
The Road to Serfdom by Friedrich Hayek

(Visualizing The True Cost Of The Clintonian Service Economy)

History of the U.S. Economy in the 20th Century Professor Timothy Taylor, M.Econ., Macalaster College.
A History of the United States, 2nd Edition Taught By Multiple Professors.
The Skeptic's Guide to American History by Professor Mark A. Stoler, Ph.D., The University of Vermont.

(Why Our Leaders Often Stink)

The March of Folly: From Troy to Vietnam by Barbara W. Tuchman
Machiavelli in Context, Professor William R. Cook, Ph.D., State University of New York, Geneseo.
A History of the United States, 2nd Edition Taught By Multiple Professors.
The Skeptic's Guide to American History by Professor Mark A. Stoler, Ph.D., The University of Vermont.
The Road To Serfdom by Friedrich Hayek
The Deep State by Jason Chaffets
Boss Tweed by Kenneth D. Ackerman

END ILLEGAL SLAVERY

All non-citizens will be identified for later relocation in new residences for manufacturing centers to be built in OZ (Opportunity Zone) along our southern border (further explained in the manufacturing video at centeredamerica.com).

Essays Dealing With This Point:

(An Indictment of The U.S. Service Economy & The Lie of *Globalism*)

United Nations Admits That The Paris Climate Accord was a fraud
The Skeptic's Guide to American History by Professor Mark A. Stoler, Ph.D., The University of Vermont.
Machiavelli in Context by Professor William R. Cooks, Ph.D., State University of New York, Geneseo.
Manufacturing Job Loss, Economic Policy Institute.
The Road to Serfdom by Friedrich Hayek
List of innocent U.S. Citizen killed by illegal aliens.
Alexander Hamilton's Manufacturing Message, Brookings Institution.
Alexander Hamilton's Manufacturing Message, CNN.
Poverty, Prejudice, and Punishment, Harvard University.edu.

GOD'S GUIDE TO THE END OF THE WORLD 337

(Clinton, Bush, Obama, the C.W.O. – Enemies Of The United States)

United Nations Admits That The Paris Climate Accord was a fraud
The Skeptic's Guide to American History by Professor Mark A. Stoler, Ph.D., The University of Vermont.
Machiavelli in Context by Professor William R. Cooks, Ph.D., State University of New York, Geneseo.
Manufacturing Job Loss, Economic Policy Institute.
List of innocent U.S. Citizen killed by illegal aliens.
Alexander Hamilton's Manufacturing Message, Brookings Institution.
Alexander Hamilton's Manufacturing Message, CNN.
Poverty, Prejudice, and Punishment, Harvard University.edu.
The Road to Serfdom by Friedrich Hayek

(Visualizing The True Cost Of The Clintonian Service Economy)

History of the U.S. Economy in the 20th Century Professor Timothy Taylor, M.Econ., Macalaster College.
A History of the United States, 2nd Edition Taught By Multiple Professors.
The Skeptic's Guide to American History by Professor Mark A. Stoler, Ph.D., The University of Vermont.

(Why Our Leaders Often Stink)

The March of Folly: From Troy to Vietnam by Barbara W. Tuchman
Machiavelli in Context, Professor William R. Cook, Ph.D., State University of New York, Geneseo.
A History of the United States, 2nd Edition Taught By Multiple Professors.
The Skeptic's Guide to American History by Professor Mark A. Stoler, Ph.D., The University of Vermont.
The Road To Serfdom by Friedrich Hayek
The Deep State by Jason Chaffets
Boss Tweed by Kenneth D. Ackerman

(Kanye West, The Only True, Modern Black American Leader)

A History of the United States, 2nd Edition Taught By Multiple Professors.

(How Tupac Shakur Taught Me How To End The Ghettos)

History of the U.S. Economy in the 20th Century Professor Timothy Taylor, M.Econ., Macalaster College.
A History of the United States, 2nd Edition Taught By Multiple Professors.
The Skeptic's Guide to American History by Professor Mark A. Stoler, Ph.D., The University of Vermont.

(The Apology Southerners Are Long Owed)

A History of the United States, 2nd Edition Taught By Multiple Professors.

(No American Can Be Environmentally Conscious)

United Nations Admits The Paris Climate Change Accord Was A Fraud/
Investor's Business Daily
China Southern Morning Post (Pollution Section).

(Where Our History Is Headed If We Don't Change)

United Nations Admits The Paris Climate Accord Was A Fraud/Investor's Business News
China manufacturing for America is polluting the world.
China Air Pollution reduces cognitive abilities.
China pollution powers storms half-way around the world.
China pollution wreaks havoc on human health.
The pollution continues from across China.
Chinese city chokes on smog specks that are 'harder than steel.'
Chinese pollution is worsening in many parts of the country.
Chinese pollution is once again destroying the Earth's ozone layer.
Devastating effects of Chinese pollution.
China Southern Morning Post (Pollution Section).

(If You Read Only One Article…)

The Skeptic's Guide to American History by Professor Mark A. Stoler, Ph.D., The University of Vermont.
Machiavelli in Context by Professor William R. Cooks, Ph.D., State University of New York, Geneseo.
Manufacturing Job Loss, Economic Policy Institute.
List of innocent U.S. Citizen killed by illegal aliens.
Alexander Hamilton's Manufacturing Message, Brookings Institution.
Alexander Hamilton's Manufacturing Message, CNN.
Poverty, Prejudice, and Punishment, Harvard University.edu.
The Road to Serfdom by Friedrich

(An Indictment Of The U.S. Service Economy And The Lie Of Globalism)

United Nations Admits That The Paris Climate Accord was a fraud
The Skeptic's Guide to American History by Professor Mark A. Stoler, Ph.D., The University of Vermont.
Machiavelli in Context by Professor William R. Cooks, Ph.D., State University of New York, Geneseo.
Manufacturing Job Loss, Economic Policy Institute.
List of innocent U.S. Citizen killed by illegal aliens.
Alexander Hamilton's Manufacturing Message, Brookings Institution.
Alexander Hamilton's Manufacturing Message, CNN.
Poverty, Prejudice, and Punishment, Harvard University.edu.

The Road to Serfdom by Friedrich Hayek

(Clinton, Bush, & Obama - Enemies Of The United States)

A History of the United States, 2nd Edition Taught By Multiple Professors.
The Skeptic's Guide to American History by Professor Mark A. Stoler, Ph.D. The University of Vermont.
Year of the Rat: How Bill Clinton Compromised American Security For Chinese Cash by Edward Timperlake.

(If Barack Obama Was the 44th White President)

Great Minds of the Western Intellectual Tradition, 3rd Edition taught by multiple professors.
The Skeptic's Guide to American History by Professor Mark A. Stoler, Ph.D., The University of Vermont.
History of the United States, 2nd Edition Taught By Multiple Professors.

(The Problem With The Major U.S. Political Parties)

The Manchurian Candidate, Motion Picture
Classical and Modern Political Theory by Professor Dennis Dalton, Ph.D., Barnard College, Columbia University.
The Skeptic's Guide to American History by Professor Mark A. Stoler, Ph.D., The University of Vermont.

(The Incontrovertible Wickedness Of Socialism And Communism)

Utopia and Terror in the 20th Century by Professor Vejas Gabriel Liulevicius, Ph.D., University of Tennessee.
The Road to Serfdom by Friedrich Hayek
Stalin's Murderous Doctor Purge shortly before his death, BBC News animation
"Stalin" by Edvard Radzinksy
"How Sweden Overcame Socialism", Wall Street Journal, January 9, 2019
Foundation for Economic Education, "Canada's Laffer Curve Lesson: Government Collects Less Revenue from High-Income Earners after Trudeau Tax Hike

(Clinton's Economic Lie)

The Manchurian Candidate, Motion Picture by John Frankenheimer (1962)
A History of the United States, 2nd Edition Taught By Multiple Professors.
The Skeptic's Guide to American History by Professor Mark A. Stoler, Ph.D., The University of Vermont.
Year of the Rat: How Bill Clinton Compromised U.S. Security for Chinese Cash by Edward Timperlake.

CVRA (CITIZEN VERIFICATION RENTAL ACT)

Only citizens will be allowed to rent or own dwellings. This will immediately reduce rents for all citizens in this epic time of trouble.

Essays Dealing With This Point:

(An Indictment Of The U.S. Service Economy And The Lie Of Globalism)

United Nations Admits That The Paris Climate Accord was a fraud
The Skeptic's Guide to American History by Professor Mark A. Stoler, Ph.D., The University of Vermont.
Machiavelli in Context by Professor William R. Cooks, Ph.D., State University of New York, Geneseo.
Manufacturing Job Loss, Economic Policy Institute.
List of innocent U.S. Citizen killed by illegal aliens.
Alexander Hamilton's Manufacturing Message, Brookings Institution.
Alexander Hamilton's Manufacturing Message, CNN.
Poverty, Prejudice, and Punishment, Harvard University.edu.
The Road to Serfdom by Friedrich Hayek

(The Curse Of Disney's It's A Small World)

Louis Theroux: Law and Disorder in Johannesburg
Louis Theroux: Law and Disorder in Lagos
Max Weber video
Great Minds of the Western Intellectual Tradition, 3rd Edition taught by multiple professors.

(Clinton's Economic Lie)

The Manchurian Candidate, Motion Picture by John Frankenheimer (1962)
A History of the United States, 2nd Edition Taught By Multiple Professors.
The Skeptic's Guide to American History by Professor Mark A. Stoler, Ph.D., The University of Vermont.
Year of the Rat: How Bill Clinton Compromised U.S. Security for Chinese Cash by Edward Timperlake.

(In Defense Of Your Fellow Americans)

Children's brains light up at their mother's voice, DailyMail.com.
Books That Have Made History: Books That Can Change Your Life Rufus J. Fears, Ph.D., University of Oklahoma.
American Mind by Professor Allen C Guelzo, Ph.D., Gettysburg College.
A History of the United States, 2nd Edition Taught By Multiple Professors.
The Skeptic's Guide to American History by Professor Mark A. Stoler, Ph.D., The University of Vermont.

END POLICE ANGER & BEGIN POLITICAL SCRUTINY

Rather than blaming the police, we will reform the politicians who systematically and racist jailed a majority of urban blacks and Latinos they robbed of traditional manufacturing jobs.

Essays Dealing With This Point:

(If You Read Only One Article…)

> The Skeptic's Guide to American History by Professor Mark A. Stoler, Ph.D., The University of Vermont.
> Machiavelli in Context by Professor William R. Cooks, Ph.D., State University of New York, Geneseo.
> Manufacturing Job Loss, Economic Policy Institute.
> List of innocent U.S. Citizen killed by illegal aliens.
> Alexander Hamilton's Manufacturing Message, Brookings Institution.
> Alexander Hamilton's Manufacturing Message, CNN.
> Poverty, Prejudice, and Punishment, Harvard University.edu.
> The Road to Serfdom by Friedrich Hayek

(An Indictment Of The U.S. Service Economy And The Lie Of Globalism)

> United Nations Admits That The Paris Climate Accord was a fraud
> The Skeptic's Guide to American History by Professor Mark A. Stoler, Ph.D., The University of Vermont.
> Machiavelli in Context by Professor William R. Cooks, Ph.D., State University of New York, Geneseo.
> Manufacturing Job Loss, Economic Policy Institute.
> List of innocent U.S. Citizen killed by illegal aliens.
> Alexander Hamilton's Manufacturing Message, Brookings Institution.
> Alexander Hamilton's Manufacturing Message, CNN.
> Poverty, Prejudice, and Punishment, Harvard University.edu.
> The Road to Serfdom by Friedrich Hayek

(Clinton, Bush, & Obama - Enemies Of The United States)

> A History of the United States, 2nd Edition Taught By Multiple Professors.
> The Skeptic's Guide to American History by Professor Mark A. Stoler, Ph.D. The University of Vermont.
> Year of the Rat: How Bill Clinton Compromised American Security For Chinese Cash by Edward Timperlake.

(If Barack Obama Was the 44th White President)

Great Minds of the Western Intellectual Tradition, 3rd Edition taught by multiple professors.
The Skeptic's Guide to American History by Professor Mark A. Stoler, Ph.D., The University of Vermont.
History of the United States, 2nd Edition Taught By Multiple Professors.

(The Problem With The Major U.S. Political Parties)

The Manchurian Candidate, Motion Picture
Classical and Modern Political Theory by Professor Dennis Dalton, Ph.D., Barnard College, Columbia University.
The Skeptic's Guide to American History by Professor Mark A. Stoler, Ph.D., The University of Vermont.

(The Incontrovertible Wickedness Of Socialism And Communism)

Utopia and Terror in the 20th Century by Professor Vejas Gabriel Liulevicius, Ph.D., University of Tennessee.
The Road to Serfdom by Friedrich Hayek
Stalin's Murderous Doctor Purge shortly before his death, BBC News animation
"Stalin" by Edvard Radzinksy
"How Sweden Overcame Socialism", Wall Street Journal, January 9, 2019
Foundation for Economic Education, "Canada's Laffer Curve Lesson: Government Collects Less Revenue from High-Income Earners after Trudeau Tax Hike

(Clinton's Economic Lie)

The Manchurian Candidate, Motion Picture by John Frankenheimer (1962)
A History of the United States, 2nd Edition Taught By Multiple Professors.
The Skeptic's Guide to American History by Professor Mark A. Stoler, Ph.D., The University of Vermont.
Year of the Rat: How Bill Clinton Compromised U.S. Security for Chinese Cash by Edward Timperlake.

GOVERNMENT TREASON TRIALS

Hillary Clinton will be prosecuted for the treason of revealing all of our spies. Anyone who received government emails from her private server and did not report it will be arrested. All individuals involved in *Spygate*, including Joe Biden, will be indicted and prosecuted for their clear treason. Port-city federal politicians who allowed the usurping of law and order in their areas will be removed in a military reorganization of the ports.

GOD'S GUIDE TO THE END OF THE WORLD   343

All those involved in the for-profit jails and opioid crisis will be investigated and prosecuted for injuring those they swore to protect.

Essays Dealing With This Point:

(An Indictment Of The U.S. Service Economy And The Lie Of Globalism)

United Nations Admits That The Paris Climate Accord was a fraud
The Skeptic's Guide to American History by Professor Mark A. Stoler, Ph.D., The University of Vermont.
Machiavelli in Context by Professor William R. Cooks, Ph.D., State University of New York, Geneseo.
Manufacturing Job Loss, Economic Policy Institute.
List of innocent U.S. Citizen killed by illegal aliens.
Alexander Hamilton's Manufacturing Message, Brookings Institution.
Alexander Hamilton's Manufacturing Message, CNN.
Poverty, Prejudice, and Punishment, Harvard University.edu.

(Clinton's Economic Lie)

The Manchurian Candidate, Motion Picture by John Frankenheimer (1962)
A History of the United States, 2nd Edition Taught By Multiple Professors.
The Skeptic's Guide to American History by Professor Mark A. Stoler, Ph.D., The University of Vermont.
Year of the Rat: How Bill Clinton Compromised U.S. Security for Chinese Cash by Edward Timperlake.

(No American Can Be Environmentally Conscious)

United Nations Admits The Paris Climate Change Accord Was A Fraud/Investor's Business Daily
China Southern Morning Post (Pollution Section).

(Where Our History Is Headed If We Don't Change)

United Nations Admits The Paris Climate Accord Was A Fraud/Investor's Business News
China manufacturing for America is polluting the world.
China Air Pollution reduces cognitive abilities.
China pollution powers storms half-way around the world.
China pollution wreaks havoc on human health.
The pollution continues from across China.
Chinese city chokes on smog specks that are 'harder than steel.'
Chinese pollution is worsening in many parts of the country.
Chinese pollution is once again destroying the Earth's ozone layer.
Devastating effects of Chinese pollution.

344 BENNETT JOSHUA DAVLIN

China Southern Morning Post (Pollution Section).

(If You Read Only One Article...)

The Skeptic's Guide to American History by Professor Mark A. Stoler, Ph.D., The University of Vermont.
Machiavelli in Context by Professor William R. Cooks, Ph.D., State University of New York, Geneseo.
Manufacturing Job Loss, Economic Policy Institute.
List of innocent U.S. Citizen killed by illegal aliens.
Alexander Hamilton's Manufacturing Message, Brookings Institution.
Alexander Hamilton's Manufacturing Message, CNN.
Poverty, Prejudice, and Punishment, Harvard University.edu.
The Road to Serfdom by Friedrich Hayek

(Clinton, Bush, & Obama - Enemies Of The United States)

A History of the United States, 2nd Edition Taught By Multiple Professors.
The Skeptic's Guide to American History by Professor Mark A. Stoler, Ph.D. The University of Vermont.
Year of the Rat: How Bill Clinton Compromised American Security For Chinese Cash by Edward Timperlake.

(If Barack Obama Was the 44th White President)

Great Minds of the Western Intellectual Tradition, 3rd Edition taught by multiple professors.
The Skeptic's Guide to American History by Professor Mark A. Stoler, Ph.D., The University of Vermont.
History of the United States, 2nd Edition Taught By Multiple Professors.

(The Problem With The Major U.S. Political Parties)

The Manchurian Candidate, Motion Picture
Classical and Modern Political Theory by Professor Dennis Dalton, Ph.D., Barnard College, Columbia University.
The Skeptic's Guide to American History by Professor Mark A. Stoler, Ph.D., The University of Vermont.

(Understanding The 2008 Meltdown)

PBS Frontline Series: Inside The Meltdown

(Bill Clinton Created A Nuclear North Korea)

You Can thank Jimmy Carter and Bill Clinton for North Korea's Nukes, New York Post Editorial Board.

(The Incontrovertible Wickedness Of Socialism And Communism)

Utopia and Terror in the 20th Century by Professor Vejas Gabriel Liulevicius, Ph.D., University of Tennessee.
The Road to Serfdom by Friedrich Hayek
Stalin's Murderous Doctor Purge shortly before his death, BBC News animation
"Stalin" by Edvard Radzinksy
"How Sweden Overcame Socialism", Wall Street Journal, January 9, 2019
Foundation for Economic Education, "Canada's Laffer Curve Lesson: Government Collects Less Revenue from High-Income Earners after Trudeau Tax Hike

(Why Our Leaders Often Stink)

The March of Folly: From Troy to Vietnam by Barbara W. Tuchman
Machiavelli in Context, Professor William R. Cook, Ph.D., State University of New York, Geneseo.
A History of the United States, 2nd Edition Taught By Multiple Professors.
The Skeptic's Guide to American History by Professor Mark A. Stoler, Ph.D., The University of Vermont.
The Road To Serfdom by Friedrich Hayek
The Deep State by Jason Chaffets
Boss Tweed by Kenneth D. Ackerman

(Hillary Clinton, The Most Powerful Person In America)

Hillary Clinton Robbed Bernie Sanders of The Democratic Nominations According To Donna Brazile, Newsweek, 11/12/17
Documents: FBI reached 'conclusions' on laptop's Clinton emails before reviewing them, World Tribune.
The Road To Serfdom by Friedrich Hayek.
Machiavelli in Context Professor William R. Cook, Ph.D., State University of New York, Geneseo.
Economics, 3rd Edition by Professors Timothy Taylor, M. Econ., Macalaster College.
Legacies of Great Economists Professor Timothy Taylor, M. Econ., Macalaster College.
History of the U.S. Economy in the 20th Century by Professor Timothy Taylor, M. Econ., Macalaster College.
Power over People: Classical and Modern Political Theory by Professor Dennis Dalton, Ph.D., Barnard College, Columbia University.
Civil Liberties and the Bill of Rights by Professor John E. Finn, Ph.D., Wesleyan University.

(Bernie Sanders, The Real Red Nosed Reindeer)

Utopia and Terror in the 20th Century by Professor Vejas Gabriel Liulevicius, Ph.D., University of Tennessee.

Economics, 3rd Edition by Professors Timothy Taylor, M. Econ., Macalaster College.
Legacies of Great Economists Professor Timothy Taylor, M. Econ., Macalaster College.
History of the U.S. Economy in the 20th Century by Professor Timothy Taylor, M. Econ., Macalaster College.
The Road To Serfdom by Friedrich Hayek
Gulag: A History by Anne Applebaum.

(Trump, America's Modern Day George Washington)

Machiavelli in Context by Professor William R. Cooks, Ph.D., State University of New York, Geneseo.
List of innocent U.S. Citizen killed by illegal aliens.
Alexander Hamilton's Manufacturing Message, Brookings Institution.
Alexander Hamilton's Manufacturing Message, CNN.
The 1944 comic book, Road to Serfdom.
Year of the Rat: How Bill Clinton Sacrificed American Security for Cash by Edward Timperlake.
China manufacturing for America is polluting the world.
China Air Pollution reduces cognitive abilities.
China pollution powers storms half-way around the world.
China pollution wreaks havoc on human health.
The pollution continues from across China.
Chinese city chokes on smog specks that are 'harder than steel.'
Chinese pollution is worsening in many parts of the country.
Chinese pollution is once again destroying the Earth's ozone layer.
Devastating effects of Chinese pollution.
China Southern Morning Post (Pollution Section).
30 second commercial spot on China's economic takeover. History of the United States, 2nd Edition Taught By Multiple Professors.
China Morning Post (Pollution Section).
Manufacturing Job Loss, Economic Policy Institute.
The Skeptic's Guide to American History by Professor Mark A. Stoler, Ph.D., The University of Vermont.

(Washington's Economic Vision In Bullet Points)

A History of the United States, 2nd Edition Taught By Multiple Professors.
The Skeptic's Guide to American History by Professor Mark A. Stoler, Ph.D., The University of Vermont.

END URBAN CRIME & THE SYSTEMICALLY RACIST MASS-JAILING OF CLINTON, W.BUSH, AND OBAMA

JMC Junior Military Corp We will immediately begin to end urban violence, mass-imprisonment, and mass-rape of mostly

GOD'S GUIDE TO THE END OF THE WORLD 347

blacks and Latinos by having certain offenders serve in the JMC (Junior Military Corp) from the age of 12 to 18. Enlistees can apply for JMC officer status. After becoming an adult, they will serve the nation for four years in our armed services and have access to job training, and later the GI Bill.

Essays Dealing With This Point:

(How Tupac Shakur Taught Me How To End The Ghettos)

History of the U.S. Economy in the 20th Century Professor Timothy Taylor, M.Econ., Macalaster College.
A History of the United States, 2nd Edition Taught By Multiple Professors.
The Skeptic's Guide to American History by Professor Mark A. Stoler, Ph.D., The University of Vermont.

(I Have A Dream" – 2018)

Books That Have Made History: Books That Can Change Your Life, Rufus J. Fears, Ph.D., University of Oklahoma.
American Mind by Professor Allen C Guelzo, Ph.D., Gettysburg College.
A History of the United States, 2nd Edition Taught By Multiple Professors.
The Skeptic's Guide to American History by Professor Mark A. Stoler, Ph.D., The University of Vermont.

(Kanye West, The Only True, Modern Black American Leader)

A History of the United States, 2nd Edition Taught By Multiple Professors.
Life Rufus J. Fears, Ph.D., University of Oklahoma.
American Mind by Professor Allen C Guelzo, Ph.D., Gettysburg College.
A History of the United States, 2nd Edition Taught By Multiple Professors.
The Skeptic's Guide to American History by Professor Mark A. Stoler, Ph.D., The University of Vermont.

(The Apology Southerners Are Long Owed)

A History of the United States, 2nd Edition Taught By Multiple Professors.

(What America A Century Ago Would Think Of Us Today)

Books That Have Made History: Books That Can Change Your Life Rufus J. Fears, Ph.D., University of Oklahoma.
American Mind by Professor Allen C Guelzo, Ph.D., Gettysburg College.
A History of the United States, 2nd Edition Taught By Multiple Professors.
The Skeptic's Guide to American History by Professor Mark A. Stoler, Ph.D., The University of Vermont.

The Road to Serfdom by Friedrich Hayek

REAFFIRM THE RIGHT OF SELF-PROTECTION

Now more than ever, a citizen's right to bear arms is paramount and will be defended for all citizens. The focus will be on gun storage and the lack of stay at home mothers whose loss coincided with the new aberration of school shooters. Our government will also remove impediments to a female's right to choose to be a mother. While there is no liturgical support for such a movement except perversely inaccurate translations by unscrupulous religious intermediaries. Both the second amendment and Row V. Wade represent politicians meddling in the same right to protect your body from the harm of criminals and over-reaching politicians.

Essays Dealing With This Point:

(Why Our Leaders Often Stink)

The March of Folly: From Troy to Vietnam by Barbara W. Tuchman
Machiavelli in Context, Professor William R. Cook, Ph.D., State University of New York, Geneseo.
A History of the United States, 2nd Edition Taught By Multiple Professors.
The Skeptic's Guide to American History by Professor Mark A. Stoler, Ph.D., The University of Vermont.
The Road To Serfdom by Friedrich Hayek
The Deep State by Jason Chaffets
Boss Tweed by Kenneth D. Ackerman

ALLOW A TRUE SHELTER IN PLACE WITH REAL PPE

.40 mm NATO gas mask systems provide 100% protection and will be manufactured in the United States, provided to essential workers first followed by a deployment to all citizens, and then non-citizens to truly allow for a real national shelter in place. Every life matters.

Essays Dealing With This Point:

(Why Our Leaders Often Stink)

The March of Folly: From Troy to Vietnam by Barbara W. Tuchman
Machiavelli in Context, Professor William R. Cook, Ph.D., State University of New York, Geneseo.
A History of the United States, 2nd Edition Taught By Multiple Professors.
The Skeptic's Guide to American History by Professor Mark A. Stoler, Ph.D., The University of Vermont.
The Road To Serfdom by Friedrich Hayek
The Deep State by Jason Chaffets
Boss Tweed by Kenneth D. Ackerman

RESTORE FREE SPEECH & END THE CANCEL CULTURE

The horror of Charlottesville was stealing free speech from Nazis so that everyone then lost that right. First people were led to believe that they could attack others with contrary political hats or attire. Now if the president can't say what he wants, Big Tech has fomented a coup and individuals like Mark Zuckerberg for some politicians censor the president? I call for their immediate execution, acting like Sanctuary politicians as unilateral leaders in conflict with the Constitution. Who is in control of the nation if the president cannot speak? Google censors VK.com web address and many more. Various Big Tech executives should be arrested and or executed by the president for warring against our constitutional rights. They censor the president's comments on COVID-19, but had no issue with a pandemic directly caused by Biden and Obama's coverup of Hillary Clinton's mishandling of files killing the spies who could've warned our president. Or Obama's treasonous lie about private wealth ownership in Communist China in his documentary *American Factory* that would've led to his arrest in any administration before Clinton. To quote George Washington, free speech is ugly but the lack of it is far worse. The press must report the truths about Communism as it did before Clinton, W. Bush, and Obama and Biden's treason.

Essays Dealing With This Point:

(Charlottesville & Free Speech)

First Amendment of the U.S. Constitution.

Civil Liberties and the Bill of Rights Professor John E. Finn, Ph.D., Wesleyan University

(How To Realize The Media Is Fixed In Three Beats)

The New Media Monopoly, Ben H. Bagdikian.
Network newscasts don't mention Brazil Clinton-DNC revelations, The Hill
1984 by George Orwell.

(The Day Comedy and Freedom Died)

The First Amendment of the U.S. Constitution.
Michael Che: Comedy Unfunny.

(The Truth No Democrat Dares To Face)

Network newscasts don't mention Brazil Clinton-DNC revelations, The Hill
18 U.S. Code7898 Disclosure of Confidential Information.
Documents: FBI reached 'conclusions' on laptop's Clinton emails before reviewing them, World Tribune.
The Road To Serfdom by Friedrich Hayek
Machiavelli in Context Professor William R. Cook, Ph.D., State University of New York, Geneseo.

(The German Who Nearly Got Me Killed In The Sahara)

The Road to Serfdom by Friedrich Hayek The German Who Nearly Got Me Killed In The Sahara
Great Minds of the Western Intellectual Tradition, 3rd Edition taught by multiple professors.
The Danger of Political Party Mobs, Townhall.com.

(Holland Insults Its Noble Legacy)

Birth of The Modern Mind by Professor Alan Charles Kors, Ph.D., University of Pennsylvania.
Philosophy as a Guide to Living by Professor Stephen A. Erickson, Ph.D, Pomona College.
Great Minds of the Western Intellectual Tradition, 3rd Edition, taught by multiple professors.

(What America A Century Ago Would Think Of Us Today)

Books That Have Made History: Books That Can Change Your Life Rufus J. Fears, Ph.D., University of Oklahoma.
American Mind by Professor Allen C Guelzo, Ph.D., Gettysburg College.
A History of the United States, 2nd Edition Taught By Multiple Professors.

The Skeptic's Guide to American History by Professor Mark A. Stoler, Ph.D., The University of Vermont.
The Road to Serfdom by Friedrich Hayek

PROFESSIONAL SPORTS REFORM

The United States will join together to unify in saluting the flag. Professional athletes who do not stand for the flag will be restricted by the FCC from appearing on TV airwaves. Instead of "End Racism" in the NFL in-zone, the president should force a change to read "End The Treason of Clinton, W. Bush, Obama, racists who systemically jailed all urban blacks and Latinos."

Essays Dealing With This Point:

(Communist China and The NFL's Failure To Salute Our Flag)

Fatal Conceit by Friedrich Hayek
A History of the United States, 2nd Edition Taught By Multiple Professors.
The Skeptic's Guide to American History by Professor Mark A. Stoler, Ph.D., The University of Vermont.

(Saluting our flag)

Hell and Back Documentary Film

(What America A Century Ago Would Think Of Us Today)

Books That Have Made History: Books That Can Change Your Life Rufus J. Fears, Ph.D., University of Oklahoma.
American Mind by Professor Allen C Guelzo, Ph.D., Gettysburg College.
A History of the United States, 2nd Edition Taught By Multiple Professors.
The Skeptic's Guide to American History by Professor Mark A. Stoler, Ph.D., The University of Vermont.
The Road to Serfdom by Friedrich Hayek

(How To Realize The Media Is Fixed In Three Beats)

The New Media Monopoly, Ben H. Bagdikian.
Network newscasts don't mention Brazil Clinton-DNC revelations, The Hill 1984 by George Orwell.

ACADEMIC REFORM

Pardons and commutations will be offered all parents offered to break the rules in the college admission scandal. Instead, we will create a blue-ribbon investigative committee on Academic Corruption from illegal entrance offers, grade inflation, to outright treason by academics at Harvard and Stanford aiding Xi Jinping's viral labs and designs.

(A Dynamic Education Proposal)

10 scientific reasons people are wired to respond to your visual marketing, Andrew Tate, Canva.com.
Great Minds of the Western Intellectual Tradition, 3rd Edition taught by multiple professors.

(How Israel Can Fix Palestine)

History of the U.S. Economy in the 20th Century, by Professor Timothy Taylor, M.Econ., Macalaster College.
A History of the United States, 2nd Edition Taught By Multiple Professors.
Legacies of Great Economist by Professor Timothy Taylor, M.Econ., Macalaster College.

(Killing Our Darlings)

A History of the United States, 2nd Edition Taught By Multiple Professors.

(America A Poem)

A History of the United States, 2nd Edition Taught By Multiple Professors.

(The Consequences of Losing Sight of Our Imminent Resurrection)

Beginnings of Judaism Professor Isaiah M. Gafni, Ph.D., Hebrew University, Jerusalem.
Jesus and His Jewish Influence Professor Jodi Magness, Ph.D., University of North Carolina, Chapel Hill.
The King James Bible.
A Serious Man By Joel & Ethan Coen
The Buddha, PBS

(Fake Flowers)

Great Minds of the Western Intellectual Tradition, 3rd Edition taught by multiple professors5.4. Going Over A Dangerous Waterfall Will Teach You...

GOD'S GUIDE TO THE END OF THE WORLD 353

Great Minds of the Western Intellectual Tradition, 3rd Edition taught by multiple professors.

(What Being Caught In A Bloody Venezuelan Riot Will Teach You...)

No Excuses: Existentialism and The Meaning of Life Professor Robert C. Solomon, Ph.D., The University of Texas, Austin.
Great Minds of the Western Intellectual Tradition, 3rd Edition taught by multiple professors.

(What Diving Face First Into A 328 Ft. Hole Will Teach You...)

Great Minds of the Western Intellectual Tradition, 3rd Edition taught by multiple professors.

(What Being Chased By A Rogue Elephant Will Teach You...)

Great Minds of the Western Intellectual Tradition, 3rd Edition taught by multiple professors.
This incident occurred in the camp where Ernest Hemingway stayed and was inspired to write The Snows of Kilimanjaro.

(The Lie of The Dark Amazon)

Great Minds of the Western Intellectual Tradition, 3rd Edition taught by multiple professors.
Matrix, the motion picture

(What Facing Danger Will Teach You...)

No Excuses: Existentialism and the Meaning of Life Professor Robert C. Solomon, Ph.D., University of Texas, Austin.
Great Minds of the Western Intellectual Tradition, 3rd Edition taught by multiple professors.

(Science's Dirty Secret)

U.N. admits The Paris Climate Accord was a fraud/Investor's Business Daily
Descartes in 90 minutes.
Great Minds of the Western Intellectual Tradition, 3rd Edition taught by multiple professors.
Birth of The Modern Mind Professor Alan Charles Kors, Ph.D., University of Pennsylvania.

(If Barack Obama Was the 44th White President)

Great Minds of the Western Intellectual Tradition, 3rd Edition taught by multiple professors.
The Skeptic's Guide to American History by Professor Mark A. Stoler, Ph.D., The University of Vermont.
History of the United States, 2nd Edition Taught By Multiple Professors.

(Science Supports Life After Death in Three Lines)

Fact or Fiction?: Energy Can Neither Be Created Nor Destroyed by Clara Moskowitz, Scientific American Magazine August 5, 2014.
Exploring Metaphysics Professor David Kyle Johnson, Ph.D., King's College
Descartes in 90 minutes by Paul Strathern.
Beginnings of Judaism Professor Isaiah M. Gafni, Ph.D., Hebrew University, Jerusalem.
Jesus and His Jewish Influence Professor Jodi Magness, Ph.D., University of North Carolina, Chapel Hill.
The King James Bible.
(The Key to Life found in Rudyard Kipling's Poem If by Rudyard Kipling)

If by Rudyard Kipling5.15. How Einstein's Theory of Relativity Can Usher in the Messianic Age
Einstein's Universe, The Movie.
Einstein's Relativity and the Quantum Revolution" Modern Physics for Non-Scientists, 2nd Edition by Professor Richard Wolfson, Ph.D., Middlebury College

(History's Most Amazing Leader)

Europe, a History by Norman Davies.
A Brief History of the World Professor Peter N. Stearns, Ph.D., George Mason University.

(Theologians' Failure To Make Great Strides)

Great Minds of the Western Intellectual Tradition, 3rd Edition taught by multiple professors.
Beginnings of Judaism Professor Isaiah M. Gafni, Ph.D., Hebrew University, Jerusalem.
Jesus and his Jewish Influence by Professor Jodi Magness, Ph.D., University of North Carolina, Chapel Hill.

(The Unrealized Wickedness of Good Intentions)

The March of Folly: Troy to Vietnam by Barbara W. Tuchman
A Brief History of the World, Professor Peter N. Stearns, Ph.D., George Mason University.

(Elijah's Message To The Israelites And Why It Matters To Everyone)

Beginnings of Judaism Professor Isaiah M. Gafni, Ph.D., Hebrew University, Jerusalem.
Jesus and His Jewish Influences Professor Jodi Magnes, Ph.D., University of North Caroline, Chapel Hill
Religions in the Ancient Mediterranean World Professor Glenn S. Holland, Ph.D., Allegheny College
The Torah.
Book of Malachi.
Complete Old Testament.

The Jewish Talmud and the Death of Christ
Analysis of Christ in The Talmud by Dr. David InStone-Brewer, Senior Research Fellow in Rabbinics and the New Testament, Tyndale House, Cambridge
Menashe, the movie.

(Unifying Science and Almost All Religions)

Beginnings of Judaism Professor Isaiah M. Gafni, Ph.D., Hebrew University, Jerusalem.
Jesus and his Jewish Influence by Professor Jodi Magness, Ph.D., University of North Carolina, Chapel Hill.
Between the Rivers: The History of Ancient Mesopotamia Professor Glenn S. Holland, Ph.D., Allegheny College.
The Fall of The Pagans Professor Kenneth W. Harl, Ph.D., Tulane University.
Late Antiquity: Crisis and Transformation Professor Thomas X. Noble, Ph.D., University of Notre Dame.
The Early Middle Ages Professor Philip Daileader, Ph.D., The College of William and Mary.
Great World Religions: Islam, Professor John L. Esposito, Ph.D., Georgetown University.
Great Minds of the Western Intellectual Tradition, 3rd Edition taught by multiple professors.
Birth of the Modern Mind by Professor Alan Charles Kors, Ph.D., University of Pennsylvania
Descartes in 90 Minutes by Paul Strathern
The Structure of Scientific Revolutions by Thomas S. Kuhn.
The Brothers Karamazov (particular focus on The Grand Inquisitor) by Fyodor Dostoevsky.
A History of Warfare by John Keegan.
Europe: A History by Dr. Norman Davies
King James Bible.

(Thoughts To Consider On Prayer)

Psychology of Human Behavior by Professor David W. Martin, Ph.D., North Carolina State University.
Passions: Philosophy and the Intelligence of Emotions Professor Robert C. Solomon, Ph.D., The University of Texas at Austin.

(Ellen G. White's The Great Controversy 2020)

The Great Controversy: Between Christ and Satan by Ellen G. White.
Descartes in 90 Minutes by Paul Strathern.
Dreamspace: the novel by Bennett Joshua Davlin.
Beginnings of Judaism Professor Isaiah M. Gafni, Ph.D., Hebrew University, Jerusalem.
Jesus and his Jewish Influence by Professor Jodi Magness, Ph.D., University of North Carolina, Chapel Hill.
Between the Rivers: The History of Ancient Mesopotamia Professor Glenn S. Holland, Ph.D., Allegheny College.

356　BENNETT JOSHUA DAVLIN

The Fall of The Pagans Professor Kenneth W. Harl, Ph.D., Tulane University.
Late Antiquity: Crisis and Transformation Professor Thomas X. Noble, Ph.D., University of Notre Dame.
Great Minds of the Western Intellectual Tradition, 3rd Edition taught by Multiple Professors
The Early Middle Ages Professor Philip Daileader, Ph.D., The College of William and Mary.
King James Bible

LGBTQ REFORM

Before representation and acceptance of LBQT in mass media, male homosexuals must come clean about the childhood molestation which most suffered in youth from older child rapists who now must be separated from their many victims before this class can be offered special legal protections. Transexual Perversions such as cross-dressing remains a person's personal business and is to be kept at home as it always was, shielded from children in public life. Transsexuals have no right to enter a lady's bathroom without security or cameras where no matter what one may think, the female is incontrovertibly the weaker of the species. While children can be scarred from such deviant behavior which is usually the vestige of early childhood rape or trauma. Politicians are not allowed to further harm the next generation, making eunuchs of at-risk minority kids but are charged with protecting the most at risk.

Essays Dealing With This Point:

(We're All Gloria Steinem's Children)

Epoch Times, Inside The Transgender Empire by Christopher F. Rufe
Stanford University Medicine News Center: Mom's voice activates many different regions in children's brains.

<u>HOLLYWOOD PEDOPHILE REFORM</u>

Hollywood pedophiles and those creating sexually reprogramming content will be investigated. Chinese funding will be removed from our media which will not be allowed to censor their material for China. When creative material became political or unilaterally censors for a Communist dictatorship they act as a threat to this nation and undermine our national security.

Essays Dealing With This Point:

(The Day Comedy and Freedom Died)

**The First Amendment of the U.S. Constitution.
Michael Che: Comedy Unfunny.**

G5 WIRELESS SYSTEM REASSESSMENT

We will pause the G5 network until more studies can be done, following Apple's reservations about this new system. Keep in mind that the prior web signal which is even less intense has been shown to cause serious personal injury.

INFRASTRUCTURE RENEWAL

Our nation will underwrite the rebuilding of eroded infrastructure, work only be done only by American firms with a priority on small and veteran-owned businesses underwritten by the SBA.

FEDERALLY LEGALIZED MARIJUANA

Marijuana will be federally legal under my executive order. I will work with Congress to make this move under federal law.

END UNCONSTITUTIONAL WIRETAPPING

Our government despite the actions begun by W. Bush and continued by Obama cannot be allowed to mass-wiretap citizens in a move that was politicized into the treasonous wiretapping of then-candidate Donald J. Trump by Obama and Biden for which they should now be indicted along with everyone else involved.

Essays Dealing With This Point:

(Clinton's Economic Lie)

The Manchurian Candidate, Motion Picture by John Frankenheimer (1962)
A History of the United States, 2nd Edition Taught By Multiple Professors.
The Skeptic's Guide to American History by Professor Mark A. Stoler, Ph.D., The University of Vermont.
Year of the Rat: How Bill Clinton Compromised U.S. Security for Chinese Cash by Edward Timperlake.

(Clinton, Bush, & Obama - Enemies Of The United States)

A History of the United States, 2nd Edition Taught By Multiple Professors.
The Skeptic's Guide to American History by Professor Mark A. Stoler, Ph.D. The University of Vermont.
Year of the Rat: How Bill Clinton Compromised American Security For Chinese Cash by Edward Timperlake.

(If You Read Only One Article...)

The Skeptic's Guide to American History by Professor Mark A. Stoler, Ph.D., The University of Vermont.
Machiavelli in Context by Professor William R. Cooks, Ph.D., State University of New York, Geneseo.
Manufacturing Job Loss, Economic Policy Institute.
List of innocent U.S. Citizen killed by illegal aliens.
Alexander Hamilton's Manufacturing Message, Brookings Institution.
Alexander Hamilton's Manufacturing Message, CNN.
Poverty, Prejudice, and Punishment, Harvard University.edu.
The Road to Serfdom by Friedrich Hayek

(Putin, Russia's Greatest Leader)

History of Russia: From Peter the Great to Gorbachev Professor Mark Steinberg, Ph.D., University of Illinois, Urbana-Champaign.
Rise and Fall of Soviet Communism: A History of 20th Century Russia Professor Gary Hamburg, Ph.D., Claremont McKenna College.
A History of the United States, 2nd Edition Taught By Multiple Professors.
The Skeptic's Guide to American History by Professor Mark A. Stoler, Ph.D., The University of Vermont.

A WORD ON DEBT

All those who might scream about rising debt from these policies should consider the unsustainable debt that 30 years of treason by Democrats and non-Trumpian Republicans created. By abandoning manufacturing, America abandoned the act of generating wealth.

It is little appreciated that the United States in times of war can draw on record debt just as it did during the 30 years of treason. Added taxation will only slow the economy and impair even our current debt repayment. Only manufacturing can grow our way out of this record debt required to continue the country alongside COVID-19. But it is an investment in an essential, thriving manufacturing society like every president from Washington to Clinton upheld. Manufacturing allows us to eventually grow out of the debt

Just as in World War II, there will probably be no financial markets or realistic currency value outside the United States after the virus and the environmental mayhem to follow from this stage of the Cold War. This general reform from the damage of treason is a temporary war-footed government supply-side-economic policy to eradicate artificially set labor prices. The price of labor is too low can further be subsidized, but removing this price control will lower the cost of manufactured goods.

Failure to follow these policies will end the United States of America. By reviewing George Washington, Alexander Hamilton, and the Founding Fathers' prophecy of our current quagmire, anyone will realize they would advocate my plan.

Essays Dealing With This Point:

(Why America Can't Help But Underpin The World Economy)

History of the U.S. Economy in the 20th Century Professor Timothy Taylor, M.Econ., Macalaster College.
A History of the United States, 2nd Edition Taught By Multiple Professors.

The Skeptic's Guide to American History by Professor Mark A. Stoler, Ph.D., The University of Vermont.

(The Wicked Lie Of Price Controls)

Economics, 3rd Edition by Professor Timothy Taylor, M. Econ., Macalaster College.
Legacies of Great Economists by Professor Timothy Taylor, M. Econ., Macalaster College.
History of the U.S. Economy in the 20th Century by Professor Timothy Taylor, M. Econ., Macalaster College.
The Road to Serfdom by Friedrich Hayek

(I Owe USA)

Legacies of Great Economists Professor Timothy Taylor, M. Econ., Macalaster College.
History of the U.S. Economy in the 20th Century by Professor Timothy Taylor, M. Econ., Macalaster College.
The Road To Serfdom by Friedrich Hayek

(History's Most Amazing Leader)

Europe, a History by Norman Davies.
A Brief History of the World Professor Peter N. Stearns, Ph.D., George Mason University.

(An Indictment of The U.S. Service Economy & The Lie of *Globalism*)

United Nations Admits That The Paris Climate Accord was a fraud
The Skeptic's Guide to American History by Professor Mark A. Stoler, Ph.D., The University of Vermont.
Machiavelli in Context by Professor William R. Cooks, Ph.D., State University of New York, Geneseo.
Manufacturing Job Loss, Economic Policy Institute.
List of innocent U.S. Citizen killed by illegal aliens.
Alexander Hamilton's Manufacturing Message, Brookings Institution.
Alexander Hamilton's Manufacturing Message, CNN.
Poverty, Prejudice, and Punishment, Harvard University.edu.
The Road to Serfdom by Friedrich Hayek Economics, 3rd Edition by Professors Timothy Taylor, M. Econ., Macalaster College.

(Visualizing The True Cost Of The Clintonian Service Economy)

History of the U.S. Economy in the 20th Century Professor Timothy Taylor, M.Econ., Macalaster College.
A History of the United States, 2nd Edition Taught By Multiple Professors.

GOD'S GUIDE TO THE END OF THE WORLD 361

The Skeptic's Guide to American History by Professor Mark A. Stoler, Ph.D., The University of Vermont.

(Why Our Leaders Often Stink)

The March of Folly: From Troy to Vietnam by Barbara W. Tuchman
Machiavelli in Context, Professor William R. Cook, Ph.D., State University of New York, Geneseo.
A History of the United States, 2nd Edition Taught By Multiple Professors.
The Skeptic's Guide to American History by Professor Mark A. Stoler, Ph.D., The University of Vermont.
The Road To Serfdom by Friedrich Hayek
The Deep State by Jason Chaffets
Boss Tweed by Kenneth D. Ackerman
(A Message To Millennials: The United States of The Damned)

United Nations Admits That The Paris Climate Accord was a fraud
A History of the United States, 2nd Edition Taught By Multiple Professors.
The Skeptic's Guide to American History by Professor Mark A. Stoler, Ph.D. The University of Vermont.
Machiavelli in Context, Professor William R. Cook, Ph.D., State University of New York, Geneseo.
The Road To Serfdom by Friedrich Hayek

(I Owe U.S.A.)

Economics, 3rd Edition by Professors Timothy Taylor, M. Econ., Macalaster College.
Legacies of Great Economists Professor Timothy Taylor, M. Econ., Macalaster College.
History of the U.S. Economy in the 20th Century by Professor Timothy Taylor, M. Econ., Macalaster College.
The Road To Serfdom by Friedrich Hayek

(What Is Lost By Not Calling "Sh*tholes", "Sh*tholes")

Psychology Today.com "Remembering Things From Before You Were Born" by Dr. Berit Brogaard.
Louis Theroux: Law and Disorder in Johannesburg
Louis Theroux: Law and Disorder in Lagos
Max Weber video
Great Minds of The Western Intellectual Tradition, 3rd Edition taught by multiple professors.

Appendix (c)
SCRIPTURAL REFUTATION OF THE PRO-LIFE MOVEMENT
(*REPRINTED FROM *SAINT MICHAEL STOOD UP*)

This appendix explores the blatant lies of the so-called pro-life movement that lacks any supporting liturgical proof for their cause.

The Pro-Life movement is scripturally unfounded in the Hebrew Bible as will be shown when we review the major scriptural verses used by this movement.[20] These verses in no way prohibit a pregnant woman's choice to not become a mother. God stresses that He controls everything and if He wants someone born as these verses prove, He'll have it so.

The pro-life campaign whether consciously or unconsciously benefits Gog, stealing liberty from citizens, and allowing bureaucrats to force motherhood upon females in a way not broached in the Hebrew Bible. More crucially, it divides Americans often by gender, extending unfounded constitutional rights to the unborn while the opposing Democrat party extends such new rights to illegal aliens. This illicit movement constitutes half of Gog's sway over Americans, revealing that most believers just take the word of their spiritual intermediaries who are by definition prohibited in the Hebrew bible.

Ironically, many of the same ministers advocating for the Pro-Life movement, lacking any scriptural foundation, likewise support the liturgically forbidden act of sodomy with the notable exception of the Westboro Baptist Church alone vociferously upholding this Divine proscription, while highlighting it in the media.

Let's examine the verses used by this movement, the first dealing with Eve who was, in fact, never a fetus.

Genesis 1:27
"So God created man in His own image, in the image of God He created him; male and female He created them."

---

[20] verses quoted from www.focusonthefamily.com.

God's modern covenant via the U.S. Constitution grants citizenship with birth.

Job 33:4
"The Spirit of God has made me, and the breath of the Almighty gives me life."

Again, this next psalm is from someone the Lord fated to be born as we decide, but He chooses our steps.

Psalm 119:73
"Your hands made me and formed me."

This next person has also been deemed worthy of being born and living as part of God's will.

Psalm 139:13-16
"For you formed my inward parts; you knitted me together in my mother's womb. I praise you, for I am fearfully and wonderfully made. Wonderful are your works; my soul knows it very well. My frame was not hidden from you, when I was being made in secret, intricately woven in the depths of the earth. Your eyes saw my unformed substance; in your book were written, every one of them, the days that were formed for me, when as yet there was none of them."

Job was allowed to be born and later reflect the following statement.

Job 10: 11-12
"You clothed me with skin and flesh,
and knit me together with bones and sinews.
You have granted me life and steadfast love."

The next verse deals with Divine pregnancy without sex, which is not comparable to normal pregnant humans.

Matthew 1:20
"But as he considered these things, behold, an angel of the Lord appeared to him in a dream, saying, 'Joseph, son of David, do not fear to take Mary as your wife, for that which is conceived in her is from the Holy Spirit.'"

Luke 1:15
"He will be filled with the Holy Spirit, even from his mother's womb."

The Lord knows everything and alone sits in judgment.

Psalm 100:3
"Know that the Lord is God. It is he who made us, and we are his; we are his people, the sheep of his pasture."

The next verse solidifies the Lord is in charge of all things, like who will be born.

Isaiah 44:24
"Thus says the Lord, your Redeemer, who formed you from the womb: 'I am the Lord, who made all things, who alone stretched out the heavens, who spread out the earth by myself.'"

Humans as the Lord's proverbial clay would best trust in their potter.

Isaiah 64:8
"But now, O Lord, you are our Father; we are the clay, and you are our potter; we are all the work of your hand."

The next verse deals with children already born.

Psalm 127:3-5
"Behold, children are a heritage from the Lord, the fruit of the womb a reward. Like arrows in the hand of a warrior are the children of one's youth. Blessed is the man who fills his quiver with them!"

God chose a prophet from the womb and Jeremiah was indeed born to serve Him as most do not as a prophet.

Jeremiah 1:5
"Before I formed you in your mother's body I chose you. Before you were born I set you apart to serve me. I appointed you to be a prophet to the nations.'"

The baby in the next verse may leap in the womb, but the mother solely decides to be a mother.

Luke 1:41, 44
"When Elizabeth heard the greeting of Mary, the baby leaped in her womb. [And she exclaimed], 'when the sound of your greeting reached my ears, the baby in my womb leaped for joy.'"

The next verse is of the prophet Isaiah who was called to be born, while others are not.

Isaiah 49:1, 5
"The Lord called me from the womb…formed me from the womb to be his servant."

Again God fates a special someone to be born.

Galatians 1:15
"But God set me apart from the time I was born. He showed me his grace by appointing me."

Christ died for women to be free in their life choices.

Ephesians 1:3-4
"Blessed be the God and Father of our Lord Jesus Christ, who has blessed us in Christ with every spiritual blessing in the heavenly places, even as he chose us in him before the foundation of the world, that we should be holy and blameless before him."

GOD'S GUIDE TO THE END OF THE WORLD

Isaiah speaks of already-born children.

Isaiah 45:9-11
"How terrible it will be for anyone who argues with his Maker! He is like a broken piece of pottery lying on the ground. Does clay say to a potter, 'What are you making?' Does a pot say, 'You don't have any skill'? How terrible it will be for anyone who says to his father, 'Why did you give me life?' How terrible for anyone who says to his mother, 'Why have you brought me into the world?' The Lord is the Holy One of Israel. He made them. He says to them, 'Are you asking me about what will happen to my children? Are you telling me what I should do with what my hands have made?'"

The Lord next makes clear that people are to use reason and not falsely assert His laws.

Exodus 4:11
"The Lord said to him, 'Who makes a man able to talk? Who makes him unable to hear or speak? Who makes him able to see? Who makes him blind? It is I, the Lord.'"

Notwithstanding whether abortion is shameful, God has set up our world to make decisions, learn, and carry shame if need be.

1 Corinthians 1:27
"But God chose what is foolish in the world to shame the wise; God chose what is weak in the world to shame the strong."

The next verse deals with shedding the blood of a man, a human long-born and matured and not a fetus.

Genesis 9:6
"Whoever sheds the blood of man, by man shall his blood be shed, for God made man in his own image."

In the context of the next verse, since life begins after birth, abortion cannot be murder.

Exodus 20:13
"'You shall not murder.'"

The next verse is also invalid, since to "kill" by law, the victim must first be born.

Exodus 23:7
"Do not kill the innocent and righteous."

A woman choosing not to be a mother is not comparable to a pregnant mother mass-assaulted and her fetus ripped from her belly against her will as depicted in the next verse.

Amos 1:13-14
"The people of Ammon have sinned again and again. So I will punish them. They ripped open the pregnant women in Gilead."

This next verse protects women wishing to be mothers.

Exodus 21:22-25
"If men struggle with each other and strike a woman with child so that she gives birth prematurely, yet there is no injury, he shall surely be fined as the woman's husband may demand of him, and he shall pay as the judges decide. But if there is any further injury, then you shall appoint as a penalty life for life, eye for eye, tooth for tooth, hand for hand, foot for foot, burn for burn, wound for wound, bruise for bruise."

In the next verse, fetuses are not individuals born of a woman who are later rich or poor. Fetuses are unborn.

Proverbs 31:8
"Speak up for those who can't speak for themselves. Speak up for the rights of all those who are poor."

GOD'S GUIDE TO THE END OF THE WORLD 371

This verse relates to living people, long-born.

Proverbs 24: 11-12
"Rescue those who are being taken away to death; hold back those who are stumbling to the slaughter. If you say, "Behold, we did not know this," does not he who weighs the heart perceive it? Does not he who keeps watch over your soul know it, and will he not repay man according to his work?"

This next verse references widows and orphans who require protection after they've been born.

James 1:27
"Pure and undefiled religion before our God and Father is this: to look after orphans and widows in their distress and to keep oneself unstained by the world."

Bullying people without God's liturgical support is nothing like the activities noted in the next verse.

Isaiah 1:17
"Learn to do good; seek justice, correct oppression; bring justice to the fatherless, plead the widow's cause."

The following four verses are related to people born and living.

Hosea 14:3
"In you the orphan finds mercy."

Deuteronomy 27:19
"Cursed is he who distorts the justice due an alien, orphan, and widow."

Psalm 41:1
"Blessed is the one who considers the poor! In the day of trouble the Lord delivers him."

Psalm 68:6
"God makes a home for the lonely;
He leads out the prisoners into prosperity."

This next verse is the Lord's indictment of the pro-life movement.

Psalm 10: 12-15
"Lord, rise up! God, show your power! Don't forget those who are helpless. Why do sinful people attack you with their words? Why do they say to themselves, 'He won't hold us accountable'? God, you see trouble and sadness.
You take note of it. You do something about it. So those who are attacked place themselves in your care. You help children whose fathers have died. Take away the power of bad and sinful people. Hold them accountable for the evil things they do. Uncover all the evil they have done."

These next verses aren't applicable for the unborn, but show what pro-life supporters should be doing.

Isaiah 58: 6-10
"Set free those who are held by chains without any reason. Untie the ropes that hold people as slaves. Set free those who are crushed. Break every evil chain. Share your food with hungry people. Provide homeless people with a place to stay. Give naked people clothes to wear. Provide for the needs of your own family. Then the light of my blessing will shine on you like the rising sun. I will heal you quickly. I will march out ahead of you. And my glory will follow behind you and guard you. That is because I always do what is right. You will call out to me for help. And I will answer you. You will cry out. And I will say, 'Here I am.' Get rid of the chains you use to hold others down. Stop pointing your finger at others as if they had done something wrong. Stop saying harmful things about them. Work hard to feed hungry people. Satisfy the needs of those who are crushed. Then my blessing will light up your darkness. And the night of your suffering will become as bright as the noonday sun."

Matthew 25: 34-40
"Then the King will say to those on his right, 'Come, you who are blessed by my Father, inherit the kingdom prepared for you from the foundation of the world. For I was hungry and you gave me food, I was thirsty and you gave me drink, I was a stranger and you welcomed me, I was naked and you clothed me, I was sick and you visited me, I was in prison and you came to me.' Then the righteous will answer him, saying, 'Lord, when did we see you hungry and feed you, or thirsty and give you drink? And when did we see you a stranger and welcome you, or naked and clothe you? And when did we see you sick or in prison and visit you?' And the King will answer them, 'Truly, I say to you, as you did it to one of the least of these my brothers, you did it to me.'"

Luke 4: 18-19
"The Spirit of the Lord is upon me, because he has anointed me to proclaim good news to the poor. He has sent me to proclaim liberty to the captives and recovery of sight to the blind, to set at liberty those who are oppressed, to proclaim the year of the Lord's favor."

The Pro-Life Movement should reexamine their goals and quit picking on other Americans without doing their liturgical homework.

Just as 1920s Prohibition fed the rule of mobsters, the Pro-Life Movement fed the country to Magog mobsters set on destroying our nation.

Doing God's will means following the laws, not abusing clearly stated words to justify new, invasive actions.

Deuteronomy 30:19
"I call heaven and earth to witness against you today, that I have set before you life and death, blessing and curse. Therefore choose life, that you and your offspring may live."

In the end, we are expected to enforce the laws, not break or alter them while affecting such basic rights. The Pro-Life Movement picked on vulnerable, low-hanging fruit while ignoring the growing threat of pedophilia through the social spread of male sodomy, despite the proscription against it in the Hebrew Bible.

Leviticus 20:13
"If a man also lie with mankind, as he lieth with a woman, both of them have committed an abomination: they shall surely be put to death; their blood shall be upon them."

Leviticus 18:22
"Thou shalt not lie with mankind, as with womankind: it is abomination."

Genesis 19:1-38
And there came two angels to Sodom at evening ; and Lot sat in the gate of Sodom: and Lot seeing them rose up to meet them; and he bowed himself with his face toward the ground;"

1 Kings 14:24
"And there were also sodomites in the land: and they did according to all the abominations of the nations which the LORD cast out before the children of Israel."

1 Kings 15:12
And he took away the sodomites out of the land, and removed all the idols that his fathers had made."

Genesis 19:5
"And they called unto Lot, and said unto him, Where are the men which came in to thee this night? bring them out unto us, that we may know them."

Appendix (d)
SCRIPTURAL INDEX BY KEY TOPIC

This appendix breaks God's message into a short list of topics with supporting biblical citation. The abbreviated term "proCom" is used to mean the U.S. enriching Chinese Communism's tyrant Gog begun by Clinton, have America as part of Magog.

Key Point	Book	Chapter	Verse	Note
Aliens	Genesis	6	2	Genesis explains these are aliens
Aliens	Numbers	13	33	Aliens, further explored in Book of Enoch
Aliens	Deuteronomy	2	11	Aliens
Aliens	Joshua	11	15	Anakim were aliens via Book of Enoch
Aliens	Psalm	104	30	Omuamua, not interrupt path of entropy
American treason/antidepressant	Isaiah	28	1	Americans on antidepressants, drugs, denial
American treason/antidepressant	Isaiah	28	7 to 8	No one follows His laws, righteousness lost
American treason/antidepressants	Proverbs	31	6 to 7	Quit taking anti-depressants, its killing the U.S.
American treason/birth control	Hosea	9	11 to 13	Birth control, sexual immorality killed the U.S.
American treason/birth control	Hosea	13	12 to 13	Sexual immorality made fatherless kids
American treason/cities	Genesis	4	23 to 24	Cities breed violent leaders, now even U.S.
American treason/cities	Proverbs	21	22	Cities are the sin of our nation
American treason/cities	Proverbs	28	11	God's message reveals suicidal rich people
American treason/cities	Isaiah	1	21	The cities are Magog, murderers, all else
American treason/cities	Isaiah	1	22	Your businesses are gone without QE1 & 2
American treason/cities	Isaiah	3	14 to 15	The Lord refutes open immigration, pro-life, China
American treason/cities	Isaiah	4	1 to 2	Women destroyed the world
American treason/cities	Isaiah	51	4 to 5	The coasts can be reformed or die
American treason/cities	Jeremiah	2	27 to 28	Your cities became your Gog and they fed Gog
American treason/cities	Ezekiel	22	6 to 7	Cities turn Americans and illegals into slaves
American treason/cities	Ezekiel	22	11 to 12	Cities are full of bribes and sexual immorality
American treason/cities	Ezekiel	22	13	Cities would be gone without QE2 & QE3
American treason/cities	Ezekiel	24	6	God condemns the cities
American treason/cities	Micah	6	9 to 12	He hates U.S. elites with no God like all before
American treason/cities	Nahum	3	3	Likewise, God feels about modern U.S. cities
American treason/cities	Habakkuk	2	12 to 14	Cities are damned
American treason/cities	Zephaniah	3	1 to 2	Likewise condemnation of U.S. port cities
American treason/conservatism	Ecclesiastes	1	9 to 10	LGBTQ and Magog lead to slavery & death
American treason/counter culture	Genesis	14	18 to 19	Belief in God is required to be a good leader
American treason/counter culture	Isaiah	28	13	The fall into Communism began with the counterculture
American treason/counter culture	Isaiah	29	13	Humans traded God's wisdom for wickedness
American treason/COVID	Leviticus	26	16 to 17	America's punishment
American treason/COVID	Leviticus	26	25 to 26	America's punishment

American treason/COVID	Leviticus	26	31	America's punishment
American treason/COVID	Deuteronomy	28	59	USA immigration
American treason/COVID	Samuel 1	15	32 to 33	The Lord detests murderers
American treason/COVID	Isaiah	10	17 to 18	The Lord will end the world (1 of 5)
American treason/COVID	Isaiah	26	20	Stay inside your dwelling when asteroid comes
American treason/COVID	Isaiah	28	14 to 15	You felt Communism wouldn't come for you but it comes
American treason/COVID	Isaiah	28	18 to 20	Our society must be reorganized by COVID
American treason/COVID	Isaiah	33	1	U.S. Magog is plundered by China's COVID
American treason/COVID	Isaiah	33	14	Our leaders will admit COVID never left
American treason/COVID	Isaiah	33	24	No COVID once the Lord arrives
American treason/COVID	Isaiah	40	29 to 31	COVID kills the next generation
American treason/COVID	Jeremiah	4	5 to 6	COVID-19 is the mark of the imminent, ongoing invasion
American treason/COVID	Jeremiah	4	4	Can't face When lab, then you will be laid waste
American treason/COVID	Jeremiah	4	10	God is why you won't face a Wuhan Lab
American treason/COVID	Jeremiah	5	5	Our leaders burst bond to the right & to life
American treason/COVID	Jeremiah	5	15 to 17	U.S. Magog is a Chinese economic & mind invasion
American treason/COVID	Jeremiah	6	22 to 23	China came in a storm on horsemen
American treason/COVID	Jeremiah	6	24 to 25	And you got COVID-19
American treason/COVID	Jeremiah	8	16	Versus a viral & political enemy of both parties
American treason/COVID	Jeremiah	8	21 to 22	This disease is incurable & workers die
American treason/COVID	Jeremiah	9	7 to 9	So He brought COVID-19 and all that followed
American treason/COVID	Jeremiah	10	22	Gog will kill you with his masked viruses
American treason/COVID	Jeremiah	11	19	USA, Ephraim is naïve about their dire leaders
American treason/COVID	Jeremiah	12	12	The USA will be cleared away by COVID-19
American treason/COVID	Jeremiah	30	5	COVID revealed war rather than peace exists
American treason/COVID	Jeremiah	30	6 to 7	He can save the USA from COVID
American treason/COVID	Jeremiah	30	12	The Lord is the one who hurt you through hosts
American treason/COVID	Jeremiah	30	13	You have no one to lead you
American treason/COVID	Jeremiah	30	15	COVID is incurable
American treason/COVID	Jeremiah	30	17	The Lord will heal COVID
American treason/COVID	Ezekiel	28	23	Plagues feed violence and false judgment
American treason/COVID	Ezekiel	38	1 to 3	The Lord condemns China's dictator
American treason/COVID	Ezekiel	38	4 to 6	The Lord calls out China's foreign cohorts
American treason/COVID	Ezekiel	38	7 to 8	The Lord notes the USA as the promised land
American treason/COVID	Ezekiel	38	9	Infected Chinese in airplanes of a viral cloud
American treason/COVID	Ezekiel	38	10 to 12	The Lord reveals China's evil plan

American treason/COVID	Ezekiel	38	13	Lord notes world doesn't suspect viral plan
American treason/COVID	Ezekiel	38	14 to 16	Lord notes China's evil plan from the north
American treason/COVID	Ezekiel	38	17	The Lord predicted and sent China attack
American treason/COVID	Ezekiel	38	18 to 20	The Lord destroys the Earth with Daniel's rock
American treason/COVID	Ezekiel	39	3 to 8	The Lord will send an earthquake on w coast
American treason/COVID	Ezekiel	39	11	The earthquake ends COVID-19 spreaders
American treason/COVID	Ezekiel	39	12 to 13	There will be a lot of dead to pick up post-quake
American treason/COVID	Ezekiel	39	14 to 16	The post-quake cleanup lasts 7 months
American treason/COVID	Ezekiel	39	23 to 25	Your lack of faith delivered you to your enemies
American treason/COVID	Ezekiel	44	23	Leaders were supposed to teach our laws
American treason/COVID	Ezekiel	45	8 to 9	My plans make USA cushy
American treason/COVID	Daniel	8	25	COVID 19 is his deceit
American treason/COVID	Daniel	8	26	An end time prophecy
American treason/COVID	Daniel	9	8 to 12	Financial destruction wrecking U.S. is same now
American treason/COVID	Hosea	5	13 to 14	Likewise, Ephraim has no cure for COVID
American treason/COVID	Hosea	13	15	U.S. abandoned manufacturing and died
American treason/COVID	Micah	6	13 to 14	The Lord thins the U.S. out like those before it
American treason/COVID	Nahum	1	12 to 13	His destruction will free you
American treason/COVID	Habakkuk	2	6 to 8	After COVID, U.S. is plundered
American treason/COVID	Zechariah	5	3 to 4	COVID-19 is the worldwide curse
American treason/equal taxation	Exodus	30	15	equal taxation
American treason/forest	Ezekiel	39	9 to 10	Enemy didn't pick up wood, weaponized w coast
American treason/immigration	Genesis	16	11 to 12	Refutation of multiculturalism/ Arabs are such
American treason/immigration	Exodus	11	7	God refutes multiculturalism
American treason/immigration	Exodus	12	49	USA immigration, one law not double laws
American treason/immigration	Exodus	23	3	USA immigration
American treason/immigration	Leviticus	24	22	One law for foreigner and citizen
American treason/immigration	Leviticus	25	46	Americans must be nice to each other
American treason/immigration	Numbers	15	16	One law for citizens and aliens
American treason/immigration	Numbers	33	55	Refutations of multiculturalism and new Israel
American treason/immigration	Deuteronomy	1	16	Immigration and arbitration
American treason/immigration	Deuteronomy	16	19	Do justice
American treason/immigration	Deuteronomy	27	19	USA immigration
American treason/immigration	Deuteronomy	27	24	USA immigration
American treason/immigration	Deuteronomy	27	25	USA politicians
American treason/immigration	Deuteronomy	27	26	USA now

Category	Book	Chapter	Verse	Description
American treason/immigration	Deuteronomy	28	43	Immigration
American treason/immigration	Deuteronomy	28	52	USA immigration
American treason/immigration	Psalm	144	7 to 8	China's dictator invades you in open borders
American treason/immigration	Psalm	147	13 to 14	Only God can strengthen your border
American treason/immigration	Proverbs	5	7 to 11	Failure to follow rules brings foreigners
American treason/immigration	Isaiah	1	7	Where our wicked west coast is right now
American treason/immigration	Isaiah	32	5 to 6	U.S. had manufacturing abandonment, jail, illegal immigration, LGBTQ
American treason/immigration	Jeremiah	2	25	You die by loving aliens over your countrymen
American treason/immigration	Jeremiah	6	11 to 13	He must hurt to destroy the USA shepherds
American treason/immigration	Jeremiah	34	9	Despite U.S. Magog's love, it is another bondage
American treason/immigration	Lamentations	5	2 to 3	an apt description of current American history in Magog's war to take our homes and kill us with COVID and violence
American treason/immigration	Ezekiel	22	9	Cities let illegals vote to further hurt Americans
American treason/immigration	Ezekiel	44	7	Lord condemnation of old curses Sanctuaries
American treason/immigration	Hosea	7	9 to 10	Illegal immigration has destroyed the U.S.
American treason/immigration	Hosea	8	7	Aliens are eating America alive
American treason/immigration	Hosea		8 to 10	U.S. is swallowed up by aliens and punished
American treason/immigration	Joel	3	17	There will be no illegal aliens ever again in U.S.
American treason/immigration	Micah	2	4 to 5	Our land is taken by immigrants
American treason/immigration	Zephaniah	1	9	Illegal aliens in U.S. threshold hurts U.S. homes
American treason/immigration	Zephaniah	2	4 to 5	The occupied territories will be destroyed, Holy promised their land
American treason/immigration	Zechariah	7	8 to 10	Lord wants no slaves including aliens & poor hurt by Magog
American treason/immigration	Zechariah	8	17	End illegal alien war on Americans, we all took a pledge of allegiance
American treason/kneel for flag	Isaiah	2	9	Kneeling for the flag and giving up power
American treason/LGBTQ	Genesis	2	23	man and women quantum merge
American treason/LGBTQ	Genesis	19	5	Sodomy feeds pedophilia, break from lesbians
American treason/LGBTQ	Genesis	19	9	Lot wanted to be in Sodom, finding newbies
American treason/LGBTQ	Exodus	4	23	Like Exodus, Americans giving up their kids
American treason/LGBTQ	Exodus	13	3	LGBTQ is the bondage of death via the Lord
American treason/LGBTQ	Leviticus	15	17	LGBTQ Semen
American treason/LGBTQ	Leviticus	20	13	LGBTQ
American treason/LGBTQ	Leviticus	20	23	LGBTQ
American treason/LGBTQ	Leviticus	26	29	LGBTQ is another of America's punishment
American treason/LGBTQ	Deuteronomy	27	21	USA what's next, no treat animals better than us
American treason/LGBTQ	Deuteronomy	28	30	Covid-19
American treason/LGBTQ	Deuteronomy	28	53	USA LGBTQ
American treason/LGBTQ	Deuteronomy	28	54	USA immigration, Democrats

GOD'S GUIDE TO THE END OF THE WORLD 381

American treason/LGBTQ	Deuteronomy	28	55	USA LGBTQ and China
American treason/LGBTQ	Judges	19	22 to 25	LGBTQ spreads like a virus (1 of 3)
American treason/LGBTQ	Judges	19	26 to 28	LGBTQ spreads like a virus (2 of 3)
American treason/LGBTQ	Judges	19	29	LGBTQ spreads like a virus (3 of 3)
American treason/LGBTQ	Samuel 2	13	14	LGBTQ bathroom, men are stronger
American treason/LGBTQ	Kings 1	14	24	LGBTQ sodomy, evil and perverted, child rape
American treason/LGBTQ	Kings 1	22	46	Child rape feeds more child rape LGBTQ
American treason/LGBTQ	Proverbs	13	16	LGBTQ Pro-China, Communist, Treason
American treason/LGBTQ	Proverbs	16	18 to 19	Anything seeking liberation, including women
American treason/LGBTQ	Proverbs	17	6	LGBT-Magog, pollution, etc,
American treason/LGBTQ	Proverbs	18	22	Families are the basis of the USA
American treason/LGBTQ	Proverbs	18	24	Abused men crave friends over family
American treason/LGBTQ	Proverbs	19	13	Family life is not nonstop fun, but it's demanded
American treason/LGBTQ	Proverbs	21	9	The family life is not perfect (2 of 3)
American treason/LGBTQ	Proverbs	24	11	LGBTQ
American treason/LGBTQ	Proverbs	25	24	The family life is not perfect, repeat of 2 (3 of 3)
American treason/LGBTQ	Proverbs	29	15	Problem with a parent not raising their kids
American treason/LGBTQ	Isaiah	45	9 to 10	A complete refutation of LGBTQ, U.S. Magog
American treason/LGBTQ	Jeremiah	6	21	Like of belief led to abominations
American treason/LGBTQ	Jeremiah	7	30	We must rid ourselves of the Chinese goods
American treason/LGBTQ	Jeremiah	8	8	Kingly deceits mask the U.S. Magog theft
American treason/LGBTQ	Lamentations	1	18	The war has driven the youth to LGBTQ
American treason/LGBTQ	Ezekiel	22	26	City priests, pro-life, pro-sodomy, bad Sabbath
American treason/LGBTQ	Ezekiel	23	39	Pro-sodomy believers profane their churches
American treason/LGBTQ	Ezekiel	33	17	Your children are persuaded to feed pedophilia
American treason/LGBTQ	Hosea	8	11 to 13	U.S. is offering up its youth for its iniquity
American treason/LGBTQ	Joel	2	17	Priests must atone for Pro-life &LGBTQ aiding Gog
American treason/LGBTQ	Jonah	4	11	LGBTQ cannot tell left from right
American treason/LGBTQ	Micah	2	6 to 7	All pro-life & LGBTQ priests but those with Michael's laws are liars
American treason/LGBTQ	Malachi	2	7 to 9	Priests should've opened the inner temple
American treason/LGBTQ	Malachi	2	10	The inner temple connect humanity
American treason/LGBTQ	Genesis	19	1	Lot drawn to gay society, like so many
American treason/manufacture	Exodus	22	1	Our politicians take our property, burden us
American treason/manufacture	Proverbs	3	9	Why the slave-made goods condemn us
American treason/manufacture	Proverbs	25	21 to 22	Why we must help save China, end purchases
American treason/manufacture	Ecclesiastes	2	24	Why USA must domestically manufacture

American treason/manufacture	Isaiah	1	23	Your government is U.S. Magog, hurt vulnerable
American treason/manufacture	Haggai	2	13 to 14	U.S. sin stains all its work
American treason/mass media	Exodus	23	1	LGBTQ and control of all media topics
American treason/mass media	Proverbs	17	18	Research your conviction over the mass belief
American treason/mass media	Proverbs	18	6 to 8	The media turned USA into divided fools
American treason/mass media	Proverbs	18	10 to 11	Trust in God over the elites' cities
American treason/mass media	Proverbs	18	13	You're told what to think by Gog
American treason/mass media	Proverbs	18	17	Why free speech is so critical
American treason/mass media	Proverbs	19	11	The perversion of political correctness
American treason/mass media	Proverbs	19	28	We are inundated with lies
American treason/mass media	Proverbs	19	29	When you're so judgmental, you're full of lies
American treason/mass media	Proverbs	21	23	How they silenced Americans.
American treason/mass media	Proverbs	21	27 to 30	Liars will perish before the righteousness
American treason/mass media	Proverbs	26	18	The truth about Democrats and Republicans
American treason/mass media	Proverbs	28	28	Freedom of speech silences everyone
American treason/mass media	Proverbs	31	8 to 9	Resume freedom of speech
American treason/mass media	Ecclesiastes	9	16 to 18	Why USA must have free speech
American treason/mass media	Isaiah	3	8	U.S. Magog has destroyed the USA's free speech
American treason/mass media	Isaiah	9	17	U.S. does not follow His rules and became wicked
American treason/mass media	Isaiah	18		God damns E. Africa/refute multiculturalism (1 of 4)
American treason/mass media	Isaiah	41	1	End censorship and let people speak
American treason/mass media	Jeremiah	6	17	U.S. silenced its outspoken critics like Lou Dobbs
American treason/mass media	Jeremiah	7	28	There is no correction without free speech
American treason/mass media	Jeremiah	13	23	God damns Ethiopia & multiculturalism (2 of 4)
American treason/mass media	Zechariah	8	14 to 16	Free speech must return to the U.S.
American treason/memorials	Proverbs	22	28	Removing Monuments after raping all black males
American treason/memorials	Proverbs	23	10 to 11	Removing Monuments causes death
American treason/memorials	Jeremiah	31	21	Return the landmarks, restore the cities
American treason/memorials	Hosea	5	10	U.S. removal of landmarks by those mass-raping blacks
American treason/memorials	Deuteronomy	27	17	Civil war monuments
American treason/Mercy	Numbers	30	2	Pledge of Allegiance and by politicians
American treason/mercy	Deuteronomy	15	11	Treat your fellow Americans well
American treason/mercy	Proverbs	3	3 to 4	The Lord urges you not to give into Magog, but love your neighbor citizen as a brother
American treason/mercy	Micah	6	8	What the Lord expects from the U.S.
American treason/presidents	Genesis	4	8	Likewise, slavery murders freedom in any age
American treason/presidents	Genesis	12	8	U.S. mirrors Israel's two state system

GOD'S GUIDE TO THE END OF THE WORLD 383

American treason/presidents	Exodus	22	22 to 24	Leave 2 of the 3 kings alone
American treason/presidents	Leviticus	4	13	Crime hidden from society & covered up by mass media
American treason/presidents	Leviticus	5	4	Pledge of Allegiance honored by doing right
American treason/presidents	Joshua	7	13	There is an accursed thing in Israel & USA
American treason/presidents	Judges	3	15 to 29	Ehud is Clinton us, both left-handed
American treason/presidents	Samuel 1	2	35	USA also created kings and screamed in pain
American treason/presidents	Samuel 1	13	13 to 14	Four traitors, power taken away
American treason/presidents	Samuel 1	26	11	LBJ with Kennedy leading to all of these events
American treason/presidents	Samuel 2	23	3 to 4	Can't rule fairly without belief, belief elects ruler
American treason/presidents	Chronicles 2	2	4	America is punished for covenant over liberty
American treason/presidents	Chronicles 2	5	10	The Ten Commandments was a burden to carry
American treason/presidents	Nehemiah	9	36	U.S.A. problem right now
American treason/presidents	Job	24	2 to 5	The three horns are guilty of removing landmarks to hide their sins
American treason/presidents	Job	34	21 to 30	Hypocrites rule U.S.A. & God sees all
American treason/presidents	Psalm	142	3 to 4	Our U.S. leaders have left us
American treason/presidents	Proverbs	14	16 to 17	Fools do not follow His laws
American treason/presidents	Proverbs	18	5	Sodomy spread enrich communism, open border
American treason/presidents	Proverbs	18	12	Your politicians not wearing masks
American treason/presidents	Proverbs	20	2	How you know our presidents are now kings
American treason/presidents	Proverbs	20	11	We must assess leadership that damned our future
American treason/presidents	Proverbs	21	13	Make Americans poorer and poorer
American treason/presidents	Proverbs	21	14	Business funds political policy, held aloft on bribes
American treason/presidents	Proverbs	21	24	Your leaders pitching radical pride over the law
American treason/presidents	Proverbs	22	7	Now the rich kill instead of merely ruling over
American treason/presidents	Proverbs	22	24 to 25	Antifa, Democrats, violence of the left
American treason/presidents	Proverbs	24	21 to 22	LGBTQ U.S. Magog, all of it ends in death, anti-conservatism
American treason/presidents	Proverbs	26	12	To enrich a communist enemy is to be wise in one's eyes
American treason/presidents	Proverbs	28	9	God's message to Democrats and Republicans who soiled Americans
American treason/presidents	Proverbs	29	2	Biden leadership must be replaced
American treason/presidents	Proverbs	29	12	Clinton & Bush betrayal corrupted the government
American treason/presidents	Proverbs	30	9 to 17	Agur prophecies modern USA from president's treason
American treason/presidents	Proverbs	30	21 to 22	Our presidents are servants, but now rule as foolish kings
American treason/presidents	Proverbs	31	4 to 5	Your leaders don't follow the law and are wicked
American treason/presidents	Ecclesiastes	3	14 to 15	Removing monuments mars present via past
American treason/presidents	Ecclesiastes	7	7	USA now freedom of speech and intimidation
American treason/presidents	Ecclesiastes	7	15	When Clinton changed the economic underpinning, all were affected
American treason/presidents	Ecclesiastes	8	1	These hard leaders of ours are not wise

American treason/presidents	Isaiah	1		12	A complete lack of law & justice including presidential wiretapping
American treason/presidents	Isaiah	2		6	U.S. Magog is pro-China, Global Warming, illegals, assault Russia
American treason/presidents	Isaiah	2		7	A description of modern U.S. from one in antiquity, both worship idols
American treason/presidents	Isaiah	3		9	U.S. Magog will destroy the world and like Sodom God will use a rock to kill it
American treason/presidents	Isaiah	5		13 to 14	Leaders ended education and polluted leaders
American treason/presidents	Isaiah	5		21	Gog controls what you think on due to presidential deceit, the Interview
American treason/presidents	Isaiah	9		15 to 16	Our leadership is killing us (including priests)
American treason/presidents	Isaiah	29		11 to 12	Your leaders and experts are not tell you the truth about vaccine & more
American treason/presidents	Isaiah	32		7	Gog and his agents intentionally destroy us
American treason/presidents	Isaiah	42		21 to 22	What U.S. Magog has done to you
American treason/presidents	Isaiah	44		9	Our leaders don't believe and are blind to their evil, cursing all
American treason/presidents	Isaiah	44		17	Our nation believes in our leaders, not God, and makes an idol of Gog
American treason/presidents	Isaiah	44		18 to 20	U.S. king presidents failure to believe destroyed us all
American treason/presidents	Isaiah	47		10 to 11	Evil-doers will be destroyed
American treason/presidents	Isaiah	47		13	Stop listening to U.S. Magog
American treason/presidents	Isaiah	52		3	You gave up your country for nothing because of president kings
American treason/presidents	Isaiah	56		9 to 10	U.S. Magog's leadership is killing you from its wicked president kings
American treason/presidents	Isaiah	56		11	God sheds light on USA leadership
American treason/presidents	Isaiah	59		4 to 5	Where USA is now
American treason/presidents	Isaiah	59		7 to 8	What your leadership has done to us brings misery & the end
American treason/presidents	Isaiah	59		13 to 15	Our lack of law & justice, even presidential wiretap
American treason/presidents	Jeremiah	4		31	Our government funded the Wuhan Lab & more
American treason/presidents	Jeremiah	5		26 to 28	USA leaders are richer & powerful than ever
American treason/presidents	Jeremiah	5		30 to 31	U.S. has communism, sodomy, pro-life, immigration
American treason/presidents	Jeremiah	6		10	Lack of belief fuels wickedness from our wicked leadership
American treason/presidents	Jeremiah	6		27 to 30	U.S. actively destroying its wealth
American treason/presidents	Jeremiah	7		5 to 7	Civil war over immigration as a Communist invasion masked as love
American treason/presidents	Jeremiah	7		8	God sees the crimes of U.S. leaders
American treason/presidents	Jeremiah	8		5	U.S. Magog's deceit is now undeniable via reason
American treason/presidents	Jeremiah	8		9 to 10	Most American men will die in Time of Trouble from presidential treason
American treason/presidents	Jeremiah	8		15	The Cold War surrender drained and then killed Americans
American treason/presidents	Jeremiah	9		4 to 6	USA preaches love but practices hate from presidential treason
American treason/presidents	Jeremiah	9		18	You must face you've made USA homeless
American treason/presidents	Jeremiah	9		25	You are now in the death of all peoples from rotten U.S. king presidents
American treason/presidents	Jeremiah	10		14	USA, Ephraim dies in a *service economy*
American treason/presidents	Jeremiah	10		21	Your U.S. Magog Leaders caused this nightmare

American treason/presidents	Jeremiah	11	9	Your leaders serve U.S. Magog
American treason/presidents	Jeremiah	12	2	Your leaders have turned on you
American treason/presidents	Jeremiah	18	15 to 16	USA forgot itself during treason of king presidents
American treason/presidents	Jeremiah	23	18 to 20	Failure to follow ends the world due to presidents' Cold War surrender
American treason/presidents	Jeremiah	30	14	Your allies flee as you fall from your U.S. king presidential betrayals
American treason/presidents	Lamentations	4	13	Your leaders and priests failed you, repeatedly
American treason/presidents	Lamentations	4	17	The United States will be destroyed
American treason/presidents	Lamentations	4	18	Everything you do and say is monitored
American treason/presidents	Lamentations	4	19	There is no escape from your government
American treason/presidents	Lamentations	5	4 to 6	China is what Egypt and Assyria were (2 of 4)
American treason/presidents	Lamentations	5	7 to 9	C19 kills off the wicked old and all lives and immigration rules us (3 of 4)
American treason/presidents	Ezekiel	22	27	Leaders ousting citizens, drug addict, jail
American treason/presidents	Ezekiel	28	16	Presidential trading in slave-made goods created our ruination
American treason/presidents	Ezekiel	28	17	So God through king presidents sold you to a king, Gog, as usual
American treason/presidents	Ezekiel	33	5 to 6	God bills Clinton, W., and Obama for USA end
American treason/presidents	Ezekiel	39	26	Lord condemns Rhino right & left from traitor presidents (read quote)
American treason/presidents	Daniel	2	41 to 42	Daniel describes republics, strength, weakness
American treason/presidents	Daniel	2	43	Daniel describes the disunity of the U.S.
American treason/presidents	Daniel	7	20	!0 kingdoms own U.S. & pompous horn president
American treason/presidents	Daniel	7	21	Gog is king of the U.S. through clients
American treason/presidents	Daniel	7	24	Daniel notes China as the Land of 10 kingdoms subduing 3 U.S. presidents
American treason/presidents	Daniel	7	25	Gog speaks through our pompous U.S. horns
American treason/presidents	Daniel	8	3 to 4	The Ram is explained to be Media & Persia (prelude to rest of Daniel 8)
American treason/presidents	Daniel	8	5 to 7	The goat is Alexander of Macedon (prelude to rest of Daniel 8)
American treason/presidents	Daniel	8	8	Greece spawns Democracy until 4 U.S. kings
American treason/presidents	Daniel	8	9 to 12	Out of the four U.S. horns, cements Gog
American treason/presidents	Daniel	8	13	U.S. rebellion makes desolate, tramples on world
American treason/presidents	Daniel	8	15 to 17	This vision in Chapter 8 concerns the end (1 o 2)
American treason/presidents	Daniel	8	19 to 22	Iran threatened Greeks spawning E & W Rome, Holland, and U.S. (2 of 2)
American treason/presidents	Daniel	8	24	Xi Jinping's power flows from Clinton, Bush, Obama, Biden
American treason/presidents	Daniel	9	27	U.S. sacrifice will end, must refute the traitorous king presidents
American treason/presidents	Hosea	4	17 to 19	The Lord condemns the U.S. wedded to idols
American treason/presidents	Hosea	5	11 to 12	Americans & Israel are deserted for failures, from its political leaders
American treason/presidents	Hosea	6	4 to 5	U.S. & Israel are destroyed for disobedience of leaders & priests
American treason/presidents	Hosea	10	4	U.S. presidents are your enemy
American treason/presidents	Hosea	10	11	U.S. always back-breaking workers now die from it

American treason/presidents	Hosea	10	13 to 14	Ignore God's laws and you transgress, our presidents caused this
American treason/presidents	Hosea	12	7 to 8	U.S. thinks in money it can hide its sin from Chinese slave trade
American treason/presidents	Hosea	13	7 to 8	Daniel saw God lets bad governments on U.S. due to Cold War betrayal
American treason/presidents	Amos	3	9 to 10	With God, Israel and likewise U.S. is lost
American treason/presidents	Amos	5	12 to 13	No one can now speak due to the wicked from presidential betrayal
American treason/presidents	Obadiah	1	5	Like Edom, U.S. took everything from Americans from presidential evil
American treason/presidents	Micah	1	1 to 2	God condemns U.S. leaders like those of old
American treason/presidents	Micah	2	8 to 9	U.S. leaders displacing Americans
American treason/presidents	Micah	2	10 to 11	Wicked U.S. presidents will distract you from the end of the world
American treason/presidents	Micah	3	1 to 3	God condemns U.S. leaders & priests destroying us
American treason/presidents	Nahum	1	14	God condemns the wicked and their leaders & priests
American treason/presidents	Habakkuk	2	9 to 11	Even the elites will be killed in the Lord's day
American treason/presidents	Zephaniah	1	5 to 6	Religious pro-gay and pro-life & pro-China slavery ended the world
American treason/presidents	Zephaniah	3	3	U.S. leaders corrupt
American treason/presidents	Haggai	2	20 to 22	God ends the earth for disobedience for pro-life, immigration, and COVID
American treason/presidents	Zechariah	1	18 to 20	4 horns hurt U.S., Clinton, Bush, Obama, Hillary
American treason/presidents	Zechariah	2	6	COVID comes from north on flying horses with us teaching virus to them
American treason/presidents	Zechariah	10	2	Modern U.S. lack of leadership to China
American treason/presidents	Zechariah	10	3	The Lord destroys earth because of leaders
American treason/presidents	Zechariah	11	1 to 3	The Lord destroys all to rid us of bad leaders
American treason/presidents	Zechariah	11	4 to 6	The bad leaders are destroyed for hurting flock
American treason/presidents	Zechariah	11	7 to 9	COVID strain kills three U.S. presidents at once
American treason/presidents	Zechariah	11	15 to 16	U.S. leadership making waste of Americans
American treason/presidents	Zechariah	11	17	Possible sickness of Biden or other wicked 3 U.S. Presidents
American treason/presidents	Malachi	2	4 to 6	Inner temple and laws kept humans alive, U.S. betrayal broke it
American treason/presidents	Malachi	2	11 to 12	Likewise aliens, U.S. Magog destroy the U.S.
American treason/presidents	Malachi	2	17	U.S. leaders now call outright evil good like priests of old
American treason/presidents	Malachi	3	6 to 7	The Lord asks U.S. & Israel to return to Him
American treason/presidents	Malachi	3	8 to 10	Our U.S. Magog presidents & priests of old cut off our temples in sin
American treason/prison	Psalm	142	7	U.S. imprisoned more people than any nation ever
American treason/prison	Isaiah	1	15	The punishment of the last 30 years of treason fueled crime & jail
American treason/pro-life	Hosea	9	7 to 9	The pro-life movement is an insane fool's task
American treason/pro-life	Jeremiah	1	5	Anti-pro-life, before formed, your destiny known
American treason/U.S. history	Proverbs	26	11	A summary of USA history & human nature
American treason/university	Chronicles 2	2	18	Few need go to college & works in management
American treason/university	Ecclesiastes	1	18	The path of knowledge beyond God is death

GOD'S GUIDE TO THE END OF THE WORLD 387

Topic	Book	Chapter	Verse	Description
American treason/war not peace	Psalm	120	6 to 7	They say peace, but are at war since Clinton
American treason/war not peace	Jeremiah	6	14	There's no peace, this is a continuing Cold War
American treason/war not peace	Jeremiah	8	11	They gave temporary aid and called it peace
American treason/war not peace	Jeremiah	23	17	Your leaders surrender Cold War & call it peace
American treason/war not peace	Micah	3	5	Our leaders war and call it peace
American treason/war not peace	Habakkuk	1	5 to 10	Likewise, COVID-19 is the same pattern
Anti-Semitism damns	Zechariah	8	22 to 23	When you hate Jews, you hate God, the New Testament births this pattern
Bacteria	Exodus	29	2	bacteria
Bacteria	Exodus	30	23	antibacterial Myrrh for showbread
Bacteria	Exodus	40	32	bacteria, washing
Bacteria	Leviticus	6	10	Linen, antibiotic
Bacteria	Leviticus	7	19	No bacteria
Date for COVID	Daniel	8	14	7 year end time via (Daniel 9:27); divide 2300 days by 365.25= 6.23 years
Date for COVID	Daniel	12	11	1290 years (1 of 2)
Date for COVID	Daniel	12	12	1,335 years (2 of 2) to reach blessed time
Date for COVID	Daniel	12	11 to 12	Overview of Chronology, 2019 end of punishment
Day of God	Genesis	8	21 to 22	Until the end, God makes seasons regular for us
Day of God	Genesis	12	3	How U.S. Magog, Illegal aliens, Pro-life ends world
Day of God	Genesis	19	24	He destroys sinful cities with asteroid/Babylon saw
Day of God	Genesis	49	10	Messiah prophesied via Judah and T
Day of God	Exodus	3	22	U.S. will later have from China like in old time
Day of God	Exodus	14	13	The Lord now fights for the USA
Day of God	Numbers	16	30	What happens to the west coast
Day of God	Deuteronomy	4	24	LGBTQ USA must keep its commandments
Day of God	Deuteronomy	26	18 to 19	Lifted the USA over all nations
Day of God	Deuteronomy	30	3 to 5	LGBTQ USA
Day of God	Deuteronomy	32	43	Lord will end the world for its sin
Day of God	Joshua	10	12 to 14	God can manipulate the heavens
Day of God	Samuel 2	7	10	Remove "sons of wicked" rulers
Day of God	Esther	10	3	The Lord saved Mordechai & can save anyone
Day of God	Psalm	9	19 to 20	The end of humanism, Greek in origin, rape
Day of God	Psalm	11	5 to 6	Effects of China pollution
Day of God	Psalm	53	4 to 5	God will destroy our leaders as well
Day of God	Proverbs	22	2	Warning to all Americans both rich and poor
Day of God	Proverbs	22	4	Point of your life
Day of God	Proverbs	27	1	LGBTQ, U.S. Magog will destroy the world
Day of God	Proverbs	29	16	At judgment everything will be truly sorted out
Day of God	Isaiah	1	8 to 9	The Lord saves a remnant from asteroid

Day of God	Isaiah	1	24 to 26	So the Lord will destroy our wealth and world
Day of God	Isaiah	1	26	The messianic age will restore wise leaders
Day of God	Isaiah	1	27 to 28	The good will be saved and evil die
Day of God	Isaiah	2	19	The elites will hide when the asteroid comes
Day of God	Isaiah	4	2	The righteous as a branch following Jesse's branch are saved
Day of God	Isaiah	11	4	I seek to save
Day of God	Isaiah	13	11 to 14	The Asteroid of the Day of the Lord (2 of 5)
Day of God	Isaiah	13	19	Asteroid comes like Sodom & Gomorrah (3 of 5)
Day of God	Isaiah	14	19	Ultimately King William was the great Satan
Day of God	Isaiah	14	21	U.S. Magog and LGBTQ will end the world
Day of God	Isaiah	24	1 to 3	The asteroid destroys the entire planet (4 of 5)
Day of God	Isaiah	24	5 to 6	Very few are alive after asteroid (5 of 5)
Day of God	Isaiah	25	5	Reverse immigration invasion
Day of God	Isaiah	26	19	Judgment comes and the living can be there
Day of God	Isaiah	26	21	Asteroid comes out of the heavens to end all
Day of God	Isaiah	28	2	Asteroid destroys world
Day of God	Isaiah	28	3	Asteroid destroy the U.S. & earth
Day of God	Isaiah	28	4	Asteroid takes everything as God's direction
Day of God	Isaiah	5	5 to 6	Messiah runs you only after world's end
Day of God	Isaiah	28	21 to 22	The world will soon be destroyed by the asteroid
Day of God	Isaiah	29	3 to 4	Destruction of the world by asteroid
Day of God	Isaiah	29	5 to 6	Gog controls the world except for Russia
Day of God	Isaiah	56	3 to 5	U.S. Magog will destroy the world
Day of God	Isaiah	57	21	The wicked burn continually
Day of God	Isaiah	59	18 to 19	The Lord will save you
Day of God	Isaiah	59	21	The Lord's covenant with the USA and world
Day of God	Isaiah	60	18	Immigration reform requires walls
Day of God	Isaiah	62	1 to 2	The Lord will come and the world will mend
Day of God	Isaiah	62	6 to 7	The USA has a firewall (1 of 2) (later Zephaniah)
Day of God	Isaiah	62	8 to 9	Immigration policy, not give wealth to foreigners
Day of God	Isaiah	65	24	Later God will be even more apparent
Day of God	Isaiah	66	24	The undead in Shoal will be seen up on Earth
Day of God	Jeremiah	2	26	The end will bring shame on the wicked
Day of God	Jeremiah	4	11 to 12	You are at the beginning of God's storm
Day of God	Jeremiah	4	3	Now you have the Viral storm of COVID-19
Day of God	Jeremiah	4	30	Xi Jinping will kill you, silences JP Morgan CEO
Day of God	Jeremiah	6	15	For U.S. treason the world will gest asteroid

Day of God	Jeremiah	8	1	The dead will come back to an animated state
Day of God	Jeremiah	8	2	This animated undead will remain alive
Day of God	Jeremiah	8	3	The undead will continue on as such forever
Day of God	Jeremiah	8	12	For U.S. violations shall come the asteroid
Day of God	Jeremiah	8	13	The China pollution will hurt food production
Day of God	Jeremiah	9	20 to 21	You've killed off the next generation
Day of God	Jeremiah	10	10	You are here to believe in God, 11/10/1619
Day of God	Jeremiah	12	15	Old Israel & USA of new both get God's return
Day of God	Jeremiah	12	17	USA that doesn't follow will be destroyed
Day of God	Jeremiah	25	30 to 32	COVID is the world's price for U.S. Magog
Day of God	Jeremiah	30	8 to 9	COVID helps you break a U.S. Magog yoke or die
Day of God	Jeremiah	30	16	The Lord will save you
Day of God	Jeremiah	30	18	The Lord will free you from U.S. Magog
Day of God	Jeremiah	30	19	USA and Israel will have Thanksgiving
Day of God	Jeremiah	30	20	Belief (not faith) will be restored
Day of God	Jeremiah	30	21 to 22	God extends his invasion through the policies
Day of God	Jeremiah	30	23 to 24	God will destroy to end the shepherds
Day of God	Jeremiah	31	31 to 32	The Lord's old covenant as husband changes
Day of God	Ezekiel	16	49 to 50	For sins like in old, asteroid destroys all
Day of God	Ezekiel	20	33 to 35	I am the Lord's little horn, pleading the case
Day of God	Ezekiel	21	27	Coming Messiah
Day of God	Ezekiel	24	26 to 27	Freedom of the press will return via God
Day of God	Ezekiel	28	18 to 19	Your wicked trade destroyed you, like all cultures
Day of God	Ezekiel	28	25 to 26	DNA kits identity old Israel and God's actions affects the new Jerusalem
Day of God	Ezekiel	32	7 to 8	The Day of the Lord & Dreamspace quote
Day of God	Ezekiel	32	26	China's fate, to be broken amongst the wicked
Day of God	Ezekiel	32	27	China is a remnant
Day of God	Ezekiel	32	31	Tyrants guide the fate of their people
Day of God	Ezekiel	34	11	The Lord will save you on judgment day
Day of God	Ezekiel	34	13 to 16	The good will live but the strong will die
Day of God	Ezekiel	34	17 to 19	Leaders dilute citizens and take homes
Day of God	Ezekiel	36	2 to 3	Lords message to the west coast
Day of God	Ezekiel	36	4	God tells the nation they're taken over
Day of God	Ezekiel	36	37	There will be ruins
Day of God	Daniel	2	44	For losing the USA, the world gets destroyed
Day of God	Daniel	3	17	Lord will save you from the furnace too
Day of God	Daniel	7	11	Our U.S. kings, this horn, feeds Gog, the 4th beast

Day of God	Daniel	7	18	The righteous get everything in the end
Day of God	Daniel	7	22	God destroys earth, judges & saves the righteous
Day of God	Daniel	7	26 to 27	God will thus wipe out Gog
Day of God	Daniel	12	10	Only the good can understand
Day of God	Hosea	1	7	U.S. is for Judah
Day of God	Hosea	2	17 to 18	Many women don't like to admit they're wrong, making them hypocrites.
Day of God	Hosea	3	5	Latter people will obey
Day of God	Hosea	4	6	Due to mothers, LGBTQ and sinful children end all
Day of God	Hosea	4	14	Death follows sexual abominations
Day of God	Hosea	5	4 to 5	U.S. worships money & sex, Israel worships rabbis
Day of God	Hosea	5	7	The United States has raised awful children
Day of God	Hosea	5	9	The U.S. will be destroyed in the day of rebuke
Day of God	Hosea	13	14	God will judge all who lived and died
Day of God	Hosea	13	16	Oppose God and die even in antiquity
Day of God	Joel	1	15 to 17	The day of destruction ends the planet
Day of God	Joel	2	17 to 20	Everyone panics at coming destruction
Day of God	Joel	2	10 to 11	The earth will be torn asunder
Day of God	Joel	2	21 to 24	Then the Lord will return the world to prosperity
Day of God	Joel	2	25 to 27	The Chinese army will be removed
Day of God	Joel	2	28 to 29	After destruction, Lord will guide firsthand
Day of God	Joel	2	30 to 31	Signs of the coming of the Day of God meteor
Day of God	Joel	2	32	Anyone who calls on Him now can be saved
Day of God	Joel	3	1 to 3	After Day of God, comes His judgment
Day of God	Joel	3	12 to 13	After the return, God will judge
Day of God	Joel	3	14 to 16	The Lord will save the returned
Day of God	Amos	2	4 to 5	Judah never returned to their inner temple
Day of God	Amos	2	6	Ephraim's U.S., immorality destroyed it
Day of God	Amos	3	1	God condemns the whole family, Ephraim U.S.
Day of God	Amos	3	2	Like Israel God used America to address all nations
Day of God	Amos	3	6	Warning sirens are His work too
Day of God	Amos	4	11	Likewise, the end is like Sodom, meteorite
Day of God	Amos	4	12 to 13	The Lord shall come to judge
Day of God	Amos	5	6 to 7	The fire of the rock will consume all not saved
Day of God	Amos	5	8 to 9	The Lord can and will destroy all
Day of God	Amos	5	10 to 11	The USA quashing freedom of speech
Day of God	Amos	5	16 to 17	The world will be terrified by the rock
Day of God	Amos	5	18	Light will be blotted out on the day of the Lord

GOD'S GUIDE TO THE END OF THE WORLD 391

Day of God	Amos	5	19 to 20	The end will be total with nowhere to hide
Day of God	Amos	5	25 to 27	Captivity will not stand in U.S. & brings Day of God
Day of God	Amos	6	3 to 7	Enemies of Jacob & likewise U.S. will be removed
Day of God	Amos	8	7 to 8	For its stubborn pride God will destroy the earth
Day of God	Amos	8	9 to 10	The sun will go dark at noon
Day of God	Amos	9	1	The Lord will annihilate all life left on Earth
Day of God	Amos	9	2 to 6	The Lord will destroy those in shelters or space
Day of God	Amos	9	8	A few will be saved from Jacob's house
Day of God	Amos	9	9 to 10	He will kill most, the sea of wicked ones
Day of God	Amos	9	13 to 15	Then the Earth will be renewed for the good
Day of God	Obadiah	1	15 to 16	For everyone in all time, Day of Lord is near
Day of God	Obadiah	1	17 to 18	U.S. and Israel shall be saved, fire and flame
Day of God	Micah	1	3 to 4	The Lord will wipe out the earth
Day of God	Micah	2	3 to 4	U.S. leaders destroy us, steal our land
Day of God	Micah	2	12 to 13	A new restoration follows the destruction
Day of God	Micah	3	6 to 7	The destruction will soon follow
Day of God	Micah	3	8 to 12	God's direct message to our leaders on the end
Day of God	Micah	4	1 to 3	A glorious vision of what follows the end
Day of God	Micah	4	7	Israel is lame and the U.S. the outcasts
Day of God	Micah	5	8 to 9	The U.S. and Israel post end
Day of God	Micah	5	10 to 15	The Lord will destroy all non-believers
Day of God	Nahum	1	6	Day of God is rock and fire from heavens
Day of God	Zephaniah	1	1 to 3	The Lord's Day will destroy all life on earth
Day of God	Zephaniah	1	4	Sin brings the end
Day of God	Zephaniah	1	7	God sacrifices humanity like they did to their kids
Day of God	Zephaniah	1	8	U.S. illegal aliens, China, and all else dooms all
Day of God	Zephaniah	1	10 to 14	Day of God ends the mighty and rich of all times and places
Day of God	Zephaniah	1	15 to 16	Day of God is worldwide for the descendants
Day of God	Zephaniah	1	17	Day of God is suffering poured on humanity
Day of God	Zephaniah	1	18	Day of God is to end elites & their wicked world
Day of God	Zephaniah	2	1 to 2	Get real with the Lord now
Day of God	Zephaniah	2	4 to 5	Resurrected are judged on Day of God
Day of God	Zephaniah	2	10 to 11	Worst is to mess with the U.S. or Israelites
Day of God	Zephaniah	2	12	The Lord condemns race of Ethiopia (4 of 4)
Day of God	Zephaniah	3	9	After God's Day, all alive speak same tongue
Day of God	Zephaniah	3	10 to 11	People will respect God after His day
Day of God	Zephaniah	3	12 to 13	Only good people live after God's day

Day of God	Zephaniah	3	14 to 15	People today don't even realize their real enemies that cause their disaster
Day of God	Zephaniah	3	16 to 17	Only the good live after God's Day
Day of God	Zephaniah	3	18 to 20	Our leaders will be punished
Day of God	Zechariah	8	7 to 8	The Lord will save Israel and the U.S. (1 of 3)
Day of God	Zechariah	9	14 to 17	The day of God saves the U.S. & Israel
Day of God	Zechariah	10	7 to 8	Americans who are good will be saved
Day of God	Zechariah	12	9	Day of God destroys U.S.'s enemies
Day of God	Zechariah	12	10	The two Joshuas will become one in the end
Day of God	Zechariah	14	1 to 2	Half of the cities overtaken by aliens
Day of God	Zechariah	14	3 to 5	How God will make his entrance on God's Day
Day of God	Zechariah	14	6 to 7	Darkness of the Day of The Lord until night
Day of God	Zechariah	14	8 to 9	The Lord saves U.S. (west) & Israel (East)
Day of God	Zechariah	14	12	Day of the Lord's asteroid causes wicked to be dissolves to ash
Day of God	Zechariah	14	15	Animals will also be destroyed on God's Day
Day of God	Zechariah	14	16 to 19	Nations opposing U.S. & Israel will later offer tribute
Day of God	Zechariah	14	20 to 21	Enemies will not be after God's Day
Day of God	Malachi	3	2 to 3	God will destroy the wicked to keep all good
Day of God	Malachi	3	4 to 5	After Day of God Lord will punish sin openly
Day of God	Malachi	3	11 to 12	God will end the world to save us from what would be our damning line
Day of God	Malachi	3	17 to 18	The Lord will serve the good in Day of God end
Day of God	Malachi	4	1	The Lord's asteroid will destroy the wicked in God's Day
Day of God	Malachi	4	2 to 3	The good will be spared and wicked made ash
Day of God/Undead	Zephaniah	2	6 to 9	Israel returned to Lord & Ammon, Moab will be undead remnant
Follow the rules or die	Exodus	19	3 to 5	God's message to Ephraim, not Israel
Follow the rules or die	Exodus	20	20	USA the current test
Follow the rules or die	Exodus	23	18 to 19	You must offer key things to God
Follow the rules or die	Exodus	23	28	controls nature
Follow the rules or die	Exodus	27	21	living under the curse
Follow the rules or die	Exodus	29	38 to 42	curse not having temple or $ to do it
Follow the rules or die	Exodus	32	1	LGBTQ given up God and found pedophiles
Follow the rules or die	Exodus	32	9	Likewise, how God feels about USA
Follow the rules or die	Leviticus	20	6	Cannot use mediums
Follow the rules or die	Deuteronomy	4	25	Failure to obey laws kill
Follow the rules or die	Deuteronomy	12	8 to 9	Do not trust your eyes, ears, heart
Follow the rules or die	Deuteronomy	28	62 to 63	COVID-19
Follow the rules or die	Deuteronomy	28	66	USA now
Follow the rules or die	Deuteronomy	29	4	Heart is over just what is seen and heard

GOD'S GUIDE TO THE END OF THE WORLD 393

Follow the rules or die	Deuteronomy	29	19	Can't follow dictates of one's heart against God
Follow the rules or die	Deuteronomy	30	11	Commandments are clear rules
Follow the rules or die	Deuteronomy	31	27 to 29	A prophecy of USA "gentiles" in latter days
Follow the rules or die	Joshua	23	6	The law allows you to judge yourself
Follow the rules or die	Judges	2	11 to 14	U.S. repeating Israel's mistake
Follow the rules or die	Judges	2	16 to 19	What the Lord is doing to the USA
Follow the rules or die	Judges	2	20 to 23	Neighboring tribes are competitive enemies
Follow the rules or die	Samuel 1	13	20 to 23	Related to Chinese U.S. manufacturing
Follow the rules or die	Kings 1	3	11	Understanding justice, USA like Solomon now
Follow the rules or die	Kings 1	12	31	When the Israelite king took breaking to extreme
Follow the rules or die	Psalm	1	4	The Day of The Lord burns up people
Follow the rules or die	Psalm	81	11 to 12	U.S. left His law and went by their own counsel
Follow the rules or die	Psalm	105	23 to 25	Likewise God put hooks in U.S. political traitors
Follow the rules or die	Psalm	106	19 to 20	Pursuing gold U.S.'s, lost glory & became like an ox
Follow the rules or die	Psalm	117	1	Praise God Gentiles because of our constitution
Follow the rules or die	Psalm	147	10 to 11	This world is a test of following His rules
Follow the rules or die	Psalm	147	19 to 20	Ancient Israel and modern world are His only land
Follow the rules or die	Proverbs	1	22 to 33	Why you need to apologize to God now
Follow the rules or die	Proverbs	3	1 to 2	Trust in His laws over your own feelings & notions
Follow the rules or die	Proverbs	3	5 to 8	His rules allow our human existence to continue
Follow the rules or die	Proverbs	16	8	The Lord helps all with their best path from free will
Follow the rules or die	Proverbs	16	25	LGBTQ, anything new
Follow the rules or die	Proverbs	16	31	You are all dead people walking
Follow the rules or die	Proverbs	17	3	The test's point is to try hearts
Follow the rules or die	Proverbs	17	11	COVID and all that follows
Follow the rules or die	Proverbs	19	27 to 29	The instruction of His laws are all important
Follow the rules or die	Proverbs	20	14	Business and politics are built on lies because it's about power
Follow the rules or die	Proverbs	20	27	Consciousness is God's test
Follow the rules or die	Proverbs	21	2	The rules are for your protection
Follow the rules or die	Proverbs	21	3	How to win the game and live.
Follow the rules or die	Proverbs	21	20	Pro-oil policy to lower gas prices
Follow the rules or die	Proverbs	21	31	The Lord decides it all in a show to exhibit good & evil for all humans
Follow the rules or die	Proverbs	23	13 to 14	Parenting is a violence caused by the actions of children
Follow the rules or die	Proverbs	28	26	LGBTQ, rules before the heart
Follow the rules or die	Ecclesiastes	2	14	Real education follow His laws despite what is felt
Follow the rules or die	Ecclesiastes	3	9 to 12	The rules govern vast time space narratives
Follow the rules or die	Ecclesiastes	3	21	It's the animal in you that is wicked, not God
Follow the rules or die	Ecclesiastes	4	1 to 3	Buying Chinese made U.S. the oppressor

Follow the rules or die	Ecclesiastes	7	16 to 18	Only trusting in God can allow survival
Follow the rules or die	Ecclesiastes	9	1	Can't trust your eyes, discerning good from evil
Follow the rules or die	Ecclesiastes	9	11 to 12	God is the puppeteer of the multiverse alone
Follow the rules or die	Ecclesiastes	12	6 to 8	The one truth that continues life.
Follow the rules or die	Ecclesiastes	12	8	Humans are full of their own vanity over God
Follow the rules or die	Ecclesiastes	12	12 to 14	A refutation of academia and book-write in a sole defense of God's precepts
Follow the rules or die	Isaiah	28	9 to 10	The reason why the young must raise Godly kids
Follow the rules or die	Isaiah	29	9	The Lord willed those antidepressants
Follow the rules or die	Isaiah	29	15	The Lord sees all
Follow the rules or die	Isaiah	29	16	Hiding 11/10/1619 births unfounded secularism
Follow the rules or die	Isaiah	42	18 to 20	"Wide Awakes" must see the wickedness
Follow the rules or die	Isaiah	43	22 to 24	Israel & USA has not believed of late and suffers
Follow the rules or die	Isaiah	48	18 to 19	USA damned all those that could've been
Follow the rules or die	Isaiah	51	7	Do not fear U.S. Magog
Follow the rules or die	Isaiah	56	6 to 7	The invitation and Sabbath can be for all peoples
Follow the rules or die	Isaiah	63	10	So the Lord struck you
Follow the rules or die	Isaiah	63	18 to 19	USA and Israel strayed from the Lord's laws
Follow the rules or die	Isaiah	64	7	USA does not believe
Follow the rules or die	Isaiah	65	2 to 5	God's specific critique of the USA
Follow the rules or die	Isaiah	65	11 to 12	Those that do not return will be killed
Follow the rules or die	Isaiah	66	3 to 4	The Lord punishes those who lie to themselves
Follow the rules or die	Jeremiah	2	20 to 22	You are punished to break your mindless yoke
Follow the rules or die	Jeremiah	2	36 to 47	As with Egypt so with China
Follow the rules or die	Jeremiah	3	1	You play a harlot with aliens, China is your Communist enemy, fetuses that aren't yours
Follow the rules or die	Jeremiah	3	6	The sexual revolution distanced us from God
Follow the rules or die	Jeremiah	4	18	USA, you brought COVID upon yourselves
Follow the rules or die	Jeremiah	5	7 to 9	The Lords message for the USA
Follow the rules or die	Jeremiah	6	6 to 7	U.S. cities are the seats of oppression & treason
Follow the rules or die	Jeremiah	6	19	For breaking the law, the world ends
Follow the rules or die	Jeremiah	7	16	Fathers against son, American versus American
Follow the rules or die	Jeremiah	7	22 to 24	The three horns sold the U.S. out
Follow the rules or die	Jeremiah	7	26	The baby boomers wrecked the U.S. & world
Follow the rules or die	Jeremiah	9	2 to 3	You live a life of lies in the USA
Follow the rules or die	Jeremiah	9	3	God punishes the U.S. now with their elites
Follow the rules or die	Jeremiah	9	13	Because you do as you will not as Americans
Follow the rules or die	Jeremiah	9	23 to 24	Safety is not guaranteed
Follow the rules or die	Jeremiah	10	15	The Service Economy made the China pollution

Follow the rules or die	Jeremiah	10	23	Going your own way, brings the rock
Follow the rules or die	Jeremiah	11	1 to 5	USA must reestablish the broken covenant
Follow the rules or die	Jeremiah	11	3 to 5	Cursed are those violating the constitution and the Bible
Follow the rules or die	Jeremiah	11	21	Wicked heresy is a false prophecy, it's death
Follow the rules or die	Jeremiah	13	22 to 23	God commands the evil USA to be good
Follow the rules or die	Jeremiah	16	12	You broke the doctrinal trust of your forefathers
Follow the rules or die	Jeremiah	17	5 to 6	The USA trusts in men over God, ruining them
Follow the rules or die	Jeremiah	23	14	Ephraim, U.S., will bring the asteroid
Follow the rules or die	Jeremiah	23	22	You cannot work to enrich a Communist tyrant
Follow the rules or die	Jeremiah	23	36	Your link to God is in His rules, without them your conscious is doomed
Follow the rules or die	Lamentations	1	6	USA lost leaders (U.S. Magog) & priests (Pro-Life)
Follow the rules or die	Lamentations	2	7	The Lord handed over the USA to Gog (China)
Follow the rules or die	Lamentations	4	14	Antifa draws blood in the streets
Follow the rules or die	Ezekiel	8	17	Following own heart, insults God, kills you
Follow the rules or die	Ezekiel	9	9 to 10	As with the old, cities are the source of evil
Follow the rules or die	Ezekiel	12	1	USA blind to C19, immigration, LGBTQ, rights
Follow the rules or die	Ezekiel	18	4 to 9	What the Lord expects from Americans
Follow the rules or die	Ezekiel	20	42 to 44	I speak for the Lord about the USA's evils
Follow the rules or die	Ezekiel	22	4 to 5	Cities are jokes, full of blood & idols
Follow the rules or die	Ezekiel	22	29 to 31	Cities use oppression, robbery no one speaks
Follow the rules or die	Ezekiel	33	10 to 11	God asks Americans to get real and be saved
Follow the rules or die	Ezekiel	33	12	Only the righteous are saved in God's judgment
Follow the rules or die	Ezekiel	33	13	The righteous who fell are damned, wicked saved
Follow the rules or die	Ezekiel	33	14	The wicked at the end can be forgiven
Follow the rules or die	Ezekiel	33	15 to 16	Wicked restore pledge, return what was stolen
Follow the rules or die	Ezekiel	33	18	Righteous are given the gift and refuse it
Follow the rules or die	Ezekiel	33	19	The wicked can turn if they follow (15-16)
Follow the rules or die	Hosea	6	6	God wants Americans merciful to each other
Follow the rules or die	Hosea	6	7	God condemns our leaders
Follow the rules or die	Hosea	7	13 to 14	U.S. transgressed and did not cry out to Him
Follow the rules or die	Hosea	12	2 to 6	Israel has always warred with God's plan
Follow the rules or die	Hosea	13	1 to 3	Like the Jews, he U.S. wicked will become ash
Follow the rules or die	Amos	2	7	U.S. sex perversions and even California wine are all cursed
Follow the rules or die	Amos	3	3	Likewise, U.S. not abide together to God's laws now
Follow the rules or die	Amos	5	21 o 24	There is no justice
Follow the rules or die	Amos	9	7	U.S. is as damned as Africa (Ethiopia) (3 of 4)
Follow the rules or die	Micah	1	5	The Lord wipes out the earth because of sins

Follow the rules or die	Micah	1		6 to 7	The Lord will consume all in flames
Follow the rules or die	Micah	3		4	Our punishment follows our crimes
Follow the rules or die	Nahum	1		9 to 11	The Lord will burn all the wicked on His day
Follow the rules or die	Malachi	3		13 to 15	For those seeking profit will soon die
God controls it all	Genesis	20		18	Pro-Choice, Lord controls births
God controls it all	Isaiah	29		10	The Lord authors your destruction
God controls it all	Isaiah	29		14	Wickedness rages without the Lord
God controls it all	Isaiah	45		12	Our punishment stemmed from a lack of belief
God controls it all	Jeremiah	8		17	The virus accompanied a loss of free speech
God controls it all	Lamentations	1		17	USA is in a Civil War after manufacturing's loss
God controls it all	Amos	3		4 to 5	God can punish by cutting off food
God controls it all	Zechariah	12		2 to 3	The Lord has Gog turn the world on the U.S.
God controls it all	Zechariah	13		7 to 9	One third of the U.S. will be saved
God controls it all	Zechariah	14		13 to 14	Wars increase in build up to the Lord's Day
God controls it all	Malachi	1		1 to 3	Love from God means He keeps line alive
God controls it all	Malachi	1		4 to 5	The Lord destroys all societies displeasing Him
God controls it all	Malachi	1		11	So the Lord went to gentiles to create a new nation for remaining Israelites
Gog	Exodus	21		28	Punish an ox for death, but not Gog for millions dead after hiding COVID
Gog	Exodus	21		30	Our politicians kill us and bear no burden
Gog	Deuteronomy	28		48 to 50	USA serving Xi Jinping
Gog	Psalm	81		8 to 10	There's always a God, like modern Gog
Gog	Psalm	106		34	U.S. aided not fought communist tyranny
Gog	Ezekiel	27		13	China uses slaves & bronze with Radhanite Jews
Gog	Ezekiel	28		2 to 3	Daniel's secret is China
Gog	Daniel	7		8	Joe Biden is the 4th U.S. king, pompous serving Clintons who serve Gog
Gog	Daniel	7		23	China destroys the earth
Gog	Daniel	8		23	XI Jinping is unmasked as the enemy
Gog	Daniel	11		40	Trump's trade war causes COVID
Gog	Hosea	14		8	The U.S. lost its faith as God & made Gog an idol
Gog	Amos	3		11	Likewise, China's allies and COVID flank U.S.
Gog	Habakkuk	1		11	Gog thinks he is God
Gog	Zephaniah	2		13	Likewise means destruction of China
Government	Genesis	22		14	The Lord provides
Inner temple	Genesis	3		7	Inner temple created, distancing them from God but allowing them to steer the multiverse
Inner temple	Genesis	3		22	The inner temple's conclusion is U.S.A.
Inner temple	Genesis	4		6	The inner temple's keeps humans moral
Inner temple	Genesis	5		29	Noah improved Enoch's DNA thereby God improved post flood people

GOD'S GUIDE TO THE END OF THE WORLD 397

Inner temple	Genesis	47	18	Where the USA is now like then
Inner temple	Exodus	20	23	Salvation from God is purely inner temple
Inner temple	Leviticus	26	40 to 42	America's solution
Inner temple	Deuteronomy	4	30	message at Time of Trouble
Inner temple	Joshua	6	25	Even a harlot can be saved
Inner temple	Samuel 1	16	7	The problem with identity politics is it doesn't take measure of the heart
Inner temple	Samuel 1	19	20 o 21	Power of group thinking, prayer and government steer us through the multiverse
Inner temple	Kings 1	8	38	Get real with the plague of your heart
Inner temple	Kings 1	15	5	Sexual adherence to laws matters even for David, involving the act of creation
Inner temple	Kings 1	19	13	Inner temple revealed to Elijah
Inner temple	Chronicles 1	29	1	Your consciousness is God's temple, building is His
Inner temple	Chronicles 2	6	22 to 23	A request to make of Him judge of our inner temples.
Inner temple	Chronicles 2	6	36	America taken captive by China over sin
Inner temple	Chronicles 2	6	24	China pollution is the world-ending sin
Inner temple	Chronicles 2	7	18 to 36	The forgiveness America must seek
Inner temple	Chronicles 2	7	14 to 15	USA is saved by returning to God &acting on it
Inner temple	Nehemiah	9	38	The bargain all Americans must maintain for God
Inner temple	Psalm	15	2 to 5	What is expected of Americans
Inner temple	Psalm	35	1 to 3	What to ask the Lord
Inner temple	Psalm	81	13 to 16	U.S. no longer follows His rules
Inner temple	Psalm	91	9 to 16	God saves the righteous who return
Inner temple	Psalm	94	22 to 23	The Lord saves those who return
Inner temple	Psalm	109	1 to 5	USA Now
Inner temple	Psalm	113	1 to 8	Follow false God and become damned
inner temple	Psalm	119	124 to 128	What the Lord expects...righteousness
Inner temple	Psalm	133	1	National unity is a blessing from common God
Inner temple	Psalm	138	1 to 3	Become righteous and you will find boldness
Inner temple	Psalm	146	1 to 4	Only God's plan delivers: only Michael
Inner temple	Proverbs	19	4	There is no truth in friends
Inner temple	Proverbs	24	25	Build the consensus to end the Civil War
Inner temple	Proverbs	29	13	The Lord controls everyone and can change
Inner temple	Ecclesiastes	4	12	Why the USA must now band together
Inner temple	Ecclesiastes	5	4	Eisenhower's pledge of Allegiance binds USA
Inner temple	Ecclesiastes	7	20	Be careful of trust in even yourself, but not God
Inner temple	Isaiah	1	16 to 17	What the Lord now expects from the USA
Inner temple	Isaiah	1	18 to 19	Let us reason & find pardon (1 of 2 of 1:20)
Inner temple	Isaiah	1	20	Refuse to face truth & be killed. (2 of 2 to 1:18-19)

Inner temple	Isaiah	1	29	Terebinth tree Elah is derived from God's name El
Inner temple	Isaiah	1	30 to 31	Lack of faith, Terebinth from Elah, God's name El
Inner temple	Isaiah	3	10 to 11	The wicked will be horrible
Inner temple	Isaiah	5	11	Get off the antidepressants and drugs
Inner temple	Isaiah	14	25 to 27	Only return to God can join Him, His hand is done
Inner temple	Isaiah	26	9	The Lord's message to the USA
Inner temple	Isaiah	28	11 to 12	No one listens to prophets, never have
Inner temple	Isaiah	32	8	We must be generous with our fellow Americans
Inner temple	Isaiah	33	2 to 4	Chapter 33 in full is what one might want to pray
Inner temple	Isaiah	33	15	What the Lord wants
Inner temple	Isaiah	58	6 to 9	If you are righteous the Lord will appear
Inner temple	Isaiah	59	1 to 3	Your sin separated you from God
Inner temple	Isaiah	61	6 to 7	The saved will live wonderfully
Inner temple	Isaiah	63	8	Get real with God inside yourself & be saved
Inner temple	Isaiah	63	11 to 13	After punishing, he recalled the good shepherds
Inner temple	Jeremiah	3	11 to 13	God demands you face your transgressions
Inner temple	Jeremiah	3	22	God invites you to return to being an American
Inner temple	Jeremiah	4	4	The Time of Trouble is His fury
Inner temple	Jeremiah	4	4	He appeals to the old & new Jerusalem
Inner temple	Jeremiah	4	14	USA, you must come clean now or die
Inner temple	Jeremiah	6	16	Made in the USA is the protection of God
Inner temple	Jeremiah	7	3 to 4	The only temple is inside people, reason, heart
Inner temple	Jeremiah	8	4	The fallen and turned will return and arise
Inner temple	Jeremiah	8	14	Loss of freedom is God's punishment
Inner temple	Jeremiah	10	1 to 2	Gentiles are dismayed; they don't believe
Inner temple	Jeremiah	10	19	Now your enslavement is undeniably clear
Inner temple	Jeremiah	11	20	Your prayer to utter against U.S. Magog
Inner temple	Jeremiah	15	19	The USA must clean up its act
Inner temple	Jeremiah	31	9	He is a father to Israel, but the USA is firstborn
Inner temple	Jeremiah	31	18 to 19	He will return when you repent for U.S. Magog
Inner temple	Jeremiah	31	20	The Lord loves the USA
Inner temple	Jeremiah	31	33	Follows his major laws or die
Inner temple	Jeremiah	46	27 to 28	God will punish, but save
Inner temple	Lamentations	1	22	The USA is punished, now turn the tables
Inner temple	Lamentations	3	7 to 9	He killed USA over a Cold War reversal U.S. Magog
Inner temple	Lamentations	4	12	Loss of speech marks an impossible takeover
Inner temple	Lamentations	5	1	This captures the USA now (1 of 4)
Inner temple	Lamentations	5	10 to 22	We are being destroyed (4 of 4)

Inner temple	Daniel	9	3 to 7	What Americans might say to the Lord
Inner temple	Daniel	9	13 to 15	If U.S. doesn't call God, suffering continues
Inner temple	Daniel	9	16 to 19	What American might also say to the Lord
Inner temple	Hosea	5	15	To be saved, one must acknowledge offense
Inner temple	Hosea	6	1	Only the Lord's will can heal COVID
Inner temple	Hosea	6	3	Dreamspace quote
Inner temple	Hosea	7	13 to 14	For lack of faith, COVID from Chinese travelers
Inner temple	Hosea	11	3 to 4	U.S. never knew God was behind them
Inner temple	Hosea	11	8 to 9	God will spare both the U.S. and Israel
Inner temple	Hosea	13	4 to 6	Then the U.S. will realize the truth of God
Inner temple	Hosea	13	9 to 11	God will save the U.S. and just believers
Inner temple	Joel	2	12 to 14	Turn to God, grain & drink offering
Inner temple	Joel	2	15 to 16	Day of Atonement by U.S. (Dec 11-WTO for China)
Inner temple	Joel	3	9 to 11	This return to God is a worldwide movement
Inner temple	Amos	5	4 to 5	Likewise save yourself by returning to the Lord
Inner temple	Amos	4	4 to 6	The rock will consume Jacob
Inner temple	Amos	8	11 to 12	Destruction came from a famine of belief in Him
Inner temple	Jonah	2	7	Most explicit explanation of the inner temple
Inner temple	Micah	7	18 to 20	God forgives those who seek Him
Inner temple	Nahum	1	7 to 8	The Lord will save those who turn to Him
Inner temple	Habakkuk	2	5	God condemns the elites of nearly any age
Inner temple	Zephaniah	2	3	The religious should seek humility from the law
Inner temple	Zephaniah	3	7	God condemns wicked modern U.S.
Inner temple	Zephaniah	3	8	God's day ends the world for legal violations
Inner temple	Haggai	2	6	God condemns the U.S. people of Chinese treason
Inner temple	Haggai	2	15	All including modern U.S. suffer for lack of belief
Inner temple	Zechariah	10	4 to 5	American must stand up now
Inner temple	Malachi	1	6 to 7	Israel priests and thereafter ended inner temple
Inner temple	Malachi	1	8	If priests stole people from leaders, would not fly
Inner temple	Malachi	1	9 to 10	Priests shut doors of people to God & some modern U.S. presidents too
Inner temple	Malachi	1	12 to 14	Closing inner temples makes flock lame like modern presidential betrayal
Inner temple	Malachi	2	1 to 2	God punished priests for theft of inner temple as U.S. presidential betrayed
Inner temple	Malachi	2	3	For theft of inner temple, punishment & Hitler
Inner temple	Malachi	2	13 to 14	God is the wife of youth disbarred by priests
Inner temple	Malachi	2	15	Unity with God connects humans to God, inner temple is everything
Inner temple	Malachi	2	16	Divorce from God brings violence
Inner temple	Malachi	3	16	The Lord will hear those who return to him

Messiah	Genesis	5	23 to 24	Enoch's DNA would affect all humanity	
Messiah	Genesis	37	9	Joseph's descendant Joshua and Messiah do it	
Messiah	Exodus	19	19	Little horn is a man speaking for God (1 of 2)	
Messiah	Exodus	20	18 to 19	Little horn is a man speaking for God (2 of 2)	
Messiah	Numbers	3	47	Once a year tax the Hasmoneans would abuse	
Messiah	Deuteronomy	18	20 to 22	What I say will come true	
Messiah	Samuel 1	11	7	One consent can be reached from fear in USA	
Messiah	Samuel 1	16	13	Example of anointing by God's intermediary	
Messiah	Samuel 2	7	9	The deal with anointed	
Messiah	Kings 1	13	18	The Lord is not an Oracle	
Messiah	Kings 1	22	22 to 23	God punishes through new prophet, all text done	
Messiah	Chronicles 1	5	20	Trust in God to defeat your enemies	
Messiah	Psalm	72	1 to 4	USA, what a real president must do	
Messiah	Psalm	81	3 to 5	From Joseph to Joshuas	
Messiah	Psalm	105	26 to 27	Israel calls out for help & He sends a political redeemer	
Messiah	Proverbs	30	4	Yahweh and Joshua, to answer query	
Messiah	Isaiah	5	26	This U.S. Magog warning goes out to the world	
Messiah	Isaiah	7	14	First Joshua is also Messiah	
Messiah	Isaiah	11	1	I am the branch and I seek branches	
Messiah	Isaiah	11	2	Light hit my parents putting this spirit upon me	
Messiah	Isaiah	11	3	I judge not what's seen but in God's sage advice	
Messiah	Isaiah	28	16	Let this foundation rise	
Messiah	Isaiah	28	17	Follow me and open up the lies	
Messiah	Isaiah	32	3 to 4	Let us open eyes and lead the nation	
Messiah	Isaiah	35	3 to 4	Our nation is the walking dead, God will save you	
Messiah	Isaiah	41	23 to 24	Our message to U.S. Magog	
Messiah	Isaiah	41	27 to 29	There is no one by me to advise you of the truth	
Messiah	Isaiah	42	1 to 3	The light striking my parents is his spirit, Elect	
Messiah	Isaiah	42	4 to 5	God now brings justice against the wicked coastlands	
Messiah	Isaiah	42	6 to 7	Why I speak to you now is from this verse...	
Messiah	Isaiah	43	5 to 7	Israel east, Ephraim west, north & south wicked	
Messiah	Isaiah	44	1 to 2	A direct refutation of Pro-Life	
Messiah	Isaiah	44	21 to 22	His message to USA and Abrahamic DNA	
Messiah	Isaiah	44	24 to 26	Return to God	
Messiah	Isaiah	45	13	We are here to survive the end of the world	
Messiah	Isaiah	45	20	I come to open the eyes of the USA	
Messiah	Isaiah	45	22	God can save	

GOD'S GUIDE TO THE END OF THE WORLD

Messiah	Isaiah	45	23	God offers salvation this one time
Messiah	Isaiah	46	12 to 13	God makes one last ditch offer
Messiah	Isaiah	48	6 to 8	We reveal hidden truths
Messiah	Isaiah	49	1 to 2	The wicked coastlands are damned
Messiah	Isaiah	49	3 to 4	Don't trust your eyes, you will be saved
Messiah	Isaiah	49	6	The Lord will save those who believe
Messiah	Isaiah	50	4	The Elect comes as a well-educated American
Messiah	Isaiah	53	8	The sin-bearing Messiah, two Messiahs
Messiah	Isaiah	56	1 to 2	All to be saved must keep the Sabbath
Messiah	Isaiah	59	15 to 16	None can speak now or would
Messiah	Isaiah	61	1 to 5	I am anointed to tell you what is coming
Messiah	Isaiah	63	5 to 6	I come because no one else would
Messiah	Isaiah	63	7	God gave the USA everything and we ruined it
Messiah	Isaiah	65	1	He sends redemption to nonbelievers in the U.S.
Messiah	Jeremiah	7	27	I'm not sure how much of the USA has light
Messiah	Jeremiah	21	8	In the end you choose either life or death
Messiah	Jeremiah	23	5 to 6	Follow the Lord and be saved
Messiah	Jeremiah	23	16	The four horns have impoverished you
Messiah	Jeremiah	23	30 to 32	The Lord is against U.S. Magog
Messiah	Jeremiah	23	33	God is not an oracle to anyone including me
Messiah	Jeremiah	23	38 to 40	Do not trust any oracles
Messiah	Jeremiah	30	10 to 11	The USA & world can't escape all punishment
Messiah	Jeremiah	33	15 to 16	The Lord will save the USA & Israel
Messiah	Lamentations	4	20	The anointed is here with you
Messiah	Ezekiel	1	10	Angels are lion (God), ox (slave). Eagle (USA)
Messiah	Ezekiel	34	1 to 6	The Lord's condemnation of leadership
Messiah	Ezekiel	34	7 to 10	The Lord is against leaders
Messiah	Ezekiel	34	23	Lord and Servant rule forever
Messiah	Ezekiel	34	29	The stain of the Gentiles scars the USA now
Messiah	Ezekiel	48	11	Warning on spread of sodomy in any age
Messiah	Daniel	7	9 to 10	Every male after their death will stand to see their judgment play out
Messiah	Daniel	7	12	Messiah makes claim & nations have time to act
Messiah	Daniel	7	13 to 14	The reign thereafter
Messiah	Daniel	7	17	Four systems of government & their leaders shown
Messiah	Daniel	10	6	Vision I saw from Omuamua
Messiah	Daniel	10	7	I only truly saw the vision
Messiah	Daniel	10	13	Michael works with the Christ figure
Messiah	Daniel	10	21	Only those with Michael can be trusted

Messiah	Daniel	12	1	On 10/27/17 Saint Michael arose
Messiah	Hosea	14	1 to 2	The key to salvation is honesty with the Lord
Messiah	Hosea	14	4 to 7	From honest prayer comes salvation
Messiah	Hosea	14	9	The laws of God are to protect humans
Messiah	Joel	2	18 to 19	The Lord will spare the U.S. after forgiveness
Messiah	Joel	2	20	Return to the Lord and Gog is destroyed
Messiah	Amos	2	13 to 16	Ephraim caused the Day of God
Messiah	Amos	3	7	The Lord reveals to His servants
Messiah	Amos	3	8	The Lord gives what is needed to survive
Messiah	Amos	5	14 to 15	Get real with God & then act upon it in this way
Messiah	Amos	7	7	The plumb line is the message of the anointed one
Messiah	Amos	9	11 to 12	The Lord will save and David will arise
Messiah	Micah	1	2	The Lord reiterates the Day of the Lord
Messiah	Habakkuk	2	2 to 4	God's speech at the end
Messiah	Haggai	2	23	Zerubbabel's progeny would be both messiahs
Messiah	Zechariah	1	1 to 6	Following God's laws alone continues life
Messiah	Zechariah	2	9	U.S. is consumed by an alien invasion
Messiah	Zechariah	3	1 to 5	Joshua opposes Satan in the end
Messiah	Zechariah	4	1 to 10	The Joshuas are also Zerubbabel
Messiah	Zechariah	4	11 to 14	There are two anointed, Joshua of old & new
Messiah	Zechariah	6	1 to 3	Joshua son of Jehozadak will be later Joshua
Messiah	Zechariah	6	9 to 14	Joshua son of Jehozadak ancestor of Second Joshua
Messiah	Zechariah	9	13	God saves both Israel and the U.S. (1 of 3)
Messiah	Zechariah	10	6	The Lord will save the U.S. and Israel (1 of 3)
Messiah	Malachi	3	1	The messengers message is the inner temple/biggest point of all!
Messiah	Malachi	4	4	The law must be upheld by those to be saved
Messiah	Malachi	4	5	Messenger is also Elijah, Joshua, & 7 others
Messiah	Malachi	4	6	LGBTQ, aliens, Pro-Life all end for kids' sakes
New Jerusalem of the gentiles	Genesis	4	16	Middle east is *east* and U.S. is *west*
New Jerusalem of the gentiles	Genesis	15	18 to 21	Promised land to Israelites, not Ephraim (who will get the U.S.)
New Jerusalem of the gentiles	Genesis	41	52	U.S.A., Ephraim, fruitful in land of affliction
New Jerusalem of the gentiles	Genesis	48	19	USA prophesied by Jacob
New Jerusalem of the gentiles	Numbers	2	18	Ephraim camps to west to symbolize the USA
New Jerusalem of the gentiles				No Levite priests for the U.S., Ephraim
New Jerusalem of the gentiles	Chronicles 1	17	9 to 12	The rest of the story for the USA
New Jerusalem of the gentiles	Chronicles 1	28	19	How He treats David, He treats you: USA
New Jerusalem of the gentiles	Isaiah	2	8	U.S. worships the things they create
New Jerusalem of the	Isaiah	11	13	Ephraim is U.S. & Judah is gentile Israel

New Jerusalem of the gentiles	Isaiah	55	5	The prophecy of the USA (1 of ?)
New Jerusalem of the gentiles	Jeremiah	10	3 to 4	USA, Ephraim, is hardworking
New Jerusalem of the gentiles	Jeremiah	10	5	USA, Ephraim goes with the group, not morality
New Jerusalem of the gentiles	Jeremiah	10	8 to 9	USA, Ephraim is ultra-materialistic
New Jerusalem of the gentiles	Jeremiah	10	16	U.S. is inheritance & Jacob is saved
New Jerusalem of the gentiles	Ezekiel	37	15 to 17	Israel and the USA (Ephraim)
New Jerusalem of the gentiles	Daniel	7	3	Daniel sees the 4 forms of future government throughout our future history
New Jerusalem of the gentiles	Daniel	7	4	The predator, man, receives God's animation
New Jerusalem of the gentiles	Daniel	7	5	Man is then eaten by dictators symbolized through the insatiable bears in history
New Jerusalem of the gentiles	Daniel	7	6	The leopard's four heads, House of Rep, Senate, Judiciary, & Exec sworn under God
New Jerusalem of the gentiles	Daniel	7	7	The beast of Ten horns (kingdoms) is the historic name of China
New Jerusalem of the gentiles	Hosea	7	8	U.S. is Ephraim, a melting pot
New Jerusalem of the gentiles	Zechariah	2	1 to 3	Jerusalem of gentiles U.S. has firewall, Daniel reveals it's the west coast
Sabbath	Exodus	16	23	No cooking and baking
Sabbath	Exodus	16	23	No cooking and baking
Sabbath	Exodus	16	29	Can't leave your dwelling
Sabbath	Exodus	20	11	Friday to Saturday is the only legal Sabbath
Sabbath	Exodus	23	12 to 15	Sabbath Friday to Saturday
Sabbath	Exodus	31	13 to 18	Sabbath rules
Sabbath	Exodus	34	21	Sabbath rule enforced further
Sabbath	Exodus	35	2	No leaving dwelling or lighting fire
Sabbath	Leviticus	23	3	Must honor the sabbath to be saved
Sabbath	Jeremiah	17	21 to 23	USA does not leave its houses on Sabbath
Sabbath	Ezekiel	20	18	Do not follow your fathers, seek Sabbath too
Science	Genesis	1	26 to 28	man in God form from evolution
Science	Genesis	2	7	man are from dust from star dust
Science	Genesis	2	11 to 14	Eden 4th river satellite verified (like 1:3-8)
Science	Genesis	6	3	Maximum life of a human post flood is 120
Science	Exodus	19	10 to 11	Anti-bacteria understanding
Science	Isaiah	10	20	U.S. not rely on leaders, but rather God (1 of 2)
Science	Genesis	1	1 to 11	Evolution is accurately described in Bible
Science/DNA	Isaiah	10	21 to 22	DNA test reunited lost tribes of Jacob/Descartes
Science/DNA	Isaiah	11	12 to 13	DNA tests already reunited the tribes (2 of 2)
Science/relativity	Genesis	7	2	Life forms are male and female only
Science/relativity	Genesis	8	21	The young are always vulnerable sexually
Science/relativity	Genesis	9	15	Branch required so not everyone drowns
Science/relativity	Genesis	18	25	Inner temple, Abraham wrestles with God

Category	Book	Ch	Verse	Description
Science/relativity	Exodus	7	11 to 12	In antiquity God offered magic to all
Science/relativity	Exodus	17	11	Moses quantum affected outcomes
Science/relativity	Proverbs	16	33	The test's God factor in the multiverse
Science/relativity	Ecclesiastes	7	27 to 28	Only men are judged, women aren't here
Science/relativity	Ecclesiastes	9	9	The point of life
Science/relativity	Song of Solomon	7	6	Unless man and woman unite, they don't continue
Science/relativity	Isaiah	55	8 to 9	Quantum Mechanics is why you must trust God
Science/relativity	Genesis	11	6 to 7	One language broken to be revived
Science/sperm	Proverbs	30	18 to 19	We've solved all but the fourth
Science/sperm	Proverbs	30	20	Eve the harlot is just eating more forbidden fruit
science/transfigurative light	Exodus	34	29	My mom saw this light
Woman as test	Hosea	2	2 to 3	Women destroyed the U.S., raped the children
Women as test	Genesis	3	13	women are the test to give in to deceit
Women as test	Genesis	3	16	women quantum cursed to choose sorrow
Women as test	Genesis	3	17 to 19	civilization is the curse for original sin, no good
Women as test	Genesis	16	4	Sexual indiscretion mars family
Women as test	Genesis	18	15	Woman lied to God, bad like Enoch said
Women as test	Genesis	18	19	Heterosexual families alone are God's way
Women as test	Genesis	31	34	Rachel (women) cursed not to be monotheistic
Women as test	Job	39	13 to 18	Liberated women have no wisdom and feed the end (1 of 3)
Women as test	Psalm	81	6 to 7	Liberated women end world (2 of 3)
Women as test	Proverbs	23	26 to 28	Rampant sex destabilizes family
Women as test	Isaiah	3	12	The modern American society is wickedly ruled by women
Women as test	Jeremiah	2	32 to 33	Lack of belief fueled wicked women
Women as test	Jeremiah	2	34	So called liberation of females was child rape
Women as test	Jeremiah	2	35	Women deny their sin from so-called liberation
Women as test	Jeremiah	3	2	Your harlotries polluted the USA
Women as test	Jeremiah	3	3	Climate change from China pollutants stems from sex immorality
Women as test	Jeremiah	6	2 to 4	Female sexual immorality (1 of 2) see Zachariah
Women as test	Jeremiah	31	22	Modern woman should stop destroying the men, ruining it
Women as test	Lamentations	2	13	The women feminized the men, now child rape
Women as test	Ezekiel	22	20	The worth of gentiles
Women as test	Hosea	1	2	The Lord accuses the U.S. of departing of law
Women as test	Hosea	2	4 to 5	Children deserted to rape and control
Women as test	Hosea	2	6 to 8	Women's wantonness damned their offspring
Women as test	Hosea	4	10	Wanton sex just releases more for women
Women as test	Amos	5	1 to 3	Women's' sexual immorality damns the world

| Women as test | Zechariah | 5 | 5 to 9 | Liberated women end world, so new one (3 of 3) |
| Women as test | Zechariah | 5 | 10 to 11 | Evil women shrine is in first society after Eden |

Appendix (e)
THE IMAGE OF THE ARCHANGEL SAINT MICHAEL
(*REPRINTED FROM *SAINT MICHAEL STOOD UP: China Is Gog*)

This appendix reveals the image of Saint Michael critical for the anointed messenger to conclude Who, in fact, anointed him.

The painting of the Archangel Saint Michael referred to in the text. The face was altered to depict the visage witnessed by the author.

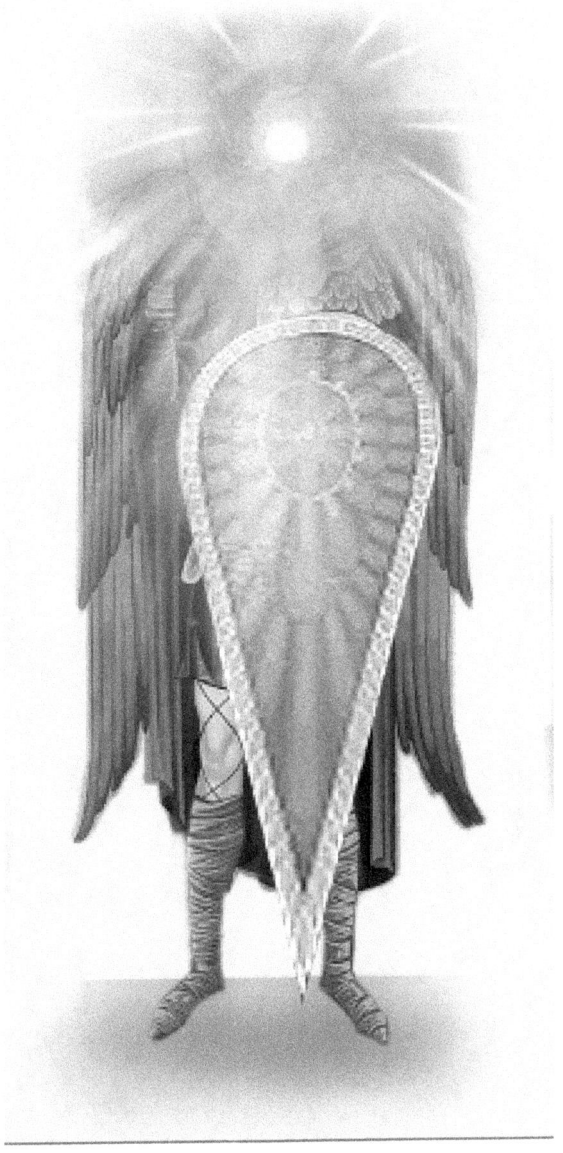

Appendix (f)
OTHER ACADEMIC SOURCES, FURTHER PROOF OF GOD'S CONDEMNATION OF BARACK OBAMA, & SPECULATION ON THE TIMING OF THE METEOR IMPACT

This appendix provides further proof of points that were not fully explored in the body of the book.

OTHER ACADEMIC SOURCES

Other major sources were the excellent college courses *Beginnings of Judaism* by Isaiah M. Gafni, Ph.D., of Hebrew University and *Jesus And His Jewish Influence* by Jodi Magness, Ph.D., of University of North Carolina at Chapel Hill. Also of inestimable value was the book *Descartes in 90 Minutes* by Paul Strathern and the lecture *The Mystical Dreams of Descartes: Exploring The Origins of Rationalism and Modernity* by Justin Sledge, Ph.D. Robert A. Caro's four part biography of then president Lyndon Johnson, based on Johnson's collected paperwork archives, lends an amazing insight into the corrupt, inner workings of our government by a politician who served in every major branch of the federal government except the judiciary. Additionally, the brave work of president Donald J. Trump, Robert Kennedy Jr., Tucker Carlson, Joe Rogan, Thomas Sowell, Friedrich Hayek, Victor Davis Hanson, and Jordan Peterson are but some of the brave voices long-speaking out against evil. BibleHub.com and BibleGateway.com were excellent, scriptural, research tools. Biblical verses were generally quoted in The New King James translation with a few exceptions when the actual Hebrew was better relayed through other translations.

PROOF OF GOD'S CONDEMNATION OF BARACK OBAMA

In the Hebrew Bible, the Lord makes clear that He decides an individual's nationality solely by their father.

Numbers 1:18
And they assembled all the congregation together on the first day of the second month, and they declared their pedigrees after their families, by the house of their fathers,

President Barack Obama's father hailed from the Rachuonyo District of what was then the British colony of Kenya, later the independent nation of Kenya. This country lays directly south of the rivers of biblical Ethiopia, marking it by God as a land cursed, most probably for their enslavement of much of Africa.

Isaiah 18:1-2
Proclamation Against Ethiopia

Woe to the land shadowed with buzzing wings,
Which is beyond the rivers of Ethiopia,
Which sends ambassadors by sea,
Even in vessels of reed on the waters, saying,
"Go, swift messengers, to a nation tall and smooth of skin,
To a people terrible from their beginning onward,

Ethiopianhistory.com
The word Ethiopia appears in the King James Bible version 45 times. When the word Ethiopia is used in the bible, it most of the time refers to all the land south of Egypt: Gen.2.[13] And the name of the second river is Gihon: the same is it that compasseth the whole land of Ethiopia. Num.12.

It's worth noting that the Africans brought to the United States as forced slaves had always been slaves in Africa. Their American migration would be their only chance of freedom in their entire lineage following the granting of U.S. citizenship at the Civil War's end. Yet Barack Obama's father was not of the "chosen" African lineage to be cleansed as an American; but an African cursed by God with that curse continuing onto his African son, Barack Obama, whom God unmasked as one of the four presidents acting as Satan to enrich Gog and end the world.

Anecdotally, this messenger as a 19-year-old-student in Kenya was approached by a Maasai warrior chieftain who presented his royal walking stick to the messenger. The chieftain claimed to have been waiting for this messenger for many years at a Maasai trading post in the Amboseli National Park. He emphatically claimed this messenger would be a most important person and do a great thing for the universe and asked him to take the walking stick at no charge and to remember the chief and his tribe. This messenger still possesses that walking stick.

CONJECTURE ON THE METEORITE'S TIMING

In the Book of Exodus, when Moses had Aaron cast down his staff and it turned into a serpent, Pharoah also had a staff cast down which became a snake. This event highlights the fact that the Lord revealed magic to pagans, most probably to control their society. And the consummate scholar of Egyptian deities will find a curious deity named *Medjed*. This minor Egyptian god has human legs, but cloaks his body from sight. Medjed was considered a great deity of the Egyptians and foretold the destruction of the whole earth from a heavenly body's impact.

The Hebrew Bible states this heavenly body impact on Earth occurs both at night and at noon because there are two blessed Israelite nations on either side of the earth. Nonetheless, Medjed reveals the meteor strikes Egypt at night. Given the deity's human form and its parallel eschatology to the Hebrew Bible, it's worth mentioning that the meteorite probably impacts Israel at night, which roughly would be noon-time in the United States of America. A good name for the world-ending, heavenly body would be CBOB, standing for Clinton, Bush, Obama, and Biden.

Appendix (g)
A COMPLETE SUMMARY OF THIS GUIDE

This appendix summarizes the entire guide in 13 pages.

Headers for different sections are shown in bold print.

Americans broke their oath to God and are soon to die except that God temporarily offers rescue to all, no matter how wicked they've been; Americans must privately confess our national crimes of enriching Chinese communism and breaking our oath to God to ensure our fellow Americans' liberties and freedoms enshrined in our founding documents. Instead, some took from their fellow citizens and gave to noncitizens and others in the false name of generosity. This work entails what we must seek forgiveness for within the confines of our minds where our Creator dwells within all. These points are given by both God through his dictated words in the Hebrew Bible and His contemporary, anointed messenger of God's modern covenant, our U.S. Constitution. It will be proven that Presidents Clinton, W. Bush, Obama, and Biden acted as the misleading force of Satan, enriching the king of China whom God codenamed Gog for reasons to be explained. By enriching China's king, Clinton became the King of Babylon, the final ruler of civilization, first begun back in Babylon, which he would wreck, earning him the title *Helel ben Shachar* often mistranslated as Lucifer, since all unfulfilled Hebrew Bible prophesies either recently came true or will soon be fulfilled because of what he started. As He promised in the Hebrew Bible, God will shortly destroy Gog, and all who support him, called Magog, namely the United States of America since Clinton. Confess now or die as God transitions us into the messianic age.

SECTION I

PART ONE: A MESSAGE TO THE NEW JERUSALEM OF GENTILES, THE ORIGIN OF SCIENCE & ITS DIRE IMPLICATIONS (pg. 1)

It is made clear that most of the end-time prophecies have already taken place. For all the end-time prophesies left to be fulfilled are all about the same incurable plague, COVID, launched by Gog, revealed through Daniel as the world-ending king of the Land of 10 Kingdoms, mainland China's historic name. The year 2020 AD, in fact, marked the end of the Israelite's 2,625-year-long-punishment foretold to Daniel, following ancient Israel's defeat to Babylon back in 605 BC. So 605 BC was when the Israelite sacrifices at their first temple turned unrightful since those sacrifices ultimately granted them protection from outside invaders, once even involving the angel of death murdering the foreign Assyrian King's entire army on a Passover evening. While Babylon sucked Israel economically dry before outright destroying them and their temple 18 years later. So in retrospect, following their loss to Babylon, the Israelite temple sacrifices became unrightful.

Behind our modern demise, God revealed through Ezekiel that He put hooks into China's Gog to dispatch "splendidly clad" soldiers in the end-times appearing as mere tourists on "ascending chariots", airplanes, flying to overtake the New Jerusalem of gentiles in a storm; the same land that our pilgrim founders in a land of the west not yet discovered in biblical times that would be symbolized by the eagle as God made clear to Ezekiel. These Chinese soldiers carried the unseen weapon, a "sword" of COVID to overtake America in Jeremiah's incurable plague for our many sins. For it was a weaponized plague funded and aided by Democrat and Rhino Republican elites masked as an act of God, hence Gog's codename sounding so close to God's moniker. A plague created in Gog's Wuhan lab only to be covered up by our wicked elites hiding their culpability in the mass murder of a million American souls thus far, in an act followed by an illegal invasion and the crushing of free speech that will eventually destroy our nation.

For our sins, God had China's Gog conquer our U.S. west coast to now fly his flag, subjugating their populations for Gog's elites to occupy the land and coopt our political system, buying it up with American money spent on Gog's made-in-China, slave-made purchases. In his final attack, God foretells that Gog will strike America and the free world, leaving them grabbing their abdomens in pain equal to that of a woman's labor, before God

GOD'S GUIDE TO THE END OF THE WORLD   421

annihilates Gog, his Chinese passengers spreading new diseases on our west coast, and all of Magog, meaning those who enriched Communist China's Gog: most notably every American citizen for the past 30 odd years.

Gog's secret plan, which God made clear to Ezekiel, was hatched to kill Americans after the U.S. quit enriching China under Trump, following three consecutive pro-China presidents shown to Daniel as three horns symbolizing our kings, Clinton, W. Bush, and Obama who enriched the world ending beast of 10 kingdoms. History reveals that Gog needs to resettle our American "unguarded homes" and lands rich in resources for his own elites after China's king, with the help of our Magog American leaders' political support, polluted China to death through made-in-China products crafted by slaves with no environmental protections.

Now God rebukes the three consecutive pro-Chinese presidents of the U.S., Clinton, W. Bush, and Obama, followed nonconsecutively, according to God, by at least a fourth pro-Chinese president, Biden, who are collectively referred to as Satan, the final arbiters misleading mankind. God makes clear China will soon wipe out all human life. After Democrats and non-Trumpian Republicans funded Covid in China's Wuhan lab, absentee ballots were then illegally legislated just before the 2020 presidential election henceforth leaving Americans politically powerless. So God comes to destroy those aiding Gog, termed Magog, most namely every American made to enrich their ultimate mass-murderer by buying his slaves' products. God, however, will soon rescue those who will go within their inner temple and confess our crimes of America's working since Clinton to enrich Chinese Communism. Absentee ballots will undermine our 2024 presidential election exposing even more the powerless status of Americans as we fall, invaded by outsiders just like Europe, including Gog's slew of military age asylum seekers accompanied by no females or children. The Service Economy ultimately rendered us clueless, homeless, and infected with an incurable disease in God's end-time war of Gog and

Magog. But as promised, God comes to rescue those who will go within their inner temple and confess our crimes of America's working since Clinton to enrich Chinese Communism and forge our modern American tyrants. Soon God makes clear He will wipe out our American west coast, and finally destroy the wicked by ending the earth from an impending meteorite to smash our planet apart. Those who now return to God will be saved and continue, according to Him on a "new Earth", possibly our own in another multiverse.

PART TWO: THE ECONOMY UNDER GOG, YOU ARE MAGOG, MADE IN USA (pg. 8).

This section explains how deadly our enrichment of communist China has been, where its lone king owns all wealth, using our money spent on Chinese purchases to destroy our nation. We introduce policies to restore American manufacturing and liberty, illustrating what in Hebrew means Mishpat, how to treat all equally regardless of class, racial ethnicity, or any other criteria: the opposite of our modern, liberal racist society.

SECTION II GOD'S M,ESSAGE TO YOU, GOD EXPOSES CHINA'S GOG VIA JEREMIAH, EZEKIEL, & DANIEL (pg. 16)

Highlights from key verses of The Books of Jeremiah, Ezekiel, and Daniel are used to show China's king is Gog, and his four pro-China U.S. presidents Clinton, W. Bush, Obama, and Biden are Satan according to God. And China's Gog will wipe out all life on earth except for those now returning to God by confessing our national political crimes within our minds to our Creator. Furthermore, a chronology of dates is presented to support God's prophetic prediction of the exact year of the "incurable" pandemic, and the fact that this message is only heard once the disease is generally admitted to be incurable.

SECTION III MISHPAT, ONE NATION UNDER GOD (pg. 54)

If We Are Powerless Then Why Discuss Policies section explains that Americans need to know how easily we can fix our nation. For this story will be of two cities, the America of those saved by God and the remaining, unrepentant masses destroyed by their Maker. **OZ (Opportunity Zone)** makes clear how America can easily return manufacturing to American soil while also helping our neighbors and creating an environment where illegal aliens on American soil will leave of their own will. **New American Entrepreneurs** makes clear how we can expand manufacturing for all citizens throughout our nation. **Manufacturing Amidst COVID** deals in ways we can responsibly manufacture while remaining safe from our incurable plague. **Future Oz** outlines future manufacturing expansion through the Americas. **Only Manufacturing Makes Wealth** drives home the point that only by making things do we truly generate wealth. **Kill The Green Energy Lie** stops the lie of climate change from carbon emissions and highlights the ungodly pollution our made-in-China purchases have spawned. **Manufacturing Alone Can Save Us** shows that domestic manufacturing alone enriched our nation and we will be slaves without it. **Raise The Shield** protects our borders and safety. Additional policies begin with **OPAH (One Parent At Home)** returns one spouse home to raise the next generation of Americans. **OYOH (Own Your Own Home)** allows Americans to own their own dwelling. **CVRA (Citizen Verification Rental Act)** will bring rents and dwelling costs down to a reasonable rate for American citizens. **End Jail Slavery** stops the immoral mass jailing of a new American slave class. **Free Speech or Die** allows a return to free discourse that our founders assured us was key to our republic. **Special Protections** will be taken away from all the so-called victims and focused on protecting our children. **LGBTQ Reform** will stop the brainwashing of our society and castration of our at-risk black, inner-city youth, simply allowing for tolerance of this minority, which would like to convert all children to their ways as a new majority. **End The COVID Vaccine Mandate** will curtail our wicked leaders who forced this dangerous, untested drug on us as a means of mass subjugation. **Real Climate Change** will reinstitute Made In America manufacturing policies to stop the insane levels of Communist Chinese pollution sowed by our made-in-China purchases. **Political Not Police Reform** will scrutinize our wicked leaders. **Port City Reconstruction**, similar to our last post-civil war reconstruction, will decommunize our port cities infected by the influx of communist imports and illegal political contributions. **Whistleblower Reform** will fund whistleblowers to expose our corrupt and communized federal government. **Reaffirm The Right of Self-Protection** will keep bureaucrats from stripping a woman's right to choose or to take guns from citizens that they need to protect themselves. **Salute The Flag** focuses on emboldening the traditions that unite all Americans. We must **End Diversity & Quantitative Easing** to allow Americans to realize their government has destroyed their entire business landscape, now held aloft on tax dollars. **Return To Our Inner Temple** drives home a necessary trust in God needed to restore our freedom while noting that **Only Those With Michael Are Righteous** and all who preach against God's ways in the Hebrew Bible thus reveal their evil.

SECTION IV PREPARING HIS WAY, THE GREAT GUILT & THE MANY SINS

PART I OVERVIEW (pg. 75)

Summarizes the following facts in the next parts.

PART II: THE REBUKE OF HASMONEAN JUDIASM & CONSTANTINIAN CHRISTIANITY (pg. 93)

Christ Spoke Only Of The Old Testament and not any new literature. **Josephus Flavius Lived To Prove Joshua's Existence,** by documenting outside of the gospels that Joshua did historically exist. **Israelite Priests Secretly Prove Joshua Was The Messiah** in the Talmud, their collective writings kept secret until the end of the 19th century. **Israelite Priests Damned Their Movement Through Pedophilia** under Greek Seleucid rule. **Sodomy's Spread Creates Permanent Biological Links** as shown by science, proving sperm burrow through human bodies to remain alive, embedded in human brains. **Sodomy's Spread Truly Destroyed Ancient Israel** so that in the end of that nation, **Christ Was Killed By Sodomy's Spread**. **Christ Opposed Rome's Illegitimate Meddling In God's Name,** most likely attacking a tax assessed by the reigning Israelite puppets under Roman occupation. The movement from **Christ Later Threatened The Roman Empire** so that **Constantine Misdirected Christ's Later Followers** with a new liturgy called The New Testament in which **Constantine Falsely Damned Any Future Joshua Messenger** and inserted spiritual intermediaries between people and God. **Satan Is A Force And In The End, Four People** proved to be Clinton, W. Bush, Obama, and Biden. **Christianity Is Truly Constantinianism** and **Christianity Mirrored Wicked Israelite Priests** breaking the rightful ways of the Hebrew Bible. In fact, Catholicism's altering of the ways and times of the sabbath marks the entire movement as antithetical to God and part of Satan's misleading force even according to Christ in the gospels, supporting the larger need for reform proffered by Ellen G. White. For **God Damns All Abrahamic Spiritual Leaders** since the Hebrew Bible does not allow for spiritual intermediaries or even priests after the fall of the Levite priestly clan, and even then they were hygiene enforcers, judges, and tendered sacrifices rather than acting as spiritual intermediaries. **Islam Was Also Part Of The Israelite Punishment** and like Christianity before it, proffered new spiritual intermediaries who soon began altering the words of their so-called Great Prophet. While Christian intermediaries, now at the end of history, support sodomy's spread and infringe on a woman's right to an abortion, making them according to God, madmen. For they divide the nation over lies with no liturgical support only to empower Satan, Gog, and the world's end. Because once the suffering of the Israelites is over, the price for such crimes is quickly extracted. According to God, **The Firm Foundation** reasserted from the Hebrew Bible is the only way, the core of God's unchangeable truth being the Torah, the first five books of the Hebrew Bible dictated by God to Moses and the remaining Hebrew scripture that followed with these end-time prophecies directly dictated or shown by God to a prophet. Where God makes clear that He worked backward in time using the ancient Israelites to inspire his "first-born" New Jerusalem of Gentiles, the U.S.A.

PART III ALIENS & MESSENGERS (pg. 111)

God Proves Extraterrestrials Exist in the Hebrew Bible's Book of Genesis. **Omuamua & The Archangel Saint Michael** explores the possible relationship between the alien probe and the anointing of this messenger by the Angel representing God in the company of witnesses. **God Speaks Through An Anointed Messenger** explores what God expects of this messenger as documented in the Hebrew Bible. **The Messenger Prepares** documents the preparation required by the anointed messenger to complete Saint Michael's order for **The Dr. Hart Meeting,** the head of Loma Linda Medical Center who was warned by Saint Michael through this messenger to stop the theft of donor dollars and to produce Dreamspace with no profit for this messenger, in order to save the world when such an opportunity existed in 2017. **Ellen G. White Caused The Hart Meeting** explains why this meeting was ordained by God and why both He and White, who back in the 19th century, knew this request would fail to bear the intended fruit of saving the world, let alone stopping the theft of donor dollars for the Loma Linda Medical-center that White founded. **God Rebuked The Catholic Church** deals with the events that led this messenger to condemn that religion and show Catholics how they could continue their belief system without being permanently doomed by God. **Hart & Biden Represent Modern Wickedness** parallels the failures of Dr. Hart and current President Biden. **God Physically Set His Spirit On The Messenger** explains a mystical event prior to the anointed messenger's birth in which his parents were struck by transfigurative light from the heavens, piercing through the roof of their car, and making their lower extremities glow. **The Messenger Lived Seven Lives** explores how the current messenger is an amalgam of Enoch, David, another son of David's father Jesse, Elijah, Zerubbabel, Joshua son of Jozadak, and the last Joshua misnamed Jesus; while making clear this current messenger is the first Joshua with the famed one from antiquity being the second as God's intervention He made clear worked backward in time from his most chosen firstborn, every single American citizen.

PART IV THE DETAILED PRESENTATION (pg. 123)

This section provides a more in-depth exploration of many of the points that were previously more briefly presented. We explore how **Science Proves God's Existence** for **Descartes Claimed To Be Visited By God. Descartes' Science Was Later Altered** by his followers, fearing persecution from the reigning Christian elites; but **The Altered Science Is Now Deadly For All** as science is perverted for murder by Godless scientific experts just as science's founder warned it would be. **Our Inner Temple Is Real & Part of God** as proven by Science's founder Descartes in Science's second work. In its first work, in fact, **Science Verifies God's Existence** through a proof that remains undisputed. **Descartes Continued To Assert God Birthed Science** on November 10th, 1619 leading his followers to alter Descartes' scientific system until years later when **Newton Destroyed the Cartesians (followers of Descartes).** But then under the philosopher David Hume, **Cartesian Lies Were Resurrected.** While in fact, **Science Proves Secularism Is A Lie** so that **The Real Project 1619 Is God.** Because of the coverup of science, Descartes urges us, **Don't Trust The Experts.** For now, **Supporting Forbidden Things Ends All.** Just as in antiquity, **Christ Died Over Sodomy's Spread** via their priesthood 150 years prior from which they never returned to their legal form of worship. But **God Loves America** and makes clear how

God's Explanations are Proven By Science. In the Hebrew Bible, **God Explained How Reality Worked.** Then He warns **Why God Comes Now** only when **God Unmasks Gog.** In the Hebrew Bible, **God Prophesied Of The Pandemic's Launch** of COVID. God explained in scripture **Why Gog Wants To Kill Everyone**: so China's king can kill us all and eventually take our land and homes. **God Alone Ends COVID. God Unmasks Magog & The King Of Babylon,** the final king of civilization first born in ancient Babylon who enriched Gog. For God warned that China's king did not become powerful by his own power but through America's four traitorous presidents, the first three acting consecutively; then broken by what was Trump to sever the China enrichment bringing a fourth defending Gog. While Magog means all those who enrich Gog, China's King, an act first instituted by Clinton whom God names the King of Babylon, noting that upon Clinton's death, he will wind up in Hell and learn his real name, Helel, mistranslated as Lucifer: the human who eventually ended humanity. **God Damns Our Four U.S. Magog Kings** who history proves can only be Clinton, W. Bush, Obama, and Biden for their policies that sowed **The Chinese Pollution** {that} **Is Embodied In Gog,** China's king. In fact, **George Washington Doubly Confirmed God's Prophecy** of our enslavement to a foreign king after outsourcing manufacturing, for **Washington Foretold Slave-Made Goods Would Damn America.** Without domestic manufacturing, **Americans Became Nazis** of the left, enriching concentration camps of innocent believers in China, funding COVID, and initiating US absentee ballot fraud to rob voters of our power while invading us with foreigners and Gog's foot-soldiers all because **Americans Quit Believing In God & Became Slavers,** which stands as **God's Proof That We Are At The End.** For **God Damns Americans Bowing To Magog.** Both the **U.S. & Ancient Israel's Servitude Were Hidden For 18 Years.** So although the Israelite's first temple was destroyed in 587 BC, the sacrifices there turned unrightful in 605 BC, 18 years prior when they were truly under foreign control after the Battle of

Carchemish. God made clear to Daniel that a total of 2,625 years of punishment would pass, leading to 2020 AD when their punishment ended and the world's end began. Likewise, America's control by China inexorably began after China with Clinton's help entered the World Trade Organization, proliferating its slave-made goods to the free world to make slaves of free men unable to compete. The loss of economic status eventually triggered their mass-invasion in the name of compassion by outside immigrants thrust upon them. Clinton's service economy was truly servitude to Communist China's despots. But soon, **Everything Ends Like Sodom & Gomorrah**, from a world-ending meteorite after **Our Politicians Except Trump Ended Our Earth** while **Our Magog Media Monopoly Mind Controls Us.** But truly, according to God, **Our Loss Of Belief Is The Real Pollution** and **Our End Is Nigh** while **Gog Controls Your Mind.** With their manipulation of the media and mass media, **The Clintons Are America's Ultimate Enemy** as **The World Died From America Abandoning Manufacturing**, first instituted by Clinton and continued by the three other U.S. presidents who, according to God, act as Satan. **Our Wickedness Now Comes For Our Children** in this future time that both **God & George Washington Damn Our Loss Of Free Speech.** But **Americans Are The Circumcised New Israelites.** In fact, **God Prophesied To The American Indians, Pre-colonial Mexico, Ancient Rome**, and **Ancient China,** all the main players in the inspiration and end of our nation: the second to be blessed by God, but in the end sanctified alone to rule. While God makes clear to his Hebrew Bible end-time prophets that **Women Truly Ended The World** by failing to raise and protect their young, fating them to servitude, perversion, and death. God further explains **Why There Must Be Two Blessed Nations,** and **Why The Second Joshua Can Only Be A Political Leader** for **God's Message Was Always Political.** While **Our Lack of Belief Brought Our Murderers.** Murder based on the loss of wealth, essential for our political power in this nation, was the reason why **Clinton**

Seeded Our 2008 Meltdown, so now **Our American Economy Is A Magog Illusion** as **Our Magog Elites Now Aim To Leave Us Homeless** while **God Demands We Quit Hurting Our Fellow Americans**. All while the COVID virus they funded kills us with no possible cure. God stresses how our loss of belief led us to elect bastards in Clinton and Obama for according to Him, **Bastards Damned Our Leadership** while **Our End Was Unknown Without God's Message;** but our Maker notes that death is an illusion and permanent life will remain for all, many full of never-ending pain and suffering so **Eternity Is At Stake.**

SECTION V (WITH WORKS CITED) A MESSAGE TO THE NEW JERUSALEM OF GENTILES, THE ORIGIN OF SCIENCE & ITS DIRE IMPLICATIONS (pg. 176)

This section uses only God's words from the Hebrew Bible along with relevant scientific and major news articles to prove the points already made in the prior sections. This use of scripture and quotations are actually the cited sources behind the first film, the Summary of God's Message, and the second short film.

APPENDICES

Appendix (a) Analysis On The Solution To Daniel's Riddle (pg. 317)

explores the dates to pinpoint God's prophesy of the COVID pandemic beginning in late 2019 and infecting the world by early 2020.

Appendix (b) Further Support For Political Policies (pg. 321)

explores prior essays and major third-party sources behind the political policies.

Appendix (c) Scriptural Refutation Of The Pro-Life Movement (pg. 363)

explores the blatant lies of the so-called pro-life movement that lacks any supporting, liturgical proof for their cause.

Appendix (d) Scriptural Index By Key Topics (pg. 375)

further explores the Hebrew Bible passages behind this message.

Appendix (e) The Image of The Archangel Saint Michael (pg. 407)

reveals the image of Saint Michael, which was critical for the anointed messenger to conclude Who, in fact, anointed him.

Appendix (f) Other Sources, Further Proof Of God's Condemnation of Barack Obama & Speculation On The Timing Of The Meteorite Impact (pg. 411)

provides further proof of points that were not fully explored in the body of the book.

Appendix (g) A complete Summary of This Guide (pg. 417)

This current summary is stated herein.

EPILOGUE (pg. 433)

This concluding section points readers to our website centeredamerica.com and other works by this author further illustrating the points presented in this guide.

Epilogue

This concluding section points readers to our website centeredamerica.com and other works by this author further illustrating the points presented in this work.

Please view more on our policies free of charge at our political site *centeredamerica.com*. The essential essays are also gathered in the nonfiction work *How To Win The War* available at major booksellers with those essays again free of charge at centeredamerica.com. SDAs will also find the link to the *Dreamspace* animatic experience Ellen G. White noted would be needed to open their eyes to the end of the world. You will also find a link to the *Dreamspace* novel available from major booksellers further exploring these points. More biographical information on the messenger, dealing with Dr. Hart, the SDAs, the formal rebuke of the Catholic Church, can all be found in the 2020 nonfiction work *Saint Michael Stood Up*. Be assured via God, George Washington, Ellen G. White, and the messenger of this covenant that no such deeds like these have befallen us in our nation's history. And what is coming will be worse than anyone can ever imagine. You can no longer fight the evil forces of Gog and Magog, enter your inner temple before it is too late. And witness your rescue from a God who has hidden Himself for eons, but hidden no longer.

Job 19:25-27
For I know that my Redeemer lives,
And He shall stand at last on the earth;
And after my skin is destroyed, this I know,
That in my flesh I shall see God,
Whom I shall see for myself,
And my eyes shall behold, and not another.
How my heart yearns within me!

Other Nonfiction works by
BENNETT JOSHUA DAVLIN

2020 *TIME OF TROUBLE* NONFICTION RELEASE FROM THE AUTHOR

FROM THE 2020 DEMOCRAT PRESIDENTIAL CANDIDATE OF THE NON-TREASONOUS WING OF THE DNC

"...I next critized the sex-abuse cover-up scandal, protected for ages by the top elites of their (Catholic) bureaucracy. I disclosed that many of my male homosexual friends, once reaching middle-age, disclosed that they were raped when young by Catholic priests. This wicked conspiracy along with the wrong Sabbath showed the wickedness wrought from the nonsensical Papal infallibility.

I then revealed that my wife and I would never be in a meeting with Catholic Officials except for one, critical fact: **The archangel Saint Michael visited me in the presence of my wife on October 27th, 2017, and altered our lives, bringing us here.**"

- *SAINT MICHAEL STOOD UP*, PAGE 94

**AT THAT TIME (SAINT) MICHAEL
SHALL STAND UP,**
THE GREAT PRINCE WHO STANDS WATCH OVER THE SONS OF YOUR PEOPLE: AND THERE SHALL BE A
TIME OF TROUBLE,
SUCH AS NEVER WAS SINCE THERE WAS A NATION,
EVEN TO THAT TIME.
AND AT THAT TIME **YOUR PEOPLE
SHALL BE DELIVERED,**
EVERY ONE WHO IS FOUND WRITTEN IN THE BOOK.

-(DANIEL 12:1)

CENTERED AMERICA BOOKS
www.centeredamerica.com

Also available as an ebook

$24.99 US
$32.65 CAN

ISBN 9781735873640

FROM THE 2020 DEMOCRAT PRESIDENTIAL CANDIDATE
OF THE NON-TREASONOUS WING OF THE DNC

SAINT MICHAEL STOOD UP

China is Gog

BENNETT JOSHUA DAVLIN

FROM THE 2020 DEMOCRAT PRESIDENTIAL CANDIDATE
OF THE NON-TREASONOUS WING OF THE DNC

CHINA LIED MASS MURDERING WITH COVID-19
REVEALED THE COLD WAR NEVER ENDED

THE SERVICE ECONOMY IS THE ILLUSION OF
AN IMAGINARY COMMON INTEREST FUNDING OUR ENEMY

TO WIN THE WAR,
AMERICA MUST:

PROTECT THE PEOPLE
LIVE FREE UNTIL COVID FREE - EXTEND UNEMPLOYMENT
ONE PARENT AT HOME - SCHOOLING SUBSIDY FOR FAMILIES
ESSENTIAL WORKERS - HAZARD PAY AND LIFE INSURANCE
STAY HEALTHY - BIFURCATE HOSPITALS AND COVID-19 CLINICS
FREE SPEECH - END CENSORSHIP SOCIAL MEDIA
DECOMMUNIZE MEDIA - REMOVE COMMUNIST PROPAGANDA

DECOMMUNIZE GOVERNMENT
TRIALS FOR TREASON -
POLITICIANS ALIGNED WITH CHINA,
WHO INSTITUTED THE DEADLY SERVICE ECONOMY,
WHO ENSLAVED CITIZENS IN FOR-PROFIT PRISONS,
WHO PROPAGATED VIOLENCE
AND DECLARED AMERICAN PORTS SANCTUARIES FOR CHINA.

MAKE IN AMERICA AGAIN- CHEXIT
MADE IN AMERICA - MANUFACTURE ESSENTIAL GOODS
CLOSE BORDERS - CONTAIN AND PROTECT FROM BIO ATTACKS
END SLAVERY - END MASS IMPRISONEMENT SLAVE LABOR

BEFORE CHINA/NORTH KOREA STRIKE AGAIN

CENTERED AMERICA BOOKS
www.centeredamerica.com

Also available as an ebook

$24.99 US
$32.65 CAN

ISBN 9781735873688

*FROM THE 2020 DEMOCRAT PRESIDENTIAL CANDIDATE
OF THE NON-TREASONOUS WING OF THE DNC*

HOW TO WIN THE WAR

The plan to save the U.S.A

BENNETT JOSHUA DAVLIN

Fiction works & feature films by
BENNETT JOSHUA DAVLIN

Dr. Hart Wouldn't Look At It, Will You?

CHINA ENTOMBED THE WORLD NOW HUMANITY FOUND AN
ESCAPE

BY 2059 Chinese manufacturing pollution triggered the worldwide flood predicted to last 7,000 years. Plagued with COVID-19 and restricted within flood-walled-zones, humanity prepares to perpetually online on *Dreamspace*, a digital diversion platform that's as real as life. To play the perpetual game, users must first find a compatible game-mate in the dating module. Once merged, the couple's minds are immersed online permanently gaming with each other, while their offline bodies are maintained in medical body-vaults.

Before the worldwide drop, FCC Web Agent Ray Kemper must solve the murder of a beta-tester who may have met his killer on Dreamspace's dating module. The web agent must date the anonymous users his victim dated in their exclusive worlds, luring each into a digital-kiss to unmask their identity and catch his real-world killer.

The mystery unravels as the detective falls for a suspect who could be the love of his life or the end of it, forcing him to question whether our species is worth saving if doing so means giving up the very thing that makes us human.

"Davlin is the only living American auteur"
-DENNIS HOPPER
Actor, Writer, Producer, Director

"The most important sci-fi story ever written."
-GLEN A. LARSON
Creator of Battlestar Galactica

"Over-the-top finale would be right at home in a De Palma movie..."
-VARIETY MAGAZINE
Review of Davlin's prior work "Memory"

CENTERED AMERICA BOOKS
www.centeredamerica.com

Also available as an ebook

$24.99 US
$32.65 CAN

ISBN 9781735873633

THE UNION 57 PETROCHEMICAL REFINERY OUTSIDE NEW YORK CITY IS OVERTAKEN BY TERRORISTS WHO WIRED IT TO BLOW UP, POSSIBLY TRIGGERING A CHAIN REACTION OF NEIGHBORING CHEMICAL PLANTS TO RELEASE A POISON CLOUD IMPERILING MILLIONS IN AMERICA'S MOST CONCENTRATED POPULATION CENTER. FBI AGENT TOM GRANT IS SENT TO NEW ORLEANS TO INTERVIEW A MYSTERIOUS FIGURE NAMED YVES ALEXANDER DUSSANT, A LONE PRISONER IN A SECRET JAIL CONSTRUCTED TO HOLD ONLY HIM. BECAUSE HEARING DUSSANT'S VOICE WILL INSTANTLY TURN A PERSON INTO AN UNWITTING SLAVE TO THE PRISONER'S TWISTED WILL THROUGH A PSYCHOLOGICAL CONDITION THE GOVERNMENT TERMS "CONTAMINATION". WHILE DUSSANT CLAIMS TO BE THE MESSIAH AND THE FREQUENCY OF HIS MANIPULATIVE VOICE CARRIES THE POWER OF GOD'S OWN. FBI AGENT TOM GRANT FEARS DUSSANT IS BEHIND THE UNION 57 TAKEOVER AND FOR HIS HELP, TOM MUST SHARE DETAILS AND SECRETS ABOUT HIS OWN LIFE, LEADING TO A SECRET THAT NO ONE COULD'VE IMAGINED.

If Constantine's Catholicism, which altered the unchangeable Hebrew Bible's Sabbath times and ways were true, then this book would depict the Messiah.

CENTERED AMERICA CA CLASSICS

CENTERED AMERICA BOOKS
www.centeredamerica.com

Also available as an ebook

$19.99 US
$26.50 CAN

ISBN 9798988146698

90000

9 798988 146698

When free will meets opportunity you find out who you really are

1990s HOLLYWOOD AGENT TRAINEE, CULLEN GERSH, HAS HIS LIFE UPENDED AFTER HE STEALS HIS BOSS'S INVITATION TO THE MOST EXCLUSIVE HOLLYWOOD PARTY. CULLEN WILL LOSE NEARLY EVERYTHING WHEN HE'S PRESENTED WITH THE ABILITY TO EXPLORE HIS UNKNOWN DESIRES WITHOUT JUDGMENT OR REPERCUSSION.

Are you who you think you are?

CENTERED AMERICA C CLASSICS

CENTERED AMERICA BOOKS
www.centeredamerica.com

Also available as an ebook

$19.99 US
$26.50 CAN

ISBN 9798988146612

90000

2020 *TIME OF TROUBLE* NONFICTION RELEASE FROM THE AUTHOR

If your memories aren't your own, then whose are they?

One man is about to find out, as he accidentally ingests a mysterious drug that throws him into a hallucination so vivid that it seems real.

Because it is...

Now Dr. Taylor Briggs will embark on a journey to unlock the mysteries of his own mind—and to find the killer of the innocent victims whose last moments are being played out in his head—in a stunning psychological thriller that explores memory, its crucial role in our consciousness, and its power to deceive...

NOW A MAJOR MOTION PICTURE
Starring

BILLY ZANE   ANN-MARGRET

and

DENNIS HOPPER

an ECHO BRIDGE ENTERTAINMENT in association with 3210 FILMS and PARADOX PICTURES presentation of a BENNETT DAVLIN film BILLY ZANE ANN-MARGRET DENNIS HOPPER MEMORY TRICIA HELFER and TERRY CHEN casting by CANDICE ELZINGA & JACK GILARDI music supervisor MICHAEL LLOYD DAVID STREJA & CHRIS MOLLERE music composed by CLINT BENNETT & ANTHONY MARINELLI co-produced by BARBARA KELLY costume designed by KAREN MATTHEWS production designed by STEPHEN GEAGHAN edited by ALLISON GRACE director of photography PETER BENISON, CSC executive produced by ROBERT J MONROE BRANDON HOGAN produced by BENNETT DAVLIN JESSE NEWHOUSE & ANTHONY BADALUCCO based on the novel by BENNETT DAVLIN screenplay by BENNETT DAVLIN & ANTHONY BADALUCCO directed by BENNETT DAVLIN

COPYRIGHT 2006 MEMORI LLC
CREDITS NOT CONTRACTUAL

NOVEL
www.penguin.com

$14.00 U.S.
$17.50 CAN

ISBN 13: 978-0-425-20705-5

NOW A MAJOR MOTION PICTURE

STARRING

BILLY ZANE.

ANN-MARGRET.

and

DENNIS HOPPER

NEVER BEFORE PUBLISHED

MEMORY

a novel

BENNETT DAVLIN

SAVE YOUR LIFE & NATION

WWW.CENTEREDAMERICA.CO

Born in South Central Louisiana, Bennett Joshua Davlin began making films at the age of five and completed his first novel at ten. He studied internationally at Semester at Sea and London's City College, graduating from Tulane University, before later attending Tulane's A.B. Freeman School of Business's graduate MBA program. Davlin was a former war correspondent in the 1990s Yugoslavian conflict. He's worked in the oilfield sector and in structured and international finance. At 23 he turned around the largest American manufacturer of high-end decorative goods, after which the policies of then-president Clinton forced him to offshore his factories to China. He lived in Hong Kong and Communist China throughout various periods for the past 30 years. Davlin became a Hollywood studio screenwriter, penning such films as the Jackie Chan blockbuster *Medallion* for Sony, Columbia & TriStar Pictures. He wrote the international best-selling novel *Memory* published by The Berkley Imprint of The Penguin Group and translated into multiple languages by Sony Books, Blanvalet, and Random House. He has been a keynote speaker at The Tennessee Williams Festival and a guest lecturer at NYU and other universities. Davlin wrote, produced, and directed the adaptation of *Memory* into a feature film, theatrically released worldwide by Warner Bros. and EBE. In television, Bennett and his TV producing partner, Randy Douthit, co-creator of CNN's *Crossfire* and *Judge Judy*, worked on projects under a *first-look* deal with CBS Paramount. He was also a 2020 non-treasonous Democrat candidate for U.S. president and a government policy thinker, political, social, economic, and philosophical essayist at his site *Centeredamerica.com* where he alerted the world about Communist China's vast takeover since 2017.

www.ingramcontent.com/pod-product-compliance
Lightning Source LLC
Chambersburg PA
CBHW050520100526
44581CB00002B/52